THE TRANSFORMATION
OF AMERICAN
QUAKERISM

Indiana Yearly Meeting of Friends, 1844, by Marcus Mote (1817–1898).
Depicted in the center are Elijah Coffin and
Jeremiah Hubbard. Drawing reproduced courtesy of the Archives,
Earlham College, Richmond, Indiana.

Religion in North America

Catherine L. Albanese and Stephen J. Stein,
Series Editors

THE TRANSFORMATION OF
AMERICAN
QUAKERISM
Orthodox Friends, 1800–1907

THOMAS D. HAMM

The Frank S. and Elizabeth D. Brewer
Prize Essay of the
American Society of Church History

INDIANA UNIVERSITY PRESS
Bloomington and Indianapolis

First Midland Book Edition 1992

© 1988 by Thomas D. Hamm

Manufactured in the United States of America

Library of Congress Cataloging-in-Publication Data

Hamm, Thomas D.
The transformation of American Quakerism.

(Religion in North America)

"The Frank S. and Elizabeth D. Brewer prize essay of
the American Society of Church History."
Bibliography: p.
Includes index.
1. Society of Friends—United States—History—19th
century. I. Title. II. Series.
BX7637.H35 1988   289.6'3   86-46236
ISBN 0-253-36004-8
ISBN 0-253-20718-5 (pbk.)

2 3 4 5 6 96 95 94 93 92

For Mary Louise

CONTENTS

Foreword

This study by Thomas D. Hamm breaks new ground with its investigation of religious and theological changes within nineteenth-century American Quakerism. Hamm's account of the transformation of the Orthodox wing of the Society of Friends provides fresh perspective on the forces of religious acculturation at work among Quakers during the period. Indeed, Hamm helps us understand why many American Quakers in the twentieth century are nearly indistinguishable from their Protestant neighbors.

The story Hamm tells is far more complex than we have commonly assumed. The players are not well known to outsiders. Nor are the Quakers of the nineteenth century consistently distinguished from the members of other religious communities by plain clothes, silence in meetings, condemnation of paid clergy, rejection of sacraments, or preoccupation with the principle of the Inner Light. In fact, it seems as though Friends in that century rarely agreed on any of these issues or practices, and often they were very unfriendly to one another.

Hamm gives a detailed historical account of the development of factionalism among the segments of the Society of Friends that rejected the innovations of the Hicksite movement. Party labels abound—Wilburites and Gurneyites; renewal and revival Friends; conservative, moderate, and holiness Friends; modernists; and even "waterites." Each of these factions formulated different answers to the religious questions posed either by the tradition or by the context. Each drew in different ways upon both the Quaker heritage and the resources available in American culture.

Surely the power of the tradition was still operative. Each party in those struggles claimed to represent some element of authentic Quakerism or to have discovered some consistency between its views and earlier traditions. Reformers rationalized their programs by pointing to the testimonies of earlier activists; evangelical Quakers saw parallels between the idea of holiness and the experiences of George Fox; all parties tried to use the established family networks among Friends to their advantage. The significance of connectional relationships among Quaker meetings was never overlooked, nor was the process of discipline within the tradition abandoned. In other words, despite schism in the ranks and radical change, most Friends remained loyal to certain distinctive Quaker patterns of religious life.

To tell this story, Hamm has immersed himself in the materials of intellectual history—the published and unpublished documents from the period—and his bibliography is a useful guide into an uncharted area. But at the heart of Hamm's reading of the material is the recognition that the gulf

separating Quakers from other Protestants in the seventeenth and eighteenth centuries no longer existed by the end of the nineteenth. By that
time, many Friends had experienced an evangelical conversion, had
accepted revivalism as a tool for evangelism, and were contributing to the
support of a paid ministry. Some Quaker meetings erected fancy buildings,
installed organs in them, and conducted regular Sabbath schools. A few
preachers even advocated water baptism. Quakerism also had its own varieties of fundamentalism and modernism. By 1900, the issues dividing main-
line Protestants had torn apart the Society of Friends, too: the authority of
the Bible, the role of the ministry, the nature of conversion, the understanding of holiness and sanctification.

In short, the attraction of American culture, with its evangelical religious
ethos, emerges as the most striking tale that Hamm must tell. In his account,
religious outsiderhood and "peculiarity" are transformed in the course of a
century to make of Quakers a people no longer peculiar but surprisingly like
the mainstream. That it is impossible to escape the influence of dominant
cultural forces is the strong lesson of Hamm's study. Thus, this volume
suggests ways to examine the process of acculturation in other outsider
groups. It tells much about the challenge and opportunity of the religious
center, about how people religiously "other" come to identify with the
mainstream. In so doing, this book sheds light on themes that help to foster a
new and comprehensive understanding of American religion as a whole.

Catherine L. Albanese
Stephen J. Stein
Series Editors

Acknowledgments

The most pleasant part of writing this book has been recalling all of the people who contributed to it in some way. It began as a dissertation at Indiana University, where it was my good fortune to have the direction and example of Lewis Perry in my graduate work. He and Stephen J. Stein, Paul Lucas, and James Madison made up an outstanding advisory committee. Their guidance as teachers as well as their thoughtful and incisive criticisms and expert editing were of inestimable help. Hugh Barbour of Earlham College also encouraged me in this project and commented on the various drafts of the manuscript. Catherine L. Albanese of Wright State University and Grant Wacker of the University of North Carolina at Chapel Hill also read the entire manuscript and made innumerable helpful comments and suggestions. A Dissertation Fellowship from the Indiana Historical Society made it possible for me to travel, and a grant from the School of Liberal Arts of Indiana University–Purdue University at Indianapolis helped with typing.

It has also been my good fortune to meet with unfailing consideration and kindness from everyone I consulted in the course of my research. This book could never have been written without the generosity of Willard C. Heiss of Indianapolis, who not only gave me free run of his wonderful collection of Quaker doctrinal literature (now largely at Brigham Young University) but also made me an outright gift of a number of books, pamphlets, and microfilms as well as aided me in other ways too numerous to mention. The interlibrary loan staff of the Indiana University Library located dozens of items for me. Damon Hickey and Carole Treadway of the Friends Historical Collection at Guilford College; Diane Altin and Elisabeth Potts Brown of the Quaker Collection at Haverford College; Albert Fowler and Nancy Speers of the Friends Historical Library at Swarthmore College; Stanford Terhune of the Cattell Library at Malone College; and the staffs of the Southern Historical Collection at the University of North Carolina, the Manuscripts Division of the Duke University Library, the Indiana Historical Society Library, and the Indiana Division of the Indiana State Library were all helpful above and beyond the call of duty. This is especially true of Phil Shore, Sara Beth Terrell, and other members of the staff of the Lilly Library at Earlham College, where I did much of my research. Others who shared memories and materials or who stimulated my thinking include Dr. and Mrs. Byron L. Osborne of North Canton, Ohio; the late Ethel Bevan of Haviland, Kansas; Kathaleen and Leland K. Carter of Valparaiso, Indiana; Elizabeth Moger of the Haviland Records Room, New York City; Robert A. and Elsie (Davis) Peirce of Dalton, Indiana; Joseph G. and Leanna (Barker) Roberts of Westfield, Indiana; George F. Parker of Bakersfield, California; Gurney B. Reece of Claremont, California; Wilmer Cooper of the Earlham School of Religion; and Ray Stewart and Errol T. Elliott of Indianapolis.

I owe a less direct but nonetheless substantial debt to the editors and staff of the *Journal of American History* from 1981 to 1984, especially Lewis Perry, B. Edward McClellan, and David Hoth. They not only imparted to me a sense of graceful writing and the importance of technical skills, but they also widened my intellectual horizons. Without them this book would have been a much poorer work.

Finally, and most important, my wife Mary Louise Reynolds provided me with unflagging moral and intellectual support throughout my research and writing. She shared an apartment with my stacks of notes and papers, cheerfully made space for the boxes of books and pamphlets that periodically appeared, and tolerated my absorption in bygone theological debates while at the same time kept me in touch with a larger world.

Introduction

In 1910 James Baldwin, publishing executive, textbook writer, and pur-
veyor of useful and moral knowledge to a generation of American schoolchildren, sought to re-create in literary form the Quaker community into which
he had been born almost seventy years before. His reminiscences were
largely of the changes brought to the Friends' "New Settlement" of Westfield, Indiana, by the technological and modernizing forces of the nineteenth
century—the railroad, the telegraph, the mass-circulation newspaper, and
the city. As Baldwin brought his memoir to a close, however, his emphasis
shifted from the material transformation of Westfield to the spiritual
transformation of the Quakerism that had shaped his youth.[1]

The Westfield of the 1840s and 1850s was, according to Baldwin, a place of
women in dove-colored "plain" bonnets and men in broad-brimmed beaver
hats and drab shadbelly coats cut in peculiar styles. The inhabitants spoke of
"thee" and "thine"; theirs was the language of seventeenth-century England.
Their favorite reading was the diaries of deceased Friends. They worshiped
in an utterly plain, barnlike building they called a meetinghouse. There the
men and women sat separately, with the elders and "weighty" Friends facing
them at the front, the silence broken only by an occasional impromptu
discourse believed to be uttered under the direct inspiration of the Holy
Spirit. "Testimonies" ruled their lives—testimonies against slavery, fighting,
"light and profane" literature, "worldly diversions," music, a "hireling ministry"—in sum, against "the world." Their lives were proscribed by "the
discipline," a "thin, dreary volume" that regulated every aspect of a good
Friend's existence, from the width of the hat brim to the height of the
tombstone. Every regulation was enforced by three overseers, "holy bigots"
whom Baldwin described as a strange cross between medieval inquisitors
and modern detectives.[2]

The Friends that Baldwin found when he returned to Westfield in 1910
left the gentle publisher bewildered. They worshiped not in a meetinghouse
but in a steepled church that, his Babbitt-like guide informed him, for "style
and comfort" rivaled any in the state. An organ for music and a pulpit filled
by a sleek and elegant minister had replaced the grim old denizens of the
facing benches. The plain language was a memory associated with long-dead
grandparents; gone too were shadbelly coats and plain bonnets. No one saw
"the use of such any longer." The Quakers of Westfield were no longer
separate from the world—they had become part of it.[3]

James Baldwin's reminiscences are important, not only for what they tell us
about nineteenth-century Quakerism, but also for what they say about the

relationship between the Quaker subculture and the larger American culture. During the mid-nineteenth century a combination of internal tensions, socioeconomic change, and the influence of non-Quaker religious thought, especially evangelicalism, subtly and gradually laid the groundwork for a near-revolution that during the 1870s would sweep away nearly all of the marks of Quaker distinctiveness. By 1900 the overwhelming majority of American Friends were no longer part of a sect but, instead, were part of a religious movement that had achieved denominational status.

Despite their importance for American Quakers, such changes have remained largely unexplored. The major Quaker historians, such as Allen C. Thomas and Richard H. Thomas, Rufus M. Jones, and Elbert Russell, gave them necessarily limited attention; two generations have now passed since Russell's work, the most recent, was published. Since the 1940s, scholarship has tended to concentrate on the earlier periods of Quaker history, those before 1800, or on the involvement of American Friends in such causes as peace, abolition, and women's rights. The result has been a major gap in the history of American Quakerism, a gap that this study seeks to fill.[4]

This volume opens with a description of the Quaker vision of religious life in the first half of the nineteenth century, a distinctive vision that, in contrast with the dominant evangelical religious culture of the United States, emphasized growth into holiness rather than the "new birth." That vision first began to disintegrate during the 1820s as the unity of American Quakerism crumbled in a bitter schism that in many ways resembled the conflicts between evangelicals and liberals in the larger religious world. This study follows the history of Orthodox Friends who, on a series of questions, took stands similar to those of non-Quaker evangelicals. Some will undoubtedly regret the exclusion of Hicksite Friends, the opposing party, from this study, but their history was so different that to include them here would have been to write two books.

In the 1830s Orthodox Friends in the United States set out on a course that brought them under the powerful influence of the dominant evangelical culture of the United States. Evangelical norms and values slowly permeated Orthodox Quakerism, often so gradually and so subtly that many Friends were not entirely conscious of what was taking place. The result was, nevertheless, another schism. Evangelical influences culminated during the 1870s, when a group of young Quaker ministers brought the revival methods of the second-experience holiness movement into the Society of Friends. The holiness revival produced a new factionalism among Orthodox Quakers, who spent the years from 1875 to 1895 attempting to reconcile those innovations with Quaker tradition. By the beginning of the twentieth century, most American Friends had become absorbed in the same questions of modernism and incipient fundamentalism that were troubling other Protestants.

The aims of this study are to bring a new understanding of the diversity and complexity of American Quaker history; to shed new light on the background of Quaker benevolence and humanitarianism as well as to make intelligible a century of doctrinal debates that might otherwise leave the uninitiated mystified; and, above all, to show that nineteenth-century Quaker history was in large part a series of interactions between American Friends and the larger political, social, and especially religious world. The reaction of Friends to those interactions and their influence determined the course of Quakerism.

To do more than merely illuminate a neglected aspect of the history of an influential but relatively small sect, however, the study also focuses on two subjects of considerable interest to students of American history and culture: evangelicalism and pluralism. The history of Orthodox Quakerism during the period under study reveals much about American religion during the nineteenth century, particularly the relationship between its evangelical center and those traditions that originally lay outside it. At the same time that evangelicalism and opposition to it were giving rise to new denominations and religious movements, thus broadening the American religious spectrum and the boundaries of pluralism, evangelicalism was also deeply influencing nonevangelical traditions and pulling them closer to the religious center. Orthodox Quakerism during the nineteenth century provides a striking example of that process.

These two themes—evangelicalism and pluralism—have, of course, been the subjects of extensive study elsewhere. We know much about the history of the traditionally evangelical groups, such as the Methodists, the Baptists, and the Presbyterians, and their vision of a Christian America. That vision had a profound impact on American life, with important consequences for politics, reform, literature, the status of women, and the nature of the family. Only recently, however, have historians begun to gauge the influence of evangelicalism on denominations outside the evangelical tradition. Evangelicalism powerfully affected both Episcopalians and Lutherans, not to mention such separatist sects as the German Baptist Brethren, the Amish, and the Mennonites. Roman Catholics in the United States adopted some of the techniques of evangelical revivalism. As pluralism increased in terms of the numbers of diverse sects, and as some of those sects expanded its boundaries, the norms of others were increasingly set by the dominant evangelical culture.[5]

Perhaps no religious group in the nineteenth century exemplifies that process so well as Orthodox Friends. The Society of Friends arose in seventeenth-century England as a protest against the dominant religious culture of its day, fortifying itself not only behind a wall of separation from the world but also with doctrinal beliefs that set Quakers apart from nearly all other Protestants. During the eighteenth century American Friends underwent a process of internal reformation that strengthened those barricades and heightened the Quaker sense of separateness and peculiarity. During the nineteenth century, however, in response to what a majority perceived as the invasion of outside heresies in the teachings of the minister Elias Hicks, Orthodox Friends reacted in a very different way. Their defense against contamination moved them significantly closer to the American religious mainstream. In a complex series of events, often intended to foster distinctive Quaker testimonies or to return to first principles, Quakers came to interpret their heritage in a way that reflected evangelical norms. This, in turn, set the foundation for the near-revolution of the 1870s, when teachings taken from the interdenominational holiness movement transformed the society. By 1900, most members of the Society of Friends in the United States had moved closer to the American religious mainstream, but at the price of a splintering that resulted in an increasing diversity within American Quakerism that reflected the larger religious world. Orthodox Quakers offer a remarkable example of the subtle means by which a dominant culture draws outgroups under its influence and closer to the mainstream.

One final word is necessary in introducing the history of Orthodox Quakerism, and that concerns its organizational structure. By the nineteenth century Orthodox Friends were living under a highly structured but somewhat decentralized system of church government with the following components:[6] (1) The lowest rung on the Quaker organizational ladder was the indulged or the preparative meeting, which can best be thought of as an individual congregation. Often Friends referred to it simply as a meeting. One or more meetings made up the (2) monthly meeting. The monthly meeting was the basic unit of Quaker organization. It had the power to receive and to disown (excommunicate) members, to hold property, and to solemnize marriages. Two or more monthly meetings made up a (3) quarterly meeting. The quarterly meeting dealt with problems, usually of doctrine and organization, deemed too important to be left to monthly meetings. Several quarterly meetings made up a (4) yearly meeting. Until 1902, the yearly meeting was the ultimate authority for the Orthodox Friends who lived within its bounds. Each yearly meeting was independent of all others; no yearly meeting could legislate for or bind any other. The yearly meeting made decisions on both doctrine and discipline and served as a court of final appeal in cases of disownment. There were six yearly meetings in America in 1800: New England, New York, Philadelphia, Baltimore, Virginia, and North Carolina. Between 1813 and 1908 Orthodox Friends in the United States formed nine new yearly meetings: Ohio in 1813, Indiana in 1821, Western in 1858, Iowa in 1863, Kansas in 1872, Wilmington in 1892, Oregon in 1892, California in 1895, and Nebraska in 1908. (A yearly meeting was also established in Canada in 1867.) These names can be misleading. After 1821, for example, Ohio Yearly Meeting included only Friends in eastern Ohio.

Those in the central and western parts of the state were part of Indiana Yearly Meeting. Ohio Yearly Meeting did include, however, Friends in western Pennsylvania and Virginia. Orthodox Friends in southeastern Michigan were part of New York Yearly Meeting until 1867, when they became part of Ohio Yearly Meeting.

It must be kept in mind that the meetings were both institutions and events. Thus in some contexts "Indiana Yearly Meeting" may refer to a body of Friends. In another context it may refer to the annual sessions when members of the yearly meeting came together for business and to deal with society affairs.

Rich Square Friends Meeting, Henry County, Indiana, 1885.
The plain dress of the older Friends and the "worldly" attire
of the younger reveal Orthodox Quakerism in transition.
Photograph reproduced courtesy of Henry County Historical
Society, New Castle, Indiana.

CHAPTER

I

THE QUAKER VISION OF RELIGIOUS LIFE, 1800–1860

Late in the year 1839, William Hobbs, an eminent minister in the Society of Friends, set down for his children "something of my religious experience." Spiritual autobiography was not uncommon in nineteenth-century America, but Hobbs's reminiscences provide a striking contrast with those of contemporaries such as Charles G. Finney and Lyman Beecher. The common vocabulary of evangelical Protestantism—conviction, conversion, revival, new birth, and even church—is missing. Instead, Hobbs wrote of "Our Society," of many baptisms, of taking up the cross. [1]

Hobbs had lived a spiritual life that differed radically from that of almost all other Christians. By the early nineteenth century, the Society of Friends had created a system of religious doctrine and moral regulations of considerable complexity. It was a system that shaped virtually every aspect of a consistent Friend's life. And it was one that offers striking contrasts with the dominant religious culture of the United States before 1850.

For half a century the starting point for understanding nineteenth-century American religion has been evangelicalism. Defining evangelicalism is no easy task. As Donald G. Mathews has noted, it is a term that annoys anyone who likes "clean-cut and precise definitions." One idea was central to evangelicalism, however: the conversion experience, a "profoundly emotional" new birth, in which a person established an acceptable personal relationship with God. Implicit in the conversion experience was the assumption of most evangelicals that this profound personal experience would not usually be achieved alone; the seeker would be led to it by a "spirit anointed" preacher. And it was a definite experience. Reborn Christians could date their new birth with the same precision that they named the date on which they came out of the womb. [2]

The Quaker vision of religious life was quite different. The label that historians have usually applied to the religious life of the Society of Friends in the eighteenth and early nineteenth centuries is quietism. It was, they argue, a life of meditation and reflection, focusing on the experience of the immediate working of the Holy Spirit on the soul. It thus had definite mystical overtones. It deemphasized preaching and all other external means of grace and instead focused on shutting out anything that might distract from the achievement of total spiritual communion with God. Quaker life-styles and concepts of worship were a conscious alternative to the asceticism in which reflective religion usually took refuge, an alternative that put Friends on the pathway to salvation by allowing them to live in the world without being contaminated by it.[3]

At the heart of that vision was the most distinctive doctrine of Friends— the Inner Light. George Fox's vision on the North Country moors in the 1640s—that "every man was enlightened by the divine light of Christ . . . and they that believed in it came out of condemnation to the light of life, and became children of it"—still guided Friends 150 years later. The Inner Light made all intermediaries—priests, sacraments, offerings—unnecessary. By following the light within, anyone could achieve salvation. Ignoring the light eventually extinguished it and resulted in damnation. Disagreement over the source and nature of the Inner Light eventually split American Friends, but virtually all Quakers agreed with the young Ohio Friend Thomas Arnett on how the Inner Light was perceived. It was a "still, small voice" in the "soul of every man . . . for the purpose of teaching him how he may pass his time in this world to obtain God's favor and blessing." As the light was of God, it taught as no mortal could teach. Thus all persons, even those who had never heard of Christ, had planted within them not only a way to salvation but also a way far above any human instrumentality.[4]

The goal of Quaker religious life thus became to allow the seed of Christ, the Inner Light, to lead believers gradually into salvation. Friends sought not a crisis experience of a single new birth but gradual growth into holiness. Growth thus became the favorite Quaker metaphor of religious life. The North Carolina minister Nathan Hunt compared spiritual life to a plant, the Inner Light being the seed that sprouts under God's guidance, gradually bringing forth fruits of salvation. Friends often compared their spiritual growth to their physical development, as was the case with Thomas B. Gould, a young New England Friend who wrote in the 1830s that he longed for "a progression from this state of childhood to that of a young man, and to a strong man in Jesus Christ." The theme of growth, of being regenerated, of "continually wrestling for an advancement," of going on "gradually and gently," is a constant one in the writings of Friends between 1800 and 1850. Often that growth took place in increments so small that they seemed indiscernible. Thus one Friend recalled of his spiritual life only that he gained "little by little . . . in many respects" until he overcame "that which was fallen" in himself.[5]

That is not to deny that many Friends experienced certain decisive turning points in their growth. The extensive Quaker journal and memorial literature often mentions specific experiences that were seen as the beginning of obedience to the Inner Light. The well-known minister Stephen Grellet had a profound awakening during a meeting for worship that was as dramatic as that of any of his non-Quaker contemporaries. Usually, however, such experiences were less abrupt. Thus Pennsylvania Friends recorded of Mercy Ellis that "in early life she was sensible of the tendering visitations of God to her inclining her to choose the good and refuse the evil." William Hobbs recalled intimations of God's love and judgment as early as age five or six. After many such visitations, at age twenty-one, while praying, he seemed to hear a voice saying: "If thou wilt be faithful in following that inward witness that has been so long pleading with thee, thy sins shall all be forgiven and I will be with thee and be thy preserver." The language of Hobbs's "voice" is significant: it did not say that his sins were forgiven outright; rather, it said that his sins would be forgiven if he followed the leadings of the "inward witness."[6]

It is important to keep in mind, however, that many memorials and reminiscences do not mention such an experience, implying that it was not seen as essential to salvation. Typical in that respect is a eulogy of a fellow member by Friends in Indiana in the 1820s: "As she yielded obedience to divine instruction in her youthful days," they wrote, "she witnessed a growth and advancement in the life of true religion, and, through its powerful operations, became a powerful and exemplary member in the church." In middle age, the New York minister Henry Hull could write only that he was on the road to salvation; whether heaven would be his reward was uncertain. Indeed, in the eyes of many Friends, the evangelical claim of salvation based on a single event led to a dangerous false rest. "Alas for that individual who relaxes in labour until safely landed on the shores of everlasting eternity," wrote one Philadelphia Friend. A Friend born in Indiana in 1842 remembered that he was a teenager before he even heard of being "converted."[7]

A comparison of evangelical and Quaker views of religious growth provides an instructive contrast. It was common for evangelicals to speak and write of the necessity of growth in grace and perseverance in faith, but they saw the new birth as the critical experience and focused most of their attention on it. For Quakers, however, growth was the experience. Thus Friends tried to aid others along the path. Growth into salvation as set forth by Friends was of an inward nature with outward manifestations.

Orthodox Friends were quick to point out that human beings could do nothing to achieve their own salvation; Jonathan Edwards himself never stated such powerlessness more clearly. There was no significant difference between the Orthodox Quaker position and that of most evangelicals as to the effect of Adam's fall on his posterity. Human beings were completely powerless; their corrupt wills would ever hinder advancement and transformation into Christ. It was impossible to take a single step alone. But for seekers there was the Inner Light, "the Divine will inwardly revealed," and the baptism of the Holy Spirit.[8]

The Quaker conception of baptism differed radically from that of most Christians. George Fox and the early Friends had rejected water baptism (along with the Lord's Supper) as one of the Jewish ceremonies that the coming of Christ had superseded. The true gospel baptism, Fox had argued, was the baptism of the "Holy Ghost and with fire." Friends saw that baptism as a peculiar visitation of God inwardly experienced to help with growth into holiness. Christ, Friends said, came into the world to end sin and to bring in righteousness; if righteousness was to conquer the heart, it had to be through the spirit of God—no outward ordinance could wash it clean.[9]

Baptisms of the Holy Spirit took many forms, but, in the experience of Friends, they usually came through suffering and tribulation. It might be illness or some personal grief, but most common was a kind of mental anguish and depression that arose from no discernible cause; "low and much stripped" was a favorite phrase. Friends living in the light learned to rejoice in such experiences, which, they believed, washed and made white the robes of believers. One Quaker mother in Indiana in the 1830s tried to comfort her daughter with the assurance that "trials and afflictions patiently endured, and quietly submitted to, prepare the Lord's people for the enjoyment of his love and power." A Philadelphia Friend wrote that trials and exercises were as necessary to spiritual health as medicines were to physical health. The prevailing tone, however, was much blunter. Stephen Grellet quoted Scripture: "Whom the Lord loveth, he chasteneth, and scourgeth every son whom he receiveth. If we had not chastening, we should be bastards and not sons."[10]

Not all baptisms involved suffering. Some were of joy and delight. The New England minister John Wilbur, an adamant opponent of doctrinal innovation, thought that those of grief and happiness balanced each other. Such was the experience of John Beals, a North Carolina Friend. Not long before his death in 1796, he had a vision of heaven with Christ enthroned in glory and surrounded by the saints. Beals received a promise that within a few days he would join their number. The experience, he told his family, filled him with unspeakable joy and a feeling of indescribable sweetness.[11]

The predominate motif, however, in the "deep baptisms" that Friends experienced was tribulation. Typical is the language of Margaret Jones, a minister in Indiana during the 1850s: "Weakness and poverty generally are my portion. . . . I think I have been most strangely and singularly tempted, proved, and tried, and in such ways that cannot be now described." One

Philadelphia Friend in the 1820s refused even to attempt to comfort one such sufferer, saying that it would be contrary to God's will. Such may account for the common description of Friends as grim, a label whose justice Friends admitted. Friends, however, thought that such an outward appearance was a sign of inward grace. As one put it in 1841: "By the sadness of the countenance the heart is made better." Of course, other Protestants, such as the evangelical revivalists of the Great Awakening, were notoriously grim in appearance and outlook; nearly all evangelicals eschewed levity and "lightness." But few groups carried dourness to the extent that Friends did, or saw such spiritual merit in depression.[12]

Those experiences, in the eyes of Friends, earned their sufferers a reward. They were a means of "refinement and purification." Friends saw the baptism of the Holy Spirit as something to be endured frequently. "O the deep baptisms I have daily to experience," Charles Osborn mourned in 1816. They gradually washed away not only sin but also the desire and propensity to sin, helping the sufferer to achieve perfection. After many baptisms Friends would be as "gold tried in the fire," completely purified. They came to surrender their wills to Christ. Thus the ultimate end of "deep baptisms" was not merely "conversion" but sanctification, a state of sinlessness.[13]

Human beings could do nothing by themselves to advance the work of salvation, but they could cooperate with it. The best means was withdrawal into solitude, where the world and all that distracted from God or drowned out "the still small voice" were distant. "To retire into the soul," Thomas Arnett wrote in 1823, "is to enter into the house of knowledge; and a perfect silence of all imagination and actings." Such solitude prepared seekers for divine instruction. Like the prophets of ancient Israel, said Arnett, seekers should dwell in retirement, awaiting the Lord. To "keep in the quiet," however, was often a struggle for Friends, and their letters and diaries are full of pleas for divine aid to remain in such a state. The constant introspection, the waiting, had as its most tangible fruits the huge number of journals and memoranda in which Friends recorded their spiritual progress or mourned their lack of it.[14]

Just as Friends sought absolute solitude on occasion, they also sought to hedge themselves against the encroachments of the world in a variety of other ways. The hedges eventually hardened into a system of mores that Friends called the plain life. Carried forward from the seventeenth century, many customs of the plain life, such as the use of "thee" and "thou" instead of "you" in the second-person singular, the peculiar dress, and the refusal to remove hats, to use titles, and to take oaths, had their origins in principles based on Scripture. By 1800 the plain life had come to serve as a barrier around Friends, one that helped to keep them separate from the world and its distractions. Peculiar dress and speech gave Friends a reputation for being odd and kept them out of popular favor. Thus Friends avoided invitations and enticements that might involve them with the world. The world was by its nature hostile to the growth of godliness, and Friends perceived their peculiarities not only as keeping them separate from the pollutions of the world but also as reminding the world of the better way.[15]

Hand in hand with the plain life came severe restrictions on amusements and diversions. Friends banned virtually all activities that did not tend toward religious reflection. Typical was the attitude of the Philadelphia journal *Friend* toward novels in 1837. The object of life, the *Friend* editorialized, was to achieve salvation, a task that required nearly all of anyone's time. To fill what spare moments were left, so much good reading was available in religion, history, and science that no time remained for lighter pursuits. Friends placed similar bans on music, including hymns. God did not need such praise; music only gratified the senses. Friends naturally shared the strictures of evangelicals against such "blatant immorality" as gambling, dancing, fornication, and drunkenness.[16]

Friends summed up that whole lifestyle—the baptisms, the tribulations, the repudiation of the world, and the plain life—in the phrase "bearing the cross." "No cross, no crown," William Penn had written in the 1680s, and Friends saw the "personal cross" as the way of salvation. Just as Christ had cleansed the world of sin by his atoning death on the cross, so Friends had to die daily to sin. "The daily cross must be experienced," Joseph Edgerton, a leading Ohio Friend, wrote in 1842, "whereby being crucified to the world, we may be made to follow the blessed captain of salvation in the straight and narrow way of self-denial." Thomas Arnett wrote lyrically of the cross as "the divine grace which . . . brings salvation to all who . . . walk under its divine influence." It would obliterate every carnal desire, subdue all sin, and ultimately sanctify the lives of all who lived under it. As Friends thus submitted to the discipline of the cross in life, they would become qualified to lead their families in the way that they should go; as they became accustomed to the yoke, it became easier to bear. Thus the cross came to symbolize both a means of grace and a way of life to Friends.[17]

From those beliefs Friends created a spirituality radically different from that of other Protestants. Friends occasionally spoke of experiencing a change of heart, but they did not regard such an experience in the same light as did evangelicals. When Friends wrote or spoke of the goal of religious life, they named it sanctification, holiness, or perfection, not conversion. Many evangelicals, most notably John Wesley in the eighteenth century and Charles G. Finney in the nineteenth, also spoke of the possibility and duty of sanctification, but they represented it as a second act. First came conversion, then sanctification. Friends instead held that justification (the divine side of conversion in evangelical eyes)—being in a state of acceptance with God—and sanctification—purification from the influence of all sin—were inseparable. A favorite Quaker text was Hebrews 12:14, which speaks of

holiness, "without which no man shall see the Lord." Thus the *Friends'*
Review proudly proclaimed in 1850 that the society had never ceased to
uphold salvation as *"sanctification* through the immediate and sensible
influence of Christ" (italics added). Friends expressly repudiated the Wesleyan and Finneyite formulation of instantaneous sanctification subsequent
to conversion, at least until the 1870s. An exhortation to Quaker youth from
an Indiana Friend a few years earlier summarized that outlook: "All unrighteousness, which is sin, must be removed . . . before we can be
reunited. . . . We must be willing to pass under the powerful operation of
that flaming sword, which turns every way upon the transgressing nature
within, before we can be partakers of the fruit of the tree of life, or enter in
through the 'strait gates' into the city." Such an experience was hard, but it
was rewarded, since "if there is a willingness to abide in humble patience,
under the operation of this holy warfare in the heart, there will be an
overcoming experienced, and in time the whole heart will be changed and
made new."[18]

The often solitary nature of religious life as Friends envisioned it might
make some question whether any form of human fellowship was necessary,
but Quakers fervently believed that gathering together for divine worship—
"meeting for worship," as they called it—was of vital importance. The
meeting not only gave Friends an opportunity to put their ideas of the nature
of true worship into action; it also became part of bearing the cross. Most
important, the meeting for worship, away from the distractions of the world,
provided the best means of waiting for God and being strengthened by
him.[19]

The meeting for worship was a logical outgrowth of the Quaker conception
of religious life. Its medium was silence, "the most sublime part of our
religious life," as one enthusiastic Friend put it. Silence was in part the
absence of all noise, since no one was to do anything in a meeting for worship
without the direct inspiration of the Holy Spirit. In order to feel such
inspiration, one had to block out all else. True silence was "a prostration of
the soul before God, having our expectation from Him, and Him only." That
expectation might take the form of prayer, exhortation, or preaching. It
might bring an inner experience, the deep baptism that Friends sought so
longingly. Silence, however, was more than a medium. In the minds of
Friends, true silence was worship itself. It was strange, one Friend wrote in
1850, to think that God needed to hear one speak aloud in order to be
worshiped: "The more mental our worship, the more it assimilates to His
likeness—the more silent, the more suitable to the language of the spirit." It
would not be correct to say that Friends rejected displays of emotion in
meeting. Weeping was not considered improper. Verbal outbursts, however, were condemned. Words and physical action were for mortals, but God
knew the language of the soul and did not need to hear words spoken.[20]

To break the silence of a meeting for worship was thus a very serious matter. Friends were skeptical of outsiders speaking in meeting for that reason. They frowned even on the approving "amen" of a Methodist hearing a Quaker minister preach. Few Friends ever spoke in meeting, but those who did apparently did so regularly. In the nineteenth century Friends recognized a gift along this line by formally recording those who spoke "in the ministry." The word *record* is important. Human beings could only recognize a gift bestowed by God. They could not advance it, nor could any human act, such as ordination, bestow special power or legitimacy on it.[21]

Friends carried the doctrine of direct inspiration to extreme ends. One of George Fox's favorite dicta was that a degree from Oxford or Cambridge did not make a minister. The result was an anti-intellectualism that made Friends lag far behind other denominations in the development of higher education even while they were leaders in primary education. Some Friends condemned all learning above bare literacy. Since preaching or other ministry had to be done under the immediate inspiration of the Holy Spirit, Friends forbade any form of preparation. Even to bring along a Bible to read in meeting was rare. Ministers had no professional status. They worked at secular employment to support themselves. And they took the silent waiting as seriously as any other member. It was not uncommon for a minister to ask Friends to hold a special meeting and then to sit silent throughout it.[22]

The nature of Quaker preaching before 1850 is shadowy, since there were no sermon manuscripts and the various Quaker diarists usually recorded only the most cursory accounts of what Friends said or heard; many Friends adamantly opposed their transcription and publication. What does survive suggests that the themes of preaching were those matters of vital concern to Friends trying to advance in holiness: baptism, growth, plainness, silence, the dangers of the world, and, especially, the Inner Light. The purpose of preaching, one minister wrote early in the nineteenth century, was "to persuade people to seek the Lord, and to be faithful to His word, *the inspoken words of the heart* . . . and then leave them to be directed by the inward feelings of the mind." The language of such discourses was usually drawn from the Bible and was filled with allegory and unusual metaphor and analogy. By the nineteenth century a set form for Quaker preaching had arisen, a kind of chant that was known as the "sing-song." The sing-song had no official sanction, and often yearly meetings cautioned ministers to avoid affectations of speech and gesture; nevertheless, this form became typical of Quaker preaching.[23]

Quaker ministry was intended not for broad-scale proselytizing but for the edification of those who already were members. Contrary to what has often been written, Quaker ministers before 1850 often held, or "appointed," meetings among nonmembers, and "Convinced Friends" could be found in almost every meeting. Some of the society's most eminent ministers during the early nineteenth century—Stephen Grellet, Christopher Healy, William Hobbs, and Jeremiah Hubbard—were converts. Friends usually perceived their mission as fundamentally different from that of evangelical religion, however. They made no regular, concerted efforts to win converts, instead depending on birthright membership to maintain their numerical strength. Thus they devoted most of their resources to strengthening and teaching those who had always been Friends. To the rest of the world, Friends were to be a leaven, an example. The Society of Friends was to be "as a light to the world" so that "men might see the good works wrought by its members, and imitating their example, 'glorify their Father which is in heaven.' "[24]

That attitude left Friends in an uncertain position toward other denominations. On one hand, Friends saw good in all churches. The very name "Society of Friends" was testimony that "church" was a word to be applied only to the universal body of believers. And Friends were explicit in their belief that obedience to the Inner Light could save even those who had never heard of Christ. On the other hand, Friends remained convinced that their society was "primitive Christianity revived," that they were to be "as a light to the nations." To take part in the worship of other denominations would risk falling back into "beggarly elements" such as the ordinances that led away from the light and the cross.[25]

The Quaker conception of community grew out of both the plain life and the idea of Friends as a leaven to the world. Friends codified the requirements of the plain life in "the discipline," which set the standard of conduct expected of every Friend in everything from behavior in meeting to the style of clothing and the height of tombstones. Each monthly meeting had overseers—"saintly, self-conceited, bigoted creatures," in the words of James Baldwin, "who, in other times and at other places would have been holy inquisitors or perhaps second-rate modern detectives." The overseers' duty was to detect and to report to the monthly meeting any violation of the discipline, both to aid members in staying in the "strait and narrow" and to ensure that the reputation of the society would not suffer reproach. Virtually all facets of life came under the care of the meeting. Even to move away from its care without being recommended to another monthly meeting was an offense that could result in loss of membership, or "disownment."[26]

Friends tried to keep entanglements with the world to a minimum. The most notable manifestation of that effort was the discipline on marriage. Marriage was to take place only with another Friend; marriage to a non-Quaker was forbidden on the grounds that to have parents of different religious persuasions would confuse their children. Such marriages, moreover, tended to lead Friends away from the plain life and the cross. The marriage regulations made for tightly knit societies with intricate family connections, as in Nantucket with its five thousand cousins. For these reasons Friends clustered in certain areas. As late as the 1860s a woman growing up in a well-to-do Baltimore Quaker family could find herself brought into contact only with other Quakers. Most Pennsylvania Friends were in five counties around Philadelphia. The overwhelming majority of Quakers in Ohio lived in three counties along the eastern edge of the state and in three in its southwestern corner. In North Carolina over half of the Quaker population lived in two counties. To leave that fellowship, even for other communities of Friends, was a matter that, at least early in the nineteenth century, required the approval of the meeting left behind. "A community of Quakers is almost a world within itself," one former Friend wrote. "It is as nearly separated from the world without . . . as any circle of mortals well can be."[27]

Even the best-known and most-studied feature of nineteenth-century Quakerism, its devotion to humanitarianism and benevolence, was bound up in the requirements of the plain life and the cross. The origins of Quaker humanitarianism are complex, but for many Friends it flowed naturally from the Quaker conception of religious life. "A spirit of benevolence is the invariable fruit of a strict and careful attention to the admonitions of grace," the *Friends' Review* editorialized in 1850, and Friends regarded good works as one of the best signs of growth in holiness. Sydney V. James has found that Friends in the eighteenth century held a similar view. In attacking slavery, for example, Quakers had dual concerns. Of course they were concerned about the outrages and hardships that slaves suffered. But, as David Brion Davis has noted, at the heart of the Quaker antislavery protest lay concerns for purity and responsibility. Slavery was an abomination for the slave because, as Thomas Arnett wrote, it deprived slaves of the freedom to work out their lives according to the light within them. As for the slaveholders, their power over their property was so great that it involved a plenitude of opportunities to indulge sinful tendencies. Thus abstaining from slavery became a sign of outward purity as well as an indication of the progress of the work of the spirit within. A similar theme runs through other Quaker reforms. Friends advocated literacy because it was necessary for reading the Bible and other useful works that furthered holiness. Friends were prominent among the proponents of the once-notorious Pennsylvania system of prison discipline in which the solitary confinement of each prisoner with a Bible was designed to lead to contemplation, repentance, and reformation. Even pacifism is partially explained by the requirements of the plain life and the cross. War and violence gave free reign to the passions, and the passions were among the chief objects of discipline under the cross.[28]

So it was that Orthodox Quakers maintained a way of religious life that differed radically from the dominant evangelical religious culture of the

United States before 1850. Friends summed up that life as one of "bearing the cross"—the cross of peculiarity, of the baptism, of the plain life, of silent worship. They sustained it only through constant adherence to the discipline and resistance to the world. But to shut out the world completely was impossible. And under the assault of the world the older vision began to break down.

CHAPTER

II

THE BREAKDOWN OF THE OLDER VISION, 1800–1850

In the 1870s, when William Hodgson of Philadelphia wrote his own pointed and very personal history of the Society of Friends in the nineteenth century, he chose a revealing subtitle: "A Historical View of the Successive Convulsions and Schisms Therein during That Period." Hodgson's summary of Quaker history from 1800 to 1860 is accurate. In 1800 the Society of Friends, not only in America but throughout the world, was remarkably compact in its population patterns and seemingly united on questions of theology. In 1860 American Friends were split into no fewer than three seemingly irreconcilable factions, each professing to be the only true Society of Friends, each hurling invective at the others. And as doctrinal unity dissolved, so did social and demographic compactness, as Friends, like other Americans, scattered across the United States.[1]

THE GREAT MIGRATION

The social fact of American Quakerism during the nineteenth century was westward movement. Some historians have tried to interpret American Quakerism as the product of the frontier experience. Friends, they argue, have always been a people in the vanguard of settlement. The freedom inherent in the frontier, those scholars assert, was in constant tension with the more conservative, restricted Quakerism of the East. That tension, they conclude, gave rise to most of the controversies that American Friends have faced. Like Frederick Jackson Turner's larger attempt of a century ago, this frontier thesis is overstated. Indisputable, however, is that by 1850 westward migration had changed the face of American Quakerism.[2]

"The Great Migration," as Friends call it, radically transformed American Quaker population patterns. Certain areas with significant Quaker populations in 1800—Tidewater Virginia, South Carolina, and Georgia—were bereft of Friends by 1850. North Carolina, a major Quaker center at the end of the eighteenth century, saw about a quarter of the meetings in the state dissolved, or "laid down," between 1800 and 1850, while the surviving Quaker communities suffered drastic decreases in population. "Our meeting is getting verry [sic] small," two North Carolina Friends wrote in 1831. "People are moving to the western Country so much that it seems we will be left alone." A similar fate befell the Quaker settlements in East Tennessee only a generation after their founding. There were similar migrations from New England and the middle states, although they were not of the same proportions. We lack definite statistics, however, and in regard to the meetings that the Hicksite schism affected, it is difficult to judge what loss was due to migration and what was due to theological controversy.[3]

The main destinations for Quaker migration before 1850 were Indiana and Ohio. Again, accurate statistics are scarce, but they suggest a massive influx of Friends. Stephen B. Weeks, using fragmentary records from the South, found over 1,400 families and 900 individuals heading west before 1850. John Hunt, a Philadelphia Friend who visited Ohio in 1813, commented: "Seldom, if ever, was there a more rapid settlement. . . . A vast number of Friends are settled there." In the year of Hunt's visit, Friends west of the Appalachians formed Ohio Yearly Meeting, the first new yearly meeting established since 1698. Eight years later, Ohio Yearly Meeting was divided, with Friends west of the Scioto River becoming Indiana Yearly Meeting. By 1843 a majority of Orthodox Friends lived west of the Appalachians: 30,000 in Indiana Yearly Meeting and 8,000 in Ohio, compared with about 35,000 in the yearly meetings along the eastern seaboard. In Ohio, elements from the middle states and from the South were in rough balance, but in Indiana Yearly Meeting there was a strong North Carolina hegemony that would spread westward for the rest of the century.[4]

The Great Migration also reveals much about the sense of community and discipline among Friends. Early westward movement by Friends was often in groups. One example is the Friends of Trent River Monthly Meeting in Jones County, North Carolina. In 1800, wishing to move out of the "Egyptian darkness" of that "oppressive part of the land" into a territory where slavery was banned, Trent Friends sent two members to look for suitable lands in the Northwest Territory. After consulting with Friends living on Redstone Creek in western Pennsylvania, the two scouts located a large tract on Colerain Creek in Belmont County, Ohio, to which the Trent Friends moved in a body. Friends in South Carolina and Georgia migrated to Warren County, Ohio, in a similar manner, having been warned by Zachariah Dicks, a minister widely believed to have the gift of prophecy, that their homes in the South would become a battleground. Such migrations of entire communities were rare after 1805, but even when Friends migrated individually, their movements required the consent and concurrence of fellow Quakers. After about 1815 even that system of consultation broke down as the meeting ceased to play any role aside from transferring the membership of migrating Friends to the meeting they would join in their new homes. In fact, to many Friends, migration out of the slavery-cursed South was becoming a holy duty. Others worried that less noble motives, such as economic gain, drew Friends west, but there were no serious attempts to curb migration. By 1819 Ohio Yearly Meeting, itself becoming a setting-off point for westward movement, could only observe that "the dissolving of old, and forming of new connections, have in some cases been attended with effects prejudicial to growth in the truth." It urged, but did not require, consultation with the meeting before Friends changed their locations.[5]

Those mixed feelings betray an uncertainty about the effect of migration on Quakerism. Some Friends were idealistic. In 1847 the *Friends' Review* expressed a hope that Quakers beginning to penetrate Iowa and Wisconsin would be a light in the wilderness, a light of civilization and religion. But other Friends set out with the idea of establishing godly communities that would remain separate from the world. "When I and other Friends came here to found this New Settlement," Isaac Baldwin, father of the chronicler James, told a visiting English minister, "we came with the fixed determination to keep ourselves and our homes unspotted from the world." Friends on the frontier tried to keep up the old standards in all of their rigor. Thus the disciplines of the new yearly meetings were just as stringent and uncompromising as their eastern counterparts. Western Friends showed the same zeal for setting up schools, faithfully attending meetings, and bringing the full force of the discipline to bear on offenders.[6]

Despite such efforts, there was a widespread feeling that frontier Friends were not measuring up to the highest standards. Too often, many Friends felt, migrants put material motives first and spiritual well-being second. In 1821 William Forster, a minister from England, mourned the "low state of religion" in the back settlements of Ohio and Indiana—ministry unheeded, meetings sparsely attended, the discipline not enforced. "Could our friends be prevailed on to stay where they are, suffer the civilized world to gather around them, and accept the benefits . . . one would have some hope for them," he wrote. Three years later, Stephen Grellet, perhaps the most eminent of Orthodox ministers in this period, was alarmed by the rampant "infidelity" that he found among Friends in Indiana and Ohio. Certainly there was no lack of offenders against the discipline. In one monthly meeting in Ohio, for example, the overseers dealt with sixty-eight members for the single offense of "marrying out" between 1804 and 1828. There is no reason to believe that the experience of that meeting was exceptional.[7]

Thus by 1850 migration had changed the face of American Quakerism. The dynamics of the migration are still not completely understood, but certain aspects are clear. Friends went west in search of both cheap land and opportunities to establish godly communities in which Friends could live apart from the blandishments of the world. West of the mountains Friends struggled to preserve the discipline in all of its old rigor, but almost from the beginning they faced high levels of deviation that created a sense of crisis and decline. And that sense of crisis coincided with a series of doctrinal crises, the first of which came in 1827.

THE HICKSITE SEPARATION

Personalities played little part in the traditional Quaker vision of religion. The generation of Friends after Robert Barclay and William Penn produced few leaders of their stature, few doctrinal writers, and no systematic theologians. There was no single work to guide Friends or to explain Quakerism to outsiders. During the period from 1800 to 1860, however, three personalities became central to the course of American Quakerism: Elias Hicks, an elderly farmer from Long Island; Joseph John Gurney, an aristocratic English banker; and John Wilbur, an uncompromising New England schoolteacher. Each of these men gave voice to powerful currents within American Quakerism, and each helped to split the Society of Friends into three factions.[8]

In many ways the most compelling of these personalities was Hicks, the farmer-preacher from Jericho, Long Island, who gave rise to the separation of 1827–1828, the watershed event in American Quaker history. In the 1820s Hicks was an old man with a career in the Quaker ministry going back to the Revolution. He had traveled for many years, visiting Friends throughout North America. By 1820 Hicks's preaching had aroused consternation and fear in the minds of many Friends, fear that ultimately led to schisms in New York, Philadelphia, Ohio, Baltimore, and Indiana yearly meetings. These separations arose not so much from a special desire on Hicks's part to found a new sect (although he sought certain changes) as from the determination of his opponents to purge the society of his heresies. The reaction to Hicks and the Hicksite Friends determined the course of the self-proclaimed "Orthodox" faction for the rest of the nineteenth century.[9]

Hicks's thought can best be described as modified quietism. Hicks was not a liberal or a modernist, although some of his ideas presaged certain modernist concepts. He was a man defending what he understood to be traditional Quakerism against the assaults of innovation and the world; he sought to reform the society by returning it to first principles.[10]

At the heart of Hicks's thinking lay his belief in the Inner Light. Like all

Friends, Hicks believed that the light guided followers into salvation, and around the principle of the Inner Light he created an elaborate system of doctrines, some of which were blatantly anti-intellectual. He opposed virtually all forms of learning beyond the rudiments of literacy and nearly all cooperative efforts toward social improvement. Hicks had other ideas that were quite progressive, such as his pioneering testimony against the use of the products of slave labor and his unflinching opposition to all creedalism.[11]

Hicks's "heresies" lay not in his championship of the Inner Light but rather in conclusions about Christ and the Bible that he drew from his perception of the light. Hicks argued that Christ was the Son of God in the same sense that all people were. The importance of Christ was in his example: he had achieved divinity through perfect obedience to the light. Along the way Hicks implicitly dismissed a variety of doctrines important to "Orthodox" Christians, Quaker and non-Quaker alike: the Atonement, Original Sin, the existence of the devil, and hell as a place rather than a condition. Hicks's approach to the Bible was equally heterodox. He admitted the value of the Scriptures, but he saw the revelation in them as far inferior to that still being imparted to human beings by the Holy Spirit and thus refused to be bound by them.[12]

There is evidence that the roots of the separation ran far deeper than doctrinal differences. Historians once tended to echo the Hicksite view that Hicks was contending for democratic liberty of thought and freedom of conscience against evangelical authoritarianism. More recent scholarship has emphasized socioeconomic factors. In a study of the separation in Philadelphia Yearly Meeting, Robert W. Doherty found that adjustment to the newly emerging capitalist order of America was at the heart of the split. The Orthodox were the successful merchants and entrepreneurs of the city and the surrounding towns, the farmers who had made the adjustment to commercial agriculture. They embraced an evangelical system of belief that allowed them to participate in worldly activities and that accepted wealth as the reward of faith. The Hicksites were a more motley group. They included artisans displaced by an industrial economy, farmers with heavy mortgages, extreme conservatives fearful of innovation, and liberals opposed to intolerance. All of those factors combined with a host of personal antipathies to produce an explosive situation.[13]

Doherty's picture may be accurate for Philadelphia Friends, but it also has limitations. It does not seem applicable to the other yearly meetings that also experienced separations, nor does it explain why three yearly meetings remained united. New England, for example, was undergoing the same socioeconomic changes as the Philadelphia area, yet it remained wholly Orthodox. Similarly, North Carolina Friends were almost all marginal farmers, but they also remained resolutely Orthodox. In Indiana, family connections and origins in the East seem to have had more to do with the few instances of separation than did social position.[14]

Thus while socioeconomic change may have played a part in the conflict, the Hicksite separation centered on questions of belief and authority, questions similar to those that agitated other denominations during the 1820s and 1830s. For Hicks's opponents, the Orthodox Friends, as they called themselves, the central question was Christ and his atoning sacrifice. On this issue the Orthodox took a position not much different from that of evangelical Protestants. The Orthodox were forthright in asserting the divinity of Christ. They endlessly quoted George Fox's 1672 letter to the governor of Barbados, which described Christ in language drawn from the ecumenical councils. He was "the glorious appearing of the great God . . . the beloved and only begotten son, in whom He is well pleased; who was conceived by the Holy Ghost, and born of the Virgin Mary . . . the express image of the invisible God." The fall of Adam, the Orthodox argued, had brought sin into the world, and Adam had transmitted his fallen nature to all of his descendants. Christ had come into the world as the means of reconciliation between God and man. On the cross he took upon himself the sins of all mankind and by his death bore the penalty for all. Through Christ's atoning sacrifice, they concluded, "we witness and know pure and perfect redemption."[15]

Without realizing it, the Orthodox were at a critical point: reconciling the Fall and the Atonement with the Inner Light. There was vague agreement that in some way Christ's death had imparted a measure of light to all and that was the Inner Light. For a century and a half Friends had eschewed systematic theological thinking. They had had no need for it. Hicks forced Friends to try to systematize their thinking about Christ, the Holy Spirit, the Bible, the Atonement, Original Sin, and the Inner Light. After 1830 those attempts would bring only more division and controversy.[16]

That, however, lay ahead. In the late 1820s Hicks's opponents were united in seeing a danger in Hicks's teachings. To many of the Orthodox, Hicks was not so much a cause as he was a symptom: a symptom that the rising tide of infidelity was overtaking Quakerism. Anna Braithwaite, an English Friend who traveled in America during the 1820s, saw "a floating, speculative spirit" abroad in the land. It had begun with Thomas Paine and Joseph Priestly and was, by 1828, openly displaying itself in "the atrocious and monstrous doctrines of the Robert Dale Owen and Fanny Wright school"—and in Elias Hicks.[17]

Infidelity was the most common charge that the Orthodox leveled at Hicks and his followers. The Hicksites, the Ohio minister Thomas Arnett asserted, had "gone out in open infidelity and deism." Charles Osborn, another minister, fulminated that the Hicksites were "deceivers," "false prophets," "evil men and seducers," moved by the Antichrist to aid the "great whore" in "warfare against the divinity of Jesus Christ." Their doctrines "tended to lay waste a belief" in Christianity, "to destroy all reverence for our Lord Jesus Christ; . . . to destroy the authenticity and authority of the Holy Scriptures; and to spread the seeds of infidelity." In the minds of the Orthodox, Hicks and his followers were not Christians, just as, in the minds of contemporary non-Quaker evangelicals, Unitarians and Universalists were not. Thus they had to be labored with, removed from positions of leadership within the society, and, finally, disowned.[18]

The break first came in Philadelphia in April 1827. Hicks's followers despaired of gaining control of the yearly meeting or of even obtaining justice within it and called a conference in which they set up what they claimed to be the true Philadelphia Yearly Meeting. The Hicksites in New York were bolder. They not only insisted on recognizing the Philadelphia Hicksites as the legitimate yearly meeting there, but in a roughshod fashion they also tried to force out all the officials who dared to oppose them. At Ohio Yearly Meeting there was a near riot in which the clerk suffered a broken rib. Even in Baltimore Yearly Meeting, where almost all Friends were Hicksites, and in Indiana, where the overwhelming majority were Orthodox, there were numerous incidents of bitterness.[19]

The separation traumatized a generation of Orthodox Friends. To Hannah Chapman Backhouse, an English Friend who traveled in the United States during the 1830s, it was "as if the powers of darkness had been let loose." A variety of horror stories circulated about the effects of the separation, stories that the Orthodox believed. Hicksites had subjected aged and venerable Friends to intense verbal abuse; they had threatened Orthodox Quakers with whips and had barred them from meetinghouses or locked them inside. Even if the reports were exaggerations, as many undoubtedly were, the process of separation broke up families and left a number of Orthodox meetings barely able to carry on. Elijah Coffin, the clerk of Indiana Yearly Meeting, saw his father and brother go with the Hicksites while his step-mother remained an Orthodox minister. Coffin's father-in-law, Benajah Hiatt, refused to speak to his Hicksite brother Silas. Backhouse reported that on Long Island there was "hardly a family in which some of the members did not go to a different Meeting house—husbands and wives, parents and children, brothers and sisters separated from each other." Backhouse's diary of visits to various Orthodox meetings is full of comments about small meetings made up of a remnant that was sound in the truth, "a chosen few, who do know what they believe."[20]

Such trauma made it easier for the Orthodox to proceed against the Hicksites. Each of the Orthodox yearly meetings, beginning with Indiana in the fall of 1827, issued a statement on Hicks and his doctrines, emphasizing the divinity of Christ, the Atonement, and the authority of the Bible. In 1829 representatives of the various Orthodox yearly meetings held a conference in Philadelphia to reassert the claim of the Orthodox to be the true Society of Friends. The conference's deliberations produced a statement of principles, the first ever circulated by Friends in America. Mainly the work of Elisha Bates, the clerk of Ohio Yearly Meeting, the statement concentrated on the Fall, the divinity of Christ, the Atonement, the authority and inspiration of Scripture, and the Inner Light. The recognition of the Orthodox by British Friends strengthened the claims of Hicks's opponents to be the true society.[21]

Having established their own legitimacy, Orthodox Friends adopted an uncompromising attitude toward the Hicksites. A "narrow scrutiny . . . into the faith" of members was necessary. Since Hicksites were no longer Quakers, the "honor of truth" demanded that they be testified against and disowned. The Orthodox rapidly dissolved meetings that showed themselves unwilling to do so. The disownment process, moreover, lumped Hicksites together with drunkards, fornicators, and swearers. Friends whose only offense was to accept some of Hicks's teachings, or to attend one Hicksite meeting, or even to read one of Hicks's books, found the overseers descending on them. The process of disownment continued for years in some areas. Under the birthright system of membership, the children of Hicksites born before the separation were, in Orthodox eyes, still members of Orthodox meetings. Thus, when such children reached adulthood, they found the Orthodox confronting them as offenders against the discipline for attending their own Hicksite meetings or for being married in them. The continuing disownments carried the bitterness of the separation into the 1840s.[22]

Those actions set a pattern that Orthodox Friends followed for nearly a century. The unity and purity of the society were all important. Separation was the greatest of all evils. Many Orthodox Friends thought that their worst mistake had been tolerating Hicks and his followers too long. Rigorous administration of the discipline became the Orthodox panacea. Thus even association with Hicksites could bring disownment. It is difficult to find a single Orthodox Friend in a position of leadership before 1870 who can be described as open-minded or tolerant. There were very few before 1900.[23]

By 1830, then, American Quakerism had split into two irreconcilable factions. The smaller one, centering on the teachings of Elias Hicks, was bound together by an amalgam of extreme quietism, religious liberalism, and antipathy to the Orthodox leaders. Opposition to the supposedly heretical views of Hicks on Christ, the Bible, and the Atonement united the larger group. Hicks's opponents, the Orthodox Friends, enunciated views on those subjects not much different from the views of evangelicals. Committed to protecting the society against heresy, the Orthodox not only forced a schism on the part of the Hicksites but also embarked on a decades-long course of trying to force unity by bringing down on dissenters the full force of the discipline.

The Orthodox, however, had achieved a consensus only on opposition to Hicks. Real unity eluded them. By 1840 new personalities and issues had come to the fore to fracture the uneasy internal peace of the Orthodox. By 1845 the Orthodox themselves had split into two factions, each dissatisfied with the Quaker status quo, each with its own solution to the problems facing the society. One faction saw the roots of decay and disunity in an inadequate devotion to Quaker tradition; the other, in inadequate devotion to the larger principles of Christianity.

THE RISE OF EVANGELICAL QUAKERISM

The relationship between evangelicalism and Orthodox Quakerism has been at the center of historical debate for decades now. Some scholars have contended that an "evangelical invasion" of the society began early in the nineteenth century and that this "invasion" explains the reaction of Orthodox Friends to the ministry of Elias Hicks. Others, however, have argued that Orthodox Friends in the 1820s were contending for doctrines that the society had always accepted and thus continued the teachings of Fox and Penn. That debate is far too complex to settle here. What is indisputable is that between 1830 and 1860 a majority of Orthodox Friends moved significantly closer to the dominant evangelical religious culture of the United States, the influence of which was to have a profound impact on Orthodox Quakerism. Curiously, however, American evangelical Friends found their most important spokesman in an Englishman, Joseph John Gurney.[24]

Gurney was born in Norwich in 1787 into an illustrious Quaker banking family. One of his sisters was the prison reformer Elizabeth Fry; another was the wife of Sir Thomas Fowell Buxton, member of Parliament and a leader in the British antislavery crusade. The latter connection says much about the Gurneys. Their Quakerism was considerably more open to the world than was that of most Friends before 1830. By age twenty Gurney had firmly committed himself to a life of service to the society, but his commitment did not stand in the way of a life that was quite liberal by Quaker standards. Gurney studied for two years with a Dissenting tutor in Oxford and over the years cultivated friendships with important non-Quaker Evangelicals such as Charles Simeon, Thomas Chalmers, and William Wilburforce. A powerful preacher, a discerning scholar, and the possessor of a charismatic personality, Gurney was the leader (albeit often challenged) among British Friends after 1830 and the most important figure in an intellectual movement that transformed both British and American Quakerism.[25]

Outwardly, Quakerism as Gurney interpreted it was not much different from quietism. He held to the spirituality of the sacraments, the importance of silence, and the traditional view of the ministry. He also accepted all of the outward regulations of the plain life. But Gurney revolutionized the Quaker conception of certain vital points of doctrine: the role of the Bible, the place of the early Friends, the guidance of the Inner Light, the nature of justification and sanctification, and the relationship of Friends to other denominations.[26]

At the heart of Gurney's system was a view of the Bible not much different from that of evangelicals in both England and America. Gurney's view that all Scripture was inspired of God and made known all the truths of religion was the same as that of Orthodox Friends in America in the 1820s. Gurney, however, carried these ideas to their logical conclusion. Since the seventeenth century, Friends had insisted that no one should exalt the letter of the Scriptures above the Spirit that gave them. The guidance of the Holy Spirit was to be the primary source of religious knowledge. To Gurney, the Holy Spirit's role was not to impart new truth, but rather to guide a correct reading of the Bible. Thus he elevated the importance of Scripture and deemphasized direct revelation.[27]

The importance that Gurney attached to the Bible led him to view the early Friends more critically. The Orthodox had always maintained that their faith was in accord with the Bible, but they had allowed the "standard works" of such seventeenth-century Friends as Fox, Penn, Robert Barclay, and George Whitehead to guide their interpretations. Gurney insisted that being guided by any authority besides the Holy Spirit in interpreting the Bible implied that the Bible was not intelligible in and of itself and was thus anti-Protestant. He then cautiously suggested that some of the early Friends had erred on two subjects that lay at the very heart of Quakerism. The first was a logical concomitant of Gurney's biblicism: he believed that Friends were carrying the doctrine of the Inner Light to dangerous and unscriptural extremes. Gurney agreed that all people had a certain illumination that enabled them to distinguish between good and evil. To compare that light with the light of Scripture, however, was, he argued, like comparing the light of the moon with that of the sun. Gurney privately came very close to repudiating the whole concept of the Inner Light.[28]

Although few historians have recognized it, the heart of the debate over Gurney's doctrines was his modification of the position of the early Friends on a second subject: the relationship between justification and sanctification. In the eyes of all Christians, justification was a state of acceptability to God. Sanctification was a state of sinlessness or empowerment. Before Gurney, Friends saw the two as inseparable—one could not be in a state of acceptance without being holy. Gurney argued that anyone could attain justification by a simple act of faith, belief in Christ, an act that imparted the righteousness of Christ to the believer. Sanctification came afterward as an

act of the Holy Spirit. Although Gurney saw justification as a single, instantaneous act, he followed the traditional Quaker vision of sanctification as
a gradual, protracted process.[29]

Gurney's debt to non-Quaker evangelicalism is clearest in his attitude
toward good works. The quietist interest in philanthropy was an impulse to
remove from the paths of Friends and others the obstacles that might
impede the way to heaven. Gurney, like non-Quaker evangelicals in the
United States, emphasized the good effects of benevolence on those who did
benevolent works. It became what one observer has called the central
paradox of evangelicalism: good works could not produce salvation, but
salvation did produce good works. Moreover, as David Brion Davis has
noted, benevolence provided an acceptable link for Quakers with non-
Friends. Gurney epitomized that tendency. He had no qualms about actively working with non-Quaker evangelicals in England and America to promote temperance, antislavery, Bible reading, and prison reform.[30]

In 1837 Gurney came to America for a three-year visit that was, as Rufus
M. Jones has put it, a "triumphal procession." Gurney's reputation for
powerful preaching and brilliant scholarship had preceded him, and Gurney
seldom failed to live up to it. Numerous witnesses testify to his winning
personality, which helped to smooth over differences with those who objected to some parts of his preaching. Nathan Hunt, the North Carolina
patriarch whose own doctrinal views differed significantly from Gurney's,
wrote: "I have never known a brother or a fellow-labourer in the glorious
Gospel of Christ with whom I could more feelingly unite." Hunt continued
with more than a small note of awe that Gurney's "capacious mind" took in
"such an extensive range that an ordinary mind cannot easily follow him."
Charles F. Coffin, a boy of fourteen in Indiana at the time of Gurney's
journey, remembered seventy years later that Gurney had made "an impression on my mind that has never been erased" with his commanding presence, personal charm, and eloquent speech. Gurney's learning and
sophistication won over many others. He disputed theology with Moses
Stuart at Andover Seminary, debated with the divinity students at Yale, held
a meeting with the president and members of Congress, and won the
friendship of Henry Clay. Everywhere, Gurney found confirmation of the
truth of the course that he was taking. No meeting was too small for his
interest, no controversy too minor to invite his attempts at mediation.[31]

Gurney's personality and charm, however important, cannot completely
explain why his ideas had such an impact on American Friends. By 1860 his
interpretation of Quakerism had become the standard for a majority of
Orthodox Friends.[32] The true explanation is that Gurney was as much a
symptom as a source of change. The English minister gave expression to the
direction that the majority of Orthodox Friends took from 1830 to 1860, a

direction they probably would have taken even if Gurney had never existed. Gurney's was the voice of a Quaker culture that was rapidly becoming a part of and was being increasingly influenced by the larger culture of American evangelicalism.

The Quaker movement from a peculiar orthodoxy to a peculiar evangelicalism is a complex story. The Hicksite separation was the immediate spur. Orthodox Friends saw "Hicksism" as part of the general wave of infidelity that threatened to overwhelm Christianity. Slowly, gradually, from 1830 to 1860 Friends rediscovered evangelical elements in their own tradition and came to see themselves as a portion of the evangelical army that was fighting for the preservation of revealed religion against deism and Unitarianism, as part of evangelical Protestantism. And once enlisted in evangelical ranks, many Friends began to adjust their heritage to fit their new role.

Some of the most interesting evidence of the gradual transformation under evangelical influences is in the surviving commonplace books, notebooks, and scrapbooks of Friends from that period. Young Quakers such as Lydia and Susanna Hockett of Guilford County, North Carolina, copied into their notebooks poetry reflecting a strongly traditional Quaker influence and bearing such titles as "On Silence," but they also transcribed such fervently evangelical hymns as "On Jordan's Stormy Bank I Stand." By the 1830s Ann Williams of Highland County, Ohio, was placing a variety of evangelical songs and poems in her commonplace book side by side with accounts of the visions and pious deaths of Friends, while a New York Friend was doing the same with the writings of the English Evangelical Hannah More. Among the rows of figures in his account book, Isaac W. Beeson of Dalton, Indiana, penned hymns with such themes, as

> Jesus, Jesus is my friend
> Oh Hallelujah
> Jesus, Jesus is my friend.

Elijah Coffin, the clerk of Indiana Yearly Meeting, approvingly pasted in his scrapbook articles on the growth of Sunday schools, the conversion of Universalists, Unitarians, and deists to evangelical Christianity, and the progress of the Gospel among the heathen.[33]

Another important indication of the Quaker movement toward evangelical culture is the choice of reading matter by many Friends. By 1833 Short Creek Monthly Meeting in Mount Pleasant, Ohio, had placed the writings of such evangelicals as William Wilburforce and Hannah More in the meeting library alongside those of Penn, Barclay, and John Woolman. Friends read and embraced the teachings of such works. The diary of Ann Taylor Updegraff, member of a leading Mount Pleasant Quaker family, is especially revealing. Her regular reading in the 1840s included the *Oberlin Evangelist* (the Updegraffs were close friends of Charles G. Finney), James Clarke's *Commentaries*, Matthew Simpson's *Plea for Religion*, biographies of the English evangelicals Henry Martyn and Edward Payson, and the works of "the pious Mrs. Hemans." After finishing the biography of one evangelical missionary, Updegraff wrote that her life would be complete if she could win but one soul to Christ.[34]

The best example of the Quaker movement toward an evangelical literary taste is the career of Joseph Tallcot. Born in 1767, Tallcot grew to maturity in the heyday of quietism. Tallcot's interest in temperance, however, brought him into contact with other denominations in New York, especially Methodists and Presbyterians. At the time of the Hicksite separation he was among the minority of New York Friends who remained with the Orthodox faction. Early in the 1830s Tallcot began traveling around New York, visiting meetings to encourage Bible study and to distribute tracts. He also published the *Friendly Visitant*, a periodical aimed at young Quakers. The contents of the *Friendly Visitant* are revealing. Some of the stories had definite Quaker underpinnings; Tallcot was concerned that Friends be familiar with their own traditions and literature. One story, for example, told of how a family of eight children all became Quaker ministers by keeping to the use of the plain language in the public schools. But Tallcot also took many of his selections from the various publications of the evangelical American Tract Society and the American Home Missionary Association. Typical of this latter strain was a little tale telling readers that "we shall be forever miserable unless we repent and experience a change of heart." Tallcot's works epitomize the melding of Quaker tradition with evangelical tenets.[35]

The most notable joining of Quakerism and evangelicalism was in reform activities. The evangelical reform crusades paralleled many of the traditional concerns of Friends. Antislavery is the most obvious example—evangelically oriented Friends joined in a variety of activities with non-Friends, ranging from North Carolina minister Jeremiah Hubbard's commitment to the American Colonization Society to the membership of hundreds of Indiana Friends in the local auxiliaries of the American and Foreign Anti-Slavery Society. By the 1830s some Friends were advocating the circulation of antislavery petitions in monthly meetings. Temperance was another favorite Quaker cause, although Friends frowned on such semisecret organizations as the Good Templars. When the Randolph County, Indiana, Temperance Society was formed in 1838, for example, Friends made up about one-third of its membership and provided five of its six officers. In a variety of efforts aimed at social uplift—prison reform, education, sabbatarianism, tract distribution, and relief for the worthy poor—Friends worked with non-Quakers. They dismissed questions about moving closer to the world. "True, genuine Quakerism," wrote New York Friend Richard Mott, was not "confin'd to the narrow precincts of a little association." "What reason is there," Ann Updegraff asked, "that we should not unite in benevolent works, because we unite our efforts with a Christian who has a different name?" Friends even came to share the confident postmillennialism of the evangelicals. "Is the state of the world advancing or retrograding, as relates to morality and piety?" Joseph Tallcot asked. After enumerating a variety of reforms, he answered: "The balance clearly preponderates in favour of advancement." Other Friends expressed thoughts that might have come from Charles G. Finney. "It is through faith in the blood of Jesus Christ," Thomas Arnett wrote, "that this gospel shall reform and evangelize the world, so as finally wars, intemperance, and slavery shall be abolished throughout the world."[36]

Even more than they pursued social reform, however, evangelically oriented Friends followed the non-Quaker evangelical example of emphasing Bible learning. They were convinced that "a want of proper scriptural knowledge" had been one of the primary causes of the growth of the Hicksite heresy. They argued that the society's most pressing need was a better understanding by its members both of "the vital principles of Christianity" and of how Quakerism was based on those principles. This new Quaker biblicism took two directions.[37]

One direction came through the Quaker version of the American Bible Society, the Bible Association of Friends in America. Organized in Philadelphia at the time of the separation, the association grew phenomenally during the 1830s. Its original goals were to place a Bible in every Quaker family and to see that every Friend owned at least a copy of the New Testament. Although statistics are not available, there was a perception of a widespread lack of Scriptures among Friends. Hannah Backhouse, for example, was horrified to find that in the Nine Partners Boarding School in New York there were but three complete Bibles for all of the students during the early 1830s. Spiceland Quarterly Meeting in Indiana reported in 1838 that 237 of the 287 member families were not "duly supplied" with Bibles. A year later all but one had been. In 1840 the national association reported that virtually every Orthodox Quaker family in the United States owned a complete Bible.[38]

Hand in hand with Bible distribution went Bible reading. On this subject a gradual change in attitudes was taking place. Later in the nineteenth century it would be a common complaint that before the Civil War most Quaker families ignored Bible reading. The constant admonitions from weighty Friends and from yearly meetings to members to keep up the "habit of a daily reading of the Scriptures in their families" indicates a perception of slackness. Joseph Tallcot, for example, mourned that in the 1820s Friends had less Bible knowledge than they had possessed a generation before. But by the 1830s concerned Friends had happily noted an increase in biblical interest and knowledge.[39]

Since families seemed such an uncertain source of Bible learning, Friends followed the lead of other Protestants in setting up Sunday schools or, as Friends preferred to call them, "First Day Schools for Scriptural Instruction." These schools grew rapidly during the 1830s; they were a particular concern of Hannah Backhouse, who agitated the subject in every Quaker community she visited. By 1860 the First Day school had become a fixture in most Friends meetings.[40]

It was not inevitable that the Bible associations and the First Day schools would take an evangelical direction. Quietist Friends could cite an array of biblical texts to justify their own views. Nor were Sabbath schools necessarily evangelical, but Friends gave them an evangelical cast by emphasizing certain portions of the Bible and by using evangelically oriented guides for teachers and commentaries from other denominations, including the venerable works of Archbishop James Ussher and Archibald Alexander. The Bible associations and the First Day schools are signs that during the 1830s and 1840s many Friends were taking a course that paralleled that of the evangelical denominations—and that they were becoming aware of it. There is no conclusive evidence that Friends yet considered themselves bound by evangelical norms; rather, perceived needs were moving them closer to the evangelical position.[41]

Perhaps the best evidence of Quaker participation in worldly activities is the changing attitude of some Friends toward politics, especially in Indiana and Ohio. In the East, Friends tended to eschew political activity, although they always voted in large numbers. On the frontier, however, Friends plunged into political life with fervor. They served in territorial legislatures and in the constitutional conventions of Indiana and Ohio. Beginning in the 1820s and reaching a peak about 1850, a few Friends were in almost every session of the Indiana and Ohio legislatures to represent the distinctively Quaker counties—for example, Wayne and Henry counties in Indiana and Belmont and Clinton counties in Ohio. At the local level, Friends held office in even greater numbers. When Randolph County, Indiana, was organized in 1818, five of the original eight county officials were Friends.[42]

Quakers, moreover, threw themselves enthusiastically into grass-roots political activism, at least west of the Appalachians. There is still much to learn about Quaker political activities, but during the era of the second party system an overwhelming majority of Orthodox Friends were Whigs. The Whigs were, in Quaker eyes, as with thousands of non-Quaker evangelicals, the party of temperance and of the Sabbath, of humanity toward Indians and blacks, of religion and morality. The Jacksonian Democrats, in contrast, were the party of slavery and liquor, led by a military chieftain. In 1840 a Michigan Friend told the governor that "we know of but two individuals in all our Society in this State . . . but what are Whigs and exerted themselves to the utmost to secure thy Election." In the same year a typical Indiana Friend was urging his family in behalf of "Old Tip," William Henry Harrison, in the presidential race against Democrat Martin Van Buren. "I want thee to do all that lays in thy power to have Van throwed out of office," Levi Branson wrote to his brother-in-law. Branson gleefully reported that conversations with travelers from the East indicated a sweeping victory for Harrison. In 1842 Orthodox Friends in Richmond, Indiana, turned out by the thousands to hear a political address by Henry Clay, giving him a hero's welcome. Elijah Coffin acted as Clay's host and seated him near the head of the meeting, afterward driving Clay about the grounds of the meetinghouse so that the Friends present might catch a glimpse of the statesman. When a Hicksite abolitionist presented Clay with a petition that urged him to free his slaves, the Orthodox went to great lengths to dissociate themselves from it, fearful that, in their own words, the taint of abolitionism might lose them "the place and influence which, as a Society" they enjoyed "with the rulers of the land." Coffin's ease with politics was not unusual; George Evans, his assistant as clerk of the yearly meeting, was one of the triumvirate that ran the Whig party in his home county, taking responsibility for getting out the "Quaker vote."[43]

By 1850, most Orthodox Friends were moving closer to the dominant evangelical culture of the United States. They reacted to the heterodoxy of Elias Hicks with a renewed emphasis on many of the same doctrines that non-Quaker evangelists contended for during the 1820s and 1830s. The Orthodox did not embrace such positions because they were evangelical; instead, they took them because of their own belief that they were thus defending primitive Quakerism. But as reform, benevolence, and politics brought Friends into contact with non-Quaker evangelicals, Orthodox Friends became conscious of shared concerns, of common goals, and they adopted such methods as First Day schools that resembled those that non-Quakers used. Such Friends still saw themselves as a peculiar people; they remained confident that they could work with godly people of the world without being contaminated by them. As Joseph Tallcot put it: "It may be well for us not to be so fearful of following the practices of other societies, as to prevent our own improvement."[44] Nevertheless, once Friends made such links, it was impossible for them not to be influenced in dozens of ways, some conscious, some not, by the larger evangelical culture. And there were other Orthodox Friends who realized this, Friends who were equally opposed to the Hicksite "heresy" but who could not accept the compromises that Gurney and his followers were making. Each new accommodation, each new sign of increasing evangelical influence, outraged them more. These Friends found their spokesman in a minister from Rhode Island, John Wilbur.

THE CONSERVATIVE RESPONSE TO GURNEYISM: THE WILBURITE SEPARATIONS

"John Wilbur, one smile might our sorrows beguile,/In mourning thou always appears." So ran a favorite rhyme of New England Quaker schoolchildren in the 1830s. It was an apt characterization of the outlook of the man who was to become the symbol of resistance to Gurneyite innovation. Born in Hopkinton, Rhode Island, in 1774, Wilbur was a model of the quietist Friend. He was reared in a sober Quaker family, had lived up to every requirement of the discipline, and was constantly attentive to what he perceived as the guidance of the Inner Light. An occasional schoolteacher and small farmer, Wilbur was recorded a minister in 1812. During the 1820s he was one of the leading Orthodox Friends in New England, in the forefront of its battle against Hicksism. Already widely traveled in the United States, in 1832 Wilbur felt drawn to Europe. Long disturbed by Gurney's writings, Wilbur naturally gravitated toward Gurney's conservative opponents in England. Wilbur vented his fears in a series of letters, later published, that attacked Gurney's views. When Gurney came to New England in 1838, Wilbur privately attempted to acquaint Friends there with the Englishman's "unsoundness."[45]

A majority of Friends in New England Yearly Meeting found Gurney's ministry acceptable and considered Wilbur's actions defamatory. In an unprecedented move, the yearly meeting appointed a committee packed with Gurneyites to silence Wilbur. When the monthly meeting to which Wilbur belonged refused to take action against the old minister, the Gurneyites dissolved it, attached its membership to another monthly meeting, and then used that monthly meeting to disown Wilbur in 1843. Wilbur appealed those actions to the yearly meeting, but to no avail. Convinced that the leadership of the yearly meeting was hopelessly unsound, Wilbur and his supporters, about 500 Friends out of the yearly meeting's total membership of 6,500, separated.[46]

More was at stake in New England than John Wilbur's membership or ministry. At the heart of the controversy was the unyielding defense by Wilbur and his sympathizers of the quietist vision. Wilburites held to the eighteenth-century faith, brooking no compromise with the modernizing forces of the nineteenth century. They feared that contact with the world, even with the most benevolent and humane intentions, would distract Friends from the great struggle of the soul toward holiness. Wilburites saw themselves as a people besieged and tested by trials: Hicksism, deism, worldliness, and now Gurneyism. Wilburites carried the plain life to extremes of austerity. They were uncompromising in the administration of the discipline. The trials they faced did not dismay them, since trials were the baptisms that burned away the chaff in the soul. But they feared that many who might otherwise work out their salvation would be seduced into the false hope of an easy way to heaven. That fear lay at the heart of the impassioned Wilburite response to Gurney and Gurneyite Quakerism.[47]

Historians of Quakerism have tended to downplay the differences between Wilburites and Gurneyites, dismissing them as abstruse theological hairsplitting. The Gurneyites usually followed this line, arguing that the Wilburites had no valid grounds for complaint. Certainly the Wilburites were in essential agreement with the Gurneyites on the issues that had divided American Quakerism during the 1820s, such as the inspiration of the Bible and the divinity of Christ and the value of his atonement. No one ever seriously challenged their status as Orthodox Friends or the sincerity of their opposition to Hicksism. But in truth the Wilburites were correct in seeing a vital question at stake. Gurney's positions and interpretations indeed had the potential to work a revolution among Orthodox Friends.[48]

Wilburites based their understanding of religion on the writings of the early Friends, a corpus that they never defined but that seems to have included all the works of the first three generations of Quaker writers and controversialists. Gurneyites read those works as well, but Wilburites tended to invest them with a sort of infallibility. In Wilburite eyes the early Friends had been given a greater measure of understanding than others in grasping the truths of Christianity. The approved writings of the early Friends were thus the standard by which to judge subsequent Friends. In Wilbur's words, the writings of the early Friends amounted to a "written confession of faith" binding on all Quakers. Here, then, was Gurney's first error. By refusing to be bound by the early Friends, Gurney had set himself up as superior to them. Gurney's self-confidence and presumption were incompatible with humble crossbearing.[49]

The Gurneyites, of course, claimed to base their views on Scripture, from which there could be no appeal. Here again Wilburites took offense. They acknowledged the Bible to be a "declaration of all of the fundamental doctrines and principles relating to salvation"; they would accept nothing contrary to it. But above the Scriptures was the spirit that gave them—the Holy Spirit that still appeared to convert, sanctify, and edify Friends. Wilburites feared that the Gurneyites had been caught in a snare of Satan, drawing "many into a spirit that would place [the Scriptures] above that which they declare themselves to be." Thus Gurneyites risked "falling back very near to that which our worthy forefathers were gathered from." Relying on the letter of the written record of the Holy Spirit's past revelations instead of heeding the spirit today risked putting religious life on a lower plane.[50]

Wilburite attitudes toward the Bible distribution and study by evangelical Friends ranged from ambivalence to hostility. Some Wilburites, especially in Philadelphia, participated in exclusively Quaker organizations such as the Bible Association of Friends. They were fearful, however, of First Day schools and Bible study. Many Wilburites, committed to the complete guidance of the Holy Spirit, refused to read the Bible unless under a special leading. In the Bible schools Wilburites saw the seeds of superficial religion. Intellectual knowledge availed nothing in the pursuit of salvation. Instead it only fostered worldly pride. Religion that was of the head instead of being painfully worked out in the heart did not bring salvation.[51]

Here lay the crux of the controversy. Wilburites argued that Gurney was attempting an easy way to heaven, one that bypassed the discipline of bearing the cross. In Gurney's insistence on simple faith in the efficacy of the Atonement as adequate to achieve salvation and in his separation of justification and sanctification, Wilburites saw a threat to the very existence of Quakerism.

Wilburites believed that Protestants had erred "in placing their trust in faith alone without regard to that work wrought by the power and spirit of Christ in the heart." By separating justification and sanctification, Gurneyites were falling into the same error. They were saying that they could be in a state of acceptability to God while retaining the "polluted garments of sin and unrighteousness." Unwilling "to die with Christ, and to abide the painful struggle of yielding up the will and wisdom of the flesh," the Gurneyites were claiming Christ's outward suffering as justification and discarding "the true obedience of faith . . . the work of sanctification wrought in the heart." Indeed, Wilbur asked, if "barely believing in Christ" could secure salvation, who would refuse a simple assent and avoid "the painful endurance of the baptism of fire and the Holy Ghost in themselves"?[52]

Although Wilburites disclaimed personal animosity toward Gurney, they had no doubts about what drove him. The English minister, they said, had been educated under Episcopalian auspices and had thus acquired his heretical views. He had been seduced by the applause that his writings had won from non-Quakers. Now Gurney was leading other Friends toward the world, and the world was ever inimical to truth. Already its deadening effects could be seen: the spirit of Antichrist was at work among Friends, as one saw in "our hoarded wealth, our worldly entanglements, our spacious dwellings, our costly furniture and attire, sumptuous tables, and dissipating assemblages of our younger Friends at the houses of their highly professing parents."[53]

The only cure, then, was unrelenting separation from the world. In practice, so far as the plain life was concerned, Gurneyites seldom took issue with Wilburites. But in other areas where Gurneyites were forging links with non-Quakers, Wilburites chose isolation. Most notable were their feelings about the participation of evangelical Friends in reform causes. Some Wilburites felt that benevolent societies, by focusing attention on one subject, weakened devotion to other, equally pressing concerns. More common were Wilburite complaints that such associations inevitably drew Friends into the spirit of the world. Such enterprises, observed Joseph Edgerton, were based on excitement and self-will instead of on waiting to know the divine will. "Joining with those who do not believe in the immediate direction of Christ in such matters, and therefore do not wait for it, you will very likely become like them," Edgerton warned. This "overactive restless spirit," Edgerton continued, in abolition, temperance, and Gurneyism was "like the locust, the cankerworm, and the caterpillar," "ready to eat up every green thing," ready to strike at the heart of Quakerism. The end result, Wilburites feared, would be deadness to the movings of the Holy Spirit. "What a pity! What a pity!" a voice in a dream warned Charles Osborn in 1833, "that for the abolition of slavery, and the spreading of the Bible, people should be turned against Christ."[54]

Thus Wilburite Friends tried to defend the old faith. In their eyes Gurneyism was dangerous because it offered a false but enticing way to salvation, one designed to appeal to a love of ease. The Wilburites would not give in to it. They would continue to uphold the old ways of bearing the cross. Nothing would sway them from it: not the popularity with the world that Gurney's evangelicalism offered, not intellectual arguments, not even causes with laudable objects but conducted according to worldly methods. They would make no compromises.

Given those fundamental differences, conflict between the two factions was inevitable. The history of American Quakerism during the 1830s and 1840s is a series of minor local disputes and squabbles that eventually widened into an unbridgeable chasm. Neither side had abandoned the tradition of using the discipline against all threats to authority, and neither had any compunction about its use. That fixation, combined with assumptions of infallibility on both sides, made tragedy inevitable.

Controversy came first in the West. In the 1830s dissension over the emerging evangelicalism disrupted two monthly meetings in Indiana. Friends in one tried to form a "Union" movement that combined Methodism and Quakerism. Members of the other split over Gurney's teachings. In 1839 many of the leading Friends in Adrian Monthly Meeting in Michigan resigned, contending that a majority of the monthly meeting was unsound in evangelical faith. The worst controversy came in Ohio Yearly Meeting, which was stunned when its former clerk, Elisha Bates, publicly denounced "heresies" in the writings of the early Friends and had himself baptized. In every case the response of Friends was the same: the stern use of the discipline culminating in the disownment of dissenters and the dissolution of meetings.[55]

These events had been but a prelude to the secession of John Wilbur and his followers in New England. The separation there polarized the rest of Orthodox Quakerism, since the other yearly meetings had to decide which New England group they would recognize for the purposes of correspondence and receiving and transferring members. In the eyes of the foes of Gurneyism everywhere, Wilbur was a martyr, a defender of the true faith who had protected Quakerism against the assaults of innovation. The Gurneyite dissolution of Wilbur's monthly meeting and the disownment of Wilbur had been contrary to discipline, the Wilburites argued; thus the Gurneyites were the real separatists. The Gurneyites responded with appeals to unity and discipline. Gurney, they said, was a fully approved minister who had come to America in unity with English Friends. It was not for Wilbur to judge his soundness. That was the province of yearly meetings, not of individuals. Wilbur had set his own judgment against that of the "weight," or the considered judgment of the most eminent members, of New England Yearly Meeting and had separated when the yearly meeting reproved him for it. Apparently most Friends found the Gurneyite version more convincing. Friends in New York, Baltimore, and North Carolina yearly meetings united against Wilbur. The Wilburite battles divided Friends in Ohio, Philadelphia, and Indiana.[56]

The division in Indiana Yearly Meeting in the 1840s was unique. Any sympathies that the yearly meeting's leaders might have had for Wilbur disappeared in Indiana's own bitter schism in the winter of 1842–1843. About one-eighth of the yearly meeting's members separated after its leadership removed eight important Friends, including Charles Osborn, from leadership positions because of their abolitionist activities. The rhetoric of the larger body in Indiana was an amalgam of the arguments of both Wilburites and Gurneyites. The abolitionists endangered the purity of the society by associating with non-Friends who did not wait for the leadings of the Holy Spirit and who were, in some cases, of doubtful religious and moral standing. Refusing to be guided by the weight of the yearly meeting, the abolitionist Friends had gone off in a spirit of faultfinding and detraction.[57]

The Anti-Slavery Friends, as the Indiana separatists called themselves, embraced what was, in the terms of discourse among Friends in the 1840s, an equally confusing set of ideas. On one hand, they, like the Gurneyites, contended that it was their duty as Friends to work with anyone to advance the cause of abolition. Thus they plunged into organized antislavery activities. On the other hand, the chief prophet of the Anti-Slavery Friends was Charles Osborn, who, from encounters with Gurney in England and New England, had concluded that the English minister was unsound on a number of questions. Walter Edgerton, the clerk of the Anti-Slavery yearly meeting, was an implacable foe of Gurney and a brother of Joseph Edgerton, a leading Wilburite in Ohio Yearly Meeting. A strong Wilburite strain runs through the Anti-Slavery Friends' tracts and addresses. The larger body of Indiana Friends, they argued, had been corrupted by wealth and worldliness. It was the duty of the Anti-Slavery Friends to raise a higher standard of discipline, reaffirming the historic Quaker position on slavery and disciplinary issues.[58]

Anti-Slavery Friends thus found themselves in a doubly isolated position. As abolitionists they repulsed the Wilburites; as separatists they were anathema to the Gurneyites. After this experience with indigenous schismatics, the larger body in Indiana had no use for Wilbur. "[We] have suffered so much" from separatists, Elijah Coffin wrote, "and undergone so much in the conflict . . . that we must keep 'hands off' from every thing which gives them strength and support."[59]

The battlegrounds thus became Ohio and Philadelphia yearly meetings. In both, the relationship with New England Yearly Meeting was the issue.

The crisis in Ohio came at the 1854 yearly meeting. For ten years it had suffered increasing tensions. By 1854 the issue was unavoidable. Both Thomas B. Gould, Wilbur's chief lieutenant in New England, and Eliza P. Gurney, Joseph John's widow, were in attendance. From the beginning the Gurneyite faction was determined to wrest control from Benjamin Hoyle, the clerk of the yearly meeting whom they perceived as a Wilburite, and to expel Gurney's opponents from positions of responsibility. They objected vehemently to the presence of Gould, who was, according to Eliza Gurney, guilty of "abominable and unforgiven" sins. The Gurneyites began by proposing a new clerk, a proposition with which most of those present did not agree. The Gurneyites nevertheless tried to install their nominee, Jonathan Binns, while Hoyle, the Wilburite, continued himself in office, since there was no unity on a successor. Thus two yearly meetings emerged along the pattern of New England. The Gurneyites pointed to what they argued were the disorderly actions of the Wilburites. The Wilburites replied that they were the true yearly meeting, holding to the old ways, and that the Gurneyites were unsound separatists.[60]

The situation in Philadelphia Yearly Meeting was similar. Here, however, the Wilburites were in firm control. The ruling powers—the meeting for sufferings (the yearly meeting's equivalent of an executive committee), the clerks of the yearly and quarterly meetings, the editors of the *Friend*—were convinced that Gurney's teachings were dangerous and that the disownment of Wilbur was contrary to discipline. As stern devotees of the discipline, however, they were troubled by the separatist tactics of the Wilburites. Ultimately they decided that New England Yearly Meeting had disowned Wilbur unfairly and that until New England annulled its proceedings Philadelphia could not remain in unity with it. The weight of the yearly meeting thus came down firmly on Wilbur's side.[61]

Philadelphia nonetheless had a powerful minority sympathetic to Gurney and unwilling to dissolve ties with the rest of Orthodox Quakerism by formally recognizing the Wilburites. As Rufus M. Jones has noted, the Philadelphia Gurneyites were the most active and dynamic members of the yearly meeting. They took the lead in founding Haverford College, were notable in reform causes, and, perhaps most important, had established the *Friends' Review* in 1847 as the organ of Gurneyite Quakerism. This talented and articulate minority was strong enough to prevent an official break with the Gurneyite yearly meetings.[62]

For ten years Philadelphia Friends lived in uneasy compromise, controlled by a "middle party" that shared Wilbur's opposition to Gurney but that also was committed to avoiding a separation at almost any price. In 1849 and 1851 the Gurneyite yearly meetings held conferences in Baltimore, ostensibly to promote "unity," but in fact to demand that Philadelphia renounce Wilburism. The Ohio separation created new strains. In 1856 and 1857 the Gurneyites, knowing that they could count on recognition from the Gurneyite yearly meetings, came close to breaking away, but in 1857 the two factions in Philadelphia reached a drastic compromise. The yearly meeting cut off correspondence with all other bodies of Friends. Philadelphia Yearly Meeting would continue to receive members from other yearly meetings, but it would not issue or receive epistles or maintain other official relations.[63]

One question remains: Was the Wilburite-Gurneyite division another example of social cleavage, similar to what took place in Philadelphia Yearly Meeting at the time of the Hicksite separation? A complete analysis is beyond the bounds of this study, but a preliminary examination of data from the 1850 and 1860 census for some members of Ohio Yearly Meeting does not indicate a clear socioeconomic cleavage. In Ohio, at least, both Gurneyites and Wilburites were predominately farm folk and artisans serving farmers; nearly all saw the value of their property increase significantly between 1850 and 1860. Both groups ran the gamut from propertyless laborers to well-to-do farmers. More extensive analysis may yield different results, but it appears that the schisms that Orthodox Friends experienced in the 1840s and 1850s must be explained in terms of intellectual and doctrinal, rather than social, factors.[64]

By 1850 Orthodox Quakerism was in a state of crisis. Two nearly irreconcilable schools of thought had developed within it. One sought to uphold what it saw as the traditional, unchanging Quaker vision of religious life. Salvation was to be achieved through a long process of testing and trial until, through obedience to the Inner Light, growth into holiness was achieved. Anything that might distract from this path, no matter how laudable its aims, had to be shunned. Thus conservative, Wilburite Friends sought to keep all the restrictions and boundaries surrounding Quakers.

Opposed to that ultraconservative view was a movement that by the 1850s was only beginning to coalesce. Inspired in large part by the English minister Joseph John Gurney, these Friends were moving slowly toward the mainstream of evangelical religion in America through ties in reform, humanitarianism, and politics. More important, Gurneyite Friends were coming to accept a religious vision not only similar to but also deeply influenced by evangelicalism. In their eyes faith brought salvation, and the foremost, incomparable means to that faith was the Bible. Gurneyites remained committed to the plain life, but an emphasis on salvation by faith was bound to undermine a testimony based on human action.

Any chance of compromise between the two groups was blasted by memories of the Hicksite separation. The schism of 1828 had so traumatized Orthodox Friends that they saw danger in virtually all dissent. Unity became the ruling ideal, but it was a unity often based on authoritarian repression. It was thus a troubled society with its own impending crisis that faced America on the eve of the Civil War.

CHAPTER

III

THE RENEWAL MOVEMENT, 1850–1870

In the summer of 1861 a Union army officer training recruits in Richmond, Indiana, decided to indulge his curiosity by attending a Quaker meeting. For half an hour the nearly one thousand people present sat in silence "so still that you could hear the heart beat . . . the men with their hats on, and eyes on the floor, the women with their hands locked in each other . . . and eyes closed like they were asleep." Then, as the army man reported to his wife, an old woman "popped up" and spoke for five minutes, followed by another woman for half an hour, then by still another Friend for about ten minutes. Soon afterward the two old men at the front shook hands and left their seats, ending the meeting. There were no familiar landmarks for the officer—no pulpit or pastor, no organ or hymns. It was a "queer" sort of religion, he concluded, so different from the rest of Protestantism that he could scarcely comprehend it.[1]

While Friends in Indiana and elsewhere seemed strange and quiescent to outsiders, in 1861 they were in fact on the verge of a revolution that would within two decades bring most of them into the mainstream of evangelical Protestantism. The 1860s were a decade of flux and change for Gurneyite Friends as a new generation assumed leadership in the society. Even greater change came during the 1870s, change so dramatic that historians of Quakerism have assumed that it must have been continuous with that of the preceding decade. In reality, the intellectual currents and goals of Gurneyite Friends in the 1860s differed in significant aspects from those in the 1870s. During the 1860s a renewal movement appeared within Gurneyite Quakerism, one that attempted to modify and reform, not to revolutionize, the society. It strove for a breakdown of sectarian barriers while preserving distinctiveness, a heightening of humanitarian and reform concerns, and a modification of worship that emphasized individual initiative and freedom. Because its goals were subtle and its methods quiet, the far more radical changes of the 1870s have obscured the renewal movement's significance.

SOCIAL CHANGE AND *MENTALITÉ*

For nearly a century historians of American Quakerism have tried to comprehend the sources of the revolution that swept over the society between 1850 and 1880. Earlier scholars found explanations in reform movements, Bible schools, and the influence of the frontier. More recent scholarship has located the roots of religious transformation in socioeconomic change, which radically altered the Gurneyite *mentalité* during the 1850s and 1860s.[2]

By 1860 the areas in which Friends were concentrated, such as New York, Pennsylvania, Ohio, and Indiana, had recently passed through or were passing through the revolution of interdependence that Thomas L. Haskell has described so well. The expansion of the American transportation and communications networks was destroying the isolated, self-sufficient agrarian communities in which Friends had lived for two hundred years and was instead integrating them into regional, national, and even international markets. For millions of Americans it was a radical, even revolutionary experience. "It is inconceivable that people could have lived through such a transformation of society without profound changes in their habits of mind, their mode of organizing experience, their very manner of perceiving human affiars," Haskell has written. "This was no ordinary transition from one generation to another, but a movement from one social universe to another governed by strikingly different conditions of action and explanation." An American born in 1800 was living in a very different world by 1860. Such was the experience of the overwhelming majority of American Friends.[3]

Probably no one described the consequences of the transformation for American Friends better than the English Quaker William Tallack, who traveled extensively in the United States on the eve of the Civil War. Tallack's account of western Quakers in 1860 leaves, at first glance, the impression of an idyllic agrarian society. These Friends lived in simple plenty, wearing plain clothes of their own making, eating the fruits of their labor with enough left over to trade for the few necessities they did not produce on their farms or in their "neat and commodious homes." Their tendency to settle close together left them largely undisturbed by "outsiders," while a general uniformity of circumstances and "mutual equality of mind and outer station" made for harmony among them.[4]

Tallack, however, saw the rural Quaker world changing. The railroad and the telegraph brought with them a world of innovation both social and economic. The foremost tendencies of the nineteenth century, Tallack declared, were assimilation and consolidation. "From this tendency the farthest west and the wildest backwoods cannot withhold compliance," he proclaimed, and Friends showed little more resistance than other people. "In their most secluded homes," Tallack wrote, "there is a growing fondness for the refinements of literature and science."[5]

Much remains to be learned about this socioeconomic transformation, but there can be no doubt of its reality. In Indiana and Ohio the railroad was the most important agent of change. Between 1850 and 1860 almost every county with a significant Quaker population in the two states was reached by railroad lines. Bernhard Knollenberg has described the impact of the railroad on Richmond, Indiana, the center of western Orthodox Quakerism: "In 1850 it was an isolated backwoods settlement dominated by the Quakers in dress, manners, and concepts," but by 1860 "it was relatively cosmopolitan and closely linked by rail to a thousand other similar communities." The experience of Friends at Spiceland in neighboring Henry County, reached by the railroad in 1854, was similar. Between 1850 and 1860 the value of real estate in the predominately Quaker township doubled. Individual Friends saw their farms soar in value, as in the cases of William B. Unthank, whose land rose in value from $2,000 to $3,500, and Samuel Griffin, who watched the value of his farm, convenient to a depot on the new railroad, go from $6,500 to $10,300. Increased income meant leisure for reading and good works, money to contemplate turning the monthly meeting school into a full-fledged academy, to bring in lecturers and lyceums, or to replace the barnlike frame meetinghouse with one of slate-roofed brick. It meant that more Spiceland young people could be educated at Earlham College for careers off the land. Easier travel; more money for books, newspapers and other periodicals, and education; and especially increasing contact with new people and new ideas—these were the results of a changing economy.[6]

Such socioeconomic changes were all part of the passing of the frontier, making it unlikely that, as some historians of Quakerism have asserted, the new Quaker outlook of the 1860s was a result of the "frontier experience." In fact, the end of the frontier was the crucial factor. The renewal and later revival movements sprang, not from the raw frontier of Iowa and Kansas, but rather from the long-settled portions of Indiana and Ohio and the even longer-settled areas of New York, New England, and North Carolina. Friends had always been a people on the frontier, and before the 1860s Quakers in newly settled areas had held uncompromisingly to the old ways. If the frontier made for deviation, why had it not done so earlier? A Friend on the frontier during the 1850s and 1860s was far less isolated from the larger society than one in 1800. Finally, if both common sense and the testimony of contemporaries can be accepted, frontier Quakers were far too busy breaking land and surviving to have time for Bible societies, reform organizations, or the doctrinal speculations that all acknowledge to have been forerunners of change.[7]

Probably the most important change that Gurneyite Friends were undergoing by 1860 was their participation in the larger intellectual world. Tallack was not alone in noting a taste for "refinements of literature" among Friends. By the 1850s newspapers, once almost unknown among Quakers, were becoming a given in the lives of Gurneyite Friends; one Virginia Quaker complained in 1853 that one could not enter a Friend's home without seeing newspapers scattered about the room. Others, however, rejoiced over how often they contained instructive and moral articles. Magazines were also becoming more common. Nereus Mendenhall, a young Friend struggling against the general backwardness of North Carolina, recorded in 1851 that his regular reading included not only the *Friend* and the *Friends' Review* but also the *National Era* to stay abreast of reform, the *True American* for politics, and *Parley's Magazine, Littell's Living Age*, and the *Westminster Review* for general edification. The reading habits of the younger generation of Friends during the 1850s and 1860s were becoming more eclectic and more appreciative of non-Quaker literature. Quakers in several localities in Indiana, Ohio, and Iowa formed reading circles to discuss, not the "standard works" of Friends, which they often found tiresome, but general works of history and biography. Many others were becoming interested in fiction and poetry. Popular novelists such as Fanny Fern and poets such as Henry Wadsworth Longfellow, William Cullen Bryant, and, of course, John Greenleaf Whittier were favorites. (A Quaker literary figure like Whittier would have been unthinkable in 1800; not so in 1860.) Arriving in Iowa to visit relatives in 1852, one young Friend was dismayed to find no reading material available. "I do wish uncle had some books," she told her diary. "I cannot see how people live without them, as so many do." In the next decade the editors of the new *American Friend* were noting that "the amount of reading done in our Society at the present time is very great compared with what was done fifty, or even twenty-five, years ago." They concluded that the effects of this "incalculable" change were only beginning to be felt.[8]

Other evidence of intellectual change among Gurneyite Friends during those years is the change in Quaker thinking about education, as indicated by the dramatic increase in the number of Quaker secondary schools. Elementary education had always been a Quaker concern, but in the 1830s a new concern about secondary education had appeared. Between 1689 and 1830 Orthodox Friends had established eight academies in North America. Between 1830 and 1860 eight new ones appeared, and in the years from 1860 to 1880 another nine were founded. Evidence suggests that only a small percentage of Quaker youths attended such institutions, but the fact that American Friends thought it necessary or desirable to establish them shows the degree to which Friends were coming to share assumptions of the larger world.[9]

Even more indicative of fundamental change was the new Quaker interest in colleges after 1850. Traditionally Friends had eschewed higher education as vain and threatening to the plain life. But by 1850 at least a few Friends in Indiana and Ohio were aspiring to collegiate degrees and, with some misgivings, were being allowed to attend Oberlin, Antioch, Amherst, and state institutions without facing disciplinary action on the part of their meetings. Many of those innovators, such as Eli and Allen Jay, would be leaders in the changes of the next decade. By 1859 Joseph Moore, an Indiana Friend with a bent for science, could enter Harvard to study under Louis Agassiz, albeit pursued by admonitions from Elijah Coffin to beware of Unitarianism. According to Tallack, Moore was one of a number of American Friends in Cambridge. Ultimately, however, most of the Friends who attended college during the 1850s and 1860s graduated, not from one of those schools, but from one of the colleges that Friends themselves founded during the period. In 1856 Philadelphia Gurneyites upgraded the Haverford Boarding School to collegiate status. Significantly, when they did so they brought in as instructors New England Friends trained at Harvard and Yale. A few years later, when Indiana Yearly Meeting decided to follow suit with its boarding school in Richmond, it hired Joseph Moore to run it. By 1870 Haverford College had become the prestige institution among Orthodox Friends, while Earlham College served less affluent Friends in the West. Within the next two decades several other yearly meetings would establish their own colleges.[10]

Some historians have asserted that education played a vital role in change among Friends because after 1850 increasing numbers of Quakers attended public schools or mingled with the large numbers of non-Quakers who were being admitted, for financial reasons, to Quaker institutions. Such influence is difficult to evaluate. Certainly peer pressure may have eroded the attachment of Quaker children to peculiarities of speech and dress in such situations, but, given the nature of children, it is unlikely that they devoted much time to theological discussions or doctrinal debates. At least one influential North Carolina Friend, Delphina E. Mendenhall, hailed the admission of non-Friends to Quaker schools because she was convinced that they would be drawn toward Quaker ideals rather than "contaminate" Friends. By 1860 a majority of Quaker children in Indiana, the state with the largest Quaker population, were no longer in meeting schools, but many Quaker children in ostensibly public schools were taught by Friends. Tallack noted that the tendency of Friends in Indiana and Ohio to settle close together made it possible for them to be the majority in the public schools they attended, with the monthly meeting serving as a *de facto* school board. The statistics for Gurneyite Friends, moreover, are not much different from those of the

Wilburites of Ohio and Philadelphia, who resisted the larger culture far more successfully.[11]

Those who have stressed the influx of non-Quaker students into meeting schools and the entry of Quakers into public schools have missed a more obvious source of change: the textbooks available to Quaker children during the 1840s and 1850s. At that time Friends began to use the McGuffey readers, the staple of the public schools; by 1847 use of such material had already become a source of concern to some Friends, who were fearful of the effects of schoolbooks that catered to "popular taste." Revealing in this respect is the work of Barnabas C. Hobbs, the headmaster of three Quaker academies. Worried by McGuffey stories that did not use the plain language and that sometimes glorified war and military leaders, Hobbs, with financial backing from English Friends, set out in the 1850s to write a series of textbooks for Quaker schools. Hobbs took most of his material from McGuffey, excluding the war stories and using "thee" and "thou" where appropriate. He included the most moralistic and evangelical selections on Christ, the Christian foundations of civilization, the nature of sin and repentance, and the necessity of conversion. Hobbs also drew on the publications of the American Tract Society and the American Bible Society, the works of educational reformer Horace Mann and abolitionist-feminist Angelina Grimke Weld, the speeches of the "learned blacksmith" and pacifist Elihu Burritt, and, of course, the poetry of Whittier. Except for the emphasis on pacifism and the use of the plain language, there is little in Hobbs's work to distinguish it from that of McGuffey.[12]

Perhaps the best way to sum up the impact of all of those changes is to return again to Westfield, Indiana. No one recognized the consequences of the social transformation more clearly than did James Baldwin in his memories of the 1840s and 1850s. His father, Isaac Baldwin, had come to Westfield determined to live in a community that would remain undisturbed by the encroachments of the world. But when the completion of the railroad to nearby Indianapolis brought the markets almost to his door, Isaac accepted it as a blessing and turned the proceeds from higher crop and livestock prices to building a new house with such modern conveniences as a cookstove. About the same time, the visiting English minister Benjamin Seebohm profoundly impressed Isaac with his arguments that Friends should be a leaven to the world rather than a city on a hill. Meanwhile, Isaac's antislavery principles led him to subscribe to the *National Era* and to become better informed about events in the larger world. They also led him to an interest in Free Soil politics; soon he was considering a run for the legislature. He also struck up a friendship with a newly arrived non-Quaker doctor, who gave him a better impression of those who were not of "Our Society." Outwardly he remained a plain Friend, but, as his son wrote, Isaac Baldwin had "gained a broader outlook upon life and the world."[13]

Still, economic and social factors cannot explain everything that was happening among Orthodox Friends during the mid-nineteenth century. It has already been seen that socioeconomic differences were probably not related to the Wilbur-Gurney schism; there is nothing in the development of American society to explain why Friends in Philadelphia for the most part resisted change while their counterparts in similar situations in New York City and Baltimore accepted it; why some Quaker farmers in eastern Ohio turned their faces against religious modernization while those 150 miles to the west did not. Further work may shed new light on these questions, but ultimately one comes down to the individual choice at the heart of all religious decisions. A minority of Orthodox Friends decided that the preservation of Quakerism depended on unyielding maintenance of tradition, resistance to all innovation. But the majority of Orthodox Quakers had decided by 1860 that they could live in the world; indeed, they were finding much in the world of which they wholeheartedly approved. Simultaneously a new generation of Quaker leaders was emerging, a generation that was in large part a product of the changing world and one that fully accepted it and its challenges.

LEADERS OF RENEWAL

In the 1860s a new generation of Friends assumed leadership in the Gurneyite yearly meetings. I have labeled the reform movement that they led a renewal movement, in part to distinguish it from the later revival movement, in part because it had as its goal nothing less than a renewal of Quaker vitality. It sought to meet that goal partly by building Quaker equivalents of the institutions it found attractive in the larger evangelical world, partly by returning to what it perceived as first principles.

The lives of the most important renewal Friends are outlined in Chart 1. Several generalizations are possible. The backgrounds of the individuals in this group are remarkably similar. Nearly all were products of long lines of Quaker ancestry; all were birthright members of the society; most were the children of prominent Friends; a majority attended the Quaker schools at Providence or Haverford. Ties of blood and marriage bound the group together: Barnabas C. Hobbs and John Butler married sisters of David Tatum; Hannah E. Bean was a sister of Samuel R. Shipley; Charles F. Coffin was a brother-in-law of William H. Ladd and a cousin of Hobbs; William and Timothy Nicholson were brothers; Mary Whitall Thomas and Hannah Whitall Smith were sisters. Nearly all were teachers, merchants, bankers, or physicians; only Allen Jay, James Owen, and perhaps John Henry Douglas and Francis W. Thomas could be called "dirt farmers" who lacked other resources and depended on their hands for a living. Most of the group were

CHART 1

Leading Renewal Friends, 1865

Individuals (By Yearly Meeting)	Date of Birth	Birthplace	Position in the Society	Secular Occupation	Education
Baltimore					
Francis T. King	1819	Baltimore	Minister, YM clerk	Merchant	Providence, Haverford
James Carey Thomas	1833	Baltimore	Elder	Physician	Haverford, U. of Maryland
Mary Whitall Thomas	1835	Germantown, Pa.	Minister	Wife of J. C.	Home, MM schools
Indiana					
Dougan Clark, Jr.	1828	Guilford Co., N.C.	Prof., Earlham	Physician	New Garden, Providence, U. of Pa.
Charles F. Coffin	1823	Guilford Co., N.C.	Clerk of YM	Banker	MM schools
Rhoda M. Coffin	1826	Green Co., O.	Minister	Wife of C. F.	MM schools
John Henry Douglas	1831	Fairfield, Me.	Minister	Farmer	Providence
Joseph Moore	1831	Washington Co., Ind.	Minister, prof., Earlham	Teacher	MM schools, Earlham, Harvard
Timothy Nicholson	1828	Perquimans Co., N.C.	Elder, former Haverford superintendent	Merchant	MM school and Providence
Murray Shipley	1830	New York City	Elder	Merchant	St. Xavier Coll., Cincinnati
Francis W. Thomas	1823	Wayne Co., Ind.	Minister	Farmer	MM schools

Individuals (By Yearly Meeting)	Date of Birth	Birthplace	Position in the Society	Secular Occupation	Education
Iowa					
Hannah E. Bean	1830	Philadelphia	Minister	Wife of Joel	Friends Select, West-town
Joel Bean	1825	Dover, N.H.	Minister, YM clerk	Farmer, banker	Providence
Lindley M. Hoag	1808	Wolfsborough, Vt.	Minister	Farmer	?
James Owen	1822	Clinton Co., O.	Minister	Farmer	MM schools
New England					
Moses Bailey	1817	Winthrop, Me.	Elder	Businessman	Providence
Eli Jones	1807	China, Me.	Minister	Farmer	Providence
Sybil Jones	1808	Brunswick, Me.	Minister	Wife of Eli	Providence
John Greenleaf Whit-tier	1807	Amesbury, Mass.	Member	Writer	MM schools
New York					
Robert Lindley Murray	1825	New York City	Minister, YM clerk	Businessman	Haverford
Ruth S. Murray	?	New Bedford, Mass.	Minister	Wife of R. L.	Providence
William H. Wood	?	New York City	?	Businessman	?
North Carolina					
Delphina Mendenhall	1810	Mecklenburg Co., N.C.	Elder	Wife of lawyer	?
Nereus Mendenhall	1821	Guilford Co., N.C.	Minister, YM clerk	Physician, teacher	Providence, Haverford
William Nicholson	1826	Perquimans Co., N.C.	Minister	Physician, teacher	Providence, U. of Pa.

Philadelphia

Name	Year	Location	Role	Occupation	Education
Joshua L. Baily	1826	Philadelphia	Member	Merchant	Westtown
Henry Hartshorne	1828	Philadelphia	Ed., *Friends' Review*	Physician	Haverford, U. of Pa.
Thomas Kimber[1]	1827	New York City	Member	Railroad official	Haverford
James E. Rhoads	1828	Delaware Co., Pa.	Member	Physician	Haverford, U. of Pa.
Samuel R. Shipley	1828	Philadelphia	Member	Imports, insurance	Westtown
Hannah Whitall Smith	1832	Philadelphia	Minister	Wife of R. P.	MM schools
Robert Pearsall Smith	1827	Burlington, N.J.	Minister	Glass manufacturer	Haverford

Ohio

Name	Year	Location	Role	Occupation	Education
John Butler	1807	Evesham, N.J.	Elder	Farmer	MM schools
Elizabeth L. Com-stock	1815	Berks, Eng.	Minister	Farmwife	Croyden Friends School
Caroline Ladd[2]	1832	Wayne Co., Ind.	Member	Wife of W. H.	Earlham
William H. Ladd[2]	1823	Smithfield, O.	Minister	Banker	Haverford
David Tatum	1822	Haddonfield, N.J.	Minister	Farmer, teacher	?
Hannah Tatum	1823	Haddonfield, N.J.	Minister	Farmwife	?

Western

Name	Year	Location	Role	Occupation	Education
Jeremiah A. Grinnell[3]	1815	Montpelier, Vt.	Minister	Farmer, teacher	?
Barnabas C. Hobbs	1815	Washington Co., Ind.	Minister, YM clerk, headmaster	Physician, teacher	MM schools, U. of Pa.
Allen Jay	1831	Miami, Co., O.	Minister	Farmer	MM schools, Antioch

Source: William Bacon Evans et al., comps., "Dictionary of Quaker Biography," typescrpt, n.d. (Quaker Collection, Haverford College Library, Haverford, Pa.).

[1] Moved to New York in 1870s.
[2] Moved to New York, 1867.
[3] Moved to Iowa, 1864.

well-to-do. Francis T. King and Thomas Kimber, for example, retired from business with comfortable fortunes while still in their thirties to devote themselves to good works.[14]

The most important of these leaders were probably Barnabas C. Hobbs and the Coffins. Hobbs was among the oldest of the renewal group. His father, William Hobbs, was an important minister and leading anti-Hicksite in Indiana Yearly Meeting. His mother was a first cousin of Elijah Coffin. While still a young man in Washington County, Indiana, during the 1830s, Hobbs attracted the notice of two important non-Quakers, a justice of the Indiana Supreme Court and the principal of the local academy. They lent him books and encouraged him to attend medical school in Philadelphia. Hobbs never practiced medicine, instead taking over the management of the newly established Quaker boarding school in Mount Pleasant, Ohio. There he married a fellow teacher, Rebecca Tatum, the daughter of a prominent Quaker family. From Mount Pleasant the Hobbses went to Richmond, Indiana, where they presided over another boarding school, this one the forerunner of Earlham College. By age thirty Hobbs was a rising star in Indiana Yearly Meeting, the holder of positions of responsibility, respected for his sanctified learning. "He held his head up with a conscious air of superiority," James Baldwin remembered. "My head swelled with pride at the thought of being in the presence of such a fountain of knowledge and storehouse of wisdom." In 1851 Hobbs moved to Bloomingdale, Indiana, to head still another Quaker boarding school. There he turned to Republican politics while remaining active in society affairs. In 1858, when Western Yearly Meeting (embracing Friends in the western half of Indiana) was "set off" from Indiana Yearly Meeting, Hobbs became its first clerk.[15]

Perhaps even more important to the renewal movement were Charles F. and Rhoda M. Coffin. Born in North Carolina and brought to Indiana at the age of one, Charles was the son of Elijah Coffin, who served as clerk of both North Carolina and Indiana yearly meetings, of the latter for thirty years. His mother, Naomi Hiatt Coffin, was a minister herself and the daughter of Benajah Hiatt, also a well-known Quaker preacher. Charles was educated in Friends schools in Indiana and Cincinnati. At fourteen Joseph John Gurney made a deep impression on him; in his early twenties he traveled with his father in the East and became acquainted with leading Friends in other yearly meetings. In 1847 he made a suitable marriage with Rhoda M. Johnson, the daughter of a well-to-do Quaker farmer and a niece of the eminent minister Thomas Arnett. While still in his twenties, Charles entered his father's bank in Richmond, Indiana, of which he became president in the 1860s. His advance in the society was even more rapid. At nineteen he was clerk of Whitewater Preparative Meeting, at twenty-four a member of the meeting for sufferings, and ten years later he succeeded his father as clerk of Indiana Yearly Meeting. In the 1860s Coffin's wealth, philanthropy, and position at the head of the largest yearly meeting in the world gave him a preeminent position among American Quakers.[16]

The career of Charles's wife, Rhoda, illustrates both the possibilities and the limitations that Gurneyite women faced in the 1860s. Rhoda M. Johnson was born to an Ohio Quaker family in comfortable circumstances in 1826 and grew up in the Quaker community of Waynesville. During the first few years after her marriage in 1847 she devoted most of her time to her children and household duties. Only when her husband's prosperity made the employment of servants possible did she attempt her own career. That career did not involve a profession; instead, it was a career of benevolence of the sort common to evangelical upper-class women of the era. She served on education and First Day school committees, distributed tracts, and relieved the suffering poor while also being active in the affairs of the society. Unlike Hicksite Quaker women, who during this period were battling their way into pursuits hitherto exclusively male, Orthodox women were content to fill socially acceptable roles.[17]

Rhoda M. Coffin's career illustrates several truths about women in the renewal movement. Most were, at best, their husbands' partners, as were Hannah Bean and Hannah Whitall Smith. Elizabeth L. Comstock is unique in achieving her own independent career as a Friend. (Delphina Mendenhall's husband was a non-Quaker who died in 1860.) Only the well-to-do had the leisure to devote themselves totally to society affairs. The careers of men such as Allen Jay and John Henry Douglas were made possible in large degree by wives who heroically kept farms going and held families together while their husbands were otherwise occupied. And even "partnerships" were the exception rather than the rule. The wives of most of the renewal Friends are obscure figures who remained very much in their husbands' shadows.[18]

Most male Friends in the renewal movement followed careers within the society that were similar to those of Barnabas C. Hobbs and Charles F. Coffin. In a denomination that equated wisdom with age, these Friends came into positions of power relatively young. The rapid rise of Hobbs and Coffin has already been described. Francis T. King became clerk of Baltimore Yearly Meeting in his thirties. Timothy Nicholson was appointed superintendent of Haverford College while still in his twenties; Nereus Mendenhall took over the same position at the New Garden Boarding School in North Carolina when he was barely thirty. About half of these Friends, however, were not recorded ministers until later in life, if ever; Bean, Jay, Douglas, the Tatums, and Comstock are notable exceptions.[19]

The renewal Friends in Philadelphia Yearly Meeting occupied a unique position. Philadelphia remained firmly in Wilburite hands until after 1900, locking Gurneyite activists out of nearly all official positions. The Philadelphia Gurneyites had two resources, however. One was Haverford Col-

lege. Unlike the lower-level schools in the Philadelphia area, it was controlled not by the yearly meeting but by a self-perpetuating board with
renewal sympathies. The school's administration and teachers attempted
some cautious innovations in the Quaker lifestyle and tried to make students
aware of wider currents in the world. Slowly they softened the requirements
of the plain life and tried to maintain a forward-looking ministry in the
Haverford meeting. And Haverford had enormous influence. Many of the
leaders of the renewal movement—James Carey Thomas, Henry Hartshorne, Dougan Clark, Jr., Nereus Mendenhall, Timothy Nicholson, Thomas Kimber, and Robert Lindley Murray, to name a few—passed through
Haverford as students or teachers. Probably more important was the influence of Haverford alumni who taught in other Quaker schools. A large
part of the Gurneyite leadership of the second half of the nineteenth century
had a "Haverford connection."[20]

The other resource for renewal Friends in Philadelphia, and the favored
organ of discourse for Gurneyites generally, was the *Friends' Review*.
Founded in 1847 after the Philadelphia *Friend* embraced John Wilbur, the
Review was outspoken in its support of Gurney and its denunciation of
Wilburism. It not only opened its columns to Friends in America, but it also
tried to strengthen ties between American Friends and the evangelical
Quakers of England. The *Review* also reprinted, with some regularity,
articles on reform, education, and humanitarian concerns taken from other
evangelical periodicals. Until the 1870s a group of rather elderly Friends
controlled it, but they were sympathetic to the renewal movement and
opened their columns to its concerns. Thus by 1860 renewal Friends had
been able to build a community of discourse based on personal friendships,
links established at the Quaker schools and through travel, and communication through a favorite journal. They used all of these to promote a program
for the reform of Quakerism.[21]

THE RENEWAL PROGRAM

If renewal Friends looked to any single person (besides Christ) as a model
and prophet, that person was Joseph John Gurney. Renewal activists were
unabashed in describing themselves as Gurneyites. Those among them who
had never met Gurney were just as taken with his character as were those
who had encountered him. To Elizabeth T. King, the wife of Francis T.
King, Gurney was "a bright example of the Christian graces" who, with
"indefatigable industry, . . . entire consecration of himself . . . to the service
of the master . . . [and] unfailing charity and deep humility" had become "a
most conspicuous ornament to the Society of Friends." Critics, wrote another admirer, simply lacked the wit to understand him. Gurneyite Friends

reprinted his essays in their publications and distributed his books as authoritative statements of doctrine and belief.[22]

Like Gurney, renewal Friends were fervent and articulate in their evangelicalism. Two themes dominate their doctrinal statements. One is the nature of the Atonement. By the 1860s all Gurneyite Friends were stressing not just the atoning sacrifice of Christ but also the efficacy of his shed blood as propitiation for sin. Between 1850 and 1870 nearly all of the Gurneyite yearly meetings issued elaborate doctrinal statements. Most included as a declaration of faith George Fox's 1672 letter to the governor of Barbados, which stressed themes important to evangelical Christians far more than did other early Quaker writings.[23]

The other half of the renewal doctrinal thrust was continuing emphasis on the Bible, especially Bible study. The young were a favorite target of the renewal movement: the movement encouraged the growth of First Day schools, and in the 1860s began to hold national conferences for their better management and promotion, meetings that provided further opportunities for contact and discussion. It even tried to attract adult "scholars," arguing that "none are too old or too wise to be studying the Bible, to be . . . occupying their mind with the gems of Truth that are to be found in its sacred pages." Renewal Friends tried to make parents assume responsibility for home instruction by emphasizing daily family Bible reading and worship. This campaign separated the renewal group from many older Friends, who feared that daily family worship would become the kind of formal ceremony that Friends had traditionally eschewed. For Charles F. Coffin it was a "matter of surprise and mortification . . . to see elderly Friends whom I have been in the habit of looking on as fathers and mothers in the church" regularly ignore yearly meeting pronouncements urging daily devotions and Bible instruction. On this subject, many Friends, either from apathy or opposition, did not fall in line with the renewal program. In Cedar Creek Monthly Meeting in Iowa in 1871, for example, only sixteen of the eighty member families had daily worship.[24]

The renewal emphasis on a biblical knowledge had a more important consequence: a subtle shift in interpreting the bases of Quakerism. By the 1860s Gurneyite Friends were increasingly finding the standard for Quaker beliefs in the Bible, not in direct revelation, or in the doctrine of the Inner Light, or in the writings of the early Friends. Gurneyites never repudiated any of those; indeed, some renewal Friends would later distinguish themselves as defenders of such traditional Quaker concepts as that of the Inner Light. But the shift was striking. M. Carey Thomas, the daughter of James and Mary Thomas of Baltimore, later recalled that "every question . . . was settled by the literal words of the English translation of the Bible. After my mother's death I found that even her Bible had 'ands' and 'buts' marked as a help to the literal interpretation of disputed texts." The Gurneyite participation in evangelical culture had brought a majority of American Friends to a new understanding of the basis of their faith.[25]

Despite the shifts toward an overt evangelicalism, renewal Friends saw themselves firmly within Quaker tradition. They still considered Quakerism to be the highest and most perfect revelation of Christianity. In 1858 Dougan Clark, Jr., waxed lyrical in praise of George Fox, to whom, wrote Clark, "were revealed clearer ideas of human perfectability, and more accurate notions of man's duty, than had been communicated since the days of the Apostles." Could the Society grow again, William Nicholson contended, not only would "souls . . . be gathered to Christ" but also "great Christian principles, hitherto practically unrecognized by other denominations, would take a firmer hold of the public conscience." In the eyes of these Friends, the enormous potential of Quakerism was going unrealized. Gradually they evolved a set of proposals that they thought would overturn "narrowness and coldness and inactivity" within the society.[26]

The first point in the renewal program was a redefinition of peculiarity. Renewal Friends saw Quakers as a people apart from the world yet actively involved in it. As the *Friends' Review* argued, Quakers were to be as "lights in your community," helping to create "a tone of soundness and uprightness." Thus renewal Friends continued the involvement in evangelical reform efforts for antislavery, temperance, Bible schools, and education that Gurney had helped to inspire. The activities of Elijah Coffin offer a good example. By the late 1850s Coffin had retired from banking to devote all of his time to Sabbath schools and the work of the American Bible Society. On his deathbed in 1862 he asked that his family read him missionary magazines so that he would die informed about the progress of the Gospel everywhere. Union Sunday schools became a special favorite of renewal Friends. New York and Cincinnati Friends were pioneers in joining with other evangelicals to "uplift" the children of the poor through education and works of charity; they were soon followed by Friends in Philadelphia, Richmond, Indiana, and Lynn, Massachusetts.[27]

Another part of the renewal program was emphasis on a nonsectarian image. In the growth of antislavery sentiment and pacifism during the 1840s and 1850s, some Gurneyite Friends saw other Protestants moving toward truths long held by Friends. The *Friends' Review* noted such tendencies in the urban revival of 1857–1858, with its lay leadership, silent prayers, and "lack of noisy demonstrations." For a time, it seemed to Gurneyites, the rest of Protestantism was willing to meet Friends halfway.[28]

A few renewal Friends even carried their desire for reform as far as working with religious liberals. Whittier and New York elder Benjamin Tatham, for example, indicated a willingness to join with Unitarians and Universalists in peace efforts. Haverford admitted Hicksites in the 1850s, although doubtless with a mind to bringing them to the light. Late in the

1860s two newly founded periodicals sympathetic to the renewal movement, the *American Friend* in Richmond, Indiana, and the Chicago-based *Herald of Peace,* ran cautious articles suggesting some sort of dialogue with the Hicksites. The journals acknowledged fundamental differences but suggested that the two groups had some basis for discourse and common action.[29]

Such sentiments were, to be sure, exceptional. In 1860 Elizabeth L. Comstock found Orthodox Friends of all types "liberal and tolerant" of "all 'Orthodox' bodies of Christians" but concluded that "they cannot endure Spiritualists, Universalists, and Unitarians. They dread and shun these as they would serpents and venomous snakes." Hicksites fell fully within that ban. William Tallack found that the Orthodox did not even accord Hicksites the name of Friends; simple courtesy toward them was viewed suspiciously. In 1866, when Gurneyite Friends held a conference on peace in Richmond to consider drafting an address on pacifism to other denominations, they made it clear that they would work only with evangelicals. A proposal not to limit the bounds of cooperation died in the face of overwhelming opposition.[30]

While they tried to break down some of the barriers that separated Friends from other evangelical denominations, renewal Friends also advocated modifying certain aspects of the discipline. Nereus Mendenhall, pondering the reasons for the decline of the Society of Friends in 1851, focused on three problems: death, marriage out of unity, and lack of aggressive proselytization. Death, of course, was beyond human control, but the other two problems were not, and the marriage regulations became the chief target of reformers. The argument against the ban on marriage to non-Quakers was twofold. First, disownment on such grounds resulted in the loss of hundreds of otherwise blameless Friends every year. More seriously, renewal Friends argued, the marriage regulations encouraged hypocrisy. Offenders could retain their membership in such cases by an acknowledgment of wrongdoing to their monthly meeting. Reformers argued that the truly conscientious could not see the wrong of such marriages and thus felt that there was no fault for them to acknowledge, while others acknowledged their wrongdoing in an insincere and perfunctory way. Thus the society lost the most valuable members while retaining the least conscientious. During the 1850s Friends began to discuss proposals for change. In 1859 New York became the first yearly meeting to revise its marriage regulations. Under its new system, a Friend who married a non-Quaker had only to indicate that he or she wished to remain a member. The monthly meeting was to wait at least a year after the marriage before requesting such a statement, during which time the "offender" remained a member in good standing.[31]

Friends in the renewal movement showed less unanimity and more uncertainty about abolishing other disciplinary restraints. They had no desire to end the prohibitions on activities of "questionable morality"—dancing, drinking, cardplaying, theatergoing, and so on. There was some disagreement on the desirability of dropping the speech and dress regulations. The painstaking rules on hats and bonnets and the cut of coats offended the evangelicalism of the renewal Friends because the regulations suggested that salvation was achieved through dead works rather than through living faith. Some renewal Friends worried (as did many non-Quaker evangelicals), however, that to abandon the plain life entirely would be to become slaves to "fashion." Ultimately renewal Friends arrived at a consensus that, consciously or unconsciously, mirrored the attitude of other evangelicals. The chief rule in dress and conversation, they concluded, should be functional simplicity, not adherence to a "Quaker uniform" and to meaningless, archaic patterns of speech. At the same time, Friends should avoid being caught up in the changing fashions of the world. In matters of dress, the 1860s were the era of transition. In 1860 William Tallack estimated that two-thirds of all western Friends were scrupulous in adhering to the plain dress. Eight years later a Quaker periodical flatly stated that the plain dress had become a thing of the past, and one Earlham student was using the dresses of women Friends visiting there as a guide to current fashion. Patterns of speech were harder to break. Most renewal Friends apparently used the plain language until their deaths, although they did not require it of their children.[32]

Just as renewal Friends tried to alter the discipline, they also tried to soften its administration. They argued that its original goal had been to hold Friends within the society, not to provide an excuse for putting them out. Too often, they contended, committees neglected patient and loving labor with offenders in favor of perfunctory visits that yielded no results. Most of the changes in the administration of the discipline were subtle, but Iowa, Ohio, and Indiana monthly meeting records show a drastic falloff in complaints relating to Quaker peculiarities after 1860. There were also some structural changes. In 1860 New York Yearly Meeting revised its discipline so that Friends who had been disowned could be received back into membership by a simple request instead of by public recantation of past sins. A few years later Western Yearly Meeting ruled that overseers were to report to the monthly meeting only cases involving "scandalous or immoral conduct." In the case of a lesser offense against the discipline, the overseers were simply to visit the offender. If they found him or her repentant, they were to take no further action and the monthly meeting was to make no record of the incident. Friends thus created a disciplinary system similar to other evangelicals, one that saw the function of church discipline as the preservation of morality rather than as separation.[33]

Statistics from monthly meetings in Indiana Yearly Meeting suggest that the changes reformers sought were effective. (See tables 1, 2, and 3.) Prior to 1860 all four monthly meetings show a common pattern: a loss of member-

TABLE 1

Disciplinary Trends in Four Monthly Meetings in Indiana Yearly Meeting

Whitewater (Wayne County)

Offense	1809–1820	1821–1830	1831–1840	1841–1850	1851–1860	1861–1870	1871–1880	1881–1890	1891–1900
Marriage contrary to discipline	63	57	59	58	41	19	0	0	0
Deviation from plainness	15	15	19	16	4	7	2	0	0
Morals	12	22	4	4	0	0	0	1	0
Nonattendance	0	16	47	85	18	6	5	15	1
Joining another denomination	0	124	30	29	3	3	16	10	10
Doctrine and Disunity	1	46	50	48	8	1	2	1	0
Total offenses	91	280	209	240	74	36	25	27	11
Deduction for multiple offenses*	1	10	63	87	17	5	1	1	0
Total membership loss	90	270	146	153	57	31	24	26	11

Cherry Grove (Randolph County)

Offense	1821–1830	1831–1840	1841–1850	1851–1860	1861–1870	1871–1880	1881–1890	1891–1900
Marriage contrary to discipline	33	16	18	65	10	1	0	0
Deviation from plainness	16	7	6	6	1	3	0	0
Morals	31	14	5	8	6	6	1	1
Nonattendance	16	17	12	21	2	2	3	0
Joining another denomination	2	4	10	5	8	6	0	3
Doctrine and disunity	2	18	47	4	1	1	0	0
Total offenses	100	76	98	109	28	19	4	4
Deduction for multiple offenses	16	15	50	16	0	2	1	0
Total membership loss	84	61	48	93	28	17	3	0

Duck Creek (Henry County)

Offense	1826–1830	1831–1840	1841–1850	1851–1860	1861–1870	1871–1880	1881–1890	1891–1900
Marriage contrary to discipline	21	34	70	68	7	0	0	0
Deviation from plainness	8	18	4	7	4	0	0	0
Morals	6	17	6	6	2	0	0	0
Nonattendance	0	7	6	8	2	1	0	0
Joining another denomination	0	4	39	16	6	0	0	0
Doctrine and disunity	42	18	60	0	0	0	0	0
Total offenses	77	98	185	105	21	1	0	0
Deduction for multiple offenses	5	16	26	9	0	0	0	0
Total membership loss	72	82	159	96	21	1	0	0

Walnut Ridge (Rush County)

Offense	1836–1840	1841–1850	1851–1860	1861–1870	1871–1880	1881–1890	1891–1900
Marriage contrary to discipline	16	30	41	17	0	0	0
Deviation from plainness	7	3	6	9	0	1	2
Morals	0	1	5	1	0	5	1
Nonattendance	5	5	2	1	1	1	0
Joining another denomination	1	6	6	3	0	0	0
Doctrine and disunity	3	10	2	2	0	2	0
Total offenses	32	55	62	33	1	9	3
Deduction for multiple offenses	2	5	2	3	0	0	0
Total membership loss	30	50	60	30	1	9	3

Source: Willard C. Heiss, ed., Abstracts of the Records of the Society of Friends in Indiana (7 vols., Indianapolis: Indiana Historical Society, 1962–1977), I, 70–191, II, 256–309, IV, 170–213, 358–87.

Note: "Marriage contrary to discipline," "Joining another denomination," and "Nonattendance" are self-explanatory. "Deviation from plainness" includes offenses that were departures from the peculiarities of Friends, such as plain speech and plain dress, pacifism, and abstaining from music. "Morals" includes offenses regarded as unacceptable behavior by all denominations, such as adultery, fornication, theft, or drunkenness. "Doctrine and disunity" includes offenses of belief rather than of action; placed in this category are Hicksites and Anti-Slavery Friends. (Many Hicksites and Anti-Slavery Friends were probably disowned for nonattendance or joining another denomination, making it difficult to get an accurate count.) "Disunity" apparently was a catchall, often not explained further in complaints.

*Necessary because some individuals were disowned for more than one offense.

TABLE 2

Marriage Trends in Four Monthly Meetings in Indiana Yearly Meeting

Monthly Meeting	1809–1820	1821–1830	1831–1840	1841–1850	1851–1860	1861–1870	1871–1880	1881–1890	1891–1900
Whitewater									
Disowned for marriage contrary to discipline (mcd)	63	57	59	58	41	19	0	0	0
Condemned mcd	43	45	10	22	17	49	33	0	0
Married in meeting	75	69	41	30	31	23	27	14	20
Cherry Grove (Est. 1821)									
Disowned for mcd		33	16	18	65	10	1	0	0
Condemned mcd		27	14	30	30	32	5	0	0
Married in meeting		34	43	22	16	12	2	0	0
Duck Creek (Est. 1826)									
Disowned for mcd		21	34	70	68	7	0	0	0
Condemned mcd		5	16	22	16	16	8	0	0
Married in meeting		19	31	37	20	12	*	*	*
Walnut Ridge (Est. 1836)									
Disowned for mcd			16	30	41	17	0	0	0
Condemned mcd			7	29	32	47	9	0	0
Married in meeting			20	55	52	13	*	*	*

Source: Willard C. Heiss, ed., *Abstracts of the Records of the Society of Friends in Indiana* (7 vols., Indianapolis: Indiana Historical Society, 1962–1977), I, 70–191, II, 256–309, IV, 170–213, 358–87.
*Records not available.

TABLE 3

Membership Trends in Four Monthly Meetings in Indiana Yearly Meeting

Monthly Meeting	1809–1820	1821–1830	1831–1840	1841–1850	1851–1860	1861–1870	1871–1880	1881–1890	1891–1900
Whitewater									
Received at request	186	59	26	43	31	101	171	246	346
Disowned	90	270	146	153	57	31	24	26	11
Resigned*	0	0	0	0	0	4	84	132	146
Cherry Grove (Est. 1821)									
Received at request		66	72	17	30	160	89	200	227
Disowned		84	61	48	93	28	17	3	0
Resigned*		0	0	0	0	0	22	40	22
Duck Creek (Est. 1826)									
Received at request		12	39	60	36	61	62	38	247
Disowned		72	82	159	96	21	1	0	0
Resigned*		0	0	0	0	0	22	40	22
Walnut Ridge (Est. 1836)									
Received at request			5	14	31	75	157	50	43
Disowned			30	50	60	30	1	9	3
Resigned*			0	0	0	0	8	6	12

Source: Willard C. Heiss, ed. *Abstracts of the Records of the Society of Friends in Indiana* (7 vols., Indianapolis: Indiana Historical Society, 1962–1977), I, 70–191, II, 256–309, IV, 170–213, 358–87.
*Before 1870 Friends did not recognize a right of resignation of membership.

ship that far outstripped the accession of new members to the society. Marriages contrary to discipline consistently outnumbered those within the order of the society; and a majority of those who "married out" chose to leave the society, apparently in growing numbers during the 1850s. After 1860 there was a dramatic decline in disownments for marriage offenses; proportional declines in disownments for such offenses as joining other denominations and not attending meetings suggest that the society was holding onto its members to an unprecedented degree. Simultaneously it was attracting a significant number of new members—the decade 1860–1870 saw a sharp increase in the number "received into membership at their own request" in all of the monthly meetings examined. By the 1870s Friends were losing their membership for the same reasons as were other evangelical denominations: nonattendance, moral offenses, or joining another church.

Just as renewal Friends made efforts to keep Friends within the society, they followed evangelical examples by reviving a missionary impulse. Orthodox Friends in the United States had followed the travels of the English missionary Friends Daniel Wheeler and James Backhouse since the 1830s. In the 1860s American Gurneyite Friends began to send out their own missionaries: Joel and Hannah Bean to Hawaii, Louis and Sarah Street to Madagascar, and Eli and Sybil Jones to Palestine. Periodicals such as the *Friends' Review* and the *American Friend* gave missions extensive coverage. And even as they began to support their own missions, Gurneyite Friends contributed to the missionary enterprises of other evangelicals. As early as 1860 Indiana and Western yearly meetings, over some strenuous objections, approved the collection of funds for the use of non-Quaker missionaries. Four years later, Indiana Yearly Meeting formed its own foreign missionary society. Most of the other Gurneyite yearly meetings soon followed Indiana's lead. From the beginning, Quaker missionaries such as the Beans and the Streets worked with other Protestants, unconcerned that they were implicated in a "hireling ministry." Later, when President Ulysses S. Grant began his "Peace Policy" of placing various Protestant denominations in charge of "civilizing" the western Indian tribes, Friends responded enthusiastically; Grant even offered Charles F. Coffin the superintendency of the Bureau of Indian Affairs.[34]

Interest in foreign missions coincided with a home missionary impulse among Gurneyite Friends. As early as 1850 Elizabeth T. King had learned German so that she could work with German immigrants in Baltimore. Throughout the 1860s Indiana Yearly Meeting took the lead in organizing home mission activities. During the Civil War leading Friends in Richmond, troubled by the growing number of street urchins and by reports of desperate poverty among the families of soldiers, banded together to organize relief work and Bible schools. In 1866, inspired by reports brought back from England by John Henry Douglas and Murray Shipley, Indiana Yearly Meeting formed a home mission association. Still, during the 1860s individual efforts remained most notable, especially those of the ministers Elizabeth L. Comstock and Sarah J. Smith, whose work in prison reform in the Midwest deserves to be classed with that of Elizabeth Fry in England. All of these efforts, individual and corporate, had by the mid-1860s created a striking missionary spirit. In 1865 Indiana Yearly Meeting was telling its members, in language that would have been unthinkable a generation earlier, that their duty was "to labor for the salvation of souls and the spread of the Gospel among men."[35]

Probably the reforms with the greatest potential for the future were those undertaken by renewal Friends to change meetings for worship. Renewal Friends did not seek a radical transformation; they remained committed to silent, unprogrammed worship. They worried, however, that too much silence was symptomatic of the domination of meetings by small groups of ministers and elders. Thus renewal Friends encouraged cautious experimentation. Their first step was to urge more members to speak when led to do so in meeting. "To be able to tell what the Lord has done for us is a happy privilege," Francis W. Thomas, the Indiana minister, wrote in 1863, and he argued that the failure of the overwhelming majority of Friends to speak in meeting indicated a lamentable spiritual condition. Part of the problem was the widespread sentiment that anyone who spoke in meeting was going to become a minister. Indeed, although the original theory behind the Friends meeting had been that anyone who felt moved was free to speak, the elders saw to it that such freedom remained carefully circumscribed. They discouraged those who were not ministers or who did not seem to be heading in that direction. Those who continued to speak in the face of such pressure usually found themselves facing disownment. Such a climate made speaking in meeting a matter of utmost gravity. Those who spoke faced it with fully as much anxiety and consternation as did young ministers of other denominations preaching their first sermons.[36]

While there were fears about suppressing the gifts of average members, there was also concern about the nature of the ministry that Friends did hear. Renewal Friends objected to the sing-song style of preaching that, although venerable in Quaker tradition, was without parallels in other denominations and had no doctrinal foundations. The *Friends' Review* described its typical features with distaste: the chanting style, the "singing tone," the speaking in broken cadences "without any regard to proper pauses or proper emphasis," and the habit of prefacing each sentence with a pronounced "Ah." Renewal activists exhorted ministers instead to avoid "peculiarities of gesture and tone" and to "endeavor to deliver themselves . . . in a dignified manner becoming the great subject." Underlying all of those criticisms was the idea that fluency in preaching was something that ministers should strive for, an idea at odds with the old belief that all ministry in all of its features was to be inspired directly by the Holy Spirit. Some renewal Friends even began to chip away at the hoary Quaker prejudice against educating ministers. They never questioned the old belief that education could not make a minister, and they certainly did not advocate a formal course of theological training. They did argue, however, that informed, systematic study of the Scriptures, guided by appropriate aids, would help ministers better to understand biblical truths and to avoid eccentric and schismatic interpretations. It is testimony to their commitment to evangelicalism that by the 1860s renewal Friends were recommending such standard Protestant commentaries as Alexander Cruden's concordance, Edward Robinson on the harmony of the gospels, Albert Barnes's *Notes*, George Bush on the Pentateuch, James Clarke's *Commentaries*, and John McClintock and James Sharp's *Cyclopedia of Biblical, Theological, and Ecclesiastic Literature*.[37]

The renewal reform that found greatest acceptance came not, however, from changes in the regular meetings for worship or in the ministry, but in alternative forms of Quaker meetings. It had never been unusual for Friends to end social gatherings with a short period of silent worship. Renewal Friends drew on that tradition to experiment with new types of meetings. In the late 1850s and 1860s hundreds of young Friends organized groups that combined the characteristics of informal prayer meetings with those of literary societies, calling themselves "social circles" or "tract-reading meetings." Members agreed on a common reading—sometimes a standard Quaker work, sometimes an evangelical text drawn from outside the society. There was usually a Bible reading, then a period of silence or brief speaking that closed with a prayer. Some have seen these meetings as the outgrowth of the cottage prayer groups that played a prominent role in the 1857–1858 revival, although they bear just as much similarity to the literary societies that were so common in antebellum America. The social circles provided a forum for young Friends to discuss religious concerns and to express themselves, free from the domination of older members. They also held potential for significant change; by late in the 1860s some Friends reported "many weeping and crying for mercy" under the influence of the prayers.[38]

One sign of the radical direction these new meetings could take appeared during Indiana Yearly Meeting in Richmond in the fall of 1860. A group of young Friends, including Charles F. and Rhoda M. Coffin, John Henry Douglas, and Murray Shipley, met in the Coffin home to discuss the domination of meetings for worship by elderly Friends. The conferees called for a special young people's meeting that evening. At the beginning Elijah Coffin, "timing" the meeting, asked those present who were in the habit of speaking to defer to the young people. The meeting went on until past 1:30 A.M., with nearly everyone present saying a few words. The most striking departure came, not from a young Friend, but from Richard J. Hubbard, a leading elder and the son of the eminent minister Jeremiah Hubbard, who rose toward the end and in a halting voice tried to sing a hymn, an almost unprecedented deviation from tradition. Although exaggerated reports aroused misgivings among eastern Friends, those present were unanimous in their endorsement of the experiment.[39]

Renewal Friends did not confine their concerns to internal affairs; they continued the Gurneyite interest in social reform. In most respects their concerns were not much different from those of other religious reformers, evangelical or otherwise. Antislavery continued to be a primary concern, although by the 1850s Friends tended to confine their opposition to slavery to maintaining the traditional testimonies and to supporting the Republican party. The antiabolitionist sentiment that had caused schism during the 1840s broke down rapidly after 1850, and in 1857 the Anti-Slavery Friends in Indiana dissolved their yearly meeting on the grounds that the larger body had come to the positions that the abolitionist Friends had embraced fifteen years earlier.[40]

While Friends maintained what one historian has called a "quiet testimony" against slavery, they were much more vocal in their support of temperance. During the 1850s yearly meetings moved toward making the use of alcohol as a beverage grounds for disownment, while Friends in the Gurneyite yearly meetings, with the tacit approval of the weighty Friends who controlled them, began to join "mixed" temperance societies. Simultaneously, when many temperance reformers espoused prohibition, Gurneyite Friends, especially in Indiana and Ohio, threw wholehearted support behind the cause. Several yearly meetings officially endorsed prohibition; they also included temperance and prohibition literature among the pamphlets that their tract committees distributed. (Elizabeth L. Comstock kept a pledge book in her sitting room so that it would be handy in case a visitor was seized by a sudden desire to take the pledge.) By the 1860s temperance, once a Quaker peculiarity, had become another tie to the larger evangelical culture.[41]

One of the ways in which Friends tried to advance their testimonies against slavery and drink during the 1850s and 1860s was a fierce devotion to the Republican party. During the 1850s the Republican party, with its antislavery and, in some cases, prohibitionist platform, drew Quakers almost as a body from the collapsing Whig and Free Soil parties, and Friends stuck by the Republicans even after they muted their temperance sentiments. It was a given that no Friend would vote for a "proslavery" candidate. Some Friends, especially Wilburites, had qualms about voting, but virtually all of the renewal Friends were active Republicans. Barnabas C. Hobbs, for example, served as a Republican state official, while Quakers in the counties around Richmond, Indiana, were the most fervent supporters of the Radical Republican congressman George W. Julian, even though Julian was a Unitarian with a Hicksite background. During the 1860s the editors of the Quaker journals made no pretense of nonpartisanship. To them the Democrats were the party of slavery and anarchy; the Republicans, that of democratic principles, morality, and reform. In 1868 the Chicago *Herald of Peace* asked rhetorically: "Is there any cripple of sound mind, who would not rather hobble miles to the polls, than incur the remotest risk of helping to elect Seymour and Blair [the Democratic national ticket] by his neglect to discharge the duty of a citizen?" Before the Liberal Republican movement of 1872, it was close to impossible to find a Friend who was not a Republican. As late as the mid-1870s, an analysis of Indiana voters has shown, 98 percent of Quakers were Republicans; the other 2 percent, independents.[42]

For renewal Friends, reform and political activism were part of a far more important cause: ushering in the millennium. In 1858 Dougan Clark, Jr., saw the personal struggle for holiness as part of a crusade that would transform the world. Those who overcame temptation, who conquered some inbred sin, were not simply sanctifying themselves but "working at the lever which is destined, with God's blessing, to reform and elevate and evangelize mankind." All of the evangelical denominations had important roles to play in the evangelization of the world and in bringing the millennium, when "the empire of love shall have become universal on earth." Friends, however, had a special part, since their principles of peace and universal love—the most distinctive of the basic Quaker testimonies—were to be the foremost characteristics of the millennium. Thus efforts to revitalize the society, to extend the reach of its testimonies, had special urgency.[43]

Renewal Friends enunciated an intellectually viable program. The main obstacles to its success were social. Some of the Friends trying to bring new life to Quakerism, especially in the West, were of the "common people," farmers of relatively small means such as Francis W. Thomas and Allen Jay. In a world in which most Friends west and south of Baltimore were still an agrarian people, however, most of the renewal leaders were urban and relatively wealthy. Francis T. King, for example, had retired with a comfortable fortune at age thirty-five; he was of sufficient social standing to be a member of the original board of trustees of Johns Hopkins University. Thomas Kimber was a railroad vice-president and president of the Philadelphia Board of Trade. To non-Friends, Charles F. Coffin seemed the epitome of gentlemanly wealth and influence—banker, philanthropist, a power in local Republican politics, well traveled in Europe and America. Even the renewal Friends who did not possess great wealth, such as Clark or Mendenhall or the Nicholsons, held positions that made them part of the Quaker elite. Their positions colored their approach to the society's problems. Their solutions usually involved change imposed from above: revising the yearly meeting's discipline, issuing minutes on various subjects, giving time and money to good causes. Most of the renewal Friends, consciously or otherwise, maintained a distance from the ordinary Friends on the farms and in the villages. Therein lay the greatest limitation and the greatest failure of the renewal movement.[44]

The consequences of that failure did not become apparent until much later. Instead, early in the 1860s the renewal program seemed to hold the future of Quakerism. Renewal Friends were putting in place a program of reform that appeared to have the potential for sweeping away the anachronisms that encrusted American Quakerism without sacrificing Quaker distinctiveness. By the 1860s the renewal movement was producing changes among Gurneyites. And those changes interacted with more popular ones that were an outgrowth of the evangelical emphases of the 1830s and 1840s.

THE NEW BIRTH

Of all of the changes that took place during the late 1850s and early 1860s among Gurneyite Friends, probably the most important was the increasing emphasis on a definite conversion experience—the new birth. Although renewal Friends advocated the doctrine, the fervent embrace of the central doctrine of evangelicalism had a basis far broader than the renewal program. It is most obvious in the doctrinal statements that the various yearly meetings and their subordinates issued. Less accessible, but perhaps even more important, was the place that the new birth was coming to occupy in Quaker preaching.

Recapturing Quaker preaching is extremely difficult. Almost no Quaker sermon manuscripts from the period survive, and few of the evangelical Quaker ministers left diaries. The reminiscences of contemporaries and the rare summaries of the sermons they heard suggest that five figures were central to the evangelical shift: Stephen Grellet (1773–1855) of New Jersey; Jeremiah Hubbard (1777–1849), Thomas Arnett (1791–1877), and Enos G. Pray (1812–1876), all ministers in Indiana Yearly Meeting; and Sybil Jones (1808–1875), a minister from Maine.

These ministers were a diverse lot. Only Pray and Jones were birthright Friends. Grellet was a French emigré and converted Roman Catholic; Arnett, a former Methodist; and Hubbard, one-fourth Cherokee. Grellet spent his life in New York and New Jersey; Jones, in Maine. Hubbard lived in North Carolina until moving to Indiana in 1837, whereas Arnett and Pray spent most of their adult lives in Ohio. All, however, shared certain characteristics. All emphasized evangelical themes, as in Hubbard's case, "the fallen and lost state of man" and the necessity of a definite conversion experience, or, as in Arnett's, the "plan of salvation." Along with an emphatically evangelical message, these five brought a new preaching style, free from the traditional sing-song but close to that of their contemporaries in other denominations. Pray, for example, delivered his messages in a stentorian voice whose power even Wilburites admired and that put some Friends in mind of Daniel Webster. Because all of these preachers traveled widely, their influence reached far beyond their own yearly meetings.[45]

By the mid-1850s the work of such ministers was bearing fruit. Unfortunately, no one at the time speculated as to why Gurneyites found such a message compelling—it was simply a logical outgrowth of the influence of Gurney and the evangelical culture in which Friends were caught up. Nonetheless, it was real and notable. A Friend from New England who attended Indiana and Baltimore yearly meetings in 1855 was struck by the emphasis placed on conversion and the new birth. Notwithstanding the leadings of the Inner Light, Friends at both yearly meetings urged the necessity of individually making a definite covenant with God and experiencing individually the regenerating work of grace in the heart. Such preaching became increasingly common at yearly meetings during the 1860s. At Indiana Yearly Meeting in 1861, the meetings for worship were so arranged that several were held out of doors, with well-known ministers present at each. The ministers exhorted everyone present to seek conversion. Two years later, when Iowa Yearly Meeting held its first session, in several meetings for worship, all were called on "to come to Jesus and receive the pardon so freely offered." In 1867 one observer of Indiana Yearly Meeting noted that many preachers were "earnestly pouring forth solemn warning or making urgent appeals to come to Christ," and concluded: "The most careless observer can scarcely fail to notice that other and more important changes have taken place . . . and not the least of these is a change in the style and character of the ministry."[46]

Other evidence of the increasing emphasis on a conversion experience emerges from a number of reminiscent accounts, which, written much later, tell of Friends undergoing conversion experiences during the 1840s and 1850s. Possibly the writers, influenced by later developments, were characterizing experiences that were not so perceived at the time. Significant, however, is that during the 1850s and 1860s some Friends were doing just that in regard to worthy Friends from earlier periods. In 1857, when Indiana Friends memorialized Nathan C. Hoag, they described his 1797 conversion experience, something utterly foreign to Friends in that period, especially to the quietist Hoag family. About the same time, Friends in Indiana and Baltimore reprinted a memoir of Martha C. Thomas, a Baltimore Friend who had died in 1836. Although Thomas's life was cast in the old mold of growth into holiness, Indiana Friends prefaced the memoir with a long essay on the necessity of the new birth.[47]

The most powerful evidence for the new emphasis on a conversion experience comes from the doctrinal statements of the various yearly meetings and their subordinates and from articles in the Gurneyite periodicals. "No man can love Christ until he is converted and his heart becomes changed," Indiana Yearly Meeting told its members in 1864. A year later Iowa Yearly Meeting included in its new discipline the simple declaration "Ye must be born again." Such Gurneyite journals as the *Friends' Review* and the *Southern Friend* ran articles on the necessity of conversion. And as a significant sign of the times, Friends began to circulate tracts on the conversion experiences of non-Quakers.[48]

Not surprisingly, by the late 1860s a few young ministers had begun to bring the message of the new birth to non-Friends through aggressive evangelistic work. For some it was simply an extension of the benevolent tradition. Women in particular—for example, Esther Frame in Indiana, Elizabeth L. Comstock in Michigan, and Mary H. Rogers in Chicago—as well as the temperance lecturer David Tatum of Cleveland, visited prisons, jails, and saloons to distribute Bibles and tracts, to pray, and occasionally to preach. All had in mind more than just moral exhortations. In 1867 Comstock lamented that in Bible times three thousand had been converted in one day; Friends were unlikely to make that many converts in a decade. Comstock's complaint would have had some validity earlier in the century, but by the late 1860s there were signs of a higher level of activity throughout the Gurneyite meetings, especially in those west of the Appalachians. Journals such as the *American Friend* and the *Herald of Peace* began to run columns of news from local meetings; previously, few meetings had had news to report. Yearly meeting statistics show steady gains in the numbers received into membership at their own request. By 1869 a few ministers were holding special meetings to try to bring back into the society some of those who had been lost during previous years.[49]

Additional sources of increasing religious enthusiasm among Gurneyite Friends were the tract-reading meetings and occasional spillovers from non-Quaker revivals. In several of the "social circles" there were outbreaks of emotionalism. We know little about such outbursts; only one minister, Francis W. Thomas, endorsed them before 1868, but incidents were reported in Indiana, Iowa, and Kansas. Similarly, in a few meetings, hymns sung by individuals were heard for the first time. There were also instances of Quakers becoming caught up in non-Quaker revivals. In Iowa, for example, some Friends in Bangor Quarterly Meeting who had taken part in a Campbellite revival "became impatient of the healthful restraints of church discipline" and ran off into "the strangest and wildest fanaticism." A few even separated from the society and refused to associate with Friends. But such instances were not common. Some Friends of conservative tendencies were apprehensive, and some elderly Friends worried that young Quakers were becoming too quick to speak in meeting and generally "too active," but the basic fabric of Quakerism at the end of the 1860s remained undisturbed.[50]

Despite the strong new evangelical emphases, as Friends preached the new birth and urged other Friends to experience it, older traditions and patterns of thought kept their power. The old ways of preaching did not disappear overnight, and the evangelical Friends never repudiated the ideas of gradual growth into holiness and bearing the cross. Thus Friends sent out conflicting signals. They did not seem to realize that they were faced with two fundamentally contradictory visions of religious life. In the 1870s those contradictions became clear. But in the 1860s they did not seem to concern Friends.[51]

By 1860, then, Gurneyite Friends had become a people in transition. Among the young elite of the society was an almost unprecedented intellectual ferment, an excitement of debates, of changes being made, of anachronisms disappearing. At all levels Friends were being swept up in the economic and social transformation of the nation and by the increasingly evangelical direction of the society. Despite such change, Gurneyite Friends felt secure in their unity. Most of the renewal program was so skillfully enunciated and executed that it aroused little opposition. What was done did not conflict with the basic structure of Quakerism. Silent, unprogrammed worship, nonpastoral ministry, the idea of Friends as a separate people remained undisturbed. Even the doctrine of the Inner Light, although deemphasized, was never challenged. During the 1860s Friends ignored the fundamental conflicts between evangelicalism and Quaker tradition and looked to the future with confidence.

THE WAR

While feeling confident about the future of the society in 1860, Friends nonetheless had a sense of foreboding about their country. "It will be no marvel if our nation should be visited with the fierce judgements of God," Earlham professor Joseph Moore wrote, "for we are surely a guilty nation." A Virginia Friend concurred. National sins, he argued, were "punishable by national judgments," and Americans merited God's "righteous indignation." Other Friends began to circulate the 1803 vision of Joseph Hoag, a Vermont Quaker minister, which ostensibly not only predicted the Hicksite separation and the antimasonic crusade but also prophesized a civil war in which slavery would be wiped out and the political power of the South broken. By 1861, as the crisis of the Union deepened, ministers in Indiana were gloomily predicting a long, bloody war.[52]

The outbreak of hostilities found Friends united in their support for the Union. The Confederacy, founded in sedition to protect slavery, seemed to many Friends to be the very incarnation of evil. "I believe that if thee or me or any other Christian could destroy their enemies by taking their lives they could do it in this ungodly rebellion," an Iowa minister wrote to a cousin who had fled North Carolina to join the Union army. Even before the war broke out, many Friends in the South made desperate attempts to move their families northward to avoid living under the Confederacy.[53]

Northern and southern Quakers faced very different problems from 1861 to 1865. Friends in the South suffered greatly during the war years, not only from the privations endured then by all southerners but also because of their reputation as staunch Unionists. The Confederate conscription laws caused horrible problems for young male Friends because of their failure to set exemption terms that conscientious Quakers could meet. Friends in the North usually did not have to contend with that sort of persecution. When the Lincoln administration resorted to conscription, it was fairly liberal in exempting religious conscientious objectors. The well-known Republican sympathies of Friends aided them, as did Secretary of War Edwin M. Stanton, who had Quaker relatives in Ohio. The problem that northern Friends faced came from within the society.[54]

It was, of course, firmly established Quaker belief that evil could not be met with evil. Nothing could justify killing in the eyes of consistent Friends, and those at the head of the various yearly meetings remained firm in upholding the peace testimony. Virtually all of the yearly meetings issued addresses to their members and adopted fairly rigorous policies on military service. Enlistment was to bring disownment, as was submitting to conscription, hiring a substitute, or paying any tax or fine for exemption.[55]

Most of the yearly meetings based their positions on an unquestioning acceptance of Quaker tradition. Few Orthodox Friends attempted new justifications of Christian pacifism. Instead, they contented themselves with reissuing a few standard peace works written before 1850. Indiana Yearly Meeting provided the significant exception. In 1863 it published *An Appeal for the Rights of Conscience*, which made the strong Unionism of the Friends the grounds for their refusal to fight. The Union was too precious a thing, the authors said, to be submitted to "the decision of means, the result of which is liable to turn on so many points independent of the true merits of the question." (Just why the Union was so precious they did not explain— apparently it was, in their eyes, a given.) War, they concluded, involved "too many elements of risk and uncertainty, arising from the fallibility, the incapacity, and the wickedness of man." Thus their pacifism rose out of the highest motives of patriotism and religion.[56]

Two problems confronted Friends who wanted to hold fast to the peace testimony. One was the hostility that pacifists always face in wartime. "A strong prejudice against our Society seems to be springing up, because of our testimony against war," Elizabeth L. Comstock wrote in 1862. "People look upon us as a sort of half-secessionists, because we will not fight for the

Union, and oppose all war." In vain did Friends protest that, while the society was an "advocate of peace," it abhorred those "who seek to destroy our general Government, and to rivet the chains of slavery in this land."[57]

An even greater problem was the number of young male Friends who flocked to the Union army as volunteers. Except for that pertaining to Indiana, the kind of systematic analysis based on monthly meeting and enlistment records that would show just how many Friends departed from the peace testimony remains to be undertaken. Numbers probably varied from place to place. Few Philadelphia Friends, Wilburite or Gurneyite, went into the army. The situation was different in Indiana and Western yearly meetings, where significant numbers of Quaker men joined the army, some with misgivings, others flaunting their defiance of the overseers. Many leading Friends had a sense of wholesale deviation. "We hear of many young Friends taking up arms for the North," one wrote, and went on to tell the story of three Union soldiers who fell into a chance conversation and discovered that one was the son of the clerk of New England Yearly Meeting, Samuel Boyd Tobey; the second, the son of the eminent minister Sybil Jones; and the third, the son of William H. Chase, a leading New York elder. Throughout the war years Western and Indiana yearly meetings issued minutes deploring widespread failure to uphold the peace testimony; some Friends privately expressed fears that even the leadership was not so firm with offenders as tradition and the discipline demanded. Certainly many Friends, at least in Indiana, were never "dealt with" for military service. Governor Oliver P. Morton of Indiana was quoted as saying that the Quakers had provided more enlistments in proportion to membership than had any other denomination in the state.[58]

Thus the Civil War brought a sense of crisis to Gurneyite Friends. In 1860 the future of the society had seemed bright: increased attendance at meetings, heightened interest among the membership, and, most of all, unity. The widespread defection from the peace testimony, or at least a perception of it, brought doubt and debate.[59]

During the war Friends were too busy aiding those who, because of their adherence to the peace testimony, faced problems to give too much attention to those who deviated from it. In 1866 the Gurneyite yearly meetings held conferences in Baltimore and Richmond, Indiana, to take up the problems of pacifism. There delegates vied with each other in horror stories about widespread deviations. One member of Ohio Yearly Meeting said that half of the membership did not understand Quaker principles on the subject. Others took a more hopeful view, but all agreed that something had to be done. After extensive debate, the conference drafted a series of memorials to Congress and to other denominations on international arbitration and established the Peace Association of Friends in America to advocate pacifism among both members and nonmembers, especially ministers in other denominations.[60]

But even after the war, the society showed signs of division over pacifism. A few Friends began to argue the morality of defensive war. Others, including some prominent renewal Friends, asserted that there were some circumstances in which governments could morally take life. Returning soldiers received a hero's welcome in Quaker communities; admiration for military figures ran high among the young. When a non-Quaker peace lecturer cast aspersions on the general character of military men at Earlham in 1867, several listeners, including some prominent Friends, indignantly defended the soldiers of their acquaintance and asked if they should have "meekly submitted" to "the outrages of the southern soldiers." Only the presence of the redoubtable Barnabas C. Hobbs kept the students from breaking into groans and hisses. A few years later Quaker Indian agents would be calling in the army to control their charges.[61]

While the war raised questions about Quaker principles, it also created an opportunity in regard to the millions of former slaves in the South. To many, both Quaker and non-Quaker, it seemed natural for Friends to continue their tradition of benevolence with work in the freedman's camps. "Never in the world's history was there so good an opportunity of giving to the poor and 'lending to the Lord,' " one Friend wrote. For Whittier it was a "blessed privilege," after their "merciful protection" during the war, for Friends to do "all in their power to aid in the good work of educating and caring for the free people."[62]

Beginning in 1863 and extending into the 1870s, hundreds of Gurneyite Friends went into the South as teachers, instructors, and camp superintendents. Most of the yearly meetings had freedmen's committees. Their proceedings and the letters and appeals from Friends working in the South were given prominent space in such Gurneyite journals as the *Friends' Review* and the *American Friend*.[63]

It is significant that these committees and most of the Friends working in the South emphasized the humanitarianian aspects of relief. Friends in the North raised money, sent food, clothing, books, and agricultural implements, built schools, and used their political influence to secure protection and civil rights for their wards in the South. Friends usually focused on education and general "uplift" and "civilization." Although they used the Bible as a classbook and actively encouraged the formation of Bible classes and First Day schools, most of the committees and Quaker workers showed little interest in proselytizing among the former slaves. The Friends held their own meetings, which blacks were always welcome to attend, but Quakers did not encourage them to become members. The reasons for this inactivity are not clear. Elements of racism may have been involved. That such was the case was the fear of certain English Friends, among them William Tallack, who, during his travels among northern Friends in 1860, found that they felt the quiet and contemplation of a Friends meeting were not suitable to "excitable" black minds. The traditional reticence about any kind of new member was probably also involved. In 1869 a black congregation in Randolph County, North Carolina, asked to join North Carolina Yearly Meeting en masse. A committee appointed to visit the black church urged rejection of the request, saying that the blacks knew absolutely nothing about Quaker principles save the traditional Quaker solicitude for blacks.[64]

Some Friends found the situation intolerable. They argued that it was the duty of the society to proselytize among the blacks. "It is by no means the 'philanthropic' aspect of the question that has interested the Society in their efforts for the elevation of the Freedmen," Dougan Clark, Jr., wrote in 1866. "The Society from its rise has recognized the importance of laboring for the elevation of the human race . . . and now we feel the pressing necessity laid upon us to instruct the freedmen in the doctrines of the Christian religion." John Henry Douglas, who made a tour of the South in late 1865 and early 1866, wrote to the *Freedmen's Record:* "It has been said that we cannot make Quakers of these people. . . . I most earnestly say that if we *would* we *can* make living Quakers of them." No one ventured open disagreement with the desirability of "making Quakers of the freedmen," but actions speak louder than words. At Helena, Arkansas, where Indiana Yearly Meeting set up a school that eventually became Southland College, an almost entirely black monthly meeting with four hundred members was established. But Southland was unique, the only black monthly meeting to appear as a result of the Quaker work.[65]

The split between the Friends who saw their mission among the former slaves as basically philanthropic and those who wanted to proselytize is vital, since it presages a wider split among Gurneyite Friends in the 1870s. Many of the central figures of the later revolution among Gurneyites—Douglas, Dougan Clark, Jr., Elkanah and Irena Beard, Sarah F. Smiley, and Calvin and Alida Clark, the Southland superintendents—were active in trying to convert the freedmen. The efforts on behalf of the freedmen put many Friends in a position to work with other denominations and to observe their methods. At least one leading worker among the freedmen, Josiah Butler, an Ohio Friend who later became a revival leader in Kansas, saw the mission as the beginning of the revolution in the Society of Friends.[66] Unfortunately, we do not know how other evangelists—Douglas and the Beards, for example—related their work in the South to their later careers. It is obvious, however, that the split over methods in the South foreshadowed divisions that became increasingly apparent for the rest of the century.

Even as Friends divided over the peace testimony and the freedmen's work, an old doctrinal controversy over the resurrection that dated back to Gurney's time flared up. The debate focused on the question of whether a physical or a spiritual resurrection would ultimately occur, with "body" advocates, apparently following the lead of non-Quaker evangelicals, insisting on a physical resurrection. The issue had not previously been a major concern of Quaker theology, at least before 1830, but the writings of the early Friends suggest that they understood the resurrection in a spiritual sense. By the mid-1860s some renewal Friends were becoming vehement in their insistence on a physical interpretation. Barnabas C. Hobbs and Eli Jessup, an Iowa minister especially active in temperance work, began to argue that belief in the resurrection of the physical body was "the beginning and the end of Christian faith," since "the believer sees in it full and complete redemption; the final triumph of Christ over Satan, sin and death." Some carried the argument a step farther and decided that their opponents denied the resurrection entirely and thus were not Christians. Most Friends tried to ignore the controversy, but many, ranging from Wilburites to incipient liberals, were offended by the dogmatism of the "body resurrection" advocates. Such doubters found ample evidence for their position in the writings of such early Friends as George Whitehead, Robert Barclay, and Isaac Penington, as well as in the scriptural statement that flesh and blood could not enter the kingdom of heaven. Armed with these, they plunged many meetings into controversy, providing concerned renewal Friends with still another cause for worry.[67]

The differences over the freedmen, pacifism, and the resurrection coincided with a dispute within Indiana Yearly Meeting, minor in retrospect, but worrisome at the time. The yearly meeting's irregular boundaries took in large groups of Quakers in northern Indiana and in southwestern Ohio, but the largest concentration was in the counties around Richmond, where most of the yearly meeting's leaders lived. Resentment over domination of the yearly meeting by Friends around Richmond had become especially acute in Ohio. In 1867 the three most isolated quarterly meetings there asked the yearly meeting to set them off as a separate yearly meeting. For reasons that are not clear, the yearly meeting refused the request. The incident caused the Indiana leadership some concern; as a concession to the isolated, disaffected Friends, the yearly meeting established a special new committee to hold general meetings.[68]

The general meetings did, at least for a time, draw the Friends of Indiana Yearly Meeting closer together. The early general meetings usually lasted three or four days. Because members of the general meeting committee, including Charles F. Coffin, members of the meeting for sufferings, and many of the best-known ministers and elders usually attended, otherwise isolated Friends had a chance to hear some of the yearly meeting's best preachers. The general meetings also brought leading Friends into contact with a cross section of the yearly meeting's membership, creating the impression, at least, that the leadership was listening to the concerns of lesser members. The general meetings proved so successful that the question of a new yearly meeting in Ohio would not come up again for twenty years.[69]

The general meetings were also clearly within the renewal movement's vision of the society's future. Many renewal Friends had been deeply disturbed by the mass defections from the peace testimony during the Civil War; that, along with the resurrection controversy, raised questions in their minds as to how well the membership understood the principles of the society. Thus the general meetings were to be teaching meetings as well. Renewal Friends would use them to instruct the membership on the Quaker view of such subjects as conversion, sanctification, worship, silence, peace (especially peace), the ministry, baptism and communion, marriage, and the plain life. The early general meetings followed a clear-cut pattern: they consisted in large part of lectures delivered by prominent visiting Friends. When discussion was allowed, visiting leaders dominated it.[70]

The general meetings, of course, also provided opportunities for worship. These featured preaching in the new evangelical mode, with some Friends hearing that sort of ministry for the first time. It was not uncommon for listeners to approach some of the ministers with individual religious concerns. Such seekers would be visited privately by one of the ministers or by members of the general meeting committee. Soon it became clear that conversion was by far the topic of greatest interest to many Friends, and the general meetings gave that subject increasing attention. Therein were the roots of a revolution that would come in the next decade. But that lay ahead. During the late 1860s the general meetings seemed to provide the answer to many of the problems that troubled renewal Friends.[71]

The years after 1850 were eventful for Gurneyite Friends. The broadening American national culture and economy, and especially the evangelical subculture, drew in increasing numbers of Friends. By 1860 a new generation of Quaker leaders was appearing in the Gurneyite yearly meetings, notably in the West. The new leaders combined an interest in modifying the discipline with a firm commitment to Quaker tradition as they understood it and carried on the Quaker interest in benevolence and social change. Along with a change in the nature of preaching, this movement laid the groundwork for a Quakerism that they saw as bereft of anachronism yet with its unique aspects preserved.

The renewal movement had its limitations. It was largely a movement of the elite. It did not wholly unify the society, as the mass defections from pacifism during the Civil War showed, and it was at times divided within itself, as when arose the differences over the freedmen's work and the resurrection of the body. The response of Indiana Yearly Meeting, the movement's stronghold, was the general meeting. But even the general meetings would soon have consequences that none of the renewal Friends foresaw.

CHAPTER
IV
THE REVIVAL,
1867–1880

Late in the summer of 1875 a Methodist minister decided to indulge his professional curiosity by attending the annual gathering of Indiana Yearly Meeting of Friends in Richmond. Unlike his military brother fourteen years before, the Methodist minister felt completely at home. The devotional meeting opened with the singing of a familiar hymn. Then the presiding preacher called for testimonies. Within ninety minutes nearly three hundred people had spoken. Then an altar call was issued, and soon seekers after conversion and sanctification crowded around several mourners' benches. To the Methodist visitor it all had a familiar feeling. "It resembled one of our best *love feasts* at a *National Camp Meeting* [more] than anything else to which I could liken it," he told the leading interdenominational holiness journal.[1] The scenes in Richmond were not unusual for Gurneyite Friends in 1875. They had set an unprecedented course.

The new direction for Gurneyite Friends was the result of competition between two movements. One, the renewal movement, tried to preserve Quaker distinctiveness while chipping away at practices it thought archaic and outmoded. By the late 1860s it was bearing fruit in social activism, disciplinary revision, and a renewed evangelism. It was, in the main, a reforming, not a revolutionary, movement. The revival, by contrast, drew its driving forces from outside the Society of Friends, from the second-experience, interdenominational holiness movement. The holiness movement among Friends fueled the revival, obliterated the plain life, revolutionized the basis and form of Quaker worship, and gave Gurneyite Friends a new understanding of the nature of religious experience.

THE EARLY ENTHUSIASMS

Since the revivals were the most notable feature of the revolution of the 1870s, an understanding of them is necessary. Friends had used the term "revival" in its literal sense since the 1850s to speak of increased religious interest and activity within the society. By 1875 Quakers were using it in the same sense that Protestants had since the Great Awakening of the 1740s. To speak of a revival among Quakers during the 1870s was to speak of an event that included five elements: (1) services focusing on a small group of preachers; (2) an emphasis on instantaneous experience, whether it be conversion or sanctification; (3) the employment of altar calls and mourners' benches; (4) the use of hymns and congregational singing; and (5) the toleration and even encouragement of extreme emotionalism.[2]

What is usually identified as the first modern revival among Friends took place at Bear Creek Meeting in Dallas County, Iowa, early in 1867. Two traveling ministers from eastern Iowa, John S. Bond and Stacy E. Bevan, held a single night meeting in which there were remarkable manifestations. "Many hearts were reached and all broken up, which was followed by sighs and sobs and prayers, confessions and great joys for sins pardoned and burdens rolled off," Bevan wrote. The two ministers did not make altar calls, nor was there singing. After one night the Bear Creek elders closed down Bond and Bevan's meeting; nothing similar took place there for seven years. The two preachers continued their journey without provoking any other outbreaks of "enthusiasm."[3]

Better known are events at Walnut Ridge in Rush County, Indiana, in the autumn of 1867. A few young Friends began to attend a series of Methodist prayer meetings. At first, the curious outnumbered the true seekers, but a few earnest young people made a deep impression on those present, including one young Friend who came under "conviction." Increasing numbers of young Quakers began to attend the prayer meetings after they were moved to the Gilboa Methodist Church. Reports of young Friends at the mourner's bench at Gilboa and in various states of spiritual anxiety led Jane Jones, a minister in the Walnut Ridge Friends Meeting, to appoint special meetings in the Walnut Ridge Meetinghouse. Here the revival exercises seen at Gilboa broke out again: "agonized crying," instantaneous conversions, work with those of other denominations in a "union," or cooperative, atmosphere. Still, there was some restraint, at least in the meetinghouse. The mourner's bench was not used, and no one sang. Early in 1868 similar outbreaks occurred in nearby Raysville and Spiceland meetings, although both were much smaller and received little attention at the time. Later in 1868, after the meetings at Walnut Ridge had ended, a few of the participants "ran off into fanaticism," which was "fruitful in unhinging the minds of several."

Some began to issue wild prophecies; one farmer left his fields unplanted for several years because of a special revelation.[4]

Rufus M. Jones says that the revival spread like a "contagion" from Walnut Ridge throughout the Midwest. Such a claim is difficult to substantiate. Walnut Ridge may properly be regarded as the first sustained Quaker revival, but there is little to show that it served as a model or inspired later ones among Friends. The only Quaker minister who took part in the Walnut Ridge meetings was Jane Jones, a minor figure in the revivals of the 1870s. Nathan T. and Esther G. Frame, later two of the most important Quaker revivalists, attended a quarterly meeting at Walnut Ridge not long afterward, but there is no evidence that any of the other major figures even visited the area at the time. The Quaker media gave the Walnut Ridge outbreak relatively little attention. The sympathetic *American Friend* in Richmond, Indiana, printed two letters that provide the only known contemporary accounts. The equally sympathetic Chicago *Herald of Peace* ignored it, as did the *Friends' Review*. Throughout the rest of the decade similar outbreaks occurred, but they also tended to be cases of revivals that began in other denominations and spilled over to take in Friends.[5]

Thus a revival impulse of sorts existed among Gurneyite Friends before 1870, but it was scattered and limited. It lacked a driving and unifying force. In the eyes of some Friends such outbreaks were signs of developing danger, but most Quakers regarded them as aberrations that did not merit excessive concern. "I think that we may no more conclude that the religious movement out of which they have sprung, is all wrong, than that the rise of Quakerism was wrong, because of the ranterism that followed it," Joel Bean, the clerk of Iowa Yearly Meeting, wrote in 1870. "What Reformation has not been attended by some excesses?" he asked. "How rare the vigorous growth that needs not the pruning hand." Edith Griffith, an elderly minister in Ohio Yearly Meeting, commented two years later that things of which she did not approve were being done, but these were the work of spiritual children, young in Christian life, excesses that they would soon outgrow. The overwhelming majority of Friends in 1870 shared Bean's and Griffith's sentiments. The success of the general meetings led the rest of the Gurneyite yearly meetings to imitate Indiana by establishing similar committees in 1871 and 1872. Signs of life were everywhere; the society appeared to be entering a new era of healthy growth and witness.[6]

Some looked at Gurneyite Quakerism about 1870 and found it still wanting. The traditional history of the revival holds that the general meetings began as part of the revival impulse and were the chief vehicle for its extension. In fact, the early general meetings included conversion as only one of several subjects for discussion. Even when conversion became the central focus of the preaching in general meetings, the hearers had no chance to respond immediately. And that upset some Friends. The problem, the *Herald of Peace* said, was that Quaker ministers knew much about the Gospel but very little about leading sinners to Christ. "We well remember many times when we would have responded gladly to an invitation to come forward and unite in earnest prayer for an immediate blessing," the journal editorialized, "but we were coldly turned away from the feast that was already spread, and sent to our homes to dissipate the influence of the occasion."[7] By the late 1860s the kind of ministry that such Friends sought was developing. Within a few years it would cause a revolution.

THE REVIVAL

To understand the whirlwind that swept through the Gurneyite yearly meetings during the 1870s, one must look to a small group of ministers and the experience that they shared: an instantaneous, postconversion sanctification that they believed, freed them from any desire or propensity to sin and filled them with the power of the Holy Ghost. They found this teaching on sanctification outside the society in the post–Civil War interdenominational holiness movement. They used it to transform first the general meeting movement and then the rest of Gurneyite Quakerism.

Ever since Timothy L. Smith published *Revivalism and Social Reform* over thirty years ago, the importance of holiness teachings during the 1850s and 1860s has been understood. Advocates of second-experience, instantaneous sanctification in the Wesleyan tradition argued, as Friends always had, that perfection, or complete freedom from sin, was possible. Unlike traditional Friends, they saw it as a second experience following conversion, attained through simple faith: the belief that the atoning blood of Christ made it possible for people to achieve a state in which they no longer had any desire or propensity to sin.[8]

In the decade from 1867 to 1877 the interdenominational holiness movement was in a state of flux. The great Protestant denominations were showing increasing ambivalence toward holiness teachings. Holiness advocates, especially those in the Methodist Episcopal church, responded by organizing the National Camp Meeting Association for the Promotion of Holiness in 1867. This organization and a host of smaller imitators and offshoots made holiness teachings their central focus, but they associated with them a growing conviction that the major Protestant organizations were, because of growing wealth and worldly pride, becoming lax and cold. The holiness movement drew sympathizers from nearly all of the evangelical denominations, although it had the greatest appeal for those with a Wesleyan heritage.[9]

Late in the 1860s the holiness movement attracted a number of young Friends, especially young ministers. Ministerial standing is significant here.

Many of the renewal Friends were not recorded ministers or were recorded long after they became active in the society. As the positions of leading revivalists' (see chart 2) indicate, however, the holiness revival movement among Friends was from the beginning one of ministers, one that exalted ministerial standing and stressed its prerogatives.

The most important and influential of all of the holiness Quaker ministers was David Brainerd Updegraff. Born in Mount Pleasant, Ohio, in 1830, Updegraff claimed an impeccable Quaker pedigree. His father, a prosperous storekeeper and farmer, was descended from the Germantown Quakers who drew up America's first antislavery document. His mother was a prominent minister and the only child of Jonathan Taylor, the clerk of Ohio Yearly Meeting who had been so roughly handled by the Hicksites in 1828, and Ann Taylor, one of the best-known Orthodox Quaker ministers of the first half of the nineteenth century. The Updegraffs were in the evangelical vanguard of Ohio Yearly Meeting. The very name they gave their son, that of an eighteenth-century missionary whose biography penned by Jonathan Edwards was an evangelical classic, shows their familiarity with evangelical culture. They were fervent Gurneyites and last-ditch supporters of Elisha Bates. They even won the friendship of Oberlin president Charles G. Finney. Updegraff's brothers and sisters read the standard evangelical works, attended a Presbyterian college, and bitterly criticized the Wilburites who controlled Ohio Yearly Meeting in the 1840s.[10]

Updegraff's boyhood, perhaps influenced by an older brother who had left the society, was lax by Quaker standards. He spent a year at Haverford before his marriage in 1852. Outwardly he was a plain Friend, but inwardly he was not at peace. That he found during a Methodist revival in Mount Pleasant in 1860. There Updegraff and his wife underwent powerful conversion experiences, but they showed no inclination to leave the society.[11]

For the next nine years Updegraff lived quietly in Mount Pleasant. Ohio was the Gurneyite yearly meeting least affected by the renewal movement, and there is nothing to indicate that Updegraff took more than ordinary interest in Quaker affairs. In the fall of 1869 John S. Inskip, a dynamic young Methodist minister and the founding president of the National Camp Meeting Association, stayed in Updegraff's home while holding a series of meetings near Mount Pleasant. He led Updegraff to holiness teachings. On the night of Inskip's final labors with him, the Mount Pleasant Friend wrote, "every 'vile affection' was nailed to the cross. . . . The Holy Ghost fell upon me just as I supposed He did at the beginning. Instantly I felt the melting and refining fire of God permeate my whole being. . . . I was deeply conscious of the presence of God within me, and His sanctifying work." On the Sabbath immediately following his sanctification, Updegraff spoke in meeting for the first time. His theme was holiness.[12]

More than any other person, Updegraff brought holiness teachings to

CHART 2

Leading Revival Friends, 1875

Individuals (by yearly meeting)	Date of Birth	Birthplace	Position in the Society	Sancti- fied	Secular Occupation	Education
Indiana						
Elkanah Beard	1833	Randolph Co., Ind.	Minister	1869	None	MM schools
Irena Beard	1833	Randolph Co., Ind.	Minister	1869	None	MM schools
Dougan Clark, Jr.	1828	Guilford Co., N.C.	Minister, prof., Earlham	1871	Physician	Providence, U. of Pa.
John Henry Douglas	1832	Fairfield, Me.	Minister	1871	Farmer	Providence
Robert W. Douglas	1834	Fairfield, Me.	Minister	Yes	Banker	Providence
Esther G. Frame	1840	Wayne Co., Ind.	Minister	1866	None	Private schools
Nathan T. Frame	1832	Pennsylvania	Minister	Yes	None	Public schools
Caleb Johnson	1820	Guilford Co., N.C.	Minister	Yes	Farmer	Spiceland, Earlham
Daniel Hill	1817	Randolph Co., Ind.	Minister, editor	Yes	Printer	MM schools
Francis W. Thomas	1823	Wayne Co., Ind.	Minister	No	Farmer	MM schools
William J. Thorn- berry	1836	Wayne Co., Ind.	Minister	Yes	?	MM schools
Iowa						
John S. Bond	1827	Randolph Co., Ind.	Minister	?	Farmer	MM schools
John Y. Hoover	1834	Miami Co., O.	Minister	1868	Farmer	Local schools
Daniel McPherson	1834	Clinton Co., O.	Minister	Yes	?	Local schools
Lawrie Tatum	1822	Burlington, N.J.	Minister	1873	Farmer	MM schools
Isom P. Wooten	1836	Preble Co., O.	Minister	Yes	?	?

Individuals (by yearly meeting)	Date of Birth	Birthplace	Position in the Society	Sanctified	Secular Occupation	Education
Kansas						
Mary H. Rogers	1836	Henry Co., Ind.	Minister	1868	Farmwife	Earlham
New York						
Thomas Kimber	1827	New York City	Minister	Yes	Railroad executive	Haverford
Thomas W. Ladd	1832	Smithfield, O.	Minister	1860s	Merchant	Haverford
Robert L. Murray	1826	New York City	Minister, YM clerk	1871	Businessman	Haverford
Ruth S. Murray	?	New Bedford, Mass.	Minister	Yes	Wife of R. L.	Providence
Luke Woodard	1832	Wayne Co., Ind.	Minister	1870	Farmer	MM schools
North Carolina						
Isham Cox	1815	Randolph Co., N.C.	Minister	?	Farmer	MM schools
Allen Jay	1831	Miami Co., O.	Minister	No	Farmer	Antioch
Rufus P. King	1841	Orange Co., N.C.	Minister	Yes	?	*
Ohio						
Jacob Baker	1828	Monroe Co., N.Y.	Minister	1870	Farmer	MM schools
Asahel H. Hussey	1832	Columbiana Co., O.	Minister	Yes	?	?
Elizabeth L. Comstock	1815	Berks, Eng.	Minister	**	Farmwife	Croyden Friends
Caroline Talbot	1824	Ohio	Minister	Yes	?	?
David B. Updegraff	1830	Mt. Pleasant, O.	Minister	1869	None	Haverford

Western						
Amos M. Kenworthy	1832	Warren Co., O.	Minister	1865	Broommaker	MM schools
Calvin W. Pritchard	1834	Henry Co., Ind.	Minister	Yes	Teacher	Earlham
Elwood C. Siler	1832	Parke Co., Ind.	Minister	Yes	?	?

Sources: William Bacon Evans et al., comps., "Dictionary of Quaker Biography," typescript, n.d. (Quaker Collection, Haverford College, Haverford, Pa.). For views on sanctification: Elkanah and Irena Beard, "A Pioneer of the Friends Foreign Missionary Association," *Soul Winner,* May 18, 1905, p. 282. For Dougan Clark, Jr.: "Notes about Friends," *Christian Worker,* 3rd Mo. 26, 1891, p. 104. For John Henry Douglas: "Personal Testimony," ibid., 6th Mo. 23, 1887, pp. 289–90. For Robert W. Douglas: "Mooresville, Indiana," ibid., 1st Mo. 15, 1871, p. 3; and editorial, *Western Friend,* 7 (4th Mo. 1886), 31. For Esther G. and Nathan T. Frame: *Reminiscences of Nathan T. Frame and Esther G. Frame* (Cleveland: Britton, 1907), 44, 452. For Caleb Johnson: "General Meeting at Salem, Union County, Indiana," *Christian Worker,* 2nd Mo. 15, 1871, pp. 16–17. For Daniel Hill: Editorial, ibid., 6th Mo. 15, 1872, p. 107. For Francis W. Thomas: Carrie T. [Johnson] to Allen Jay, Nov. 18, 1892, Miscellaneous folder, M-R box, Allen Jay Papers (Archives, Earlham College, Richmond, Ind.). For William J. Thornberry: "Center Quarterly Meeting," *Christian Worker,* 9th Mo. 1, 1875, p. 267. For Daniel McPherson: Joel Bean to Timothy Nicholson, 9th Mo. 14, 1881, Timothy Nicholson Papers (Archives, Earlham). For John Y. Hoover: "Sketches from Life," *Evangelical Friend,* Aug. 8, 1907, p. 501. For Lawrie Tatum: *Iowa Yearly Meeting Minutes, 1901,* p. 72. For Mary H. Rogers: "My Experience," *Friends' Expositor,* 1 (April 1887). 52. For Thomas Kimber: "Editorial Notes," ibid., 5 (April 1891). 525. For Thomas W. Ladd: "Brooklyn General Meeting," *Friends' Review,* 12th Mo. 30, 1871, p. 233. For Robert L. and Ruth S. Murray: [Ruth S. Murray], *Under His Wings: A Sketch of the Life of Robert Lindley Murray* (New York: Anson D. F. Randolph, 1876), 127–28. For Luke Woodard: Luke Woodard, *Sketches of a Life of 75 in Three Parts: Biographical, Historical, Descriptive* (Richmond, Ind.: Nicholson, 1907), 9–10. For Rufus P. King: "Editorial Note," *Friends' Expositor,* 4 (Oct. 1890). 457. For Jacob Baker: "Testimony of a Minister," *Christian Worker,* 8th Mo. 13, 1891, p. 515. For Caroline E. Talbot: A. H. Hussey, "Memorial of Caroline E. Talbot," *Friends' Review,* 3rd Mo. 1, 1894, pp. 198–200. For Asahel H. Hussey: "Ohio Yearly Meeting," *American Friend,* 9th Mo. 6, 1894, p. 185. For David B. Updegraff: J. Brent Bill, *David B. Updegraff: Quaker Holiness Preacher* (Richmond, Ind.: Friends United Press, 1983), 14–16. For Amos M. Kenworthy: Lydia M. Williams-Cammack and Truman C. Kenworthy, *Life and Works of Amos M. Kenworthy* (Richmond, Ind.: Nicholson, 1918), 3–4. For Calvin W. Pritchard: "Now," *Christian Worker,* 6th Mo. 23, 1887, p. 294. For Elwood C. Siler: *Minutes of the Ministerial Conference of Western Yearly Meeting of Friends Held at Bloomingdale, Ind., Eleventh Mo. 1880* (Indianapolis: Baker and Randolph, 1881), 44–52.

*King received no education until after joining Friends in the 1860s. He then attended Quaker schools in Indiana. See Emma King, "Rufus P. King," in *Quaker Biographies,* Series II (5 vols.: Philadelphia, 1921–1926), II, 173–99.

**Comstock is the one person whose views on holiness defy classification. The best conclusion that can be drawn from her writings is that in the 1870s the teaching attracted her, but she never underwent the experience. Later she became skeptical about it. See Caroline Hare, comp., *Life and Letters of Elizabeth L. Comstock* (London: Headley Brothers, 1895).

Friends. His converts included some of the revival's most important figures: Luke Woodard, Asahel H. Hussey, Jacob Baker, and, most notably, Dougan Clark, Jr., and John Henry Douglas. Clark became Updegraff's chief lieutenant and the closest thing that the revival had to a theologian; Douglas was the only Quaker holiness preacher who rivaled Updegraff in power and appeal. The lives of both illustrate the transforming power of holiness teachings.[13]

Dougan Clark, Jr., was born in North Carolina in 1828. His parents were both eminent ministers, and his grandfather, Nathan Hunt, was the patriarch of North Carolina Yearly Meeting. Clark was educated in Quaker schools in North Carolina and New England, finishing at Haverford. Subsequently he studied medicine at the University of Pennsylvania. In 1856 Clark moved his family to Westfield, Indiana, where he began a medical practice. A few years later he went to Earlham to teach foreign languages.[14]

As a young man Clark identified with the renewal movement. He participated enthusiastically in the reform efforts that he saw transforming the world. During the 1860s his confidence in the movement disappeared as he found himself questioning his religious experience. Thomas C. Upham's *Principles of the Interior, or Hidden Life* (1845), one of the most influential Wesleyan holiness works, struck a responsive chord in Clark, and about the same time he became aware of the National Camp Meeting Association. Clark's commitment to holiness was sealed by Updegraff, who told the Earlham professor that all he needed to do to become sinless was to lay claim publicly to the experience through faith. "O it filled me," Clark later wrote, "all my being was filled with this wonderful peace. . . . Dead to self and sin, alive to Christ, and filled with the Holy Ghost!" Clark was a thoroughly changed man. Before a shy, retiring figure, the very picture of the introverted scholar, Clark, glowing with new fervor, now became an aggressive revival preacher and holiness writer. "In the three weeks that followed my sanctification I did more good than in three years before," he wrote.[15]

Like Clark, John Henry Douglas was well known in Quaker circles during the 1860s. Born in Maine in 1832, he grew up in a home that mixed evangelical faith with rigid adherence to the discipline. In his early twenties he moved to Clinton County, Ohio, where he married, farmed, and was recorded a minister. He was a stalwart of the renewal movement in Indiana Yearly Meeting, an intimate friend of Charles F. and Rhoda M. Coffin, active in freedmen's work, and the first secretary of the Peace Association of Friends in America. Late in the 1860s he took the lead in aggressive proselytizing among non-Quakers.[16]

Throughout the 1860s Douglas's religious views were changing. He had undergone a dramatic conversion experience at age nineteen, but his "mind was not clear as to doctrines or doctrinal terms." Early in the 1860s he rid himself of the last vestiges of "mysticism" by accepting conversion as the result of faith, while he still viewed holiness as something attained by constant striving and frequent baptisms of suffering. Yet Douglas found himself constantly struggling against what he called "the old man." Finally, through "complete consecration," he found the inward battle at an end. Only later, when about 1870 he first encountered holiness teachings, did Douglas understand that he had been sanctified. Despite his own experience, he resisted holiness doctrines, since he was "careful" about his reputation and the society's and was determined that neither should suffer because of "unwise and imprudent teaching." At a general meeting in Brooklyn in 1871 attended by Updegraff and Caroline Talbot, Douglas saw his error. He publicly embraced the teaching, laying aside his concerns about reputation and tradition. "This," Douglas later wrote, "began a new era in my work for God."[17]

Many other Quaker ministers experienced holiness at about the same time as Updegraff, Clark, and Douglas, or perhaps even earlier. Mary H. Rogers, an Iowa minister who became one of the revival's most important figures, was sanctified in 1868. John Y. Hoover, another Iowa holiness stalwart, first encountered the experience by reading Phoebe Palmer's *Guide to Holiness*, one of the most influential holiness works. To Esther G. Frame, perhaps the most important woman revivalist, her sanctification in 1868 brought not only relief from a host of besetting fears but also the strength for the preaching career to which she felt called.[18]

Unfortunately we do not have detailed accounts of the experiences of many of the other revivalists. Like Lawrie Tatum in Iowa, some carefully recorded the exact date of the event; others were like Amos M. Kenworthy, the burly, uncouth Indiana broommaker who terrified three generations of Quaker children with his reputation for reading minds and seeing the future, who remembered only that he was sanctified while digging a ditch. Tatum and Kenworthy left no indication of how they first encountered the teaching. In regard to many other leading figures of the revival, we know only that they claimed the experience and taught it. As second-experience holiness teachings increased in power in the society, so did the power and popularity of revival methods. Only two of the prominent revivalists of the period, Francis W. Thomas and Allen Jay, were not holiness advocates.[19]

Historians of Quakerism often observe how deeply many of the revivalists had been influenced by non-Quakers, especially Methodists. In some cases the influence is obvious. Nathan T. and Esther G. Frame were Methodists who became Friends in 1867 so that Esther could be a recognized minister. Caroline Talbot, after Updegraff Ohio Yearly Meeting's leading revivalist, had been a Methodist prior to her marriage to a Friend in the 1840s. Rufus P. King was also a former Methodist, whose experiences in the Confederate army brought him to pacifism, which, in turn, led him to Quakerism. Such men and women may have carried familiar methods with them into their new denomination. In other cases the influence was more subtle. Updegraff was converted in a Methodist revival, whereas John Y. Hoover was deeply influenced as a boy by a Methodist hired girl who lived with his family. But it is not clear that there were such influences in the lives of the other revival Friends. John Henry Douglas and his brother, Robert W. Douglas, were raised "according to the strictest sect" of New England Friends, as were Luke Woodard in Indiana and Thomas W. Ladd in Ohio. Our knowledge of the early lives of Daniel Hill, Mary H. Rogers, Asahel H. Hussey, Elkanah and Irena Beard, Calvin W. Pritchard, and others suggests that they had unremarkable Quaker upbringings. Even apparent links can be misleading. Dougan Clark, Jr.'s father had been a Methodist exhorter before becoming a Quaker. The elder Clark, however, like many other converts, once a Friend became "more Jewish than the Jews"; he and his wife were Wilburites. Far more than previous exposure to other denominations, the influence of the holiness movement offers an explanation for the revolution within the society between 1870 and 1880.[20]

Thus armed, holiness advocates set out to create a revolution. No longer would revivals be confined to a few areas, the overflow from Methodist enthusiasm or the product of small groups of seemingly overwrought young people. Scenes like those described below became the rule, not the exception, among Gurneyite Friends:

Spiceland, Indiana, 1873: "There were a number engaged in exhortation and vocal supplication, besides many others singing, while others were down at the mourners' benches, and the most of the rest on their feet, who had arisen at the call of the preacher, all going on at the same time. Meanwhile children, and even young women, evidently terrified and wild with fright, were crying, women hastening through among the men, and men among the women." Over seven hundred people, virtually the entire membership of the meeting, ministers and elders, young and old, were converted or sanctified by a team of revivalists led by Updegraff.[21]

Damascus, Ohio, 1874: In the course of a meeting conducted by Amos M. Kenworthy, thirteen people lay at one time prostrate in the gallery, and one seeker was unconscious for almost two days.[22]

Bear Creek, Iowa, 1877: Benjamin B. Hiatt, leading a revival, called on all who wished to lead a new life to come to the front seats. About twenty people scrambled forward, some climbing over the benches—Friends who remained at their seats were visited there by others and had prayer groups form around them. Some prayed aloud, some wept, some broke out in anguished testimonies, some sang snatches of hymns. Horrified, conservative Friends began to move toward the doors of the meeting-house. As they did, one elderly woman climbed upon a bench and spoke in meeting for the first and only time in her life: "The Society of Friends is dead. This has killed it."[23]

Two questions arise here: Why did holiness teachings work such a transformation in the Society of Friends? Why did the overwhelming majority of Friends accept such revolutionary change?

THE INEXORABLE LOGIC OF HOLINESS

To understand the impact of holiness teachings on Gurneyite Friends, one must consider the holiness critique of Quakerism. The revivalists began by urging conversion and sanctification as instantaneous acts of faith. "Jesus saves me and saves me now; Jesus sanctifies me and sanctifies me now" were the lines they taught their audiences as embracing everything necessary to salvation and holiness. Faith in the efficacy of the atoning blood of Christ, when confessed publicly, brought first salvation and then holiness—nothing more was needed, and nothing less sufficed. From that vantage point, the revivalists applied a merciless critique to contemporary Quakerism, which they saw as "swallowed up in dead formality and ceremony."[24]

The revivalists dismissed the value of the traditional Quaker plain life. They had no desire to be worldly, and they said that a Christian should speak and dress plainly, but they felt that wearing the traditional Quaker garb and holding to the archaic forms of speech fell into the category of dead works, from which they were free. To holiness Friends the plain dress no longer even served the function of separating Friends from the world, since Hicksites also wore it. Plainness, in their view, had become a source of false security for many Friends, a snare from which they had to be set free. Thus one young woman converted in an Ohio revival told her mother, a minister, that it was her plain bonnet that stood in the way of her sound conversion; as for her father, it was his watch chain. A holiness Friend from New England complained bitterly that during his boyhood traveling Friends spent hours arranging their bonnets and shawls but never preached the Atonement.[25]

Revival Friends reserved their most withering criticism for silent waiting. Such waiting was unnecessary for the sanctified since, as one of them put it, "those who were baptized by the Holy Ghost as a second definite experience after conversion . . . always had him with them and did not need to wait." They argued, with some justification, that silence had been the exception rather than the rule among the early Friends. For the revivalists silence and composure were almost always signs of spiritual deadness. They attacked Friends who always remained silent: "It is a sin for people not to praise the Lord," Amos Kenworthy proclaimed. A Kansas revivalist told Friends in Hesper meeting that "those who sat down with their arms folded were going down to the devil and damnation."[26]

From all of that the revivalists drew an inexorable conclusion: the majority of the Society of Friends had not been soundly converted: "They were not saved and were on the road to ruin." The old methods of preaching did not produce converts, and the revivalists bitterly resented that; indeed, they openly mocked the old ways. The holiness revivals outside the society, with their thousands of conversions and sanctifications through aggressive, uncompromising preaching, were the model for holiness Friends. Instead of "reserve, coldness, shyness, and silence," they "recommend[ed] religion by beautiful exhibitions of joy and peace and love and comfort and power." As for music, it aided in producing conversions and thus could not be dismissed. Critics observed not just that Friends were singing but that singing had become a mania among them.[27]

Seeing little value in the plain life, in the old ways of worship, and in works generally, revivalists had little use for the idea of Friends as a peculiar people, separate from other believers. One boasted that he experienced sanctification only when he renounced Quaker exclusiveness. Distaste for "peculiar doctrines," combined with devotion to new practices in preaching, transformed the general meetings. Updegraff summarized the change:

> Many could not see that the blessing of God rested upon an attempt to convey to perishing sinners "accurate *information*" about our "distinctive *tenets*." I was one of that number and joined with others in imploring that "the dead" might be left to "bury the dead," and that we might unite in preaching the gospel and in getting converts to *Jesus*. In the providence of God such counsel prevailed, and then it was that our General Meetings became "Revival Meetings."[28]

Thus less than twenty years after his death, John Wilbur's prophecy was fulfilled. No longer did most Gurneyite Friends see the need to *await* the baptism of the spirit and with fire; they *claimed* it instantaneously. No longer would most of them abide the humiliations of plainness and the tests of tribulation. In a religious milieu that envisioned salvation as something toward which to strive throughout life, all of those had their place. In a world in which salvation and holiness were obtained by simple acts of faith, however, the plain life no longer offered the way to salvation. The outward cross had supplanted the inward one.

More than that, the plain life lost its meaning because it no longer defined a community. After the revival had done its work, many Friends eschewed expressions of distinctiveness. Their first loyalty was not to the society but to the larger community of evangelical Christians. They insisted that Friends were in complete agreement with other evangelicals on every fundamental doctrine of Christianity, a clear shift from the renewal position that, while Friends held evangelical views on such subjects as the Atonement and the inspiration of Scripture, they were called to bear a testimony to the world on the spirituality of true worship, the non-necessity of the ordinances, and the power of silent waiting. But for holiness Friends none of the peculiarities was essential. The revivalists argued instead that all true Christians would be in harmony and that anything that made for divisions among them was necessarily of Satan.[29]

Thus the revivalists saw no reason to apologize for working with holiness preachers of other denominations. While such Friends as Clark and Updegraff professed loyalty to Quaker tradition, they reduced that tradition to little more than the possibility of perfection. Clark saw no difference between the teachings of George Fox and those of such fathers of the evangelical tradition as Richard Baxter and John Bunyan, explaining away the pamphlet wars they waged with seventeenth-century Friends. Updegraff contended that Quakerism lost its power early in the eighteenth century with the institution of birthright membership and elders. He argued that Fox's real successor was John Wesley, the greatest advocate of sanctification.[30]

Why, then, did the overwhelming majority of Gurneyite Friends acquiesce in or embrace such radical changes? The most important reason is that the revival apparently met a deep need in the lives of many Friends. For a generation Quakers had heard that they should experience conversion and strive to achieve holiness. Friends had always believed in the possibility of holiness, and a desire for it was common. Take, for example, Ann T. Updegraff, the sister of David B., writing to a friend in the 1840s: "For years my soul has mingled with thine in *longing* desire and aspirations after a higher and holier and more perfect existence. . . . I feel the deepest reproach that I have done nothing to encourage and help thee forward in the path of holiness." Not even Friends ultimately skeptical about instantaneous sanctification questioned the appeal of an experience that promised an easy deliverance from all temptation and a quick entrance into a sinless state. "I am very much interested in the 'Higher Christian Life,'" Elizabeth L. Comstock wrote in 1873. "To me there is sweet *rest* in the thought that all responsibility, all care, all dependence are given up to Him who careth for us." The revival offered an easy way to that experience.[31]

The problem with the old way was that, while there had been exhortations to conversion and holiness, it was never clear how they were achieved. Hannah Whitall Smith, a Philadelphia Friend who became a convert to holiness teachings in the 1860s, remembered that "the most we ever heard was how to walk and live, how to be good." While valuable in urging a holy life, that teaching "failed to tell the secret by which this holiness could be realized." "All my young life," Smith recalled, "how eagerly and hungrily I watched and waited to be told how, and how continually I was disappointed."[32]

In truth the old plain Friends had shown a way, but it was the long, tried

tried path of tribulation, depression, and inward examination. It was for thousands a grim, gloomy way. Its favorite readings were the interminable introspections and the dry-as-dust accounts of the travels of long-dead ministers and elders. Its self-view was most commonly expressed as "mourners in Zion." The silence that it found so meaningful was often at best a forum for daydreams, at worst a trial, for many members.[33]

The revival offered a way not only different but also happier. It offered preaching, music, and liberation from the prying of the overseers and the frowns of the elders. Often the revival brought the wonderful sight of those weighty Friends who, having so long oppressed the young, were now kneeling at the altar and being forced to confess the inadequacy of their own spiritual lives. No longer would Friends be subject to the exactions of the discipline, the humiliations of peculiarity, the seemingly endless silent meetings. Instead of "bearing the cross" and "taking up the yoke," Friends were called to the "liberty of the sons of God." In place of silence came excitement, in the place of grimness was ecstatic joy, and all in the name of a higher vision of religious life.[34]

While the revival Friends brought new ways to the society, they also made brilliant use of traditional Quaker language and ideas. The concept of perfection, of course, had a long history among Friends. The holiness movement taught that perfection came through the baptism of the Holy Ghost, an idea that had similarities to the older conception of the nature of baptism. In the holiness vision, baptism need be experienced but once, and then it brought joy, not suffering. More than any other denomination, Friends had emphasized a theory of unstructured worship. That very lack of structure played into the hands of revivalists and made it possible for them to bend meetings to their own ends. The traveling ministry was one of Quakerism's most familiar and venerable institutions. The revivalists were simply traveling ministers with a radically different message.[35]

Much about the precise sequence of events in the revival is yet to be learned. A few things are certain. One is that the general meeting movement, still confined to Indiana Yearly Meeting, was not a vehicle for revival practices before 1870. The revival manifestations were still usually in unsanctioned, unofficial settings. Reports from the general meetings before December 1870 show that while the necessity of conversion was emphasized in all, and although singing took place in one, they followed the earlier pattern. The general meeting in Waynesville, Ohio, in December 1870 was the first real departure: it consisted entirely of devotional sessions. Afterward David B. Updegraff held additional meetings in the village. In 1871 the future direction of the general meetings became clearer. Holiness Friends increasingly emphasized instantaneous sanctification. Late in the year one Indiana Friend noted how the general meetings were giving increasing attention to the "Higher Life," a trend that was also becoming prominent in preaching outside the general meetings. At Indiana Yearly Meeting that fall, William Wetherald, another sanctified minister, held meetings for young people that a local newspaper thought had "a wonderful similarity to Methodism . . . rather in the revival style."[36]

In the fall of 1871 and spring of 1872, most of the other Gurneyite yearly meetings followed Indiana's example by holding general meetings. Late in the former year, the *Christian Worker* called them "the order of the day." The justification given by New York Friends was typical: they hoped that the meetings would convert nonbelievers and strengthen knowledge of Quaker doctrines among members. The unanimity with which the proposals were received and the readiness with which Friends of conservative views served on supervisory committees suggest that the movement still had no especially radical connotation: Iowa, for example, established a general meeting committee even as it took steps to discourage "social-religious" meetings.[37]

The first clear signs of radicalism appeared in New York. In the spring Friends there took part in "union" meetings, in which they welcomed ministers of all denominations. In August a general meeting was held in Farmington with nearly all of the revival leaders present. Their preaching was aggressively evangelical with holiness prominent. The clearest breaks with tradition, however, came in a general meeting in Brooklyn in December. Five holiness ministers—Updegraff, Woodard, Talbot, Esther G. Frame, and Sarah F. Smiley—ran the meeting aided by John Henry Douglas, who accepted holiness teachings while there. The ministers began by telling those present that conversion and sanctification were instantaneous— "All are either in or out of Christ." Updegraff demanded that those who wished to be sanctified rise and make an immediate decision. The women preachers made a vivid impression on a newspaper reporter, who found them "eloquent and dramatic beyond description." "They work the audience to such a pitch of excitement," the reporter wrote, "that some cannot contain themselves, but screech and scream, cry amen and groan. It would take but a slight stretch of the imagination to suppose oneself in a redhot glowing camp meeting." When one Friend tried to hand out a pamphlet of early Quaker writings, the ministers condemned his action as inappropriate to the "Christian" nature of the occasion. Also in attendance was Philadelphia Friend Henry Hartshorne, who was struck by the fervor of those present but also noted regretfully that there was virtually no silence.[38]

Thus the conversion of general meetings into revival meetings began. By 1873 other Quaker ministers were emulating Updegraff's techniques. Any occasion was suitable—the devotional sessions of monthly, quarterly, and especially yearly meetings, general meetings, and, increasingly, "protracted meetings" that often lasted for two weeks or more. The revivalists put themselves in complete charge, making altar calls and singing universal. By 1875 the revival was general in Indiana, Ohio, Western, Iowa, and North

Carolina yearly meetings, which contained about 70 percent of all Orthodox Friends. Kansas lagged a bit behind, as did New England, but New York was powerfully moved. Baltimore, as will be seen later, remained immune. Philadelphia, under firm Wilburite control, opposed the revival just as it had opposed everything else that had come out of Gurneyite Quakerism since the 1840s.[39]

The revivals usually followed a common pattern. They did not arise spontaneously. They were instead the work of cadres of holiness ministers who moved into a meeting, created havoc or a wonderful outpouring of the spirit, depending on one's point of view, and then moved on. The relatively small number of Quaker communities and the tendency of Friends to settle close together made it possible for revivalists to visit almost every Quaker community within a few years. Cyrus W. Harvey, a young minister of conservative views, provided a vivid account of how the revival came to Kansas. In 1877, according to Harvey, the entire yearly meeting included only four "fast" (the Conservative term for revival enthusiasts) ministers, who produced occasional but isolated eruptions. Then, he wrote, "all at once we were literally overrun by this class of ministers from abroad. They swarmed into the yearly meeting in 1877. . . . There were about 35 in attendance that year." After controlling the devotional sessions of the yearly meeting, Harvey remembered, "they scattered into all parts of the yearly [meeting] to break up the old way of worship and ministry." By 1879 they had succeeded. But even to those who acquiesced in the changes there was no gradual transformation. "You cannot understand it here," Barnabas C. Hobbs told London Yearly Meeting in 1878. "No one can without seeing it. Our meetings were shaken as by a vast whirlwind."[40]

A few ministers employed some of the methods of the revival while remaining committed to a moderate course. The most important of these was Allen Jay. A small Indiana farmer from a long line of Quaker ancestors, Jay was recorded a minister early in life. He spent most of the 1870s in North Carolina trying to help Friends there rebuild the society and their own lives. To Jay must go credit for the relatively moderate course of the revival in North Carolina during the 1870s. He began holding meetings in High Point to aid young Friends who had come under conviction in a Methodist revival; when Friends began to come forward asking for aid in one of his services, he did not forbid them. He had no quarrel with singing, although he would not lead it. Jay refused to do anything to which a portion of the meeting objected, and he eschewed the fire-and-brimstone preaching so dear to the other revivalists. "No doubt it is right to preach at times the terrors of the law," Jay wrote to his wife in 1875, "but there is so much danger of getting a little of self in with it—wishing to bring everybody to our idea of what is right—that I often think it is safer for me to leave the judging with my heavenly father." Jay's success as an evangelist rivaled that of the holiness revivalists, but the course he pursued later in life was radically different from that of the sanctified.[41]

Jay's moderation and willingness to compromise were exceptional. After 1874 the revivalists moved toward institutionalizing their revolution. One of the first fruits of their efforts was disciplinary reform. During the 1870s the Gurneyite yearly meetings wrote new disciplines that significantly weakened or entirely abolished the older ways. Almost all of the distinguishing marks of the old disciplines—the rules on speech and dress, the marriage regulations, the restrictions on tombstones—disappeared. The doctrinal sections that had first appeared during the 1850s became longer. A comparison of the 1859 and the 1876 Ohio Yearly Meeting disciplines is instructive. In 1859 the Ohio discipline devoted seven pages to the details of the plain life, threatening disownment for a variety of infractions. The 1876 discipline gave plainness and moderation two paragraphs, never mentioning disownment. It is significant that the revision went through with virtually no opposition.[42]

Nowhere was the effect of the revival on the discipline more apparent than in the marriage regulations. Their reform had been a priority of the renewal movement, but renewal Friends had shown no inclination to set aside the traditional Quaker ceremony, in which members repeated vows in meeting without the supervision of clergy, or to discourage members from seeking the guidance of the meeting in marriage. After the revival redefined religious community, distinctions between Quakers and non-Quakers had little meaning, and the holiness revivalists were determined to obliterate what remained of them. By 1880 the marriage regulations were gone. Not only were Friends free to marry whomever they chose, but also they were free to choose the form, and they flocked to more conventional ceremonies. By the 1880s the old way of marriage had all but disappeared in most of the Gurneyite meetings, and Quaker ministers were performing weddings like those performed by other ministers.[43]

Some moral regulations remained as part of the discipline, of course: strictures on cardplaying, dancing, attending theaters, drinking alcohol, and violating the sabbath were retained. What was left was a system of mores similar to that of rural and small-town evangelicals across America.[44]

Equally important for the future of the society was the power shift from the elders to the ministers during the 1870s. The traditional duty of elders was to restrain and direct ministers, but their attempts to do so early in the revival had created bitter resentment. Some of the revivalists attacked the office of elder as unscriptural and tried to abolish it, but they never succeeded. Most of the yearly meetings instead limited the terms of elders to three years, thus allowing meetings to dismiss those whom they found recalcitrant and uncooperative.[45]

The prestige of the ministry increased as that of the eldership declined.

Most of the revival converts had an understandable loyalty to the ministers who had brought them to salvation and would brook little opposition to their spiritual "parents." The revivalists often imbibed non-Quaker ideas about ministerial power. No one could judge a minister, the revivalists said, since the call to preach came from God, and the minister was responsible only to him. Gradually the idea of a Quaker clergy with distinctive offices and privileges emerged. Ministers came to play increasingly important roles in the Quaker colleges, converting them into institutions for the preparation of religious workers and forcing them to justify their continued existence in such terms.[46]

The revival, of course, was not aimed solely at those who were already Quakers; the hundreds of new members that the revivals brought in posed the greatest problem for the society. Some were former Friends who had in the past fallen victim to the discipline, but many were strangers to Quaker tradition. All had been converted in a setting that was very different from the traditional Quaker meeting. The worship of Friends seemed utterly foreign to many, since as late as the 1880s most meetings were unprogrammed. Some converts took advantage of the silence to unburden their consciences in unseemly ways, and others insisted on singing hymns. Trying to hold these new members in the society would give rise to even more radical innovations during the 1880s.[47]

Thus by 1880 a revolution had taken place among Gurneyite Friends. The old ways were fast disappearing. Worship was on a new basis. Hundreds of new members were coming in. Significant opposition to such changes arose in every yearly meeting; in its most extreme form, that opposition resulted in separation.

The separation in Western Yearly Meeting is a good example of this process. There had been tensions in Plainfield Quarterly Meeting during the 1860s, but the yearly meeting began holding general meetings with general unanimity in 1871. Within little more than a year, however, conservative Friends on the general meeting committee, led by Robert W. Hodson, an elder, and Eleazer Bales, a well-known minister, resigned in protest over the increasing use of revival methods. Nevertheless, conservatives showed little interest in separatism, hoping that the revival was an aberration that would soon disappear. By 1876 it was clear that it was instead increasing in strength, and the conservatives made one final effort to clear themselves of innovation. They began by holding a series of conferences to discuss the state of the society. They then climaxed their attack by using their tenuous majority in Plainfield Quarterly Meeting to dissolve its committee on general meetings and abruptly to close a revival being held at Sugar Grove Meeting. Their action split the quarterly meeting, and when Western Yearly Meeting met in the autumn of 1877 it had to decide between the parties.

The yearly meeting brought in a report in favor of the revivalists. After it was read, Hodson and Bales, both octogenarians who had "borne the burdens and heat of the day for half a century," announced that they "no longer had any rights or privileges" in the society and invited those in sympathy with them to withdraw. Moderate Friends such as Barnabas C. Hobbs, the clerk, and Stanley Pumphrey, a visiting English minister, appealed to the conservatives not to take that final step, but the conservatives were not moved. Led by the two venerable old plain Friends, they began to move slowly toward the doors of the meetinghouse. As they went out, one of the revival ministers began a hymn at the top of his voice:

> See the mighty host advancing
> Satan leading on.

The revivalist turned to a neighbor and exclaimed that he wanted the conservatives to hear one more hymn before they left.[48]

Conservative Friends in Iowa also began to separate in 1877, although the process there was not complete until 1881. The separation in Kansas did not begin until 1879, largely because of the influence of the clerk of the yearly meeting, William Nicholson, who was himself skeptical about the revival. In 1877 a small group of separatists in Indiana Yearly Meeting joined the newly formed Western Yearly Meeting of Conservative Friends.[49]

The revivalists made little or no effort to assuage Conservative fears. Some reveled in the separations. After the division of Bear Creek Meeting in Iowa in 1877, one member rejoiced that with the departure of the "old drones" revival Friends could "make honey." When William Nicholson's diplomacy prevented a separation in Kansas the same year, Nicholson noted that the revival Friends were disappointed. They wanted a separation, "the sooner the better." Another revivalist in Iowa told Walter Robson, a visiting minister from England, that they were determined to "crush" all who opposed them. Revival Friends, while significantly loosening disciplinary restraints, were willing to use them on their opponents when convenient.[50]

The saddest such incident of the 1870s took place in Indiana Yearly Meeting. In 1876 Walter Edgerton, an elderly member of Spiceland meeting, published a devastating critique of the revival and its departures from Quaker tradition. Spiceland had been revived in the winter of 1873–1874 and although several "weighty" Friends were appalled, they were "coerced" into silence. That was not Edgerton's nature. He was, moreover, a cantankerous soul. During the 1840s he had been a leader in the antislavery separation, and there were rumors that he had driven his first wife to suicide. Edgerton's family ties with leading Wilburites in Ohio made him

even more suspect. He soon found himself disowned for "creating disunity."
In vain did he and his supporters rightly protest that every statement in his
pamphlet could be proved and that he had never been charged with false-
hood. No dissent was to be allowed among the revived.[51]

Most of those who had doubts about the revival did not separate. A
majority of Friends had too many bitter memories of previous schisms. And
there were some who, despite their doubts, could not bring themselves to
oppose the revival on the chance that it might be a true work of God.
Doubtless there were many whose experience paralleled that of Levi T.
Pennington, an elder in James Baldwin's community of Westfield, Indiana.
When Amos M. Kenworthy and Calvin W. Pritchard began a full-blown
revival in Westfield in 1873, Pennington found many of their practices
offensive and finally became determined to use his influence to close down
their meetings. Then his youngest child, for whose spiritual welfare he had
long been concerned, came home and told him that she had been converted.
Thereafter Pennington could not bring himself to oppose the revivals. "The
car of salvation is rolling on," he reportedly said, "and if some of us do not get
out of its way, we will be crushed."[52]

Some Friends chose neither to separate nor to acquiesce in changes they
considered unreconcilable with true Quakerism. In the 1870s they coalesced
into a middle party. This sometimes amorphous group was small numerically
but included many of the most influential Gurneyite Friends in America,
the clerks and leaders of most of the Gurneyite yearly meetings. More
simply put, the new middle party embraced most of the old renewal
movement.

Doubts about the revival bound moderates together. They had welcomed
the early signs of renewed life in the society. Typical was Joel Bean, the clerk
of Iowa Yearly Meeting for most of the 1870s. Until 1873 he had "long been
praying for a greater prevailing of the presence and power of the Holy
Ghost." While he could not approve of some manifestations, he found that
"like ripples upon the surface, they were lost, in the deeper waves of
feeling." But as the radical holiness advocates came to control the revival, he
felt that he had to "stand aloof from the movement, where it had adopted
means" he viewed as "hazardous and scattering."[53] All of these Friends
agreed that separation was no solution, but there consensus broke down.

Some of the renewal Friends, such as Bean in Iowa, John Greenleaf
Whittier in New England, and Francis T. King in Baltimore, took an openly
critical view of the revival. A few opponents, such as Nereus Mendenhall in
North Carolina, who quietly retired from society affairs into the relative calm
of a teaching post at Haverford, held themselves aloof. But most of the
middle party, such as Hobbs in Western Yearly Meeting; Charles F. and
Rhoda M. Coffin, Timothy Nicholson, and Eli and Mahala Jay in Indiana;

William Nicholson in Kansas; Elizabeth L. Comstock in Michigan; and John
Butler in Ohio, tried a delicate balancing act. Initially favoring the revival,
and in many cases actively participating in it, they became increasingly
skeptical as the revivalists seemed bent on overthrowing all of the old
landmarks. At the same time, they continued to appreciate the new energy
and vitality it seemed to create. Thus they tried to carve a middle way. They
would accept "orderly" revivals. They would accept converts, if they were
schooled in Quaker practices after becoming members. They would accept
singing, if "done in the spirit." But they eschewed second-experience
sanctification and feared the arrogance they perceived in the revival ministry. Strongest in Indiana, New England, New York, and North Carolina
yearly meetings, the middle party tried to preserve tenuous unity among
Gurneyite Friends.[54]

The Philadelphia renewal group occupied an even more uneasy position.
There was some holiness agitation among Philadelphia Friends, led by
Hannah Whitall Smith and Sarah F. Smiley, but they had left the society by
1872. The *Friends' Review* provides the best barometer of the attitudes of
Philadelphia Gurneyites. Until late in the 1870s the journal's commentary
on the revival was cautiously positive. It praised the large number of
converts reported while it expressed doubts about certain practices. Its
editors, William J. Allinson, Henry Hartshorne, and James E. Rhoads, may
have been overwhelmed by the flood of favorable reports sent in by revival
supporters. More than that, the politics of Philadelphia Yearly Meeting
dictated that they not take an openly critical stance. For two decades the
Friends' Review had contrasted what it saw as the increasing spiritual life of
the Gurneyite yearly meetings with the deadness of Philadelphia, dismissing
the Wilburite fears about the ultimate consequences of Gurney's thought.
When the revival fulfilled Wilbur's prophecies the *Friends' Review* could
hardly capitulate. It went on publicly minimizing the adverse consequences
of the revival while Hartshorne, at least, privately took a much dimmer
view. In 1875 Hartshorne went to Indiana (he attended the very meeting
conducted by Updegraff and John Henry Douglas described at the opening
of this chapter), and what he saw left him horrified. The tactics of the two
ministers, Hartshorne told Updegraff, were "diametrically *opposite* to those
of the early Friends—and irreconcilable with their *fundamental principles.*"
Hartshorne liked Updegraff; he considered him "a young man of great
natural talent and enthusiasm," but, he continued, Updegraff's "views in
regard to worship, preaching, and evangelizing have . . . been *overmuch
influenced by the Methodists with whom he has been associated.*" As the
1870s wore on, the *Friends' Review* diverged more and more from the
western-based *Christian Worker* to become the editorial bulwark of the
middle party.[55]

RENEWAL VERSUS REVIVAL

The factional lineup of the 1870s brings us to two final questions: What was the relationship of the renewal movement of the 1860s to the revival movement of the 1870s? What would have happened to American Quakerism had there been no holiness revival? There are no simple answers.

There can be no doubt about the links between the renewal and revival movements. Both were interested in evangelism, in bringing new life to meetings. Both were committed to evangelicalism. The tolerance of debate and the openness to new ideas that the renewal movement brought to Quakerism played an important role in opening Friends to the influences that brought the revivals. Yet those links cannot obscure the major differences between the renewal and the revival movements. The renewal Friends were reformers—they wished to modify the plain life, to loosen the rules on marriage, to encourage more participation in meetings while maintaining their traditional character, and to work with other denominations while preserving the distinctiveness of Friends. The methods and aims of the revival were revolutionary—to smash the plain life and the assumptions behind it, to sweep away the marriage regulations as unchristian, to demand participation in meetings instead of encouraging it, to dismiss silence completely, and to use whatever methods produced converts, regardless of their origins or effect. Most revivalists had little use for reform or humanitarianism; for the concept of Quaker distinctiveness, they had none.

A glance at the participants in the two movements also highlights the discontinuities. The opposition of such Friends as Bean, King, and Timothy and William Nicholson to the revival has been outlined, as has the ambivalence of many others who were prominent in the 1860s. Some renewal Friends threw themselves wholeheartedly into the revival: Clark, Jay, Hill, John Henry Douglas, Thomas Kimber, Thomas W. Ladd, and Robert Lindley Murray are the most notable. All except Jay, however, had in common an experience of sanctification that marked, with the possible exception of Douglas, the beginning of their aggressive evangelistic careers; Jay's lack of the experience melds with the unique course that his revivalism took. Some of the revivalists, such as Woodard and the Frames, saw the revival as a gradual, continuous outgrowth of the 1860s, but opponents such as Bean emphasized the lack of continuity between the trends of the 1860s and those of the 1870s. Contemporary writers such as Updegraff and William Nicholson also saw a dramatic difference between the movement that gave rise to the general meetings and the one that transformed them, and they agreed on what the source of that latter movement was—holiness. More important, most of the leading revivalists—Updegraff, Talbot, Hoover, Woodard, Hussey, the Frames, Wetherald, Pritchard, and Kenworthy—played unimportant roles in the society before 1868. Before their sanctifications they were mostly obscure ministers, if even yet recorded. The holiness movement brought them into prominence.[56]

That brings us to the other question: What would have happened to Quakerism had there been no revival? For generations Quaker historians have more or less reluctantly defended it as the only alternative to a dead Wilburism.[57] That position should be reconsidered. Before a single hymn was sung, before a single altar call was issued, the severities of the plain life were being softened, the marriage rules relaxed, distance from the world narrowed, participation in meetings increased, and evangelism encouraged. Before Updegraff and Woodard and the Frames, a newly effective ministry was emerging. And all of those changes were taking place in a way that avoided divisiveness, that blended tradition with adjustment to the times without destroying Quaker distinctiveness, and that avoided the intellectual havoc of the revival.

There was, moreover, one yearly meeting that resisted the revival, and its example suggests what might have happened had the renewal movement been allowed to come to fruition. At the end of the Civil War, the Gurneyite Baltimore Yearly Meeting had barely four hundred members in only two quarterly meetings. Its leading members, however, such as Francis T. King and the White and Thomas families, were pillars of the renewal movement and tried to put its ideas into effect. They softened the discipline, tried to build up the traditional ministry, and emphasized works of humanitarianism both within and outside the society—aiding the freedmen, helping rebuild Quakerism in North Carolina after the Civil War, working in a host of reform causes, and playing a leading role in the founding of Johns Hopkins University. In the 1870s the yearly meeting began holding general meetings on the original lines and kept them on course. The revivalists, save for an occasional incursion from Ohio Yearly Meeting, gave Baltimore a wide berth. Despite the lack of revivals, significant outmigration, a low birthrate, and a slower loosening of the discipline, the yearly meeting expanded into new areas and tripled its membership by 1900.[58]

But the path that Baltimore Friends choose was one that no other yearly meeting followed. After 1875 the future of Gurneyite Quakerism lay largely in the hands of a small group of ministers committed to holiness theology. And within a few years that small group almost obliterated two hundred years of tradition and moved American Friends very close to the Protestant mainstream.

CHAPTER
V

THE REALIGNMENT OF AMERICAN QUAKERISM, 1875–1890

"Quakerism," wrote John Nicholson, Baltimore businessman and brother of William and Timothy, in 1885, "is getting to be a very indefinite term." Defining a Friend had once been as easy as defining a Methodist or a Presbyterian or a Catholic, but by the 1880s Quakerism had an uncertain meaning. To the Baltimore Friend its future seemed bleak. "The Society seems to be getting ripe for a general disintegration"—a disintegration that he was coming to think inevitable.[1]

John Nicholson was not alone in fearing for the future of the Society of Friends during the 1880s. Although Orthodox Quakers had split into three mutually antagonistic factions that feuded bitterly over the direction that the society was to take, a remarkable consensus on one point remained. The revolution of the 1870s had destroyed most of the landmarks that two hundred years of tradition had built. New institutions had to be established in their place. Their nature was the focus of discussion and debate for nearly twenty years, a debate that continued to divide the society. At one extreme were the Conservative, or Wilburite, Friends, whom the revivals of the 1870s had traumatized and driven out of the society and who wanted to blot out the untoward events of that decade and to return to the good old ways. At the other extreme were the holiness revivalists and their converts, determined to maintain the fervor of the 1870s and to complete the revolution they had initiated. Between those two, small in numbers but powerful and influential, were the heirs of the renewal movement of the 1860s, moderate Friends trying to hold the society on a middle course that preserved the best of the old ways while it instilled the society with the new vigor that the revival had released.

The problems of American Quakerism between 1875 and 1895 flowed from those divisions. The Conservative Friends, having formally repudiated the other two factions through formal separation, withdrew into self-imposed isolation, seeing an occasional glimmer of hope for the moderates but regarding the revivalists as apostates who had forfeited the right to the name of Friends. The holiness revival Friends, trying to expand the evangelistic outreach of the society, dismissed the Conservatives as irrelevant fossils while they battled with the moderates for the leadership of the masses of Friends. The moderates tried to steer a conscious course between the other two factions, sometimes fighting both, but usually concentrating their resources on counteracting the influences of the revival, which they regarded as having gone awry.

CONSERVATIVE FRIENDS

The story of the Conservative Friends, as the antirevival, anti-Gurney separatists came to identify themselves, is the easiest to tell. Conservatives sought to follow as closely as possible the old ways, not "that which is popular among men," but rather the ways ordained by "the one who should be our leader." Truth was unchangeable and unchanging, and Conservatives felt that the ways of Friends in the early nineteenth century continued to bind them.[2]

Conservative Quakerism came from two streams. One consisted of the Wilburite yearly meetings in New England and Ohio that had risen out of opposition to Gurneyism during the 1840s and 1850s. They were joined by tiny groups of Wilburite separatists in New York and Baltimore. Here also belongs Philadelphia Yearly Meeting, which under firm Wilburite control resisted the "errors" of Gurney well into the twentieth century. The Wilburites themselves were not immune to controversy, however, and between 1855 and 1865 several Wilburite groups became involved in a series of obscure controversies concerning their relationship with each other and with the Gurneyites. The result was the separation of a tiny group of ultraconservative Wilburites who assumed the name of Primitive Friends. By the 1870s, however, the Wilburite bodies had settled down to relative peace and stability.[3]

The other stream of Conservative Quakerism was made up of the Friends in Iowa, Indiana, and Kansas who separated from the Gurneyite yearly meetings in reaction to the holiness revival during the 1870s. Union between the Conservative separatists of the 1870s and the older Wilburite bodies was not a foregone conclusion, since the latter sometimes viewed the former as having tarried too long amidst Gurneyite error. Real differences between the two groups were minor, however, compared with their common commitment to the importance of the plain life and traditional forms of ministry and worship. By 1890 their yearly meetings had established official relations with each other through exchanging correspondence, ministers, and members. Thereafter "Wilburite" Friends and "Conservative" Friends were indistinguishable, and the two terms were used interchangeably, although most of the yearly meetings officially adopted the title of Conservative Friends.[4]

The Conservative Friends, of course, came out of the Orthodox tradition, and their beliefs and practices were those sketched in chapter one. Their theology on such points as the divinity of Christ and the authority of the Bible continued to be stated in the same terms used by the opponents of Elias Hicks during the 1820s. They felt called to maintain the spirituality of worship, the immediate guidance of the Holy Spirit, the existence of the Inner Light, and the necessity of holiness. They felt called to be "lights in the world, and hold up a standard of righteousness in the earth." Given their background, however, it was natural for them to strike a primarily negative chord. Thus the dominant tone of the Conservative Friends was opposition: "Body Resurrection," "Second Advent views," water baptism, instantaneous conversion and sanctification, and the entire apparatus of the revival.[5]

It was to Philadelphia Yearly Meeting that Conservative Friends elsewhere looked for leadership, but the response from Philadelphia was mixed. There was much from which Conservative Friends could take comfort. Visiting Conservative Friends were given places of honor in Philadelphia meetinghouses and heard with respect, whereas the treatment that visiting revival ministers received was at best cool and at worst often rude. The Philadelphia *Friend* offered editorial encouragement, stating flatly that although separatism was usually an evil, it was difficult to discern who the real separatists were in the divided yearly meetings. Traveling ministers from Philadelphia visited Conservative meetings, and money from a special Philadelphia Yearly Meeting fund helped build Conservative meetinghouses all over the country. But official recognition by correspondence (the formal exchange of letters of encouragement, exhortation, and so on, among yearly meetings) for the Conservative yearly meetings never came. The Gurneyite element in Philadelphia continued to oppose putting Philadelphia officially out of unity with the other Gurneyite yearly meetings, while many Philadelphia Wilburites thought that they could oppose the revival more effectively by not becoming involved in the vexing correspondence issue.[6]

West of Philadelphia, Conservative Friends found their champion in Cyrus W. Harvey of Spring River Meeting in Kansas. Harvey's early life gave little indication of his future career. Born in Indiana in 1843, he had volunteered for the Union army early in the Civil War. His experiences made him a confirmed pacifist, and his marriage to a granddaughter of

Robert W. Hodson, a leading opponent of the revival in Western Yearly Meeting, brought him into the scattered network of antirevival resistance. After the war Harvey moved to Kansas and was soon afterward recorded a minister. As the revival gained ground there, Harvey established himself as its leading opponent. In 1879 he began publishing the *Western Friend,* the organ of Conservatives west of the Appalachians. The *Western Friend* billed itself "the avowed and fearless advocate of the ancient type of Quakerism," maintaining the doctrines of Fox, Penn, and Barclay, pressing "the necessity of inward experience" and spiritual worship, and pointing out the "danger and inconsistency of 'Mourners' Benches,' 'Sanctification Altars,' 'Outward Consecrations,' and all human dictation of outward acts as 'means of grace' in worship."[7]

The *Western Friend* is a fascinating document, especially when compared with the Philadelphia *Friend*. While the latter was staid and restrained, the former was witty, vituperative, and personal. Harvey consistently printed details of (from the Conservative viewpoint) particularly horrendous revivals, praised any signs of soundness reappearing among "Fast Quakers," and took delight in highlighting rumors of quarrels and friction between the revivalists and their opponents in the middle party. Harvey never shrank from controversy or ferocious editorial wars with those who dared to oppose him, especially revival journals such as the *Christian Worker* and the *Gospel Expositor*. Harvey's favorite target was David B. Updegraff, who was for the Kansas editor the incarnation of everything that was wrong with American Quakerism.[8]

Opponents often dismissed the Conservative Friends as hopeless reactionaries, and there was some truth to the charge. The Ohio Conservatives used an 1819 discipline, with only minor revisions, until 1922. Long after other Friends had accepted public schools, Conservatives kept up monthly meeting schools and boarding schools to provide the "guarded" education that had once been the ideal of all Friends. Some individuals among the Conservatives took the plain life to impossible extremes, as, for example, did Joshua Maule of Colerain, Ohio, who eschewed politics, voting, and photography. Maule burned every book by Joseph John Gurney on which he could lay his hands and separated from the Ohio Wilburites because he thought even them too liberal.[9]

Many Conservatives, however, were willing to adjust to changing times. Kansas Conservatives held First Day schools. In the 1890s Ohio Conservatives moved cautiously to develop literary societies and social activities for their young people. Harvey threw himself into Prohibition party politics and woman's suffrage agitation with almost as much enthusiasm as he showed for battling the revival. A few Conservative ministers tried to make converts among both non-Quakers and revived Friends; one even undertook missionary work in Africa and Japan. Thus while the prevailing note was caution, signs of life and movement were apparent among the Conservatives.[10]

Conservative Friends were always few in number, probably never more than a few thousand. Throughout the nineteenth century their number declined. The separatists in Indiana, Iowa, and Kansas had been disproportionately elderly, and strict adherence to the discipline meant the loss of many members. For most Conservatives such attrition was not a cause for concern. They saw themselves as a remnant, witnesses to the truth who, if they remained faithful, would someday be raised back to prosperity and see their enemies confounded.[11]

During the last years of the nineteenth century, Conservative Friends lived in a largely self-imposed isolation. Yet they kept alive the older ways of life and worship that other Orthodox Friends were abandoning. During the early years of the twentieth century, when a new generation of Conservative Friends began cautiously to reach out toward other Friends, they found many of them coming to appreciate the witness that the Conservatives had maintained.

THE REVIVALISTS

The most visible force within American Quakerism during the 1880s continued to be the holiness revival. Virtually all of the revivalists active during the 1870s continued their work into the following decade, and they were bolstered by new recruits from both within and outside the society. During the 1880s revival Friends usually followed the course of the larger holiness movement. They splintered slightly over some details of holiness theology, but they showed an increasing interest in faith healing and premillennialism, combining these with the old emphases on justification and sanctification in what became known as the "Four-Fold Gospel." They also were united in opposition to what holiness people everywhere saw as the chief dangers of the 1880s: higher criticism, evolution theory, sectarianism, and apathy.

While the revivalists of the 1870s remained prominent, a number of younger ministers also came into prominence during the 1880s. Most having been born in the 1840s or 1850s, they came largely from solid Quaker backgrounds. Among the most important were John Pennington (1846–1933) and Seth C. Rees (1854–1933), both from Westfield, Indiana; Hulda Rees (1854–1898), Seth's wife; Micajah M. Binford (1852–1902), from Walnut Ridge in Indiana; David Hadley (1842–1915) in Western Yearly Meeting; Anna J. Winslow in Iowa and Kansas; J. Walter Malone (1857–1937), a Cleveland businessman turned preacher; and William P. Pinkham (1844–1925), a native of Maine who spent the 1860s and 1870s teaching in Quaker schools in Indiana before turning to the ministry in the 1880s. All, with the possible exception of Pinkham, were revival products who were recorded as ministers at an early age and who made evangelism their life's work.[12]

Perhaps even more important for the future course of revival Quakerism was the influx of holiness preachers from other denominations between 1875 and 1890. A disproportionate number were members of Ohio Yearly Meeting: Noah McLean and William Allen, both former slaves; George W. Willis, the son of Presbyterian missionaries; and David J. Lewis and O. L. Olds, who left Methodism for Quakerism. Among those in other yearly meetings were William F. Manley, a former Free Methodist minister; David Sampson, a member of the Plymouth Brethren who became North Carolina's most important Quaker evangelist; and Harvey and Almira Bergman, who left the Methodist church to become evangelists in Indiana Yearly Meeting. The revivalists made such accessions so easy that many new preachers began evangelistic work with little or no understanding of Quakerism. One such instance took place in Ohio Yearly Meeting. A young convert from a Methodist background showed some preaching ability and was promptly recorded a minister by Ohio Friends. He decided to make western New York the scene of his first evangelistic campaign. He was mystified when Friends there reacted badly to a sermon on the necessity of water baptism. He had assumed that the views of Quakers were the same as those of the Methodists, since they were so similar on other subjects. An even more extreme case is that of James Grandstaff, who early in 1882 was a saloonkeeper in Van Wert County, Ohio. That spring his invalid wife was converted and subsequently "healed" in a revival conducted by the Bergmans. Her experience led Grandstaff to profess conversion, give up his saloon, and undergo sanctification. By the fall he and his wife were conducting revivals under the auspices of Friends in Indiana. But within a few years he would be at the center of an obscure but bitter schism that would come close to destroying several Friends meetings.[13]

As the revival became solidly established among Friends, it found its organ in the *Christian Worker*. Published since 1871 in New Vienna, Ohio, the *Christian Worker* had originally been the revival's chief publicist and defender, but later in the decade Daniel Hill, its editor, began to waver on subjects important to holiness Friends. In 1883 a group of revivalists purchased the journal, moved it to Chicago, and installed Calvin W. Pritchard, a holiness stalwart, as editor. In the reorganized *Christian Worker* the revival party found a reliable mouthpiece. "First a Christian, second a Friend," was the *Christian Worker*'s motto. It advocated a thoroughgoing revival platform that included preaching, singing, vocal prayer, altar calls, and mourners' benches. It was an uncompromising defender of "scriptural holiness"—instantaneous, second-experience sanctification—and an enemy of Unitarianism, infidelity, sectarianism, and traditional Quakerism.[14]

Pritchard epitomized the attitudes of holiness Friends in the last quarter of the nineteenth century. Revivalism had become a permanent feature of Quakerism, they asserted, and should be part of the life of every Quaker. No meeting could do without revivals, because no other method worked so well in producing conversions and sanctifications.[15]

Little more can be said about the continuing revival impulse. Revivalists in the 1880s used the same methods as in the 1870s and with the same results. During the winter, the favorite time for revivals, accounts of successful meetings filled the columns of the *Christian Worker*. The following, from one issue in 1884, give a sense of holiness Quakerism:

> Maple Grove, Illinois: A meeting commenced at Maple Grove, Douglas County, Illinois, by Elwood C. Siler and Ira Newlin and wife 1st Mo. 25th. It continued with interest until the close. . . . As a result there were forty-nine converted, and most of the membership professed full salvation. At a meeting appointed for the children, twenty testified to the love of Jesus in their hearts; this little army for the Lord ranged in age from 5 to 12 years old. Number applied for membership, 8. . . .

> Greenwood Meeting, Hortonville, Hamilton Co., Ind.: Willis Kenworthy and Allen, his son, held a series of meetings here of nineteen sessions, commencing the 23rd. Their services were endued with Holy Ghost power; their gospel teaching reached the hearts of many, strengthening the church and warning sinners to flee from the wrath to come. Sixteen special blessings were received, three were sanctified, four converted and nine reclaimed. Much good seed was sown; we hope it will bring forth to the glory of God.

> Oak Run, Iowa: Oak Run Monthly Meeting was held 1st Mo. 12, 1884. . . . Daniel McPherson arrived on the evening train and began a series of meetings and continued until the 29th; holding meetings in the day at dwelling houses (schools being in session, and we have no meetinghouse of our own).

> The Lord was with us in wonder-working power, and we had a feast of good things from his bountiful store-house; backsliders were reclaimed, souls converted to God, and the church greatly strengthened.[16]

The Quaker revival had become indistinguishable from those of any other evangelical denomination.

While the revival was simple and direct, the holiness movement among Friends was becoming more complex, as holiness Quakers explored the implications of their beliefs. They increasingly became involved in union movements and revivals. They espoused faith healing and premillennialism. And their beliefs hardened into an uncompromising dogmatism characteristic of the emerging movement within American Protestantism that was to become known as fundamentalism. Although they remained the most visible and apparently the most powerful faction within Orthodox Quakerism, the holiness Friends were a troubled group, troubled by continuing opposition within the society, by a lukewarm commitment on the part of a large portion of the membership, and by backsliding on the part of the once faithful. The strange combination of confidence and fear mirrors the experience and the influence of the larger holiness movement during the period.

The decade 1880–1890 was a critical time for the larger holiness movement. Initially united by enthusiasm over the camp-meeting movement of the 1870s, by 1885 the group was splitting along Reformed and Arminian lines. Both sides agreed that a sinless, holy life was possible, but they disagreed as to how it was achieved. The *Christian Worker* succinctly summarized the difference between the two views in 1887. Advocates of Arminian holiness theories, mainly Methodists, held that the "sin-destroying baptism of the Holy Ghost . . . destroyed, crucified and made dead" the carnal mind, the desire to sin. Those in the Reformed tradition, such as Dwight L. Moody, argued that "our victory is by overcoming, through faith in Christ, while sin remains alive but powerless within us."[17]

The Reformed position attracted some Friends because of its similarity to older Quaker teachings. A few holiness Friends active in the revivals of the 1870s, most notably Thomas Kimber of New York, came to embrace gradualist views and gravitated away from the revival. But the overwhelming majority of holiness Friends rejected such views. "*Holiness is sanctification in perpetuity,*" Dougan Clark, Jr., proclaimed. "*It implies heart purity,* or *freedom from sin. . . .* It is freedom from the *guilt* of sin, freedom also from its *power,* from its dominion, nay, from its very *existence.*"[18]

For holiness Friends the distinction between gradual and instantaneous sanctification was not a mere splitting of theological hairs. It went to the heart of religion. Holiness Friends saw commands to experience instantaneous sanctification on every page of the Bible. Only holiness guaranteed a sanctified judgment that could distinguish gospel truth from heresy. Only sanctified ministers were endued with the power that converted sinners. Gradualism encouraged one to remain in a sinful state, to shun the promises of God, to retard the spread of truth. Thus one Friend was deadly serious when he wrote that "the theory of . . . a gradual sanctification is sufficient to keep thousands out of the kingdom," and another predicted eternal damnation for all who opposed instantaneous sanctification.[19]

Perhaps the most notable feature of the work of holiness Friends was their continuing deemphasis of denominationalism. While holiness Friends thought it unrealistic to expect denominational lines to disappear before the millennium, all agreed that the Bible taught only one truth, and if there were 500 interpretations of it, 499 had to be wrong. Holiness Quakers blasted preaching the "peculiarities" of Friends; they saluted truth wherever they found it. Updegraff liked to boast that he was raised a Quaker, sanc-tified under the guidance of a Methodist, married to his second wife by a Presbyterian, and baptized by a Baptist. He even condemned setting up new Friends meetings in areas where evangelical churches already existed. The *Christian Worker* and the *Gospel Expositor* (a short-lived Quaker holiness journal edited by Dougan Clark, Jr., and Asahel H. Hussey) were far more likely to reprint articles from other holiness journals than to run pieces on Quaker traditions. (Harvey did a little counting in 1883 and found that in twenty-five issues the *Expositor* had published one extract from the writings of a Friend before 1800, forty-one articles written for it by non-Quakers, and forty pieces reprinted from other holiness journals.)[20]

Holiness Quaker nondenominationalism reached its peak in union revivals and camp meetings in which Quaker holiness preachers worked with Methodists, Baptists, Wesleyans, United Brethren, and the Salvation Army. Clark and Updegraff in particular became regular fixtures of the great holiness camp meetings held at such places as Ocean Grove, New Jersey, and Mountain Lake Park, Maryland. There were no better places, Updegraff wrote, in which to find salvation and sanctification.[21]

The course of holiness Quakerism paralleled the larger holiness move-ment in other ways. The most notable was the increasing interest in faith healing. Holiness Quakers held that the Scriptures taught the healing of the body as clearly as any other evangelical truth, and "not to believe God's word is to dishonor God." Healing was the logical outgrowth of sanctification, since God hardly intended for those filled with the Holy Ghost to be at the mercy of "fallible, self-contradicting physicians."[22]

The form that divine healing was to take became a subject of some debate. A few Friends—for example, Asahel H. Hussey and especially Amos M. Kenworthy—claimed special gifts as healers. Some, citing James 5:14–15, argued that the proper procedure for healing the sick was to call in the elders of the meeting to pray and to anoint the sufferer with oil. Others argued that the believing prayer of the sufferer sufficed. Still other Friends were in-terested in "healing homes," which, like those conducted by Dr. Charles Cullis of Boston, combined "modern" medicine with holiness teachings. But such differences did not occupy the attention of holiness Friends overmuch. Methods were not important; results were. Holiness Quakers claimed sub-stantial results, and accounts of faith healing became a regular feature in the *Christian Worker* after 1883.[23]

Of even greater consequence for the future of revival Quakerism was its movement toward premillennialism during the 1880s. Before the Civil War the dominant outlook of American Protestantism had been postmillennial, a confident belief that reforms and the progress of Christianity would make the world better and better until the millennium was achieved, at the end of which Christ would return to earth. After the Civil War the holiness movement, along with many other evangelicals, began to move toward a pre-millennial view. Premillennialists taught that the world, in accordance with prophecy, would grow worse, degenerating into unprecedented wickedness; at the climax Christ would return, change the earth, and establish his thousand-year reign of peace and righteousness. It was essentially a pessimistic view, one that was skeptical of the possibility of universal reform and improvement.[24]

Leading revival Friends, most notably Updegraff, Clark, and Woodard, became committed premillennialists during the 1870s. Unlike many other premillennialists, who devoted enormous energies and ingenuity to calculat-ing the precise time of the Second Coming, holiness Friends kept their premillennialism on a rather simple level. They devoted most of their energies to attacking the postmillennial outlook that had dominated the society since Gurney's day. In the Bible, especially in Revelation, holiness Friends found proofs of the premillennial interpretation so conclusive that they could not tolerate any other view. Postmillennialism was the result of a loose and twisted reading. "Nothing beyond such a dangerous license as this," Updegraff wrote in 1878, "is needed to extinguish all reliance on the Bible as an inspired volume." Thus premillennialism became an indispens-able part of holiness teachings. By 1883 William Nicholson was writing that Christ's Second Coming had "a peculiar fascination for some of our preachers—no matter what they start out with they are apt to get on second adventism before they get through."[25]

Closely associated with Quaker premillennialism was an extremely pessimistic mindset. "The religious optimism of our day is as senseless as it is vicious, as wicked as it is foolish," Updegraff wrote. Holiness Friends saw decline everywhere. Infidelity, liberalism, and blasphemy were creeping into the pulpit. Heathenism was increasing infinitely faster than Christian-ity. Catholicism was growing in strength. Politics were corrupt. Vice, crime, and open immorality were everywhere.[26]

Premillennialism turned some holiness Friends against the historic Quak-er devotion to reform. The Society of Friends, Clark told London Yearly Meeting in 1879, was "not an association for the promotion of certain moral reforms." Instead of giving time to temperance agitation, he argued, Friends should devote all of their energies to conversion, which would remove the evil and thus resolve the problem. Updegraff took a position remarkably similar to that of the Wilburite Friends of the 1840s in condemning reform movements generally. By allowing the participation of deists, Unitarians, and Universalists, he argued, reform movements violated the scriptural injunction not to be yoked with unbelievers and thus were unfit for Christian participation.[27]

Nowhere is the impact of premillennialism on holiness Friends clearer than in their attitude toward the historic Quaker peace testimony. Holiness

Quakers stopped participating in movements for peace and international arbitration on the grounds that universal peace would come only after Christ returned to earth and that their time was better spent in revivals. Pacifism also posed a problem for holiness Friends in their relations with the larger holiness movement. Under traditional Quaker teaching, participation in war or fighting was a sin. Yet many non-Quaker holiness believers, whose sanctified state holiness Quakers could not doubt, had fought in the Civil War, were serving in the military, or advocated the use of force under certain circumstances. Faced thus with a choice between Quaker pacifism and attitudes about the war, on one hand, and loyalty to other holiness believers, on the other, many revival Friends chose the latter.[28]

The issue first surfaced in the *Christian Worker* in 1878. Updegraff, responding to an editorial, argued that there were situations in which war might be moral—it could be an execution of God's judgment, as in the Old Testament conflicts. In subsequent letters Updegraff elaborated his position. War, he said, would not stop until the millennium. Therefore, Friends would be well advised to give up the hopeless task of trying to educate people about the sinfulness of violence and to concentrate on winning souls. Holiness enthusiasts such as Luke Woodard echoed Updegraff's position, but they were a minority. This was one of the few occasions before 1880 when Updegraff overreached himself. His letters brought down a storm of protest. He permanently alienated Daniel Hill, the *Christian Worker's* editor, who publicly accused him of undermining Ohio Yearly Meeting's peace efforts. Numerous Friends wrote to the *Christian Worker* to brand Updegraff a "New War Advocate" and to argue that his letter showed that he had fallen from grace. Updegraff was forced to modify his position, saying that he personally thought all acts of violence, defensive or otherwise, sinful. But he never repudiated his statements that the sanctified could fight and that Friends should give up peace agitation.[29]

Many holiness Friends followed Updegraff's teachings in a less obvious way. Some holiness revivalists paid lip service to the peace tradition and a few were fully committed to it; most of the yearly meetings continued to issue addresses on arbitration and capital punishment. Yet the conclusion is inescapable: the stronger the revival impulse, the weaker the commitment to pacifism. The move away from pacifism may have been the result of holiness theology. John Henry Douglas, for example, had been the executive secretary of the Peace Association of Friends in America in the 1860s. After his sanctification he gave no attention to the subject. Pragmatism may also have been behind the deemphasis of pacifism. In 1893 one Friend complained that evangelists refused to mention pacifism in their meetings because they feared alienating potential converts who had served in the Union army. By the 1880s complaints about apathy and disinterest in the cause of peace were the rule rather than the exception in yearly meeting minutes.[30]

One tradition that many of the revivalists carried over from the Quaker past was heresy hunting. The revivalists proved the adage that sometimes extremes will meet. They shared with the Conservative Friends a sense that they were surrounded by infidelity, worldliness, and constant attacks on true religion.

The focus of holiness fears during the 1880s was gradually changing. The revivalists were as adamant in their opposition to infidelity and (in revival eyes) its Unitarian and Universalist offshoots as was the most fervent Hicksite hunter of the 1820s. During the 1880s, however, holiness Friends shifted their fears away from the older forms of liberal religion and concentrated on the emerging "higher criticism"—the application of techniques of scientific and literary analysis to the Bible. In the United States there were almost no trained biblical scholars among Orthodox Friends, but there were a few in England, and these, along with the pioneers of modernism in other denominations, were enough to precipitate holiness fears. Updegraff used the columns of his new journal, the *Friends' Expositor*, to score higher criticism unmercifully. Christianity was endangered, he wrote, by the "fearless attacks of unsoundness in high places. . . . It seems sometimes that if a man can get 'Prof.' or L.L.D. or D.D., or get to sit in a 'chair,' people will just gulp down anything that he offers, and think it good, no matter how tainted." Calvin W. Pritchard, editor of the *Christian Worker*, agreed. "Infidelity is working inroads," he told Allen Jay in 1886, and it had to be opposed at every turn.[31]

While holiness Friends shared the fears of other evangelicals about modern biblical scholarship, they also showed more receptivity than might be expected to the theory of evolution. A few firebrands such as Asahel H. Hussey labeled the theory the Antichrist's forerunner, but they were a minority. The prevailing attitude was negatively cautious. In 1886 Iowa Yearly Meeting, second only to Ohio in its commitment to holiness and revivalism, confronted the question of whether an evolutionist could be recorded a minister. The yearly meeting took no action, effectively refusing to disqualify ministerial candidates for such views. The *Christian Worker* commended the decision, concluding that not enough was known about the various interpretations of evolution and their implications to make any binding pronouncement.[32]

Despite their gloom about the larger world, holiness Friends were in a stronger position within the society than were their counterparts in other denominations. In the 1880s the Methodist church was on the verge of officially condemning second-experience sanctification, while Baptists and Presbyterians were beginning to take action against holiness enthusiasts in their own ranks. In contrast, holiness Friends were entrenched in positions of power. By 1885 they controlled Ohio and Iowa yearly meetings, were very close to control of Kansas and Western, and had strong wings in Indiana, New York, and North Carolina. The *Christian Worker* declared that five-sixths of all Gurneyite Quaker ministers accepted holiness teachings. There can be no question that virtually all of the leading revivalists were among them.[33]

Despite their apparent strength, revival Friends showed considerable uneasiness over any kind of opposition. They attacked the Conservative Friends unmercifully, accusing them of being blind to religious truth, hardhearted, unsound, and of being allied not only with the Hicksites but with Satan as well. Conservatives, in Updegraff's words, were "fossil remains" living in a "valley of shadows." All of that vituperation was directed at a handful of Friends who posed no threat to the revival after 1880. More powerful, and in revival eyes infinitely more dangerous, were the moderates. They, Dougan Clark, Jr., wrote, accepted holiness as a vague concept but were "practically and uncompromisingly" opposed to it. In holiness eyes, their position was tantamount to that of the Wilburites; they wanted only the "kind of holiness . . . that somebody had two hundred years ago." Their opposition was all the more dangerous because it was subtle. Moderate opponents were everywhere, Clark warned: they were "leaders of the people in nearly all the Yearly Meetings—ministers, elders, influential men, and writers for the periodicals."[34]

Holiness Friends had other reasons to worry. The overwhelming majority of the rank-and-file membership had accepted the loosening of restraints that the holiness movement had brought, but this did not mean that they accepted the experience itself. In the yearly meetings that kept such statistics, the number of sanctifications reported was invariably a fraction of the number professing conversion. Even the constant succession of revivals could not prevent tendencies toward apathy and indifference. In 1884 Kansas Yearly Meeting collected some unusual statistics. After seven years of revivals, about half of the members attended meeting any given First Day; 10 percent or less of the membership frequently spoke in meeting or could be considered as "active" in church work. Further evidence of resistance to revival teachings can be found in the statistics on family worship that other yearly meetings collected. Despite constant admonitions, less than half of all member families held daily devotions in the 1880s. Evidence of apathy, or perhaps of social change, can also be found in the decline of midweek meetings, traditionally held on Wednesday or Thursday mornings. By the 1880s attendance was so small that many meetings had abolished them entirely (in Kansas seven-eighths of the membership regularly stayed away) or had changed to Wednesday night prayer meetings, adopting the practice of other evangelical churches.[35]

Revival Friends were thus a people of paradox. They maintained, with considerable justification, that the innovations they had introduced in the 1870s—revivals, singing, and protracted meetings; the heightened prestige of the ministry; and nondenominational holiness evangelism—had become institutions in the Society of Friends. Holiness ranks were constantly strengthened by new ministers from both within and outside the society. Holiness Friends published journals with the largest circulation among Friends, controlled several yearly meetings, and professed to be part of the most important interdenominational movement in Christendom. Yet holiness Friends were a troubled people. Their view of human society and its potential was darkened by the premillennialism they took from outside the society. They saw infidelity rearing its head in new and varied forms. They saw holiness under constant attack both within and outside the society. They saw spiritual complacency even among the professedly revived. They had accomplished much, but they saw themselves locked in a never-ending battle.

THE MIDDLE PARTY

Between the Conservative Friends and the great mass of revived Quakers led by the revival preachers stood a self-conscious group of moderately evangelical Friends. They had emerged during the 1870s as a compromise group in the Gurneyite yearly meetings, steering a course between the unbending conservatism of the Wilburites and the radicalism of the revivalists. The middle party was a continuation of the renewal movement. It found its voice in the *Friends' Review*. The only yearly meeting completely under its control was Baltimore, but moderates held positions of power in North Carolina, Indiana, New York, and New England yearly meetings, and were fighting brave but losing battles in Western and Kansas yearly meetings. Many of the middle party's leaders had been active in Quaker affairs since the 1850s. Some, such as Allen Jay, Thomas Kimber, and Charles F. Coffin, had initially been active in the revival but had come to have reservations about it. Others, such as Joel Bean and the Baltimore leadership, had been skeptical since the beginning. The differences among the moderates continued into the 1880s. Bean, for example, was openly at odds with the revivalists. Others, such as Coffin and Kimber, still hoped that the revival could be brought back into "sound channels." Still others, such as Timothy and William Nicholson and Henry Hartshorne of the *Friends' Review*, privately found the new direction of Quakerism appalling but suppressed their opinions for the sake of unity.[36]

The moderate group received new strength from younger Friends during the 1880s. James Wood in New York and Allen and Richard H. Thomas in

Baltimore were the latest generation of their families to assume leadership in their yearly meetings. John B. Garrett and David Scull in Philadelphia were products of the Gurneyite Twelfth Street Meeting and Haverford College. A number of the younger moderate leaders were associated with Quaker schools: Lewis L. Hobbs and his wife Mary (Nereus Mendenhall's daughter) at Guilford in North Carolina; Thomas Newlin, who from 1885 to 1915 taught in almost every Quaker college; Isaac Sharpless, who became president of Haverford in 1888; and Joseph J. Mills, president of Earlham for most of the last quarter of the century. Symptomatic of the direction the middle party took is William L. Pearson, who began teaching at Penn College in Iowa in the 1880s. Pearson was probably the first American Friend to take a divinity degree (at Princeton Theological Seminary in 1877). Encouraged by important Friends, Pearson spent several years in graduate study in Berlin and Leipzig, receiving a Ph.D. in ancient languages from the University of Leipzig in 1885. His articles on biblical interpretation in the *Friends' Review* had a scholarly erudition that holiness preachers could not hope to approach.[37]

The moderate Friends were not so visible as a group as were holiness and Conservative Friends, perhaps because they professed to abhor all factionalism. Nevertheless, they were a conscious group, bound together by a common view of Quakerism. They were consciously in the middle— between, in Hartshorne's words, the "dear old Friends laboring with their wagons in *deep ruts;* and . . . young men, moving . . . at a speed which is attractive, but less safe for them and their neighbors." They were for "true conservatism" and "secure progress." Moderation, they agreed, was usually not a popular course, but it was the only safe one. For the middle party, moderation was so inseparable from true Quakerism that they were much more likely to describe themselves as "loyal Friends" or "sound Quakers" than as moderates.[38]

The other distinguishing feature of the middle party was its elitism. Save for Baltimore, it is impossible to find any yearly meeting in which the moderate party embraced large numbers of members. It had no single leader because it was a party made up of leaders. Moderates were always aware of their lack of numbers. William Nicholson, complaining of the instability and lack of judgment of the membership, often gives the impression that he was fighting singlehandedly to hold off a complete revival victory in Kansas. Joel Bean betrayed a certain spiritual arrogance when he wrote of the revival's adherents in Iowa as "rabble." The urgings of the *Friends' Review* that spirituality was not to be measured in numbers reflect the worries of a conscious minority.[39]

When forced to make a choice between the Conservatives and the revived, most of the moderates probably preferred the Conservatives. A few, such as Bean, openly sympathized with the separatists. Others, such as

Barnabas C. Hobbs and Coffin, understood their complaints but thought them wrong to abandon the society rather than trying to work out the problems of the revival. Nevertheless, moderates never ceased to regard Conservatives as Friends. (Ironically, by the early 1890s the moderate organ, the *Friends' Review*, originally the chief critic of Philadelphia Yearly Meeting, was hailing the yearly meeting as a "centre of gravity.")[40] They were far more concerned about the growing power of the revival. In the late 1870s and 1880s they left the Conservatives to hold to the old ways and devoted all of their resources to struggling with holiness Friends for control of the society. The history of Quakerism for the rest of the century is largely a history of that struggle. Thus an understanding of the moderate critique of the revival is vital.

Moderate Friends shared certain attitudes and beliefs with the revivalists. The most important was a firm commitment to evangelical doctrines of the Gurneyite variety: insistence on acceptance of the blood Atonement, the necessity of a conversion experience, and the inspiration of the Bible. Open infidelity horrified them just as much as it did the revivalists. In 1882, for example, the *Friends' Review* urged a constitutional amendment making atheism a disqualification for political office. Most moderate Friends were equally hostile to Universalism and Unitarianism, and they shared the fears of holiness Friends about the consequences of "destructive criticism" of the Bible.[41]

An excellent example of how holiness and moderate Friends could cooperate is found in the Quaker missionary movement. Between 1875 and 1895 each of the Gurneyite yearly meetings selected for itself a foreign "field," set up mission stations and schools overseas, and dispatched ministers and other workers to staff them and to seek to "rescue" the heathen. Tiny in comparison with those of larger denominations, they were supported bravely by the yearly meetings. The copying of the methods of other denominations is striking: home support was largely the duty of the Woman's Foreign Missionary Union, which published the *Friends' Missionary Advocate* to keep enthusiasm for the cause alive. The missionaries themselves, particularly before 1900, tended to be holiness stalwarts, as were Elkanah and Irena Beard in India, Samuel A. Purdie in Mexico, and Esther Butler in China.[42] Nevertheless, they had the enthusiastic support of the moderates.

In all of their stands, however, moderate Friends tended to be more tolerant and less vehement than revived Friends. Their thinking on conversion offers a good example. Many Friends, the moderates said, were undoubtedly converted without being able to name the specific time or place; that such was the case was perfectly acceptable. "They are saved," Barnabas C. Hobbs told an Earlham audience in 1880. "We may cross the line which separates two states. We may or may not know when, and yet be assured that the line has been passed." At Indiana Yearly Meeting two years later,

Hobbs said that he felt his own conversion experience had been spread over most of his life and was still going on. Elizabeth L. Comstock thought revived Friends flippant and fulsome "in telling the day, hour, and place of conversion. . . . To me it seems awful such experiences are lightly told, as it usually is by those whose daily walk by no means confirms their words."[43]

Moderate Friends took an equally broad view of the Bible. They did not question its authority or inspiration, but they had little use for biblical literalism. "If you take the utterances of this book literally," Israel P. Hole, Updegraff's *bête noire* in Ohio Yearly Meeting, said in 1887, "you will find it full of contradictions, unworthy of confidence, and much of it impossible of belief." The idea of biblical infallibility, William Nicholson wrote in 1883, was contrary to the genius of Quakerism, which was the immediate guidance of the Holy Spirit. To many moderate Friends the scriptural "idolatry" of the revivalists threatened the centrality of Christ in Quakerism. "In proportion as we take up a more literal view of the Bible," Richard H. Thomas wrote, "we lose our position and our testimony." Christianity rested on experiencing Christ, not on a written revelation of him. Moderates warned against calling the Bible "The Word of God," since that title, they felt, belonged to Christ. "Let us never say that He became a book," one wrote.[44]

The attitude of the moderates toward biblical scholarship was in keeping with their attitude toward the Bible. While some of the moderates were critical of the trend to apply scientific and literary analysis and techniques of textual criticism to the Bible, most did not see anything innately harmful in the emerging higher criticism. They were usually much more critical of what they saw as the crude and uninformed attempts of some revival Friends to undertake complicated problems of exegesis with only slight knowledge of Greek and none of Hebrew. Such efforts invariably led to doctrinal "hobbies," William L. Pearson told readers of the *Friends' Review*. The implication was clear: knotty problems of doctrine and interpretation were better left to the learned.[45]

Nowhere is the break between the moderates and their opponents on either wing of Orthodox Quakerism more apparent than in attitudes toward the theory of evolution. The theory horrified Conservatives, and it held little attraction for holiness Friends, but moderates embraced it. The *Friends' Review*, which as early as 1865 had dismissed those credulous enough to think the world only six thousand years old, tried to preserve an air of calm, scientific objectivity. It opened its columns to both advocates and critics of Charles Darwin, but in its editorials it embraced theistic evolution—the idea that evolution through natural selection was the process chosen by God for creation—a theory that had great appeal for many Protestants in the 1870s. Friends, the *Friends' Review* maintained, had to accept that nearly all men of science were evolutionists. The real question was whether the interpretation of the theory of evolution had to be atheistic. To Hartshorne and the editorial writers for the *Friends' Review*, the answer clearly was no. Such moderate educators as Joseph Moore freely taught the theory of evolution to students at Earlham and Guilford with relatively little criticism.[46]

Thus while moderate Friends were relatively confident about the problems facing American Protestantism, they also saw forces at work that caused them to fear for the future of the society. They were inward forces. Attempting to continue the program that renewal Friends had laid out in the 1860s, the moderates saw much of what they thought essential to the growth and health of Quakerism threatened by the holiness revival.

The starting point for moderate Friends was opposition to the doctrine of immediate, second-experience sanctification. Moderates were vocal in their devotion to the cause of "true" holiness. "Let it ever be remembered," the *Friends' Review* editorialized in 1883, "that the standard of the Society of Friends was in the beginning and is now holiness."[47] But moderates saw a teaching they could not accept in the modern holiness movement. Early in the 1870s most of the criticism of immediate sanctification came from Conservative Friends. By 1880, as if it had taken them a decade to realize the implications of the doctrine, moderates had begun a searching critique of holiness teachings.

Moderates looked back to the older Quaker belief that sanctification was gradual. They dismissed instantaneous freedom from sin. "It is a *theory reasoned out*," Hartshorne told Luke Woodard in 1886, "misusing for the purpose passages in the Scriptures which the great majority of readers have never thought of in such a sense." Moderates were equally opposed to making holiness a "distinct separate experience." In their minds such a teaching denigrated the conversion experience, and in so doing it approached blasphemy. Could anyone, an opponent asked, really say that "the new creation, created in Jesus Christ, begotten of God, born of the spirit, is . . . in degree, morally leprous?" Justification and sanctification, they said, were inseparable. Like the older Friends, they were fond of the text that without holiness no one could see God. And their view of how holiness was achieved was similar to that of Friends earlier in the century. William Nicholson, in an influential pamphlet published in 1884, summed up the moderate view. Sanctification, he wrote, was a long process that began with conversion. Believers gradually moved toward complete holiness, struggling against the sinful inclination inherent in themselves until, as Nicholson put it, "we constantly and steadfastly overcome it, by prayer and faith and grace." Moderates did not continue the emphasis of Friends on eroding the base self through tribulation, but they did emphasize the baptism of the Holy Ghost. They saw that baptism, not as the sort of pentecostal experience so dear to holiness Friends, but as an event repeated again and again in "seasons of solemnizing power." As Richard H. Thomas put it: "The work is not completed at once; but our Lord does not stand off from us. . . .

On the contrary, as we submit to Him we are . . . in an ever increasing likeness to his character."[48]

What moderate Friends found most objectionable in holiness teachings was their tendency to crowd out almost everything else. The revivalists made sanctification a "hobby." Even worse, those who made the loudest profession of sanctification did not "make it manifest to those who, with longing hearts, pray every day and night that they *may* see it." Moderate Friends saw instead the antithesis of perfect peace and love in the works of holiness enthusiasts. "One of the saddest parts of this erroneous teaching is the fearful havoc, resulting in spiritual deadness," Timothy Nicholson wrote in 1881. "It engenders strife, distraction, and disreputable maneuvering . . . the dire effects of which it will require years to remove." The opponents of the revival reeled off scores of examples of how holiness practice did not live up to the profession of sanctification. In California a revivalist damned all who dared disagree with him. Revivalists in Indiana tried to set themselves up as virtual bishops. In Iowa what had once been the largest quarterly meeting in the state found itself losing hundreds of members, laying down a meeting, being split by bitter factionalism, and finally becoming involved in a separation after a few visits from Updegraff. No wonder that there one saw "a most dangerous heresy, a fearful delusion, wrapped up in this modern sanctification doctrine." Explaining those unholy acts of the professedly sanctified was not difficult for the moderates: the proponents of "instantaneous eradicationism" were at a false rest. Thinking themselves perfect on the basis of one experience, they became arrogant, refusing to submit to guidance or to close examination of their motives and actions.[49]

As if holiness teachings were not bad enough, moderates found additional cause for worry in the ideological baggage that holiness Friends brought with them, ideas "not only erroneous but especially dangerous." William Nicholson summarized the teachings presented at Kansas Yearly Meeting in 1881. One could be saved and yet engage in a variety of sinful behavior—the eradication of the bases of sin had to await the second experience. There was no need for the sanctified to wait in silence for the guidance of the Holy Spirit, "for they always had him with them." They had no need to ask forgiveness of their sins, "for they were always under the blood." And any mention of the necessity of a Christian life or good works was followed by a denunciation of all works. In brief, holiness teachings had the potential to undermine the whole basis of Quakerism.[50]

Despite their almost unanimous opposition to instantaneous sanctification, moderate Friends differed over the correct course regarding the revival. Virtually all of them had welcomed new signs of life during the early 1870s, but as "wildfire" became the rule, they became doubtful. How open and strident their opposition to the revival was to be became a subject of disagreement in the 1880s.

There were a few moderate Friends who, although they would not separate, openly opposed the revival. Of these the most prominent was Joel Bean. Born in New Hampshire in 1825, Bean was educated at Providence, where he became the close friend of Dougan Clark, Jr., and Timothy Nicholson. In 1853 Bean moved to Cedar County, Iowa. Recorded a minister while young, in 1859 he married Hannah E. Shipley, the daughter of a prominent Philadelphia Quaker family. Together the Beans played a prominent role in the renewal movement. In 1861 they became the first Friends to visit Hawaii as missionaries; simultaneously they became leaders in Quaker Sabbath school work. In 1867 Joel Bean was chosen clerk of Iowa Yearly Meeting.[51]

Joel Bean responded enthusiastically to the early revival manifestations of the 1870s. "We hear of 'many voices,' of 'creaturely activity,' of 'strange fire within our borders,'" Bean wrote to the *Friends' Review* in 1870. "But beneath all the surface-heaving, there is, my soul believes, the stirring, in healthful motion, of a deeper wave. The Lord has a genuine work." Bean missed the most critical year of the revival, 1872, by traveling in Europe. When he returned he began to have doubts about what he was seeing. He especially disliked holiness teachings, but when Iowa Yearly Meeting divided in 1877, Bean, still the clerk, remained with the revived portion.[52]

The turning point for the Beans came early in 1880. Hitherto Bean's home community of West Branch had escaped the revival. It did, however, contain a faction of holiness sympathizers, led by Lawrie Tatum and several members of the family of future president Herbert Hoover. They invited Updegraff to hold a series of meetings in West Branch. Updegraff stayed three weeks, later boasting that in this short time he had revolutionized the teachings of thirty years. The entire quarterly meeting split irreconcilably into two factions, destroying the unity and harmony that Bean had prized so highly.[53]

Early in 1881, after considerable soul searching, Bean published a manifesto titled "The Issue" in the Glasgow-based *British Friend*, which had long cast a skeptical eye on American Quaker "enthusiasm." "The Issue" was a devastating critique of the revival. Bean opened it with praise and thankfulness for the new life that Friends had manifested since 1850, then showed how the holiness movement had turned the new currents into unhealthy channels. Instead of judging the revival by the number of converts it claimed, Bean used different criteria: the answers to the queries, attendance at midweek and business meetings, attachment to the society, knowledge of Quaker doctrines and history, and evidence of humility and reverence. By all of those standards, according to Bean, the revival was clearly retrogressive. "Disorganization and disintegration are confessedly making rapid progress," he concluded, "and most rapid where protest is silenced and conservatism is inert."[54]

Moderate and Conservative Friends alike acclaimed "The Issue." Cyrus
W. Harvey quickly reprinted it in the *Western Friend*, and New York
Friends circulated it as a pamphlet, as did John Greenleaf Whittier and
Joseph Cartland in New England. "The Issue" also enraged the revival party
and made Bean a marked man in Iowa Yearly Meeting, which by 1881 was
under the control of holiness forces.[55]

Most moderate Friends did not go as far as Bean in their criticism. The
Friends' Review set their public stance. Moderates were willing to accept
the use of revival methods that seemed to deepen the religious life of many.
But there were limits. While such methods had their place, they were not
appropriate in all situations. Often they produced an unhealthy degree of
emotionalism. And many of the converts that they produced were not truly
converted, the *Friends' Review* concluded, soon falling away from all
religious life.[56]

Privately many of the moderate Friends were even more critical. Hartshorne, the editor of the *Friends' Review*, was typical. A revival, he said, was
needed to counteract "the stagnation and formal traditionalism with which I
have been familiar," but, he continued, "in breaking loose from the bondage
of this, the reaction has in many places gone too far." Others were equally
critical of the revival but had more confidence. Timothy Harrison, a prominent Friend in Richmond, Indiana, who had himself experienced the revival's appeal, compared it to a cyclone: it soon passed, but it wrought great
destruction. Similarly, Harrison's neighbor, Timothy Nicholson, was appalled by the "sensational and dogmatic preaching" of the revivalists but
thought that the rising generation of Friends was too intelligent to be taken
in by it.[57]

Other moderate Friends shared the view that all that was necessary was to
thresh out the chaff in the revival and benefit from what was good. In
London Yearly Meeting in 1878, Barnabas C. Hobbs acknowledged that
there was an upheaval in America and that there was much in it that was
wrong, much that had not lived up to its early promise. But, Hobbs concluded, "we know that there is something there which the Lord has sent," so
that Hobbs and like-minded Friends waited with "patience and forbearance"
to guide the new enthusiasm into safer channels. In a long exchange with
Cyrus W. Harvey, Charles F. Coffin struck a similar note: "Many of us see
defects in the church at present, but feel that inside is the proper place to
labor for their remedy." There were excesses and "imprudencies," but he
was convinced that they could ultimately be turned to good.[58]

The testimony of the moderate Friends was not wholly negative. They
continued a vision of Quakerism that had at its heart Friends as a separate
and distinct people. They would accept the essential truths held by other
evangelicals, but they would, in addition, set forth higher views of Christian

worship and practice. They would cooperate in any good work with all orthodox believers, but *"still as Friends."*⁵⁹

In their efforts to maintain the "higher views" of Friends, the moderates contended for some ultimately hopeless causes during the 1880s. Among them was silent worship. Moderates did not argue that silence was always good in itself but asserted instead that it was necessary to prepare for true worship. "We believe great advantage results from intervals of silence in our meetings for worship," William Nicholson wrote in 1884. "Indeed, if we do not cultivate and earnestly seek after a reverential, worshiping frame of mind, vocal exercises may *entertain* rather than profit us." Here was the fear of many moderates: there was so much *din* in Quaker worship that the rising generation of Friends would not know how to seek true silence.⁶⁰

The ideal of silent waiting also shaped moderate attitudes toward music. Moderates did not want to exclude it entirely. Joel Bean, for example, condemned a Friend who resigned from his meeting because "thrice in 2½ years one dear member has sung a verse or two." Moderates accepted music when sung "in the spirit." If a member or a group of members felt moved to sing, that was worship. It was not acceptable to preset the hymns or to appoint a chorister to lead them, or to have an organ or any other musical instrument at hand for accompaniment. All of those detracted from the leadings of the spirit.⁶¹

A critical difference between revival and moderate Friends lay in their views of the millennium. Moderates united in opposition to premillennialism as based on a distorted reading of history. William Nicholson complained in 1883 that some revival ministers seemed to see signs of the Second Coming in everything: "Sunspots and perhaps comets and wars and rumors of wars and distress of nations are all pressed into service to prove that His coming is very near—although in the whole history of the world, there have been few periods with so little war and distress." Daniel Hill broke with the holiness group for the same reason. Looking at the world in 1880, he saw evil in abundance, but he also believed that because of the whole apparatus of evangelicalism—ministers, revivals, evangelists, missionaries, Sabbath schools, hospitals, orphanages, and Bible, tract, and peace societies—evil was on the decline. The *Friends' Review* agreed, commenting that only a handful of leading Christian thinkers accepted premillennial teachings. Trying to decide why premillennialism attracted so many Friends, Barnabas C. Hobbs concluded that holiness Quakers were thoughtless fanatics, and "second Adventism" had always been a favorite resort of fanaticism.⁶²

The postmillennial hope inspired moderate Friends to continue the reform tradition. The revivalists were interested in work among the Indians and blacks and in promoting temperance, but they saw those as works of evangelism, of spreading the Gospel and bringing individuals out of individual sins. Although moderate Friends did not condemn such motives, they worked in those causes and in many others in which the revivalists showed little interest—fighting lynching in the South, improving conditions in prisons and asylums, promoting peace and arbitration—as part of a vision that was consciously postmillennial. Summarizing the various reform concerns of Friends at the end of the century, Richard H. Thomas concluded that "they are only different sides of one reform—the establishment of the Kingdom of God on earth."[63]

Orthodox Friends thus faced the last quarter of the nineteenth century a badly divided people. The revivalism of the 1870s had fractured them into three antagonistic factions. At one extreme, the Conservative Friends tried to hold fast to the old ways in self-imposed isolation. Here they succeeded, but at the cost of declining membership and increasing irrelevance to Quakers outside their bounds. At the other extreme, the holiness Friends tried to keep up the revival fervor of the 1870s. Closely tied to the interdenominational holiness movement, they followed it into faith healing, premillennialism, and increasing dogmatism. Between the two were the moderates, a self-conscious middle party trying to hold to the best of the old ways while adapting the society to changing conditions. Although relatively few in number, moderate Friends held positions of power and influence in the society. Because they saw the revival as more of a threat than was Conservatism, they devoted most of their resources to battling holiness Friends for control of the society. Moderate and holiness Friends split in part over issues that were agitating the larger religious world—premillennialism, evolution, higher criticism—but more often over questions unique to Quakerism—the nature of worship, conversion, and sanctification. The gaps separating these bodies of Friends were wide by 1880. What came in the next decade would make them even wider.

CHAPTER
VI

THE QUAKER SEARCH
FOR ORDER, 1875–1895

"The Religious Society of Friends has ceased to exist; and the Friends Church is inevitably moving in the direction of Methodism."[1] With those words a distraught Friend in 1892 summed up the preceding quarter-century of American Quaker history. It was a drastic judgment, but one that had a certain validity and that was shared by a sizable number of American Friends. During the years since the Civil War, the majority of American Friends had moved away from almost everything that had once distinguished them from other denominations. The old standards were gone; new ones had yet to emerge. And the search for new certainties was proving both painful and divisive, with many Quakers fearful about the outcome.

During the 1880s and early 1890s American Quakers were in the final stages of adjusting the society's traditions to the evangelical and holiness teachings that they had embraced. It says much for the power of the broad American evangelical culture and for the appeal of the holiness movement that within forty years they could work such a dramatic transformation. Friends were not the only religious "out" group in the United States to undergo such change. Some, such as Roman Catholics, managed to adapt revivalism to traditional church teachings. Other sects, such as Mennonites and the German Baptist Brethren, split just as Friends did. Friends grappled with many of the same problems that other Protestants faced in this era: premillennialism, evolution, critical study of the Bible. Among Friends, however, those questions took second place to issues that grew out of the conflict between Quaker tradition on one side and the new teachings imported from the larger religious culture on the other. Between 1880 and 1895 Friends absorbed themselves in debates that had few parallels outside the society but that were vital to subsequent Quaker history: the existence of the Inner Light, the nature of Quaker ministry, and the spirituality of the ordinances. These struggles climaxed in the closest thing nineteenth-century Quakerism ever saw to a heresy trial, the fifteen-year ordeal of Joel Bean, a case that defies almost every generalization that has ever been made about heresy trials. American Friends, as so many other Americans during the 1880s and 1890s, were trying to bring order to their world. Their search only created new problems and divisions.[2]

THE INNER LIGHT

No other issue says as much about the impact of evangelicalism on Quakerism in the last quarter of the nineteenth century as the debate over the Inner Light. The tortured arguments both for and against the doctrine showed little understanding of what its meaning had been to the early Friends. The conclusions reached are indicative of how far Gurneyite Friends had moved since 1800.

When seventeenth-century Friends spoke of the "Inward Light," or "the light of Christ within," they often were imprecise in their language and conceptions. The most careful early Quaker writers, such as William Penn and Robert Barclay, distinguished between the light, which to them was Christ, guiding the believer, and a seed or germ of Christ that they believed to have been planted in all humans. From this seed and by the leadings of the light, men grew into new life. Thus Quaker teaching and tradition urged hearers to turn inward to the seed and the light's leadings. Gradually the difference between the two became less and less distinct. By the end of the eighteenth century, the seed and the light had become synonymous.[3]

The difficulties had become clear by the time of the Hicksite separation in the 1820s. Orthodox Friends united in rejecting Elias Hicks's virtual identification of the light with conscience, but there unity broke down, as the views of a few important early nineteenth-century Friends show. For Charles Osborn the Inner Light was "the light of Christ, as manifested in the heart." For Nathan Hunt it was "the still small voice" within. Samuel Bettle wrote of the "witness of God within"; William Williams, of "the inspoken words of the heart." It was Aaron White, a prominent elder in Indiana, who presaged the future. For him the Inner Light was "the Holy Spirit walking and moving on the mind in a miraculous manner."[4]

Partly for those reasons, partly because of the increasing emphasis given to evangelical doctrines, the concept of the Inner Light was declining in importance among Friends by 1860. Renewal Friends occasionally alluded to it, and when they wrote about the essential doctrines of Quakers, they always included it. At times they harked back to the original understanding, but more often they cast it in terms not offensive to other evangelicals. The

Inner Light was Christ in his role of "The Light of the World," or the Holy Spirit in the role of the reprover for sin, or the inward working of God on the soul.[5]

The revival brought the issue to the fore. As early as 1872 an anonymous writer in the *Friends' Review* expressed a fear that the emphasis on conversion then prevalent would lead toward denying the influence of the Holy Spirit on the unconverted. As the revivalists came increasingly to emphasize the utter depravity of humans because of Original Sin, they found it impossible to perceive anything that was "of God" in the unsaved.[6]

The revivalists' discussion of total depravity and Original Sin was not especially original or sophisticated, but it was prominent and omnipresent. A few quotations from leading revival Friends give a sense of their position:

Luke Woodard: Mankind was "a race of beings, all of whom are misadjusted in their moral nature, dead in trespasses and sins; unable to develop anything further of themselves but deeper ruin and corruption."

David Hunt: The "depraved and fallen state of man" was such that he could only be "perverse, deceitful, and desperately wicked."

Dougan Clark, Jr:" "In our fallen condition—all our faculties and powers are crippled by sin, our bodies subject to disease and death, our minds intimately associated with them, and partaking of their infirmity. . . . Our senses, the avenue through which information reaches us from the eternal world, may deceive us."[7]

With such a vision, it was impossible to see any light in an unregenerated soul.

Thus the concept of total depravity led revival Friends to repudiate that of the Inner Light explicitly and entirely. They could find nothing in the Bible to indicate that there was any "seed, light, principle, or Spirit" of Christ in the unregenerate. The Holy Spirit dwelt only in believers after sanctification and appeared to sinners only to reprove them.[8]

The issue reached a head in Ohio Yearly Meeting in 1878. Ohio, under the firm control of David B. Updegraff, surpassed all other yearly meetings in its commitment to holiness doctrines. That year, seeking to clear itself of "all unsoundness," the yearly meeting issued a minute on the "inner light." There was, it told its membership, no "principle or quality in the soul of man, innate or otherwise," that could in any way "save a single soul." Souls were saved through preaching that urged repentance and salvation through faith in the shed blood of Jesus Christ. Thus the yearly meeting "repudiated the so-called doctrine of the inner light, or the gift of a portion of the Holy Spirit in the soul of every man, as dangerous, unsound, and unscriptural."[9]

No other yearly meeting was quite so explicit as Ohio in repudiating the doctrine of the Inner Light, but holiness Friends everywhere applauded the Ohio action. Joel Bean brought down a storm of protest when he criticized it during Iowa Yearly Meeting in 1881. Mary H. Rogers said that the Inner Light was a Hicksite doctrine, and Noah McLean and Updegraff agreed that it was a source of infidelity. Its place in the thought of the early Friends was, in Updegraff's words, a "matter of unprofitable discussion."[10]

The reaction of moderate and Conservative Friends to the revival attack is instructive. Conservative Friends found it horrifying but not surprising. Philadelphia Yearly Meeting, while refusing to take official notice of the Ohio action, since it came from a group it had always considered schismatic and unsound, nonetheless made it clear that the light was in all. Cyrus W. Harvey rushed the *Western Friend* to the attack. Harvey branded the Ohio action "The Confession of Non-Belief." In his judgment, it was now abundantly clear that the yearly meeting was "given up to . . . apostasy." "In the language of Jude," Harvey editorialized, "they 'run greedily after error' and glory in 'foaming out their own shame.' "[11]

Moderate Friends reacted more uncertainly. The Ohio statement brought little response from them. A few moderates—for example, Joel Bean— continued to preach the doctrine of Inner Light. The *Friends' Review* upheld it in editorials. Barnabas C. Hobbs lectured on it. Privately, William Nicholson considered the Inner Light "the foundation of all religious experience." But even these Friends were hobbled by confusion over whether they were defending "the Light of Christ in the heart" or "the indwelling of the Holy Spirit." A comparison of the energies that moderate Friends gave to the Inner Light debate with those they devoted to other controversies leads inexorably to the conclusion that the hearts of many simply were not in it. Moderates were too firmly enmeshed in evangelicalism to fight a sustained battle for a concept that was so hard to reconcile with evangelical doctrines.[12]

THE PASTORAL DEBATE

Perhaps no innovation of the last quarter of the nineteenth century did more to change Quakerism than the introduction of the pastoral ministry. For two hundred years Friends had steadfastly resisted the establishment of a clerical class. Between 1880 and 1900, however, most Friends moved away from the early forms of Quaker worship toward concepts and methods that were not much different from those of other Protestants. Once again, assumptions taken from the larger evangelical culture, in this case the centrality of preaching, triumphed over Quaker tradition.

The pastoral debate began with the huge influx of converts from the revivals of the 1870s and 1880s. From 1881 through 1889, for example, Indiana Yearly Meeting had over nine thousand applications for membership (and this in an organization with only eighteen thousand members). The yearly meeting expanded into areas in northern Indiana and Ohio in which Friends had never lived. In Van Wert County, Ohio, where in 1875 not a single Friend had lived, there were by 1890 nearly one thousand members in seven different meetings. Even in old, established meetings half the members were not birthright Friends. Western Yearly Meeting reached into new areas in southern Indiana and Illinois. Iowa Yearly Meeting ranged as far south as Texas and Louisiana and as far west as the Pacific coast. In 1888 Charles Brady, a traveling English Friend, found many meetings in Iowa Yearly Meeting without a single birthright member.[13]

New members faced several problems. Those who joined older, established meetings often found themselves, even in meetings with several ministers, enduring long periods of unfamiliar silence. Such customs bewildered newcomers. In theory it was the duty of the entire meeting to help them to understand Quaker beliefs, but in practice what was everyone's business was no one's, and many of the converts drifted away. The situation was worse in the meetings made up almost entirely of new members, who could not believe that a minister would gather them in and then leave them to drift unguided.[14]

During the 1880s the proper means to deal with new members became a subject of intense debate. Some moderate Friends were skeptical about the large number of converts and urged caution in accepting them without testing the genuineness of their interest. A few Friends suggested some sort of probationary period. Most moderates, however, acquiesced in the new growth and agreed with the notion of forming in each monthly meeting pastoral committees of elders, overseers, ministers, and other concerned members to see to the spiritual welfare of new Friends. The idea proved popular in the Gurneyite yearly meetings; by 1885 all had endorsed the use of such committees. But revival Friends had come to their own solution, and on the pastoral question, as on so many others, they effectively outmaneuvered the moderates by introducing the one-person pastorate that the moderates dreaded.[15]

The revival's commitment to pastors was inextricably linked to its view of the ministry. The revival centered on preaching, impossible without ministers. Furthermore, ministers were a divinely appointed class, "the noblest of the race, called of God to teach and lead the rest of us." Luke Woodard was frank in undermining the older concept of the priesthood of all believers. "It is a dangerous abuse. . . . to carry it to the extent of nullifying that respect, honor, and authority which God himself has assigned to the office of Gospel ministry," Woodard wrote. "The very terms *pastor* and *shepherd* imply a position of leadership."[16]

The revivalists' vision of the nature of the ministry involved more than a vested authority, however; the true minister, in their eyes, was a person who had experienced a "call." That inevitably led Friends into the vexed and divisive issue of financial support of ministers. One of the most venerable of all Quaker beliefs was that ministers should support themselves in a secular trade. It was acceptable for ministers undertaking long journeys to receive some financial help; Elizabeth L. Comstock thought that some ministers traveled just for that reason. Nonetheless, the funds available were never, in revival eyes, sufficient.[17]

During the 1880s the revivalists carried those ideas to their logical conclusion: it verged on sin for those called to the ministry to continue in secular pursuits. "If a man or woman is really called to preach the Gospel," Esther Frame said in 1892, "God intends every energy and mind-power to be used in that direction." Updegraff, as usual, was even more vehement: "Such a calling, and such a work, demands the dedication of one's entire life and powers to spiritual work, and a complete separation from every secular pursuit." The ministry was no longer merely vocal service in meeting—it was an office.[18]

Finally, the revivalists continued the emphasis on preaching. During the 1870s the Gurneyite yearly meetings had implicitly accepted the revival assumptions about the necessity of preaching by collecting statistics on meetings without ministers and by urging ministers to consider moving to meetings that lacked them. For the revivalists that was not enough. "Every church must be provided with a living gospel ministry," Elwood C. Siler, one of the most active revivalists in Western Yearly Meeting, wrote. The inescapable fact was, he argued, that "a *regular teaching ministry* was necessary to the growth and development of the church, and that congregations could not thrive on silent prayer alone, and prophecy in the sense of a few words dropped by way of exhortation and encouragement."[19]

All of those beliefs melded with the revival's concern for converts. "Every analogy of nature teaches us that when life is produced it must be nourished," one evangelist wrote. The pastor would "look after the newly awakened," encourage them, pray with them, and "teach them the way of salvation more perfectly." The revivalists had endless tales of converts lost to other denominations or to religion entirely because of lack of proper pastoral care. All that was needed, they assured Friends, was a regular pastoral ministry.[20]

Many forces thus pushed Gurneyite Friends toward a pastoral ministry during the 1880s. Quakerism had come to focus on revivals, and revivals focused on ministers. In keeping with their importance, the revival ministers evolved a theory that, in unprecedented fashion, transformed the Quaker ministry into a clerical class. Combined with a genuine concern on the part of almost all Gurneyites for the welfare of new Friends, the revivalists had an opening to ensure that meetings would be conducted along their ideas of proper worship.

The first meetings to employ regular pastors were, for the most part, new ones organized as a result of revivals or older meetings that had received large numbers of new members from revivals. Several evangelists—Robert W. Douglas, Luke Woodard, and Nathan and Esther Frame—claimed to have been pastors before 1875, but their tenures were brief and unofficial. The first true pastorates were those of the Frames in Muncie, Indiana, and John Henry Douglas in Glen's Falls, New York, in 1878; Isom P. Wooton in Des Moines and Jacob Baker in Selma, Ohio, in 1880; and Dougan Clark, Jr., in Cleveland in 1882. Thereafter the number of pastoral meetings steadily increased.[21]

Iowa Yearly Meeting moved most aggressively to institutionalize and support the pastoral system. While Joel Bean and more traditionalist Friends remained active in the yearly meeting, they stymied any movement toward a paid ministry; but by 1883 Bean had stopped attending the yearly meeting, and the last-ditch Conservative Friends had separated, leaving the holiness party in firm control. In 1886, after considerable discussion, the yearly meeting adopted two minutes urging all meetings to "call" a pastor and authorizing the yearly meeting's pastoral committee to provide financial help when appropriate. The justification for the new measures freely employed the language and assumptions of the revival. "Wherever the regular ministration of the gospel has been wanting there has been weakness and decline or at least no growth and aggressive work," the committee drawing up the minutes reported. "Many meetings" suffered from this problem; "they longed for clear exponents of the truth to come and labor among them." They wanted pastors but were uncertain about the attitudes of other Friends and about their ability to provide the requisite financial support. The report also discussed the needs of new members, but it emphasized the pastorate as an "aid to the evangelization of the world." Iowa set a pattern for the other Gurneyite yearly meetings. By 1900 pastors had been accepted by every Gurneyite yearly meeting save Baltimore.[22]

The revivalists' triumph did not come without considerable struggle. The factional breakdown was familiar. A few ministers of holiness sympathies, such as Alexander M. Purdy in New York, found the pastoral system unacceptable. A few moderates, such as William Nicholson, were won over to it. For the most part, the opponents of the pastoral system were the same moderates who had for so long been skeptical about the revival: Henry Hartshorne and the group around the *Friends' Review;* the weighty Friends in Baltimore; Nereus Mendenhall in North Carolina; Thomas Kimber and James Wood in New York; Timothy Nicholson and Charles F. Coffin in

Indiana; Barnabas C. Hobbs in Western Yearly Meeting; and, of course, Joel Bean. Throughout the 1880s they fought a losing battle against the pastoral system.[23]

The antipastoral Friends' assumptions about the nature of worship and ministry differed radically from those of pastoral advocates. The latter assumed that ministers were the focal point of worship. Moderates summed up worship in another word: waiting. The essential, vital principle of Quakerism, Hartshorne wrote in 1892, was "a waiting worship and a waiting ministry," waiting for the leadership of Christ and the guidance of the Holy Spirit in everything.[24]

In the eyes of moderate Friends, the pastoral ministry threatened the traditional view in two fundamental ways. First, a programmed service seemed implicit in pastoral worship. The meeting would expect the pastor to preach, and that would take up most of the time. Singing and vocal prayer would fill remaining time. Moderates visiting pastoral meetings invariably found no silence or worshipful waiting. "The idea with the people is to have a good sermon," Richard H. Thomas of Baltimore noted sadly. It was obvious to Thomas that they no longer understood what a real Quaker meeting was.[25]

Closely related to misgivings about programmed worship was the fear that pastors would destroy the freedom of meetings for worship and institute a "one-man rule." Many ministers of undoubted talents were not called to pastoral labor; what were they to do? The reply of the pastoral Friends that they should be "sweet," stay quiet, and obey the pastor was of no comfort. In moderate eyes the pastoral movement was fraught with intellectual baggage carried over from Methodism that threatened and undervalued the offices of elder and overseer as well. What would happen, Thomas Kimber asked, if the pastor were carried away "by any of the modern dogmas or novelties of the hour?" All those under the leadership of the pastor would inevitably follow him into error. And from the look of the society during the 1880s and 1890s, that seemed all too likely. The pastoral system, James Carey Thomas of Baltimore wrote, would "eliminate the influence of an older period" and instead "entrust the main interests of the church to a rather inferior class of men."[26]

Most of all, however, the antipastoral Friends feared that ministers would become a "class with special privileges and authority." Pastoral Friends avoided such terms as "laity" and "clergy," but in the minds of opponents the drift was unmistakable. The moderate opponents of the pastoral system usually did not advance beyond this level of argument. A clerical class was so foreign to Quakerism that no elaboration seemed necessary. The whole idea of a Quaker clergy, the Friends' Review editorialized, was "radically unsuited to the Society of Friends, and will tend either to its rapid dissolution or its entire transformation."[27]

Once again the moderate Friends fought a losing battle, as the pastoral system became widespread throughout the Gurneyite yearly meetings. In some—Kansas and Western, for example—the pastoral forces simply overwhelmed the opposition. New York, New England, and North Carolina adopted what was in effect a policy of local autonomy, with some meetings calling pastors and others eschewing them. As late as 1889 Timothy Nicholson maintained that Indiana Yearly Meeting was overwhelmingly opposed to the innovation, but even in Indiana pastors became increasingly common.[28]

The pastoral system, while it did not destroy the society as the moderates feared it would, did not live up to the hopes of advocates. In 1887 Stephen Breed, a holiness minister who did extensive evangelistic work in southern Illinois, put his finger on the source of difficulty. Not one-fifth of all meetings, he said, could afford to support a pastor full time. Thus financial considerations would force several meetings to join together as a circuit, dividing the pastor's time and attention and defeating the whole purpose of the system. Breed's prediction was accurate. Although a circuit arrangement became the exception, many meetings gave pastors the choice between finding an outside source of income or starving. Iowa Yearly Meeting in 1889 paid its pastors an average of $130 per year. In Indiana $18 per month was considered generous. The papers of Allen Jay, who served as evangelistic and pastoral superintendent of Indiana Yearly Meeting during the system's early days, are filled with poignant pleas from ministers living in grinding poverty for money to buy a Bible or to pay medical bills, stories of near starvation and of being forced to send sons and daughters to work. "I have seen the time more than once in the last two years," one minister wrote, "that I have had to wait for the children to return with their day's wages to get food for supper."[29]

Fears about the quality of ministers also proved well founded. The first pastors were former evangelists, and it was natural for the most successful to gravitate toward the largest meetings. "Where the biggest money is our evangelists seem to have the most peculiar drawing," one skeptic observed. Many ministers, happily settled in secular occupations, had no desire to move, so that the demand for pastors often exceeded the supply, particularly in small meetings. As late as 1907, less than a third of the meetings in Indiana Yearly Meeting had full-time pastors. Old members of one small, rural meeting in Indiana remember how they felt compelled to have regular preaching but could pay almost nothing. Often they simply opened their pulpit to anyone willing to fill it, subjecting themselves to a procession of cranks. There were few criteria, educational or otherwise, for recording ministers besides a "call," and harried yearly meetings often recommended untested and unsuitable fledgling preachers for pastorates.[30]

A revealing incident occurred in Indiana Yearly Meeting in 1892–1893. A Young Men's Christian Association worker named Frank Smith heard Allen

Jay preach in Michigan. Smith wanted "to preach the Gospel" and "tell sinners how Jesus died to save them." Within a few months, not yet recorded a minister, Smith was pastor of the Onaway, Michigan, Friends Church. His tenure was a disaster. The Friends in Onaway welcomed him but soon discovered that, as one member wrote, "he cannot preach, and his bible readings and talks became monotonous and do all we could; the people lost interest." This Friend urged patience and kindness, but "No," Smith answered, "I'll fight the devil in his works, by telling them what I think of dancing, and staying away from church, drinking, etc." Soon Smith had driven away a considerable portion of the membership, and Michigan Friends were badgering Allen Jay for action.[31]

Such difficulties notwithstanding, the pastoral system transformed worship. Ministers became a clerical class, directing all aspects of meetings, now indistinguishable from the services of other denominations. Only the administration of the ordinances—the observance of the rites of communion and water baptism—was missing. And, for a time during the 1880s, it seemed that even that might become general among Friends.

THE ORDINANCE CRISIS

From the standpoint of other Christians, one of the most unusual Quaker testimonies was that against water baptism and physical communion. Friends did not recognize them as sacraments; their true meaning, they argued, was spiritual. The true baptism was that of the Holy Ghost; the true communion was the worshipful fellowship of believers.[32]

As Friends moved toward the evangelical mainstream, it was natural for them to give some thought to these subjects, but before 1878 even revival Friends showed little disposition to challenge tradition. In 1872 Sarah F. Smiley, a holiness minister from Philadelphia, was baptized in New England, but she immediately left the society. In 1876 Stacy E. Bevan, leader of one of the first revivals in the 1860s, was baptized in Iowa, and he lost his ministerial standing. Neither case attracted more than passing attention. Nor did that of Louis Street, the Quaker missionary to Madagascar who baptized a few native converts when they requested it.[33]

The first major controversy came in 1879. At its center was Helen Balkwill, an English Quaker minister and intimate of Hannah Whitall Smith. Balkwill spent two years traveling in the United States. Toward the end of her stay, her reading of the New Testament convinced her that water baptism was required of all Christians. Astonished English Friends soon called her home, where she resigned from the society.[34]

In America, Balkwill, a holiness believer, had identified herself with the revival, and her misgivings about the traditional Quaker position on water baptism apparently reflected the thinking of some of the revival's leaders. Before her decision to return home became public, Balkwill met in Glen's Falls, New York, with several holiness Friends, including Luke Woodard, John Henry Douglas, Thomas W. Ladd, and David B. Updegraff. The *Christian Worker* contended that their aim was to lay strategy for agitating a new understanding of the ordinances among Friends, an accusation that the participants denied. In the fall of 1879, however, Updegraff, Woodard, and Ladd, along with Dougan Clark, Jr., began just such agitation.[35]

Updegraff opened the campaign with letters to the *Christian Worker*, followed by a pamphlet, *Open Letters for Interested Readers*. Updegraff's publications presaged most of the themes that ordinance Friends—or the "water party," as they became known—would use into the 1890s. The water party claimed no saving efficacy for baptism or the supper; instead, they saw the former as a symbol of entry into Christian life, the latter as a simple memorial, and both as clearly commanded by Christ and the Apostles. If Friends could spiritualize such unequivocal commands of Scripture or, as some Friends implied, if the Apostles were misguided in baptizing believers, then the authority of the Bible was open to challenge, and that was inconceivable for Orthodox Friends. The early Friends had sometimes observed water baptism, Updegraff argued; they certainly never had made nonobservance a condition of membership. The opposition to Balkwill and similar-minded Friends, Updegraff concluded, showed an unchristian lack of charity and tolerance. Other holiness Friends moved to support Updegraff. In meetings held in New York and Indiana, Woodard and Ladd said that they were "commanded" to preach on the subject. While not making observance of the ordinances mandatory, they were, it seemed to many, clearly edging in that direction. They characterized all opposition as "cruel persecution."[36]

The ordinance Friends had little success. Both the *Christian Worker* and the *Friends' Review* condemned their agitation. Stanley Pumphrey, a popular English minister who had traveled widely in America, showed in a devastating article how Updegraff had twisted and misused the writings of the early Friends. Other Friends tried to prove that baptism and the supper were not commanded by Christ and that they were denigrations of spiritual worship. Meanwhile, moderate Friends in New York and Indiana revoked Woodard's and Ladd's credentials for religious service. The representative meeting (the yearly meeting's equivalent of an executive committee) in New York, where Woodard was evangelizing, forced him to sign a statement effectively recanting his views on the ordinances, and New Garden Monthly Meeting in Indiana, where Woodard had kept his membership, removed him from his honorary position as "head of the meeting."[37]

Indiana Yearly Meeting, with Charles F. Coffin and Timothy Nicholson in firm control, took aim at Updegraff. When the Ohio minister appeared at its sessions in 1879, silence greeted his request to hold devotional meetings; Coffin told him that his assaults on Quaker principles had made Indiana Friends wary of him. Updegraff responded in language that was, in Nicholson's words, either unfortunate or "exceedingly stupid." In the spring of 1880, Woodard and Updegraff counterattacked by complaining to Whitewater Meeting in Richmond that Nicholson had defamed them. Their move backfired when they were unable to prove their charges. When Updegraff attended Indiana Yearly Meeting in the fall, it refused to receive him officially; when he tried to take over one of the devotional meetings, a committee headed by Nicholson rebuked and silenced him, announcing that the yearly meeting preferred "sound" ministers. Updegraff, Nicholson exulted, had finally been brought to heel.[38]

Updegraff's power in Ohio Yearly Meeting was beyond challenge, however, and so long as he retained its confidence, no other group of Friends could take disciplinary action against him. For a time Updegraff gave up the agitation and the ordinance debate waned, but his opinions had not changed. In 1884 he began the controversy anew.

By the mid-1880s Updegraff had begun a regular "circuit" of attendance at yearly meetings and holiness conventions. April always found him in Philadelphia for that yearly meeting's sessions. Updegraff was anathema to the Philadelphia leadership, but he found a warm welcome in the home of Elizabeth H. Farnum, a fervent holiness Friend. Farnum regularly hosted gatherings at which holiness preachers of all denominations were welcomed. While in Philadelphia for those meetings in 1884, Updegraff was baptized by the pastor of the Berean Baptist Church.[39]

For reasons still unclear, Updegraff kept his baptism secret for a considerable time. Subsequent events suggest that he was laying plans for a concerted campaign to win a place for the ordinances in the Society of Friends. He reportedly told Allen Jay that "he would bring the ordinances into the Society or tair [sic] it to peaces [sic]." In the spring of 1885, William J. Thornberry and Noah McLean, two ministers from Ohio with close ties to Updegraff, arrived within Indiana Yearly Meeting's province. They created a furor by publicly partaking of the supper in West Elkton, Ohio; they then parted to agitate privately for "toleration." Meanwhile, Updegraff pursued a similar course in Ohio Yearly Meeting, and such associates as Asahel H. Hussey also submitted to baptism.[40]

The Ohio actions galvanized the strong antiordinance sentiment in other yearly meetings. In 1885 the spring yearly meetings, New York and New England, went on record that no minister who had been baptized or who had partaken of the supper was to be received as a minister. The other yearly meetings took similar action through their representative meetings. The sole exception was Ohio, which, after a bitter debate during its annual session that September, refused to adopt a similar minute. Ohio's refusal put it in open conflict with the other Gurneyite yearly meetings and laid the ground-work for nearly ten years of debate.[41]

The Quaker debate over the ordinances referred to traditions and prac-tices that mystified most outsiders. On the surface, it seems to have had little relevance for non-Friends. But the debate is important for two reasons. First, it shows the strong impact that the larger evangelical culture and the holiness movement had had on the society. Friends felt compelled to chal-lenge or to defend traditional practices, not on the basis of tradition, but on those of biblicism and a shared evangelical theology. Second, the ordinance debate divided and distracted the holiness Friends at a time when they may have been close to becoming the dominant group within the society, so strong as to be beyond all challenge. Without the ordinance controversy, the course of American Quakerism might have been very different.

The debate was not, in theory, over the value of the ordinances. No one even in the "water party" ever contended that they possessed any saving efficacy. No one ever suggested that a Friend who was baptized or who partook of the supper should be disowned. The issue was one of toleration for ministers: whether ministers who felt compelled to be baptized or to take communion could do so and not lose their ministerial standing.[42]

The ordinance debate produced a temporary factional realignment among Friends. It split the holiness group. Most of the leading holiness revival-ists—Updegraff, Clark, Woodard, John Henry Douglas, Hussey, Rogers, Baker, the Pritchards, and the Reeses—favored toleration, although several were never baptized themselves. Many other important holiness Friends, such as William P. Pinkham in Indiana, J. Walter Malone in Ohio, and Lawrie Tatum in Iowa, however, opposed toleration. Interestingly, the leading tolerationists were birthright Friends, whereas the most notable revival converts from Methodism, Nathan T. and Esther G. Frame and Rufus P. King, were opponents. Thus the ordinance issue left the holiness group splintered. The moderates, on the other hand, were united in oppos-ing toleration.[43]

As the debate progressed, three major lines of argument developed. One centered on the place of baptism in the apostolic church and among the early Friends. Another concerned the relationship of the ordinances to the Quak-er ideal of spiritual worship. The third revolved around the problem of balancing the demands of denominational order against liberty of con-science.

Biblical literalism lay at the heart of the movement toward the ordinances by Updegraff and his followers. Christ clearly had commanded his disciples to baptize in his name. Traditionally Friends had interpreted that command as the baptism of the Holy Ghost, but according to holiness theology, the baptism of the Holy Ghost was the prerogative of God alone. A human being could not administer it. Thus the only logical alternative for fulfilling the command of Christ was water baptism. Given the holiness commitment to biblical literalism, it was inevitable that many of the revivalists and their followers would move toward a literal observance of the ordinances. The only mystery is why some holiness Friends such as the Frames resisted. Perhaps they were influenced by the elaborate arguments of the opponents, who tried to prove that baptism was a Jewish ritual that had only been tolerated in the early church. Others were committed to the idea that the spirit of the Gospel was against all ritualism, whether it be water baptism or plain dress.[44]

Finding a basis for toleration of the ordinances in the early Quaker writings was much more difficult, but Updegraff, at least, argued that the early Friends were tolerant on the subject. First, from the works of Barclay, Penn, and Edward Burrough, he quoted some general sentiments on the evils of religious persecution; then, from the writings of Barclay and John Crook, another seventeenth-century Friend, he quoted passages stating that Friends did not condemn those who felt compelled to be baptized. Here opponents had an advantage, and they pushed it. To find support also for an antiordinance position in the early Quaker writings was easy. Updegraff, moreover, was vulnerable in his use of the same writings. With considerable justification, Thomas Kimber accused Updegraff of using "mutilated extracts" and "perverted constructions" "to make the writers . . . say *precisely the opposite of what they really do say.*" Israel P. Hole, an Ohio Friend whose speech in 1885 against Updegraff's position was widely circulated, commented that only dishonesty could explain Updegraff's misconstructions.[45]

The second issue, the relationship of the ordinances to spiritual worship, tended to be one-sided. It was a favorite theme of opponents. The duty of the Society of Friends, Hole proclaimed, was "to call man back from these outward forms and concentrate his thought and attention upon the inward and spiritual life; to call him away from ceremonies, from the . . . outward form, to the inward, to the inward and spiritual worship of God." Emphasis on the material, the opponents argued, detracted from the true baptism of the Holy Ghost. The water party's answers tended to be simple negations. Following a command of Christ could never detract from the true spiritual life, adherents argued, and no one could seriously accuse ordinance Friends, with their commitment to sanctification, of derogating the baptism of the Holy Ghost.[46]

Both of those debates were really sidelights to the central one: the controversy over balancing tradition and conscience. The ordinance Friends maintained that they had every right to indulge their consciences and that the society had no right to judge them for doing so. The actions of the various yearly meetings showed that the society not only was intolerant but also was out of step with the rest of evangelical Christianity. Updegraff struck the prevailing note in a long speech in Ohio Yearly Meeting in 1885. No member could be judged an offender "except for some *moral* offense, or one against the *evangelical* faith, or teachings of the Bible." Christ himself, tolerationists said, would have been shut out of the society by the standards some wanted to impose. In the eyes of Updegraff and his followers, to create standards of faith not found in the Scriptures was to "violate the constitutional law of the universal church" and to stand revealed as schismatic. No one wanted to make the ordinances mandatory, they argued; all they asked was to be left in peace.[47]

Intolerance was, in the eyes of the "waterites," wreaking havoc in the society. Here Updegraff, at least, edged toward making the ordinances mandatory. He reprinted an article by John P. Brooks, a leading Methodist holiness evangelist, which said that giving up the ordinances always led to fanaticism and infidelity. A missionary in Mexico used the pages of Updegraff's *Friends' Expositor* to argue that the refusal of Quaker missionaries to baptize converts there was confusing the natives and hindering the work of other Protestants. Updegraff angrily noted that nonobservance of the ordinances had kept Friends from being recognized as evangelical by such organizations as the National Christian Association. If Friends would only accept the ordinances, he concluded, they would bring in thousands of new members.[48]

Most of the tolerationists saw something darker behind the opposition to the ordinances. The real aim of the antiordinance campaign was, they asserted, to "invite *out* of the church those whom others have invited into it." They fervently believed that the whole controversy was a "club" to beat the cause of holiness, that "opposition to the ordinances is striking at the sanctification doctrine." Updegraff noted that the most zealous opponents of the ordinances were the unsanctified. Unsuccessful in directly opposing holiness, they were now trying a more devious route. All around them, tolerationists saw "infidelity . . . working inroads" among Friends: restorationism, destructive biblical criticism, opposition to revivals. With all of those enemies already in the camp, Calvin W. Pritchard wrote, it seemed incredible that some Friends wanted to expel the society's most zealous evangelical workers. Thus the ordinance issue became even more entangled with holiness and the revival.[49]

The antiordinance Friends were also fearful, but for different reasons. The society had changed greatly since 1860. Innovations had created problems but also great good. The ordinances were different, however. Baptism and the supper made no converts, saved no souls; they only relieved a few misguided consciences. For such negligible gains the price was too high: the denigration of the spirituality of the Gospel, the setting at naught of nearly all discipline, the disappearance of the last vestiges of Quaker tradition. The time had come for moderates to take a firm stand. No one holding the views of Updegraff could, in their minds, for a moment consider himself or herself a real Quaker. Now that the revolutionaries had by overt acts roused opinion against themselves, there should be no turning back. Only love of place and prominence kept the ordinance ministers in the society. It was time to make them choose.[50]

Thus the antiordinance forces worked methodically to secure unity against baptism and the supper. At the 1886 and 1887 yearly meetings, they pressed for reaffirmation of the 1885 statements and overrode all opposition. They held firm even against officially receiving a baptized minister. When Calvin W. Pritchard, the editor of the *Christian Worker*, and his wife, Esther, who edited the *Friends' Missionary Advocate*, took a tolerant position, opponents first set up a rival journal in Indianapolis, the *Star and Crown*. They then bought sufficient stock in the *Christian Worker* to force tolerationists off the editorial board and to give Pritchard a choice of modifying his position or resigning.[51]

One holdout against complete unity remained: Ohio, itself deeply split on the subject. Opponents of the ordinances rallied around John Butler, an octogenarian elder from Damascus, Ohio. Butler, a brother-in-law of Barnabas C. Hobbs, was one of the few moderates left in a position of power in Ohio; Cyrus W. Harvey thought him "the last flickering spark of Quakerism" there. He had been active in society affairs for half a century, and although revivalists derided him as a "Rip Van Winkle," his prestige outside the yearly meeting was so great that even Updegraff had to treat him with respect. Convinced that the "water party" had to be stopped, and backed by three of the yearly meeting's six quarterly meetings, Butler in 1886 again urged Ohio Yearly Meeting to adopt a minute similar to those adopted by the other yearly meetings. The debate was acrimonious, with several of the young revival ministers denouncing the notion that they could be bound by the ideas and practices of the early Friends. The final vote on the "intolerant" minute was close, but Updegraff's position was upheld 198–183.[52]

The Ohio decision left opponents both within and outside the yearly meeting distraught. They feared that Updegraff would use his slim majority to pack key positions and committees with his supporters. By the summer of 1887, Butler had concluded that the only course left for "sound Friends" was separation. He sounded out such sympathizers as Timothy Nicholson and Henry Hartshorne. "No religious Society can expect to Continue in Existance [sic] long that will Tolerate Teachings and usage inconsistant [sic] with the principles on which the *organization* is *Founded*," he wrote to Nicholson. "The invaders has [sic] become more bold and Persistent in their movements; and we see no other way for relief but a *Separation*." The separation never came. In the *Friends' Review* Hartshorne had called for "sound Friends" in Ohio Yearly Meeting to separate and to join Indiana

Yearly Meeting, but Butler fell ill not long before the yearly meeting's sessions and was unable to do much more than attend. By the end of the year he was dead. With him passed the last significant moderate influence in Ohio Yearly Meeting.[53]

THE RICHMOND CONFERENCE

It is likely that the moderates discouraged John Butler's plans because they had in mind another solution, one that Friends had used at the time of the Hicksite separation and again during the Wilburite controversies—a conference of all the yearly meetings. In September 1887 that conference convened in Richmond, Indiana.[54]

Several Friends had suggested a conference in 1886, but the formal proposal was the work of moderates in Indiana Yearly Meeting. In 1887 all of the Gurneyite yearly meetings in America, along with London and Dublin, endorsed the idea and appointed delegations. Four leading Philadelphia Gurneyites, including Henry Hartshorne and Bryn Mawr president James E. Rhoads, were also invited. Most of the leading figures of the debates of the past twenty years were present, although the two most prominent tolerationists in Indiana Yearly Meeting, Dougan Clark, Jr., and Luke Woodard, notably were not.[55]

The conference was the scene of wide-ranging debate on the mission of the society, the nature of worship, and the proper place and function of the ministry. Disagreement was sharp but usually not acrimonious. Refusing even to discuss the ordinances, the conference resolved, despite some dissent, that the actions of all the yearly meetings except Ohio had settled the question. The conference carefully couched its conclusions in language that submerged areas of disagreement and satisfied all but the most extreme radicals and conservatives.[56]

The most important result of the conference was the Declaration of Faith, prepared to "prevent the tendency towards the disintegration of society." The committee named to write it was heavily weighted with moderate Friends. The declaration that emerged was almost entirely the work of the Englishman Joseph Bevan Braithwaite, assisted by James E. Rhoads and James Carey Thomas.[57]

The Richmond Declaration of Faith has often been hailed as the pinnacle of the revival. It certainly is a monument to the impact of evangelical thought on the society. Its statements on God, the Holy Spirit, the Fall, the Bible, and conversion would have satisfied almost any evangelical denomination; it gave little attention to the Inner Light. Yet the document was hardly a revival triumph. The statements on sanctification, vague in many respects, were closer to the moderate definition than to the holiness one, as were those on worship and the ministry. The sections on baptism and the supper were anathema to tolerationists. Summing up the conference, one observer thought that "the conservative element was largely in the majority," explaining the "coldness" that the conference had shown toward "the evangelical work of the day."[58]

The reaction to the Richmond Declaration mirrors these realities. Its most enthusiastic supporters were the moderate opponents of the ordinances. Richard H. Thomas of Baltimore spoke for them in hailing the conference and declaration as "a check . . . upon growing divergencies in faith and practice." This group, combined with those of the revival party who opposed toleration, received endorsements in one form or another from all of the Gurneyite yearly meetings, usually with the reservation that the declaration would not supersede their own statements of faith and was not to be considered a creed. One holiness Friend commented that at least three-quarters of all revival Friends found the statement acceptable. The opposition came from the extreme poles of Orthodox Quakerism. To Cyrus W. Harvey in Kansas and to the Philadelphia leadership, the conclusions of the Richmond conference represented the ultimate apostasy. Updegraff, on the other hand, although he thought that the conference had made for harmony, complained that too little attention was given to soul saving and practical evangelism. And in his guise of champion of freedom of conscience, he blasted the declaration as a dangerous creed.[59]

Ultimately as important as the declaration was an idea set forth by William Nicholson in the conference's closing stages. The trend of Quakerism, Nicholson argued, had "been in the direction of disruption, disintegration, and dissolution." The cause, he concluded, lay in lack of central organization and authority. All bodies needed a head, one that brought "unification, compactness, strength, solidity, power of resistance, and an effective wielding of our forces." Nicholson proposed, as the means to bring order to the society, a triennial conference of the yearly meetings with ultimate authority and legislative powers and with delegates appointed by the yearly meetings in proportion to their membership.[60]

Nicholson's proposal became the focus of sharp debate between 1887 and 1890, splitting older factional lines. The tolerationists blasted it. To Updegraff, "the whole scheme was unspiritual in its conception, revolutionary and anti-Quaker in its doctrine, and utterly visionary as to any practical utility whatsoever"; in other words, it was just another scheme of oppression. On the other hand, some moderates, including Henry Hartshorne, were equally opposed, fearing that the revival party would use a central organization to impose its own uniformity on the society. The *Friends' Review* created horrific pictures of ranting Western preachers being forced on Philadelphia meetings. Nevertheless, the idea steadily gained ground among both moderate and revival Friends.[61]

Thus the ordinance controversy had a paradoxical effect on the Society of Friends. It created new factional lines that split the holiness group. For a time moderate Friends who had doubts about the revival found themselves in accord with holiness Quakers who, despite all of the innovations they had championed in the past, could not accept a departure that brought no discernible benefits. Together they apparently represented a majority of Friends. The opponents of the ordinances undermined Updegraff's influence and discredited many of the leading holiness revivalists. The preoccupation of Updegraff and his followers with the ordinance issue may have been the major factor in allowing the moderates to retain their positions in such places as Indiana and North Carolina, where they had lost so much ground to the revivalists. The ordinance battle also brought an illusion of unity that was symbolized by the Richmond conference of 1887. Moderates came away hopeful that the worst excesses of the revival were over, that some order had been restored. They ultimately found themselves proved wrong.

THE BEAN CASE

If moderate Friends produced anything close to martyrdom in the revival era, it was in the case of Joel Bean, the leading moderate in Iowa Yearly Meeting. The controversy that surrounded Bean during the twenty years after 1880 is important in three respects. It says much about the dogmatism and fears of the revival party. It helped widen the split between the revivalists and their moderate opponents. Most of all, it shows how different the issues that confronted Friends in this period were from those that challenged other Protestants. The best-known "heretics" and heresy trials outside Quakerism between 1870 and 1900 involved innovators, those who were challenging old orthodoxies.[62] In contrast, the Bean case involved the continual harassment of a Friend whose offense consisted almost entirely of his stubborn opposition to departures from tradition.

Throughout the summer of 1881, the holiness revivalists in Iowa bitterly criticized Bean for publishing "The Issue" and for refusing to join in revival work. The attack climaxed at Iowa Yearly Meeting early in September. David B. Updegraff was present and devoted considerable time to an attack on Bean's article and the doctrine of the Inner Light. The yearly meeting left Bean distraught. When Iowa Friends gave Updegraff a "returning minute" (a meeting's formal statement of gratitude to a visiting minister), signifying approval of his work, Bean felt repudiated. West Branch offered no refuge from the controversy, which was heightened by still another revival there. Early in 1882, unable to withstand the troubles any longer, the Beans sold their farm. "We need rest and change," Bean wrote to Timothy Nicholson. "I need retirement from all pressure for a while." He had not altered his views, but, he sadly concluded, "a Faction rules now, & when faction becomes *authority* from sanction of the Y[early] M[eeting], it becomes *disorder to resist it*." The Beans' new home was to be San Jose, California, where Joel Bean's favorite brother already lived and where the climate promised a respite from the Iowa winters.[63]

Unfortunately, San Jose offered no escape from controversy. There was strenuous opposition from the revivalists at West Branch to allowing the Beans to transfer their membership in good standing, but the Beans still had enough support in the monthly meeting to overcome them. The removal to San Jose posed a greater problem, one that the Beans apparently had not considered, in that it took them out of the limits of a quarterly meeting where they were well known and respected into Honey Creek Quarterly Meeting, a holiness bastion dominated by an elderly, argumentative revival minister, David Hunt.[64]

The Beans faced harassment almost from the moment of their arrival in California. San Jose itself was quiet enough, since most of the Friends there shared the Beans' view of the revival. Joel Bean's holiness opponents back in West Branch, however, gave him no peace. Writing privately to David Hunt, a group of twenty-five repeated four charges of "unsoundness" that West Branch Monthly Meeting had investigated and dismissed before transferring the Beans' membership. Honey Creek Quarterly Meeting forwarded the charges to San Jose in 1882, demanding that the Beans clear themselves. San Jose Friends responded by forwarding to Honey Creek a testimonial to the Beans' ministry signed by ninety West Branch Friends, including most of the other ministers and elders there. For a time that seemed to end the controversy.[65]

Early in 1885 a scene familiar to the Beans was reenacted in San Jose. Two zealous Iowa holiness evangelists, Mahlon Stubbs and Samuel Lloyd, arrived to hold meetings. They found little support. Bean maintained that only five members of San Jose Meeting accepted their teaching; the revivalists' complaints about "the low state of the church" in San Jose suggests that he was correct. The revival minority, however, irreconcilably split the monthly meeting. This, along with the reports of Lloyd and Stubbs, once again brought in Honey Creek Quarterly Meeting. After addressing a series of questions to the monthly meeting, Honey Creek pronounced the leaders of San Jose Monthly Meeting unsound and dissolved it, attaching its membership for disciplinary and business purposes to Honey Creek Monthly Meeting in Hardin County, Iowa, two thousand miles away.[66]

To revival Friends, the reason for those actions was self-evident—the monthly meeting was, by its own admission and behavior, out of unity with aggressive soul saving. Moderate and Conservative Friends decried the action as aimed at the much-respected Beans. The *Friends' Review* was typical in calling the whole affair an "inquisition." Moderates in the East, along with almost all Friends in England, where the Beans were widely known and respected, condemned Honey Creek's actions as arbitrary and absurd.[67]

For the next six years, the Beans and the other opponents of the revival in San Jose lived in a kind of disciplinary limbo. In the suburb of College Park, the Beans built, at their own expense, a small meetinghouse, where they held meetings in the traditional way. Meanwhile, the revival party brought in a pastor and established the "San Jose Friends Church." After the pastor arrived, Honey Creek reestablished the "Friends Church" as a monthly meeting but drew its limits so as to leave the Beans still members of Honey Creek Monthly Meeting back in Iowa. Later, when Iowa Yearly Meeting established monthly meetings in Oregon and in the Los Angeles area, the Bean group asked to be transferred to one of those (only five hundred miles away), but Honey Creek denied that also. Finally, some adjustment was made. The College Park Friends were transferred to New Providence Monthly Meeting in Hardin County, Iowa—two and a half miles closer to them.[68]

In 1893 the whole affair came to a final crisis. Professing hope for a restoration of unity, New Providence Monthly Meeting and a yearly meeting committee offered to strike all previous proceedings from the record if the Beans and the other minister living at College Park, Benjamin Jones, would give unequivocally affirmative answers to nine questions that Iowa Yearly Meeting required to be put to all of its ministers. The nine covered essentially the same subjects as those in the document sent to San Jose in 1885. Tacked on was an additional question from New Providence asking for a general expression of unity.[69]

The Beans and Jones answered yes to eight of the nine yearly meeting questions and gave the expression of unity. The one question they did not answer unequivocally dealt with eternal punishment. New Providence asked for an explanation. Joel Bean answered by citing the words of Christ that at the day of judgment it would be more tolerable for Tyre and Sidon than for those who had heard and rejected him. To him that suggested "possibilities of repentance" beyond this life and degrees of punishment that he was not ready to deny categorically. Bean concluded with a powerful statement that hinted that he was moving toward a progressive understanding of religion. "The New Testament abounds in passages of deeper meaning than we are yet able to fathom," he wrote. "The tenor and teaching of it as a whole must be the ground of our doctrine, rather than our partial interpretation of isolated texts." God was ever leading seekers on to deeper thoughts and larger views. Because he himself was uncertain on the subject of eternal punishment, Bean concluded, he had never referred to it in his public ministry. But he could not make the definite statement that Iowa required.

New Providence was not impressed. It deposed the Beans and Jones from the ministry (despite the fact that Jones had not endorsed the Beans' answer) for "entertaining and advocating doctrines . . . contrary to the fundamental principles held by our church."[70]

New Providence's action created a furor both in the East and in England. In London Yearly Meeting hundreds of prominent Friends, including many who had been sympathetic to the revival, condemned the Iowa proceedings as "inquisitorial" and contrary to discipline. They circulated a public letter in which they effectively announced that they still considered the Beans to be divinely called ministers. In many ways the Bean case was a turning point for English Friends. Once badly divided over the attitude they should take toward the revival in America, after the Bean case they were ever in sympathy with the opponents of pastoralism and revivalism.[71]

In America the controversy surrounding the Beans once again divided Friends along the familiar moderate-revival lines, helping to dissolve the fragile unity that the Richmond conference had built. In revival eyes Joel Bean was an inveterate opponent of holiness and effective soul-saving work and had now been publicly proved unsound on the subject of eternal punishment. Moderates took a different view. However unorthodox the Beans' opinions on some subjects might be, they were private, divulged only when the monthly meeting demanded that they be disclosed. A world of difference lay between publicly proclaiming unorthodox doctrines and privately pondering them. Throughout the affair the supporters of the Beans saw "an evident lack of true charity and brotherly kindness." They hailed the Beans as sufferers for righteousness, the victims of "narrow minded, . . . ignorant, self sufficient dabsters in theology."[72]

In practical terms, the deposition of the Beans had little meaning. They could continue to preach at College Park or in any other meeting that would receive them. And with Joel Bean nearing seventy, it was unlikely that they would undertake any further substantial religious labors. But the symbolic importance of the case was immense. The Beans had fought the revival in Iowa and had lost. Defeated, they had tried to withdraw into the relative solitude of California to live out their old age worshiping with like-minded Friends in the traditional way. But the revival party could not bear the thought of a minister opposed to revivalism within its bounds. First, by dissolving San Jose Monthly Meeting, it deprived the Beans of a role in church business. Then, when Joel Bean finally divulged what really was an unorthodox opinion, it found grounds to depose the Beans from the station they had held so long. The Bean case says much about the dogmatism and fear of heresy into which the revival was hardening, and about the cautiously liberal direction in which some moderates were moving. Real unity, seemingly within reach for Gurneyite Friends in the late 1880s, had proved to be an illusion.

Thus, as the Gilded Age neared its end, Gurneyite Friends had confronted many of the issues that agitated other Protestants. Questions of holiness, evolution, the millennium, and the infallibility of the Bible all divided Friends in this era along lines similar to those dividing American Protestantism. In the twenty-five years after the Civil War, Gurneyite Friends, once a united people, faced their own spiritual crisis.[73]

That crisis, however, involved issues in many ways unique to the Society of Friends more than it did the problems that agitated the larger religious world. The central issue during the 1870s was the revival. Friends who wished to retain the traditional ways of worship, conservative by Quaker standards, were by temperament and by their stand on such issues as evolution akin to the "liberal" factions emerging in other Protestant denominations. In the same way, the Friends who worked for radical reform of Quakerism were inspired in large part by their links to the interdenominational holiness movement, one of the most important forces behind the eventual emergence of fundamentalism.[74] By the 1880s the debate between conservative and moderate Friends on one hand and radical revival Friends on the other had shifted to other unique Quaker issues, like the Inner Light and a pastoral ministry. These factional alignments broke down temporarily in the debate over whether Friends would take the final step of allowing and administering water baptism and the supper, a step that the society ultimately refused to take.

The 1880s were to be the last decade in which Gurneyite Friends would occupy themselves largely with issues unique to the Society of Friends. The Bean case showed that modernism, and fear of modernism, was beginning to appear within the society. During the next fifteen years Friends would join the larger debate that pitted the forces of modern, liberal thought against the emerging forces of fundamentalism.

CHAPTER
VII
THE RISE OF MODERNIST
QUAKERISM, 1895–1907

Within a few months of each other in the late 1890s, two American Friends published books embodying their vision of Quakerism. Superficially, Seth C. Rees and Richard H. Thomas had much in common. Both were well-known, active Gurneyite Friends; both were recorded ministers; both had even been born in the same year, 1854. There the resemblance ended.[1]

Thomas, a leading Baltimore moderate, cast his views in a novel titled *Penelve; or, Among the Quakers*. It recounted the conversion of a fashionable young New York businessman to Quakerism during a stay in a rural Pennsylvania community. The Quakers of Thomas's Penelve lived a religion that melded tradition and progress. They had discarded the plain dress, but they tried to avoid being slaves to fashion. They still used the plain language in their families, justifying the practice with a comparison to the use of the familiar German *du*. They read the Bible faithfully, but they did not fear critical study of it. They still held their meetings on the basis of silent waiting, dreading alike the ramblings of traveling Wilburites from the East and the rantings of visiting revivalists from the West. The Quakers of Penelve were a confident people, active in peace, temperance, and other reform causes, certain that their lives were part of God's plan to establish his kingdom on earth.[2]

A few months before Thomas finished *Penelve*, Seth C. Rees published *The Ideal Pentecostal Church*. A religious persuasion more different from Thomas's is difficult to imagine. Rees's ideal church was one of constant "holy ghost revivals," with "old-fashioned conviction followed by old-fashioned conversion" and sanctification. In worship it was a place of shouting, laughing, weeping, "holy" dancing, and other signs of pentecostal joy. It eschewed denominationalism, evolution, higher criticism, and social reform;

it had no room for politics, art, and literature that was not religious. Its sole purpose was to save as many sinners as possible before the imminent return of Christ.[3]

These two works were indicative of a continuing fundamental split within American Quakerism. On one side were the heirs of the renewal movement, trying to adjust Quaker tradition to modernity while preserving Quaker distinctiveness. On the other were the heirs of the revival, who saw Quakerism as a small cog in the great holiness soul-saving apparatus. Many Friends did not accept either vision exclusively, but by the beginning of the twentieth century, the society was becoming increasingly polarized. Even as old issues passed away, new ones arose to widen the old divisions.

RESOLVING THE OLDER ISSUES

The 1890s were a decade of transition for American Quakerism, transition most apparent in the ranks of the society's leaders. Many of the old moderate leadership—Thomas Kimber, William Nicholson, Barnabas C. Hobbs, Francis T. King, Nereus Mendenhall, Henry Hartshorne, and Elizabeth L. Comstock—died between 1890 and 1900. The holiness faction also lost four of its most important figures—David B. Updegraff, Dougan Clark, Jr., Caroline Talbot, and Calvin W. Pritchard—between 1894 and 1896. There were departures for other reasons. Charles F. and Rhoda M. Coffin withdrew from society affairs after undergoing bankruptcy in 1884; some of the holiness faction's leaders—for example, Mary H. Rogers and the Reeses—were increasingly devoting their time to nondenominational evangelism.[4]

As old figures passed away, some of the issues that divided Friends during the 1880s lost their immediacy, most notably those of the ordinances and pastors. The deaths of Updegraff, Clark, and Pritchard deprived the tolerationists of their most effective spokesmen; the stringent regulations that most yearly meetings adopted on baptism apparently cowed the rest. Many of the baptized ministers, such as the Reeses, the Rogerses, and John Pennington, left the society or as independent evangelists took up posts beyond its control. Their departure left the tolerationists who had not themselves been baptized with little to defend. The revivalists were more successful in their advocacy of the pastoral system. Many Friends continued to have doubts, but by 1900 the system was so entrenched and widespread that debate over it ceased.[5]

Another issue resolved in the 1890s was the Joel Bean case, although not without additional controversy. After their deposition from the ministry in 1893, the Beans remained in San Jose, still members of faraway New Providence Monthly Meeting. In 1898 a new, inexperienced clerk at New Providence, apparently unaware of the consequences of her action, dropped the Beans and a number of like-minded San Jose Friends from membership for "disinterest." When the action became known it created a new storm of protest. To many moderate Friends, it was just another incident in the campaign of systematic harassment of the Beans. But this time New Providence, apparently tired of the controversy, reversed itself. It restored the Beans' membership and then gave them letters stating that they were members of the society in good standing, leaving them free to associate with any group of Friends that would receive them.[6]

During the 1890s Friends continued to rationalize their organizational structure. After conferences in 1892 and 1897, all of the American Gurneyite yearly meetings except Ohio joined together in 1902 in a legislative body with a uniform discipline, the Five Years Meeting. The effects of the movement toward centralization are difficult to assess. Many Friends hoped that the Five Years Meeting would be a stabilizing influence, allowing the weight of the whole body of Friends to come to bear on deviations. Instead, it probably exacerbated tensions. Not only did it bring together parties with fundamentally different points of view, but also it produced another set of institutions over which they battled for control.[7]

The decline of older issues and causes thus did not produce new unity. By 1900 a new series of divisions formed as a new Quaker movement emerged.

THE RISE OF MODERNIST QUAKERISM

The seeming universalism of the concept of Inner Light and the devotion of Friends to social activism has led some scholars to believe that Quakers have always been liberals. Indeed, seeds of liberal religion are implanted in the writings of various early Friends, particularly those of William Penn. The Hicksite minority moved comfortably toward modernism during the 1880s and 1890s. But before 1890 the attitude of the Orthodox majority toward modernist thought had usually been unfavorable, ranging from the wariness of most moderate Friends to the implacable hostility of the revivalists.[8]

According to William R. Hutchison's influential study, modernist Protestantism made three claims: that religious ideas must be adapted to modern culture; that God is immanent and is revealed through human cultural development; and that the human race is moving fitfully toward realizing, if never quite attaining, the kingdom of God. Glimmers of such ideas can be seen in the thinking of moderate Gurneyite Friends of the 1870s and 1880s.[9]

Modernist tendencies among Gurneyites are the most apparent in the writings of the prominent North Carolina educator Nereus Mendenhall. Beginning in the 1860s, Mendenhall moved privately toward a vision that was at odds with that of virtually all of his Quaker contemporaries. Mendenhall saw the immanence of God in the Inner Light, "that of God which lighteth every man." By means of the light, God was leading all into his kingdom through "art, science, literature, matters civil, political, domestic, religious—to everything good pertaining to life." The revelation of God through the light was, moreover, progressive, becoming clearer from age to age. Thus Friends had to avoid committing themselves to static creeds, especially to biblical literalism and "bibliolatry." "Much which has been written and believed about the Bible must sooner or later fall to the ground," Mendenhall wrote; those who railed against "higher criticism" and "new theology" seldom understood what they were fighting. Mendenhall's influence on other Friends is difficult to gauge. His thinking was a major factor in shaping that of his sons-in-law, Lewis Lyndon Hobbs and J. Franklin Davis, as well as that of his daughter Mary Mendenhall Hobbs, and they in turn were among the leading early Quaker modernists. For the most part, however, Mendenhall confined his thoughts to private letters and essays, allowing only hints to appear in print.[10]

Other moderate Friends, most notably Joel Bean, foreshadowed modernist themes before 1895. But they were exceptional. During the 1890s modernism came to the fore among Quakers through the efforts of a trio of gifted Quaker educators: Elbert Russell at Earlham, Mary Mendenhall Hobbs at Guilford, and, above all, Rufus M. Jones at Haverford.

Jones is the central figure in American Quakerism after 1895. He was born into an old Quaker farm family in China, Maine, in 1863, and received his education in Quaker schools, culminating with a Haverford degree. Jones enjoyed special advantages as the nephew of the ministers Eli and Sybil Jones, whose names opened doors for him throughout the Quaker world. The revival did not affect Friends in Maine as much as it did those elsewhere, and Jones grew up in a world guided by the moderate Gurneyism of Haverford and the *Friends' Review*. In his early twenties he consciously chose a career of service to Quakerism when he turned down a prestigious fellowship for a teaching position in a Quaker boarding school. In 1893 he returned to Philadelphia to take up two tasks: teaching philosophy at Haverford and editing the *Friends' Review*.[11]

Jones came to the *Friends' Review* with high hopes and plans for extensive changes but found instead that he had to devote most of his time and energy to grappling with declining circulation and growing financial problems. Early in 1894 Jones and the well-to-do Philadelphia Friends who subsidized the journal came up with a radical solution: namely, merging it with the Chicago-based *Christian Worker*. The scheme appeared visionary, but a peculiar combination of circumstances made it viable. The *Christian Worker* was also losing money, and its major stockholder, J. Walter Malone of Cleveland, although a firm advocate of holiness, was at the time more concerned with battling the "water party" than with opposing moderate

Friends. Thus, to the astonishment of most Quakers, the two journals united
in July 1894 as the *American Friend*, based in Philadelphia with Jones as
editor and a variety of moderate and holiness Friends as his associates.[12]

Jones walked a tightrope and, initially at least, did it successfully. He
opened the journal's columns to all factions of Friends (save the waterites),
balancing blasts at the "dead Wilburism" of Philadelphia Yearly Meeting
with criticism of the excesses of the revival. A few of the old readers of the
Christian Worker and the *Friends' Review* felt betrayed, voicing outrage
over the inclusion of pieces favorable to pastors or protesting the absence of
"real, spiritual, holiness" articles. But most Friends expressed satisfaction
with Jones's editorial practices. "I praise the Lord for thee and for the
American Friend," Malone wrote, and Timothy Nicholson told Jones
that the new journal was the best Quaker periodical published in recent
times.[13]

The turning point for Jones and the *American Friend* was his trip to
Europe in 1897. Jones's editorial success enabled him to arrive in England as
a rising star among American Friends. He was quickly drawn toward a circle
of young modernist Friends who were committed to lifting English Quakerism out of the evangelical channels in which it had run since Gurney's day.
These Friends—J. Rendel Harris, William Edward Turner, William C.
Braithwaite, and especially John Wilhelm Rowntree—had enthusiastically
accepted the theory of evolution and the critical study of the Bible. Convinced that the Scriptures did not offer the firmest of foundations for
religious life, they melded the modernist concept of progressive revelation
with the older Quaker idea of the Inner Light. God, they argued, adapted
his revelation to the capacities of mankind. Some sections of the Bible,
suited to the standards of more primitive days, might be unreliable guides
for later generations. The true guide for all Christians, they concluded, was
personal religious experience, an experience verging on mysticism. Along
the way, the young English modernists challenged many of the central
doctrines of evangelical Quakerism—the Atonement, Original Sin, and eternal punishment. They continued an emphasis on social reform and activism
and turned increasingly sympathetic eyes toward the Quaker past. Rowntree
spent the last years of his short life planning a multivolume history of
Quakerism researched and written according to the most rigorous standards
of scientific history, a project that Braithwaite and Jones completed.[14]

Jones returned from England with a new vision of Quakerism, a vision that
a year of graduate work in philosophy at Harvard University in 1900 and
1901 further broadened. Harvard was the center of the "Golden Age of
American Philosophy," and Jones studied under George H. Palmer, Hugo
Munsterberg, Josiah Royce, and George Santayana. Royce's treatment of
mysticism as "one of the major pathways to reality" particularly impressed
Jones. In Jones's own estimation, however, the most lasting influence of his

stay in Cambridge came from Harvard Divinity School professor Francis G. Peabody, a committed modernist and pioneer of the social gospel.[15]

After his return from England, especially during and after his year at Harvard, Jones became more open in his modernism. By 1901 his thought had taken the form to which it would hold for the rest of his life. It had three major elements: progressive revelation, mysticism, and the social gospel.

A commitment to progressive revelation shaped Jones's thought and reaction to higher criticism, evolution, and the emerging forces of fundamentalism. As early as 1888 Jones had argued that Friends had to adjust their thought and practices to changing circumstances, a theme that he continued to emphasize. "This is the age of the dynamo," he wrote in 1907. "We must meet the age with a *dynamic religion*—not with a horsecar religion—a religion that works and is good for every stage of intellectual attainment." There was no need for Friends to be fearful of change and advance, since both were part of God's plan. "Each age finds out something new about the universe," he wrote in 1897, "but the more we learn about it we realize that there must be a Being who controls and guides it all, and who has an infinite purpose which He is working out." Everywhere, proclaimed Jones, men were coming to a purer, more basic understanding of the essential truths of Christianity—the need for a spiritual, personal religion.[16]

Central to Jones's vision of spiritual progress was critical study of the Bible. For him, higher criticism was simply the application of the wonderful new tools that progress was providing. Jones was aware that some higher critics did not approach the Bible with the reverence it deserved, but he dismissed them as both foolish and exceptional. "The honest modern thinker destroys no single truth of Evangelical Christianity," Jones wrote in 1906. "He brings the discoveries of truth—the great searchlight of historical study—to bear on the supreme realities of life, and . . . he helps see how marvelous, how wonderful are the ways of God, how measureless is His goodness." The critics did not undervalue the Bible—the painstaking study that they gave to almost every word belied that charge. The enemies of biblical learning, Jones charged, were those who wrapped it up "in a medieval napkin . . . without taking any pains to discover the real spirit and meaning of it."[17]

Jones thus was adamant in his opposition to all forms of creedalism, dogmatism, and heresy hunting. In his view, modernism did not endanger great doctrines such as the divinity of Christ, the inspiration of Scripture, and the Atonement. What was in danger was freedom to continue along the new paths that God was showing. "Faith is not endangered by the advance of science," Jones told readers of the *American Friend* in 1901. "It is endangered by the stagnation of religious conceptions. If religion halts at some primitive level and science marches on . . . there will be difficulty." Thus if Friends wedded themselves to "theological definitions and medieval thought" by insisting on creeds and crusades against "unsoundness," they would destroy Quakerism and work against the purposes of God. The worst offenders, in Jones's view, were the "holiness cranks," who, having got hold of "some little half truth . . . push[ed] it . . . until they almost lost sight of all the deeper truths of God."[18]

"The deeper truths of God" were important to Jones; they informed his vision of religious life. Since traditional dogma and interpretations of the Bible were not infallible guides for believers, a new way was required. Here Jones drew not only on modernist thought but also on the philosophy of Ralph Waldo Emerson's "Oversoul" and of Josiah Royce, and especially on Quaker tradition, to find that way in a religion, not of doctrines, but of the mystical, personal experience of God.

Jones had a firm belief in the divine immanence. God had "direct relations and dealings" with everyone, dealings Jones identified as the Inner Light. God was a spirit, a light, that illuminated the world and everything in it. Jones held that God needed human beings just as much as they needed God, and God revealed himself to them in Jesus Christ.[19]

Jones's conception of Christ was clearer and more complex than his conception of God. He never doubted the divinity of Christ, but he rejected the extreme evangelical formulation that the sole purpose of Christ's life was his atoning sacrifice. Instead, in Jones's eyes, Christ's life was the model of the perfect, "a life which settled forever that the ultimate reality is love." His sacrifice on the cross was the ultimate act of love, to show how sin brought pain to God.[20]

How, then, was one to be saved? For Jones, the answer lay in mystical union with God. Jones's influence brought mysticism back into high repute among Friends. Mysticism was the "immediate experience of God" in the soul, based not on belief in some "plan of salvation" but on actual conscious contact with the divine. Jones argued that by constant waiting and seeking and prayer and "dwelling on the goodness of God," one gradually appropriated Christ into one's life and transformed the old nature. Without realizing it, Jones was very close to the concept of growth into holiness that had dominated Quaker thought a century before.[21]

Jones recognized the danger that mysticism could degenerate into asceticism. Although he saw religious experience as something profoundly personal and private, he nonetheless viewed its manifestations as social. While God commanded that individuals experience union with him, he also commanded that they help to realize his kingdom on earth by wiping out the evils that plagued it. Those evils could be eliminated in a variety of ways: "by a political method, or a legal act, or by a campaign of education or on a definite religious basis." Thus Jones was inevitably drawn toward the social gospel in religion and toward the Progressive movement in politics.[22]

Jones's thought was thus firmly within the modernist impulse.[23] And from it Jones drew inspiration for a new vision of American Quakerism. To understand that vision, one must understand its debt to the new biblical scholarship and its links with the older moderate resistance to the revival. These are exemplified by the two other leading Quaker modernists: Elbert Russell and Mary Mendenhall Hobbs.

Russell was born near Friendsville, Tennessee, in 1871. His parents, both Quaker ministers who had come south from Indiana for reasons of health, died late in the 1870s, leaving Russell to be raised by his grandfather in West Newton, Indiana. He grew up in a meeting that the holiness revival had transformed. He then went on to Earlham, where he was converted in a revival conducted by John Henry Douglas but soon came to doubt the value and reality of his experience. His record at Earlham was so good, however, that when in 1895 the Earlham trustees forced Dougan Clark, Jr., out of the biblical department because of his waterite views, they asked Russell to take over the post. Russell's training consisted of a one-semester course on the Bible and a few weeks of Greek, but a month at the Moody Bible Institute in Chicago and a summer Chautauqua course in Hebrew left him sufficiently prepared in the eyes of the Earlham officials.[24]

Russell later realized that it was his very lack of training that made him right for the post he assumed—the absence of association with "tainted" divinity schools and his unfamiliarity with the higher criticism made him acceptable to Indiana Yearly Meeting's powerful holiness wing. But as Russell set out to rectify that lack, he was drawn irresistibly to the works of higher critics and such modernist scholars as George Adam Smith and Shailer Mathews. A visit from John Wilhelm Rowntree, and Rowntree's subsequent gift of a number of important modernist works, sealed Russell's conversion to modernism. In 1901 Russell left Earlham for two years of graduate work at the University of Chicago, a modernist stronghold. In 1903 he returned to Earlham to transform its biblical department from an adjunct intended to produce preachers into a regular course of study for both undergraduate and graduate students—and to become the most embattled figure in American Quakerism.[25]

Russell did not become well known outside Quaker circles until much later in life. He was not a theorist or a prolific writer. Russell's importance lies instead in the pronounced and combative modernist outlook he brought to an exposed and sensitive position. In addition to teaching courses at Earlham, he delivered countless lectures and sermons between 1900 and 1910. Through the pages of the *American Friend,* he assumed the role of interpreter of the new theology and the higher criticism for American Quakers.

Russell began with progressive conceptions of the nature of society and religion. The opening lines of his only major book from this period, *Jesus of Nazareth in the Light of Today,* reveal Russell's methods and assumptions:

The twentieth-century man who is in harmony with the historical and scientific spirit, who thinks in terms of the evolutionary philosophy, who presupposes commonly accepted results of the historical and literary criticism of the Bible, especially of the Gospels—what shall he think of Jesus of Nazareth? Let us attempt to form an estimate of his character and importance as a force in history in the same spirit and by the same methods by which we would attempt to estimate the significance of any other historical personage, such as Napoleon or Hannibal, Buddha or Mohammed.

Russell ultimately confirmed the uniqueness and divinity of Christ, but few critics read beyond these lines.[26]

Russell's chief contribution to the growth of the modernist impulse among American Friends lay in his writings on the Bible. After 1900 he became the recognized authority on Scripture among Quaker modernists; even Rufus M. Jones deferred to him. Russell's writings on the Bible had two purposes: to acquaint Friends with the Bible's progressive revelation and to bring within their purview the findings of modern scholarship on the dating and composition of the Scriptures.

Russell fervently believed that all Scripture pointed toward "a progressive revelation of God and duty." On many subjects, such as divorce, peace, the nature of God, and the immortality of the soul, the earlier portions of the Old Testament made "a temporary accommodation to a low state of morals and religion, . . . which was to be done away with altogether or modified essentially in the course of time." Thus it was necessary for one to fight a false view of the Bible that focused on its scientific and historical inerrancy in order for one to clear the way for its "purely spiritual use." Russell summarized the progressive understanding of God and Scripture in a controversial paper at the 1907 session of the Five Years Meeting. "Men understood Him differently in different ages, because of dim visions and hard hearts," Russell said, but God remained the same; he was only leading the way to a better understanding of him. Thus the real enemy of revealed religion was one who wanted to shut out continuing revelation and to bind Christians to outmoded conceptions.[27]

To wean Friends from their traditional, outdated views of the Bible, Russell initially embarked on a quixotic crusade to introduce the society to modern scholarship on the authorship and writing of the canon. Russell had visions of bringing his newly acquired wisdom to the masses of Friends, a delusion that came to an end after a few disastrous lectures. Thereafter he confined his campaign to more appropriate audiences, primarily his Earlham students, pastors attending special institutes and meetings, and, in a less scholarly fashion, the readers of the American Friend. By 1905 Russell had become well known to and respected by the small but growing group of modernist Friends. But he had also become a byword to the holiness faction.[28]

While Russell was giving Earlham and Indiana Yearly Meeting a modernist tinge, far to the south one of the most remarkable women in Quaker history was waging the same battle among North Carolina Friends. She was Mary Mendenhall Hobbs, for many years the power behind Guilford College president Lewis L. Hobbs and the leading member of North Carolina Yearly Meeting.

Mary Mendenhall was born in the New Garden, North Carolina, Quaker community in 1852, the daughter of Nereus Mendenhall. She was educated in Quaker schools in North Carolina and New York. In 1880 she married Lewis Lyndon Hobbs, a Haverford alumnus who in 1888 became the first president of the newly organized Guilford College. Mary Hobbs became as much a part of the institution as her husband. An important but unappreciated figure in southern women's history, she was also active in a variety of educational, temperance, and even political causes. For Friends, her importance lies in her place as a transitional figure between the renewal movement and modernist Quakerism.[29]

Mary Hobbs had early come to abhor the holiness movement. As a young woman in boarding school in New York, she had encountered David B. Updegraff. "He put me through all the paces," she later remembered. After a long and agonizing experience on her part, he pronounced her "wholly sanctified." Soon she repudiated "the whole performance," becoming instead her father's intellectual heir, opposing the revivalists and the intellectual baggage they brought with them. She and her husband tried to instill in Guilford's students the broad, progressive vision of her father, to produce "men and women with well-trained minds and good hearts; people who can think for themselves and not be blown about by every wind of doctrine." They recruited faculty from Haverford and from the best eastern graduate schools, resisted bringing a pastor into the college meeting, and generally made Guilford "a modernist island" in a sea of fundamentalism.[30]

Mary Hobbs's chosen task within the society was to battle for a progressive understanding of revelation. Like Jones and Russell, she resisted all attempts to invest the Bible with historical and scientific infallibility. In her view, such attempts denied the fundamental doctrine of Friends, the immediate guidance of the Holy Spirit. "The Bible has been made a kind of Pope," she wrote bitterly in 1901, "and has been degraded in the making." Thus for her the great struggle of the Society of Friends in the twentieth century was for freedom of conscience. The future, in her mind, lay with the Friends who were attempting to bring the society to a deeper understanding of truths of religion and of the Bible.[31]

Other Friends chose a similar path during the years from 1890 to 1910.

They fall into two groups. One was made up modernist scholars teaching in the Quaker schools: Thomas Newlin at Pacific College in Oregon; Rayner W. Kelsey and Charles E. Tebbetts at Whittier College in California; Isaac Sharpless, Allen C. Thomas, and George A. Barton at Haverford; Murray S. Kenworthy and Robert L. Kelly at Earlham; Albert J. Brown at Wilmington; and J. Franklin Davis and J. Edwin Jay at Guilford; in addition to Jones, Russell, and the Hobbses. These Friends often lacked extensive graduate training themselves (only Kelsey took a Ph.D. before 1910), but they identified with the trend toward graduate training and specialization. They made brave efforts to integrate the new religious and biblical scholarship into their classes and writings.[32]

The other portion of the "liberal" faction in this period consisted of Friends who, if not overtly modernist themselves, preferred the modernists to the holiness activists. They were the heirs and survivors of the renewal movement. They usually were urban, held prominent positions in the society, and often possessed some wealth. They included the Philadelphia Friends who subsidized the *American Friend* and Jones's position at Haverford, Richard H. Thomas in Baltimore, James Wood in New York, and Timothy Nicholson and Allen Jay in Indiana. Jay's position is vital. He was probably the best-loved Friend in America before his death in 1910, perhaps the one Quaker beyond attack from any faction. Without his support the liberals might never have established a foothold west of the Appalachians; certainly Russell would not have survived at Earlham. Jay's own theology remained faithful to the evangelical Gurneyism of the 1860s, but he believed that the openness of the modernists was more likely to assure the health and prosperity of the society than was the dogmatism of their opponents. Jay's open identification with the liberals, especially with Russell, gave them respectability in quarters that might otherwise have been closed to them and may have made some of their opponents more cautious in their attacks.[33]

Although drawn from two somewhat different streams, the modernist faction was relatively united. They found their inspiration in Jones ("We are looking to thee—we younger men of the church—to lead us," Albert Brown wrote); their goal was a new, progressive vision of Quakerism; their enemy was a "cramped conception of Christianity." Their chosen means were logic and persuasion; they would "quietly, steadily . . . work to broaden the thought of the church," as Jones wrote to Russell in 1898.[34] And by 1900 they had created a program to accomplish just that. Its theological basis has been described. In terms of action it had three main features: a firm reliance on Quaker history and tradition, an attempt to unite all persuasions of Friends, and a commitment to the social gospel.

One important accomplishment of the liberals was the stimulation of a new interest in the study of Quaker history. Some of that enthusiasm was antiquarian, but Friends such as Jones had more important objectives.

Jones, Russell, and Allen C. Thomas became the first American Friends to produce scholarly histories of the society. Friends suffered, Jones wrote, because they had no sense of background or perspective, no comprehension of real Quakerism. "They are at the mercy of any new teaching," he sadly concluded. "They have no steadying force; they have no roots which make use of the accumulate[d] experience of their people." To understand Quakerism, Jones argued, one had to understand George Fox and the other early Friends. Only historical study could clear away the distortions of quietism and the revival and recapture what was unique and vital in Quakerism. By 1910 modernists were happily noting an upsurge of historical interest among Friends.[35]

As liberal Friends plunged into Quaker history, they were overjoyed to find much that to them had a modern ring. "The central truth which our fathers discovered, lived by, and suffered for," Jones wrote in 1910, was that "religion to be real must be the life of God experienced in the life of man." *"God ever present with every soul,"* as another modernist told Indiana Friends, had been the message of George Fox, and it was "a message for all times." The liberal Friends began to examine again the once-central doctrine that the revival had nearly obliterated—the Inner Light. "That of God in every man" fit neatly into a scheme that emphasized the immanence of God and individual experience.[36]

The liberals were not always in accord on how to carry out Quaker principles in worship. Most probably sympathized with traditional forms based on silence. Mary Hobbs spoke for them at the 1897 session of the Five Years Meeting when she deplored "the readiness with which we are dropping our manner of worship." If Friends only returned to their original principles of an expectant, waiting silence, she concluded, there would be a "wonderful ingathering." Many liberals, such as Russell, Tebbetts, and Brown, however, served Friends as pastors, and nearly all accepted the pastoral system as established fact within the society.[37]

Liberal Friends could not abide revivalism. Here they allied themselves with many of the older moderates and set themselves against the continuing revival impulse within holiness Quakerism. The modernists were notorious for remaining calm in the midst of enthusiasm. Jones recalled with relish the astonishment of Walter Malone that Jones could preach for half an hour with the tail of his coat turned up and never shake it down. Russell created a sensation at a devotional meeting conducted by Esther G. Frame at Western Yearly Meeting in 1899 when he refused to take part in a Chautauqua-style handkerchief salute to loved ones looking down from heaven or to rise when Frame asked all of those who wanted to be saved to stand.[38]

Modernist Friends opposed such demonstrations not from a desire to appear staid and intellectual. They always affirmed that religion necessarily involved the heart and the emotions. "A Christless religion, or one without atoning sacrifice does not suit me at all. . . . I know too well the strength and terror of sin to offer men a mere human savior or a religion of self-culture," Russell told a critic. In the eyes of the modernists, the emotionalism of the revival, however, was dangerous. "There are meetings held, ostensibly as Friends meetings, where scenes are enacted that are dangerous to physical, mental, and moral health—meetings marked by emotional disorders that ought not to be allowed anywhere, in this era of intelligence," Jones wrote in 1907. "Those who encourage a type of religion which paralyzes the will under storms of emotion, those who push meetings to the verge of hypnotism or trances to get results . . . are thoroughly unsuitable persons to deal with human souls." Mary Hobbs thought revivals "disgraceful" and refused to attend them. Other modernists dwelt on how ephemeral the results of such excitement usually were. Typical was one monthly meeting that, after two years, retained only twelve of ninety-two members brought in by a revival.[39]

Their commitment to older forms pulled modernists into cautious dialogue with the Hicksites. "The Other Friends" had regarded the revival with a combination of amusement and horror, but, since tolerance was an essential Hicksite doctrine, they remained open to overtures from the Orthodox. Late in the 1890s signs of thaw appeared. Hicksite and Orthodox Friends in Indiana began to hold joint "social meetings" and set up an informal joint committee to petition the legislature for a change in the divorce laws. Joint meetings for worship became increasingly common in the East after 1900. Even in Philadelphia, where the separation began and where the greatest bitterness remained, there were signs of a relaxation of tensions. Nowhere was the change more apparent than in the attitude of Jones. In 1898, when liberals in London Yearly Meeting proposed reaching out to Hicksites and Wilburites in America by addressing a general epistle to all Friends everywhere instead of only to the Orthodox bodies, Jones opposed the action as ill-advised. By 1904, however, he had made an abrupt about-face to endorse the idea. A year later Jones created a considerable stir when he attended the Hicksite yearly meeting in New York and preached a conciliatory sermon. While reaching out to the Hicksites, Jones especially remained hopeful about revival Quakers farther west. "There are great possibilities in Western Quakerism," Jones wrote to an English Friend in 1899, and he hoped "to see those possibilities realized." Visiting among them, he found them generally opposed to "pure emotionalism" and "hobbyists." Jones was convinced that most pastoral Friends could be drawn into the vision that he saw the *American Friend* advancing: "the unification of American Friends on the eternal principles of Christian truth, expressed in modern terms."[40]

Of greater importance for the future of the society was the reforming outreach of modernist Friends through the social gospel. The modernists gave Quakerism the activist, reforming tinge that most associate with it today. The liberals combined older Quaker reform concerns with the tenets of the social gospel to create a new vision—a fundamental shift from philanthropic benevolence to the hope of a more basic transformation of society.

The reform impulse was not confined to the modernists. Prohibition activism, for example, involved Friends of virtually every stripe. Quakers formed the backbone of the Woman's Christian Temperance Union in many areas, and S. Edgar Nicholson, a Quaker minister from Indiana and Jones's successor as editor of the *American Friend,* headed the Anti-Saloon League when the Eighteenth Amendment was ratified. Prison reform and educational work remained priorities in many yearly meetings. Quaker liberals, however, took the reform impulse in a new direction that, after 1890, emphasized the coming of the kingdom of God.[41]

Modernists continued the postmillennialism that had been a prominent part of Quaker thought since Gurney's day. "There is a kingdom of the Spirit," Jones wrote in 1895, "for the Spirit of God is in His world, shaping history, . . . putting down evil, and making for righteousness, silently guiding the forces in the great battle of Armageddon." Liberal Friends saw a vague, endless progression ahead, as the world grew better and better. There was, however, a fundamental difference between the reforming visions of the modernist Friends and their predecessors. Earlier generations of Quakers had taken aim at specific evils that seemed antithetic to the spread of the Gospel. Modernists continued to do so, but within a broader vision of remaking American society along the lines of the teachings of the New Testament. The greatest failure of Christians in the past, Thomas Newlin declared in 1897, was that they had failed to realize that "a new society was quite as emphatic in Christ's teaching as a new man."[42]

Although vague about what the nature of the kingdom would be, modernist Friends tried to be definite about how it would come about. It would be realized, they argued, through the spread of the "Gospel of Christ as the remedy for the ills of mankind." Modernists were as quick as any other faction of Friends to denounce attempts to overemphasize secular concerns. They took a deep interest in efforts to strengthen Quaker home and foreign missionary work. But modernist Friends also felt that the Gospel could be preached through political and economic reform.[43]

Political activism was nothing new for American Quakers, and the modernists introduced few innovations. An identification with the Progressive wing of the Republican party was natural for most, although some Quaker liberals were Prohibitionists, and a few, such as the Hobbses in North Carolina, were Democrats. Whatever their partisan preference, liberal Friends united in backing the political reforms that Progressives favored. Jones used the columns of the *American Friend* to score "bosses" and election fraud. Earlham president Robert L. Kelly and Elbert Russell campaigned against the local "machine" in Richmond, Indiana, and Russell later ran for Congress on the Progressive party ticket.[44]

The most significant contribution of the modernists to Quaker reform thought was a new focus on economic justice. The relationship of Friends to economic liberalism is one of the least explored areas of Quaker history. There are tantalizing hints of an earlier reform impulse, such as the activities of Archibald Crosbie, the Iowa minister who gave years of his life to agitating Henry George's Single Tax, and Cyrus W. Harvey's and other Kansas Friends' fervent support of the Populists. But the predominate view among renewal Friends, and among revivalists as well, toward economic reform was molded in the classical liberalism of the mugwumps. Elizabeth L. Comstock, for example, was quite sure in 1889 that American workers could "go where they like, do what they like, and earn good wages anywhere." The *Friends' Review* combined support for free trade with an intense aversion to anything that tended to disturb the workings of the marketplace. Occasionally it condemned "immorally low" wages and poor working conditions, but it always saw the solution in making Christians of employers, not in passing legislation or forming unions. Anything smacking of socialism filled it with horror. Given a choice between the tyranny of capital and that of labor, the *Friends' Review* editorialized in 1892, it preferred that of capital as more intelligent and orderly. The *Christian Worker*'s editorial stance was virtually indistinguisable from that of the *Friends' Review*.[45]

Rufus M. Jones accepted the same economic and social orthodoxies when he began editing the *American Friend*. His reaction to the Pullman strike, in progress when the journal began publication, is instructive. Applauding the use of troops to break the strike, Jones wrote that although Friends abhorred the use of force, it was better "to compel the dangerous element to maintain peace, than that by a timid policy of irresolute dallying [w]e should permit life and property to be at the mercy of unrestrained rioters." The vigorous public support for breaking the strike, he concluded, made "a man's heart throb with joy." Soon afterward Jones approvingly printed a piece by James E. Rhoads, who argued that the wage system was divinely ordained and that American workers had to accept it.[46]

Later Jones and other Friends began to cast a more critical eye on the workings of American capitalism. Jones himself urged compulsory arbitration as a means to avoid strikes. Articles urging the prohibition of home work and the regulation of working conditions began to appear in the *American Friend*. In 1897, in a remarkable address, Thomas Newlin proclaimed that "every prophetic thinker today has his face set squarely against the ancient individualism." Modern life seemed to produce widespread degradation, misery, and suffering, Newlin observed, and it was the duty of Christians to transform the system that created such conditions. During the first decade of the twentieth century Friends began to respond. "We have heard a distinct call to social service," New York Yearly Meeting told its members in 1907. It was committed to "trying to solve the great problem of poverty," to encouraging employers to pay "just wages" and "mitigate the evil of undue competition and above all things to lighten the pressure of toil on the nation's womanhood and childlife." The same year at the Five Years Meeting, Benjamin F. Trueblood, Joseph J. Mills, and a parade of other speakers, many of them not previously open liberals, embraced the movement. At the same time, Haverford, Earlham, and Guilford began to include social service, creating a "social order based on love and justice," as part of their missions. It is a mark of how far Friends had come that in 1912 the *American Friend* published a series of articles by Elbert Russell on the evils of child labor, sharecropping, and the wage system that culminated in a rather sympathetic piece on the textile strike led by the Industrial Workers of the World (IWW) in Lawrence, Massachusetts. Socialism and anarchism were inevitable, Russell warned, if Americans continued to tolerate economic oppression.[47]

When it came to solutions, modernist Friends once again were vague. They applauded progressive legislation to regulate working conditions, to set minimum wages, and to improve slum housing and sanitation. Often, however, they offered only "timely Christian sympathy and love." Like the larger Progressive movement, nearly all liberal Friends remained committed to a capitalist society. And there is little evidence that the modernist exhortations had much impact even on fellow Quakers such as the great Quaker businessmen of Philadelphia and the Quaker millowners in North Carolina.[48]

While the social thought of modernist Friends was often vague and of an uncertain impact, it mirrored the vagueness and uncertainty of the larger social gospel. Rudimentary examination shows the debt that modernist Friends owed to non-Quakers. Rufus M. Jones was deeply influenced by Francis G. Peabody at Harvard. He reprinted articles by Washington Gladden and praised him as one of the great religious prophets of modern times. Elbert Russell was an admirer of Walter Rauschenbusch, who often lectured under Quaker auspices. Friends certainly were influenced by their reform heritage. But they also drew liberally on non-Quaker thought in reacting to the modern world.[49]

Modernist Friends were in many respects the heirs of the renewal movement. The personal continuities are the most obvious, but a similarity of methods is also apparent. The modernists were a self-conscious elite. Although not as wealthy as their predecessors, they were much better educated and more self-consciously middle or upper class than were most other American Friends. Like renewal Friends, they placed their faith largely in exhortation and education. The leading modernists, such as Jones and Russell, traveled extensively and sought to meet Friends of all walks of life, but even then their attitudes bore a hint of condescension. Occasionally one of the modernist group, most often Allen Jay, would warn against that failing, but usually his admonitions went unheeded.[50] More notable is the debt of modernist Quakers to thinkers and figures outside of the society, who were deeply influenced by the new biblical scholarship and by the social gospel. From those elements the modernists constructed a program that has endured to the present.

THE HOLINESS QUAKER RESPONSE TO MODERNISM

The modernists did not go unopposed. The holiness wing of Gurneyite Quakerism, although undergoing changes, remained strong and active. The rise of liberal Quakerism energized and reunited holiness believers.

The holiness ranks had lost many of their most important leaders by 1900. Updegraff, Clark, Pritchard, Caroline Talbot, and Hulda Rees were dead. Many of the activists who had begun their careers during the 1870s were now elderly. Of the leading revivalists of that decade, only John Henry Douglas, Luke Woodard, and Amos M. Kenworthy remained active after 1905. The holiness faction also lost some of its younger stalwarts—for example, Edgar P. Ellyson, Seth Rees, and John Pennington—to such nondenominational groups as the Holiness Band and the emerging Church of the Nazarene.[51]

Into the void stepped an unlikely figure, J. Walter Malone. Born in southwestern Ohio in 1857, the son of an Irish father of uncertain religious leanings and a devoutly evangelical Quaker mother, Malone grew up in New Vienna, Ohio, the original home of the *Christian Worker* and an early center of revival enthusiasm. While in his twenties he moved to Cleveland. There he entered an older brother's stone business and joined a small Friends meeting that had just been revived by Nathan T. and Esther G. Frame. In 1883 Malone married Emma Brown, a young Quaker who had been converted by Dwight L. Moody.[52]

The turning point of Walter Malone's life was the pastorate of Dougan Clark, Jr., at Cleveland in 1883. Under Clark's guidance, both of the Malones experienced sanctification. Thereafter, although his business was increasingly profitable, Malone turned his attention to religious concerns. In 1892 he used his savings to open the Friends Bible Institute and Training School in Cleveland. It grew steadily during the next twenty years, and Malone's prestige and influence increased with it. His commitment to an antiordinance position and his mild, engaging personality made him acceptable even to Philadelphia Friends, while the institute's uncompromising holiness orthodoxy made it a rallying point for the holiness faction.[53]

By 1900 Malone had gathered around him in Cleveland a group of Friends that had assumed the leadership of holiness Quakerism. Foremost was William P. Pinkham, a teacher in Quaker schools since the 1860s. Pinkham's success as a preacher previously had been limited, but at the institute he found his niche as teacher of theology, editor, and controversialist. Among the other faculty members at the institute were such Friends as Lewis I. Hadley, Edward Mott, and Eli Reece, who would provide modernist Quakerism with its chief adversaries throughout the following half-century.[54]

The Friends Bible Institute set an example that other holiness Friends increasingly followed. Between 1900 and 1920 holiness Quakers in Oregon, California, Kansas, Indiana, and Western yearly meetings set up similar institutions, partly to train preachers without the expense of a regular college education, partly to serve as bastions of unquestioned "soundness." Such institutions became part of the network of bible colleges of many denominations that provided the shock troops of the emerging fundamentalist movement. Holiness Friends increasingly looked to these schools for leadership, contributed to their support, subscribed to their publications, and called their alumni as pastors. By 1910 at least two yearly meetings, Ohio and California, were controlled in large part by training-school groups. Malone's Cleveland school remained the largest, and it made its head the leader in the Quaker battle against modernism.[55]

Holiness Quaker thought during the period extending from 1890 to 1910 is more simply sketched than is modernist, largely because it was continuous with that of the 1870s. Holiness Friends emphasized the necessity of a definite conversion experience and subsequent sanctification, revivalism as the most effective means to accomplish those, and the repudiation of quietism and the doctrine of the Inner Light. There is, however, one striking difference between the earlier and the later holiness positions. Before 1890 holiness Quakerism had been on the offensive, attacking quietist complacency. After 1890 it was mainly reactionary, defending the old faith against heresy.[56]

The most common theme of the holiness crusade against modernism was the rejection of modernist theories about the Bible. Holiness arguments usually were not very sophisticated but depended rather on appeals to authority. Typical was William P. Pinkham's statement in 1895 that the Bible was infallible in all respects, a "self-consistent and logically impregnable system of truth." Apparent contradictions were the result of lack of faith. In holiness eyes, modernists were attempting to pick and choose what truths they would accept on the basis of their own limited powers of reason.

"The entire drift of such teaching," Walter Malone warned, "was to deprive the Scriptures of all inspiration, all that is supernatural, and bring them down to the level of any other book of history, leaving no place for prophesy or miracles." Faith in Christ, according to the holiness group, was indissolubly bound to faith in the Bible's testimony concerning him. The higher critics and modernists were thus creating loopholes "by which the unbelieving may escape the obligation of reverent obedience," and which often destroyed faith entirely. As the exaltation of reason increased, the "genuine soul-saving power of the society" waned.[57]

Holiness Friends gave even more attention to the "New Theology." The key point was the Atonement. Salvation was achieved only through faith in the efficacy of the literal blood shed on Calvary. Modernists replaced faith with a teaching that emphasized "the Divine Love to such an extent as to almost do away with divine judgment." That done, the holiness Friends argued, it was easy for modernists to minimize the equally important doctrines of a definite conversion experience and eternal punishment. The modernists never did so openly, of course; they cloaked their dangerous theories in "the most beautiful Christian phraseology." Nevertheless, they were wolves in sheep's clothing with "naught but death in them."[58]

The end result of modernism, holiness Friends feared, would be exaltation of culture and intellect over heart experience. To many, Rufus M. Jones seemed the epitome of that tendency. Jacob Baker, an aging holiness minister, described one instance of Jones's preaching: "The whole trend of the discourse was, if people desire knowledge they should resort to the learned, the cultured, placing culture before spirituality, or at least exalting it as the ideal channel to obtain light." Baker noted that "there was much display of intellectual skill and a tame, cool delivery, a frigid benediction, and it was over." An old woman in New England was more succinct. She remarked pointedly to Jones: "Jesus said feed my sheep, not my giraffes." Anti-intellectualism was never far below the surface of holiness Quakerism, and after 1900 it gained strength. "Learning and culture may be all well enough for the world, but only that which we can make conserve to God's glory is really of any use," Hulda Rees had preached. Some holiness Friends became suspicious of all higher education.[59]

What disturbed holiness Friends most, however, was a perceived link between the modernists and that ancient *bête noire* of all evangelical Friends, the Hicksites. Modernist views of the Bible, of Christ, and of the new birth all resembled Hicks's teachings, at least in holiness eyes. Holiness Friends suddenly discovered a sinister significance in the motto that Jones had chosen for the *American Friend* in 1894: "That They All Might Be One." Hicksism and modernism, holiness Friends declared, were mutually reenforcing. They had no objections to modernists' joining the Hicksites, but they did object to the Hicksites' trying to infiltrate the true society.[60]

The reaction of holiness Friends to the most important contribution of the modernists, the social gospel, was inextricably bound to the holiness commitment to premillennialism. After 1890 the imminence of the Second Coming became an increasingly common theme in the discourse of holiness Quakers. "Jesus is coming again. He may come any moment," one proclaimed in 1895. The various Quaker holiness publications filled their pages with articles on how the prophecies concerning the last days were being fulfilled. Premillennialism predisposed holiness Friends to take a pessimistic view of world progress. Holiness Friends saw, instead of an advancing kingdom of God, increasing vice and crime, with "evil men and seducers . . . waxing worse and worse, deceiving and being deceived, and every kind of ism that the devil ever invented . . . captivating the minds of men and laying waste the heritage of God." To holiness Friends the world showed only the inevitable degeneration that prophecy foretold.[61]

The holiness response to the social gospel was, however, more complex than one might expect. As was the case with other turn-of-the-century evangelicals, holiness Friends were divided. The dominant note among them was opposition to any type of reform activity. The great duty of Christians, they proclaimed, was not to save the world, but to make men separate from it. "We are not here in this world to reform it," Seth Rees thundered. "We do not believe that the world is going to be saved as a whole. Our duty is to get people to the lifeboats and be rescued."[62]

Yet while skeptical about the possibilities of general reform, many holiness Friends applauded specific actions. They were staunch Prohibitionists. And they looked favorably on some of the goals of the Progressive movement. "The MONOPOLIES that curse the people are coming to judgment," Malone's journal, *Soul Winner*, cried in 1905. "AMEN! Death to all monopolies!" A year later the *Soul Winner*'s successor, the *Evangelical Friend*, told its readers that they had duties as citizens to support good legislation and to create a sense of public loyalty. But holiness Friends never attempted the sort of social analysis to which the modernists were drawn. Usually when they supported reform it was only to clear away obstacles from the path of evangelism.[63]

The rise of modernist Quakerism was not the only source of worry for holiness Friends. They also faced internal problems. By 1900 two major ones had emerged: the attitude of holiness Friends toward excessive emotionalism and the relationship of holiness believers to the world.

Holiness Friends remained committed to the revival methods that had become popular among Friends during the 1870s. They continued to believe in healing, in "wide-open" revivals, even in casting out demons. Wherever such methods had given way to "modern" practices, they argued, "real soul-saving work" had declined. They took pride in the fact that their churches were "in a state of chronic revival." On the other hand, holiness

Friends were doubtful about some of the emotional experiences that many
on the fringes of the holiness movement were embracing after 1900, experiences such as trances that sometimes lasted for hours. "I hope we may keep
out of lustful, emotional things," David Hadley wrote in 1899; and after that,
Friends of holiness views became more specific about dangers: excessive
noise, "morbid" and lurid public confessions, extreme claims of private
revelation. Edward Mott warned against those who wanted "to sing and
shout just as they please and call this the freedom of the spirit." Fanaticism
was a favorite device of Satan in his war on holiness, and the duty of the
sanctified was to reproach it.[64]

The one facet of traditional Quakerism that holiness Friends preserved
was alienation from the world, an alienation that increased as the churches
seemingly grew more worldly. One of the revival's chief sources of appeal in
the 1870s had been freedom from the exactions of the discipline, but by 1900
holiness Friends had created an almost equally exacting system of mores.
They continued to denounce such "seminaries of vice" as the ballroom, the
card table, and the theater. Many holiness Friends found new abominations
to attack. One blasted football as unworthy of the attention of the sanctified;
another proclaimed that union cards were the mark of the beast. An enthu-
siast in Fairmount, Indiana, included among "open mouths to hell" not only
secret societies but also life insurance, church "festavels," and Christmas
trees. (One holiness minister considered it her duty to tell young children
that there was no Santa Claus.)[65]

Such an outlook explains much of the subsequent course of holiness
Quakerism. It tended to be strongest in areas where the holiness movement
was strongest: the rural areas of Kansas, Oklahoma, and Iowa; southern
California; and such cities as Marion, Indiana, and Alliance, Ohio, where
there were large numbers of displaced native rural whites. The elite of the
cities were caught up in Unitarianism and dissipation, whereas the "common
people," "the bone and sinew of society," were committing themselves to
holiness. Because they were fighting much the same battles that anti-
modernists in other denominations were fighting, holiness Friends identified with the emerging fundamentalist movement: both worried about
higher criticism; both bitterly opposed modernist theology; both were
ambivalent about the social gospel. Conflict between holiness and modernist
Friends was inevitable. Between 1900 and 1910 the two factions battled over
the future of Quakerism.[66]

THE MODERNIST CONTROVERSY

The modernist controversy among American Friends involved fundamental disagreements over the direction that the Society of Friends was to

take. It also involved relatively few people. It was a battle of elites—a handful of modernist ministers, educators, and laymen on one side; a somewhat larger group of holiness believers, but still a minority of all Quakers, on the other. Both sides were conscious of the relatively narrow groups involved. "What always amazed me," Rufus M. Jones wrote later, "was the fact that so few persons seemed to know that the battle was on, and that so many, who did vaguely know that it was being fought, appeared not to care very much which way the issue turned." Few of the holiness Friends were so frank, but their constant exhortations to Friends to "awaken" to danger suggests that they also sensed apathy and lack of interest.[67]

Was it apathy? Some evidence suggests that the masses of Friends were in a state of confused and uncertain neutrality. The battles were being fought in a denomination of fewer than one hundred thousand members. To many Friends, Rufus M. Jones and Elbert Russell were not distant monsters but real people who had visited them and preached in their meetings, eaten at their basket suppers, stayed in their homes. Jones remembered numerous occasions when he disarmed potential critics with his rural New England charm. The case was similar with Russell, as one revealing incident in 1907 shows. Ira C. Johnson, an uneducated but beloved minister in Indiana Yearly Meeting, was outraged by an editorial on miracles in the *American Friend*. He wrote immediately to "Mr. Editor" to cancel his subscription. About the same time, some holiness compatriots were trying to persuade Johnson to attack Russell, quoting various "unsound" statements that the Earlham professor was supposed to have made. But Johnson knew and liked Russell; he wrote to Russell and asked him to explain. To Johnson it seemed impossible that so upright and amiable a young man as Russell could be unsound. "Thee don't talk like that to me," Johnson concluded unhappily.[68]

The lines of division, moreover, were not always hard and fast. Modernists and holiness Friends were able to cooperate on a variety of matters, such as the desirability of Prohibition, extending and supporting Quaker missionary work, and creating a uniform discipline. Occasionally issues arose that divided Friends along lines quite different from the usual modernist-antimodernist cleavage. A good example is the uniform discipline's abolition of birthright membership in 1902. Long advocated by a number of prominent revivalists such as Updegraff on the grounds that birthright membership made members of those who had not experienced the new birth, modernists also embraced abolition of birthright membership from a desire to ensure that all members made a positive commitment to the society. Opposition to the change came from an equally unlikely alliance of traditionalist and holiness Friends, who worried that it would diminish the church's nurturing role and would ultimately lead to a decline.[69]

Nonetheless, the divisions were real, and after 1900 disputes became open and bitter. They seldom focused on individual meetings or churches.

Instead, controversies revolved around the Quaker colleges, the Haverford Summer School, and especially the *American Friend*. The struggle had three stages. In the first, from 1895 to 1901, the two sides crystalized. The second period, from 1901 to 1905, was a time in which holiness Friends strengthened the institutions under their control and tried to set up alternatives to those in modernist hands. Finally, after 1905, the holiness faction attempted to "purify" the society by forcing the modernists out of it.

The most obvious source of factionalization was the course of the *American Friend*. Before Jones's trip to England in 1897, holiness complaints had been minor. Some believers thought that the journal did not give sufficient attention to holiness teachings, or that it was misguided in its postmillennialism, or that it was not printing enough accounts of local revivals. After 1897 the complaints became more bitter as Jones increased his coverage of modernist topics and became more outspoken in his editorials. "It seems to me that the dikes are rapidly giving way and the floods of skepticism are sweeping in," one subscriber wrote in 1897, protesting such journalistic notice of the "cavils of destructive criticism." Another was more blunt: the *American Friend*'s contents made him feel like "fainting and vomiting." By 1901 the protests had reached a crescendo. Holiness ministers were publicly criticizing the journal, and at least one quarterly meeting went on record as objecting to its general trend. An important holiness minister, David Hadley, warned Jones that there would be a "stampeed" away from the *American Friend* unless it rid itself of its modernist taint.[70]

While holiness Friends were worrying about the *American Friend*, they were also casting a critical eye on Quaker educational institutions. At the center of most of the controversy were Thomas Newlin at Pacific College and Elbert Russell at Earlham. Newlin was attacked as an "atheist," a "Hicksite," and an "infidel" because he allowed some of his students to read works implying that the Bible was not historically inerrant and because he subscribed to Lyman Abbott's liberal journal, *The Outlook*. Strenuous efforts were made to force him out. Russell was the target of fierce attacks from John Henry Douglas and Esther Tuttle Pritchard. Russell exacerbated the situation when, in 1901, he went to Iowa Yearly Meeting, a holiness bastion, to argue that the higher criticism posed no threat to Christianity and that Friends would be better off concentrating on preaching the Gospel than on hunting heretics. At times the holiness attacks reached into the smaller schools. The principal of the Quaker academy in Bloomingdale, Indiana, mourned that he had "to watch not to use the word 'evolution' or 'higher criticism' or all the good committees in the church are after me."[71]

Worst of all in holiness eyes was the Haverford Summer School. The summer school was organized by Jones and funded by modernist Friends in the East as a means of bringing together Friends from England and America and introducing them to the latest advances in biblical scholarship. When the first session was held in June 1900, non-Quaker modernists such Washington Gladden and William N. Clark dominated the program. Those in attendance, including Allen Jay and Joel Bean, were delighted, but holiness Friends were horrified. William P. Pinkham sent a furious protest to the *American Friend*, alleging that some of those on the program were "unsound." Esther Pritchard took a similar line, writing that the summer school teachings were "irreconcilable with the Christian faith" and that "the mouths of false teachers must be closed."[72]

The modernists responded to those attacks with a blend of conciliation and defiance. A few urged silence; some worried that they were moving too fast; but others, such as Joseph Moore at Earlham, told Jones and his compatriots to "Keep ON!" Ultimately, the modernists took a middle course, which Allen Jay called "Christian statesmanship." Newlin joined the faculty of Guilford. Russell obtained a leave of absence from Earlham for graduate work at the University of Chicago. The summer school continued, but in a less visible way. Jones, in a stinging series of editorials, asserted his orthodoxy on such fundamental doctrines as the divinity of Christ, the Bible, and the Atonement. He scored the "little group of dissatisfied and disaffected Friends" who wanted to adopt "the ostrich's method of hiding the head in the sand." Nevertheless, Jones privately admitted he was "generally over bold," and for the next year or so, he muted the modernist message of his editorial columns.[73]

The first phase of the struggle was something of a draw. Since Philadelphia Friends sympathetic to modernism owned and subsidized the *American Friend*, holiness Friends had little leverage over Jones. The impact of the holiness faction on the Haverford Summer School was similar, since holiness enthusiasts had no influence at Haverford. The personal popularity of Russell was such that he was able to retain his post at Earlham. Although Newlin left Pacific College, his departure may have had as much to do with his lack of enthusiasm for fund raising as with any of his "heresies."[74]

After 1901 those in the holiness faction began to look toward the institutions under their control. They began with the colleges. They kept careful watch over the two they considered free of unsoundness, Penn in Iowa and Friends University in Wichita. They tried to build up the Malones' school in Cleveland. They strengthened ties with such non-Quaker institutions as God's Bible School in Cincinnati.[75]

Holiness Friends also tried to provide some sort of alternative to the *American Friend*. Serving that purpose for a time were two holiness journals, the *Bible Student*, or its successor, *Soul Winner*, published by the Malones in Cleveland, and the *Witness*, put out by the Huntington Park Training School in California. Although both had a holiness Quaker flavor, neither was aimed specifically at Friends. In 1905 Walter Malone made the final break with Jones and began publication of the *Evangelical Friend*, with

William P. Pinkham and Edward Mott as editors. The first editorial in the new journal was significant. The *Soul Winner*, Pinkham and Mott wrote, had been a holiness paper, but now "unbelief in various guises" was "so vigorously and so insidiously attacking all the fundamental doctrines of the Gospel" that a wider outlook was needed. The next few issues of the *Evangelical Friend* left no doubt that it intended to undermine modernism generally and the *American Friend* in particular.[76]

The most important work that evangelically oriented Friends accomplished in this period was at the grass-roots level. Their impact on the masses of members is uncertain, but they were successful in winning allies in the lower ranks of the Quaker hierarchies—pastors, quarterly meeting superintendents, individual representatives to yearly meetings. The holiness Friends were, Allen Jay noted, "attending Quarterly meetings, Conferences, and public occasions of all kinds, writing private letters and reaching Friends in every way." The holiness forces made strenuous efforts to increase the circulation of the *Evangelical Friend*. They gave a year's subscription for one dollar, and allowed dozens of agents a 60 percent commission. By 1907 the circulation of the *Evangelical Friend* had surpassed that of the *American Friend* in some areas; in California it was "unsound" even to subscribe to the latter.[77]

By 1905 the holiness forces were in a position of considerable strength. They dominated Ohio Yearly Meeting, keeping it out of the Five Years Meeting. California Yearly Meeting, with the Huntington Park Training School group and the relocation of such leading holiness figures as Amos M. Kenworthy, Lewis I. Hadley, and John Henry Douglas to areas within its bounds, was coming to rival Ohio as a holiness bastion. Kansas, Oregon, and Iowa yearly meetings were all under firm holiness control. There was also a strong holiness wing in North Carolina. Of all of the yearly meetings west of the Appalachians, only Indiana remained openly tolerant of modernism, and even it had a very strong holiness faction.[78]

While the holiness forces gathered strength, the modernists were also quietly regrouping, perhaps trying to avoid anything that would hinder the final organization of the Five Years Meeting. In the early months of 1902, Jones felt "badly discouraged" and took a conciliatory line, chuckling that he was heaping burning coals on the heads of his opponents through friendliness. But with spring came new hope; by May, Jones was seeing an "evident improvement." In August he made a trip to Indiana and Ohio. While in Richmond he and a dozen others—"the leading young Friends of the west"—met to discuss the situation and pledged "to take every opportunity to forward the truth—i.e., true and solid Quakerism." Jones was soon writing editorials and printing articles that the holiness wing found offensive. Russell also returned to Earlham in 1903 and promptly touched off new controversy by suggesting to an assembly of Indiana Yearly Meeting ministers that parts of the Bible might be allegorical or mythical.[79]

By the end of 1905 the two sides were farther apart than ever, and the holiness faction was gaining the upper hand. In 1906 it increased its pressure on the modernists. The *Evangelical Friend* was at open war with the *American Friend*, trading editorial for editorial. More seriously, holiness Friends mounted an attack on Russell by attempting to persuade Earlham's major financial backers to withhold contributions; some of the other Quaker colleges, feeling that Earlham's loss was their gain, abetted the campaign. Malone, meanwhile, was making strenuous efforts to gain the holiness yearly meetings' official endorsement of the *Evangelical Friend*. Late in the summer of 1906, California Yearly Meeting adopted a set of questions for ministers and elders designed to weed out the small modernist group at Whittier College. Some in the holiness group associated with the Huntington Park Training School even openly attacked Allen Jay. By the end of the year, Jay was almost in despair. Malone, Pinkham, and their sympathizers had "deep and well-laid" plans, he wrote to Jones and James Wood; they wanted "to run the *American Friend* out of existence . . . to turn Elbert Russell and some others out of the Earlham College faculty," and to humiliate Indiana Yearly Meeting, "which had stood in the way . . . of their revolutionary schemes." The modernist Friends, Jay feared, were unprepared, a view echoed by others. As if to confirm their worst fears, the *Evangelical Friend* opened the year with a call to purge the Quaker colleges. But the modernists' nightmares were never realized. Even as their plans were reaching fruition, holiness Friends found themselves thrown into confusion by a figure from their own ranks, the driven evangelist Levi Lupton.[80]

Lupton is one of the most fascinating figures in Quaker history. Born into an old Quaker family near Beloit, Ohio, in 1860, he was converted to holiness teachings in the 1880s. For several years he worked as an evangelist under the auspices of Ohio Yearly Meeting, associating with some of the most uncompromising disciples of David B. Updegraff. He cast out demons, preached faith healing, was uneasy with denominationalism, and conducted "wildfire" revivals. In 1901 Lupton settled in Alliance, Ohio, as pastor of the Friends church, which had been established there as the result of one of his evangelistic campaigns.[81]

After settling in Alliance, Lupton had increasingly grandiose visions of his own destiny. In 1902 he founded the World Evangelization Company, whose purpose was to use every means possible to evangelize the world "in this generation" and thus speed the Second Coming of Christ. He set up a missionary training school in Alliance, bought a railroad car as a traveling revival headquarters, and began publishing a holiness weekly significantly titled *New Acts*. Lupton expected the same signs of success to accompany the efforts of the new apostles of the World Evangelization Company as had accompanied those of the original apostles. In 1904 he and a handful of prospective missionaries went to West Africa to set up a mission there. Lupton and his associate, William M. Smith, recorded for publication every detail of their journey, certain of their central role in the revival they thought would soon sweep the globe.[82]

But by 1906 Lupton's world was crashing down around him. His African mission lasted little more than a year before the workers became discouraged and returned home. Lupton's strictures on denominationalism upset even Ohio Yearly Meeting, in which he was still nominally a minister; it appointed a special committee to "investigate and advise" his work. A June tornado in Indiana destroyed Lupton's revival tent, and funds began to run low at the training school. At times the little group of students and teachers was reduced to praying that a local believer would be moved to donate a chicken or a few canned goods so that they might have supper. Nevertheless, Lupton remained confident of his mission. In October 1906, beset by all of the difficulties, he stopped publishing his newspaper and dismissed classes at the school. He and his associates began a prayer vigil to seek guidance and power to overcome their problems. And by divine sign or strange chance, within a few days pentecostal preachers fresh from the Azusa Street revival in Los Angeles reached the area, teaching that there was a third definite experience following sanctification, an endowment of power by the Holy Ghost that was shown by speaking in tongues.[83]

In pentecostalism Lupton found the answer to his yearning and questions. Some of his associates in the World Evangelization Company, including William M. Smith, resisted the new movement and left him. But Lupton, who was by November speaking in a tongue that he identified as Syrian, was convinced that the power that he and other Friends needed to fulfill their mission had come. At his suggestion, two of the pentecostal missionaries moved in January 1907 to the Friends Bible Institute in Cleveland.[84]

When the pentecostals arrived, the institute and the adjacent First Friends Church were in the midst of their annual winter revival. Holiness ministers of all denominations were always welcome among Cleveland Friends, and, once in the church, the two pentecostals assumed control of the revival. They swept in many of the students. Some spoke in tongues; others claimed to cast out demons. The emotionalism was extreme even for Cleveland Friends. The congregation was badly divided, with some opposing the new teaching and others embracing it.[85]

Those who counted in Cleveland—Malone, Mott, and Pinkham—soon made up their minds, and their judgment was that the new movement was not of God. They did not doubt that God could impart the gift of tongues, but to teach that it was to be received by all or that it was the only sign of the baptism of the Holy Ghost was, they felt, unscriptural. Pentecostalism was instead just another device employed by Satan to appear as an angel of light, delude believers, and create "confusion and fanaticism." The representative meeting of Ohio Yearly Meeting met in emergency session to issue a statement condemning pentecostalism. It then disowned Lupton, who later fell from grace and abandoned his wife to elope with the secretary at his school.[86]

The tongues issue continued to plague holiness Friends after the Ohio actions. Judging from articles in the *Evangelical Friend* and in its west coast counterpart, the *Pacific Friend,* it persisted in some meetings for months. A few holiness Friends were not convinced that the movement was wrong. Among them was A. J. Tomlinson, scion of a leading Quaker family in James Baldwin's Westfield, Indiana, and the founder of one of the largest pentecostal denominations.[87]

More important, the tongues excitement, breaking out as it did in the very heart of holiness Quakerism, gave modernist Friends a handy club with which to beat their opponents, and Rufus M. Jones led the way in wielding it. At first Jones airily dismissed pentecostalism as a kind of emotional disease that was "no more religious than a headache." But when it appeared among Friends in Cleveland, Jones attacked. The tongues excitement was, he wrote, "a symptom of a larger trouble which threatens to swamp American Quakerism." The holiness zealots were advocating an unbalanced, "thoroughly unhealthy type of religion" that inevitably led to "ranterism, bigotry, division, and emotional upheavals." Jones concluded his editorial on a note more strident than he had ever allowed himself to put into print. "One thing is as sure as the pole star," he wrote. "The young Friends of America are determined to have a Quakerism characterized by the genuine spiritual power, breadth, and health of the apostolic period or none. . . . If the leaders of our church allow things to drift toward the rocks they will have themselves to blame."[88]

The pentecostal episode breathed new life and fighting spirit into the modernists. When the *Evangelical Friend* printed a ferocious response to Jones's editorial, Jones in turn responded with "One More Serious Call," in which he pointed to the excesses of Lupton and the pentecostals as the logical outgrowth of holiness teachings. The society had to choose, he wrote, between realizing "a future of power and influence" and running "off into emotionalism and ranterism." Proponents of the latter were circulating "insidious rumors" and spreading "unfounded suspicions and charges . . . to get control of our entire church and winnow it to their liking." That, Jones defiantly concluded, would not happen. Late in January 1907, while the holiness Friends were preoccupied with the pentecostals, Jones set off on a lecture tour that included stops at Wilmington, Earlham, and Penn colleges as well as at Friends University. First, in Cincinnati, he met with Albert

Brown, Elbert Russell, and a few other sympathizers to discuss "every phase of the situation." He then passed on to the colleges, increasingly pleased with his reception. "The Friends I met," Jones wrote, "are sick and tired of attacks on education and attempts to carry the church into a type of effervescent Christianity." The tour climaxed at Friends University, where he almost single-handedly faced down the holiness leadership of the yearly meeting and "completely turned the tide." "The victory in Kansas was extraordinary," Jones told his wife. "I believe that we could win the cause if we could only circulate enough." Surveying the results of the past three months, Thomas Newlin in March wrote ecstatically to Jones: "You have got them whipped for all time now."[89]

Nowhere was the new modernist confidence more visible than at the 1907 session of the Five Years Meeting. Before it convened in October, the modernist group held an informal conference to plot strategy. The modernists were buoyed by the cool reception that attacks on Earlham and the *American Friend* had received at Western Yearly Meeting, usually a holiness stronghold, the month before. They decided that Jones and Russell, in the papers they were to present, should elaborate modernist views. The two papers outraged holiness delegates; when Russell concluded his address, one woman from California immediately fell to the floor to offer an agonized prayer for his soul. But when David Hadley and Luke Woodard tried to keep Russell's paper out of the printed proceedings, their motion was voted down by a substantial majority. Jones wrote exultantly that he had witnessed the greatest triumph of his life; the modernists considered themselves vindicated.[90]

The events of 1906–1907 are a watershed in Quaker history and the natural stopping point for this account. The holiness attacks on "unsoundness" did not cease after 1907; if anything, they became more fervent and pronounced. But after 1907 the existence of modernist Quakerism was never in danger. American Quakerism had become a microcosm of American Protestantism. It had a primitivist faction, desperately attempting to preserve the old ways, the Wilburites. It had one liberal faction that had grown out of the Unitarian-Universalist liberalism of the 1820s, the Hicksites. It had another liberal faction, symbolized by Jones, that had grown from evangelicalism into modernism. And finally, a faction calling itself evangelical, the product of the holiness revival movement of the 1870s, was rapidly hardening into fundamentalism.

The history of American Quakerism during the twentieth century has reflected those realities, as Friends of all persuasions have struggled to meld their heritage with the influences and challenges of the larger world. Liberal Quakerism became the dominant force in the Gurneyite, Wilburite, and Hicksite yearly meetings in the East after 1907; by the 1960s Friends in New England, New York, Philadelphia, and Baltimore were again united. Liberal

Quakerism also spread throughout the United States in small, unprogrammed meetings found largely in college and university towns or in major urban centers. Combining traditional patterns of worship with modernist theology and an often radical social activism, these Friends have usually set the image of Quakerism for most Americans.[91]

West of the Appalachians (and in North Carolina), the American Friends show considerable diversity. Conservative Quakerism has been transformed by the influx of new members who embrace unprogrammed worship but who show little regard for the theological underpinnings of Wilburism. The Gurneyite Friends of the Five Years Meeting (renamed Friends United Meeting in 1960) have remained the largest and most strife-prone Quaker group. Modernists rooted themselves in colleges like Earlham and Guilford, in the pastorates of some of the larger urban meetings, and in the bureaucracies of the Five Years Meeting. Friends with fundamentalist sympathies responded by taking three yearly meetings (Oregon, Kansas, and Nebraska) out of the Five Years Meeting between 1925 and 1956; in 1965 they joined Ohio Yearly Meeting and formed the Evangelical Friends Alliance, which has eschewed the National Council of Churches in favor of the National Association of Evangelicals and like-minded groups. Friends United Meeting remains the most diverse Quaker group, including pastoral and nonpastoral meetings, its clergy drawn from the whole spectrum of American seminaries, its congregations ranging from the most restrained mainstream Protestantism to charismatics, and in many ways still debating the same questions that it was debating in 1907.[92]

But what of the masses of Friends in such places as the community in which we started, Westfield, Indiana? They had given up almost all of the marks that once distinguished them. The plain speech and the plain dress were confined to the rapidly declining group of Conservative Friends. The old burying ground with its small plain stones had been abandoned for the town cemetery. The academy, the last remnant of a guarded education, had been forced out of existence by competition from a public high school. There was little, aside from the absence of the ordinances, to distinguish the Westfield Friends Church ("Meeting" had been dropped as archaic) from any other church in the community. Modernists were hard to find in Westfield—the few to come out of the village soon headed for the more hospitable confines of Earlham or the East. The holiness fervor that had produced Seth Rees and A. J. Tomlinson, however, was also dying down. Levi Lupton's old associate, William M. Smith, moved to Westfield in 1911, but after little more than a decade he led a holiness remnant out of the Westfield Friends Church on the grounds that it had become tainted with modernism and was opposed to holiness. In other words, it had become worldly. Smith was right. Westfield Friends, like other Quakers throughout the country, were inextricably tied to the larger world and its ways.[93]

Appendix I

Membership Statistics
for Orthodox/Gurneyite Friends, 1845–1908

Yearly Meeting	1845	1871	1890	1908
Baltimore	562*	600*	1,012	1,179
California	NA	NA	NA	3,893
Indiana	30,000*	17,200	22,015	20,346
Iowa	NA	8,599	11,391	10,305
Kansas	NA	NA	9,347	11,370
Nebraska	NA	NA	NA	1,791
New England	8,021*	4,403	4,020	4,351
New York	11,000*	2,858	3,895	3,433
North Carolina	4,500*	4,000	5,905	6,763
Ohio	8,000*[1]	2,855	4,733	6,043
Oregon	NA	NA	NA	2,051
Philadelphia	8,686*	5,500*	4,513	4,389*
Virginia[2]	331	NA	NA	NA
Western	NA	9,749	13,784	15,628
Wilmington	NA	NA	NA	6,243
Total membership	71,600[3]	55,764	80,615[4]	97,785

Sources: "Number of Friends in America, 1845," *Bulletin of Friends Historical Association*, 4 (3rd Mo. 1911), 43–44; "Friends in America," *London Friend*, 3rd Mo. 1, 1872, p. 47; "United States Census of Friends, 1890," *Christian Worker*, 4th Mo. 7, 1892, pp. 211–13; "Statistics for 1909," *American Friend*, 1st Mo. 6, 1910, p. 4; Elbert Russell, *The History of Quakerism* (New York: Macmillan, 1942), 434; James H. Norton, "Quakers West of the Alleghenies and in Ohio to 1861" (Ph.D. diss., Case Western Reserve University, 1965), 259; Allen C. Thomas and Richard H. Thomas, *A History of the Friends in America* (Philadelphia: John C. Winston, 1919), 256.

*Approximation.

NA—Statistics unavailable or yearly meeting not in existence.

[1] Elbert Russell gives the membership of Ohio Yearly Meeting in 1845 as 18,000, which must be an error. In 1826 its membership was 8,873. Given the Hicksite separation, which took away many members, and continuing outmigration, the figure here seems reasonable.

[2] Virginia Yearly Meeting was dissolved in 1845 and its membership was joined to Baltimore.

[3] There were approximately 23,000 Hicksite Friends in the United States in 1845.

[4] In 1890 there were 4,329 Conservative Friends and 232 Primitive Friends in the United States. At that time Hicksite Friends numbered approximately 22,000.

Appendix 2

The Evolution of American Quakerism, 1800–1907

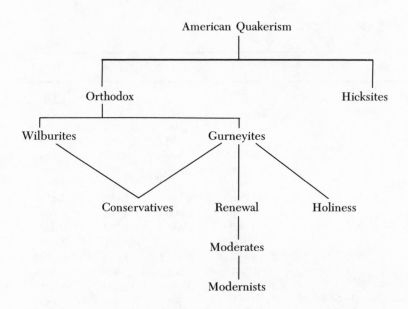

American Quakerism

Orthodox   Hicksites

Wilburites   Gurneyites

Conservatives   Renewal   Holiness

Moderates

Modernists

Notes

INTRODUCTION

1. [James Baldwin], *In My Youth: From the Posthumous Papers of Robert Dudley* (Indianapolis: Bobbs-Merrill, 1914); Donald E. Thompson, comp., *Indiana Authors and Their Books* (3 vols., Crawfordsville, Ind.: Wabash College, 1966–1981), I, 14.

2. [Baldwin], *In My Youth*, 12–42, 86–111, 187–209.

3. Ibid., 488–93.

4. Allen C. Thomas and Richard H. Thomas, *A History of the Friends in America* (Philadelphia: John C. Winston, 1894); Rufus M. Jones, *The Later Periods of Quakerism* (2 vols., London: Macmillan, 1921); Elbert Russell, *The History of Quakerism* (New York: Macmillan, 1942). For an evangelical rebuttal, see Walter R. Williams, *The Rich Heritage of Quakerism* (Grand Rapids: Eerdmans, 1962). For some of the outstanding work of the last forty years on Quakers in the colonial and early national periods, see Frederick B. Tolles, *Meeting House and Counting House: The Quaker Merchants of Colonial Philadelphia, 1682–1763* (Chapel Hill: University of North Carolina Press, 1948); Thomas E. Drake, *Quakers and Slavery in America* (New Haven: Yale University Press, 1950); Sydney V. James, *A People among Peoples: Quaker Benevolence in Eighteenth-Century America* (Cambridge: Harvard University Press, 1963); Edwin B. Bronner, *William Penn's "Holy Experiment": The Founding of Pennsylvania, 1681–1701* (Philadelphia: Temple University Press, 1962); Mary Maples Dunn, *William Penn: Politics and Conscience* (Princeton: Princeton University Press, 1967); Richard Bauman, *For the Reputation of Truth: Politics, Religion, and Conflict among the Pennsylvania Quakers, 1750–1800* (Baltimore: Johns Hopkins University Press, 1972); J. William Frost, *The Quaker Family in Colonial America: A Portrait of the Society of Friends* (New York: St. Martin's, 1973); Arthur J. Worrall, *Quakers in the Colonial Northeast* (Hanover, N.H.: University Press of New England, 1980); Richard H. Dunn, ed., *The Papers of William Penn* (5 vols. to date, Philadelphia: University of Pennsylvania Press, 1982–); Jack D. Marietta, *The Reformation of American Quakerism, 1748–1783* (Philadelphia: University of Pennsylvania Press, 1984); and Jean R. Soderlund, *Quakers and Slavery: A Divided Spirit* (Princeton: Princeton University Press, 1985). Some of the best recent scholarly studies of the involvement of nineteenth-century American Quakers in reform and humanitarianism are Peter Brock, *Pioneers of the Peaceable Kingdom* (Princeton: Princeton University Press, 1970); Hiram H. Hilty, "North Carolina Quakers and Slavery" (Ph.D. diss., Duke University, 1969); John B. Pickard, ed., *The Letters of John Greenleaf Whittier* (3 vols., Cambridge, Mass.: Belknap, 1975); Clyde A. Milner II, *With Good Intentions: Quaker Work among the Pawnees, Otos, and Omahas* (Lincoln: University of Nebraska Press, 1982); Marjorie Horsepian Dobkin, ed., *The Making of a Feminist: Early Letters and Journals of M. Carey Thomas* (Kent, Ohio: Kent State University Press, 1979); and Margaret Hope Bacon, *Valiant Friend: The Life of Lucretia Mott* (New York: Walker, 1980). For differing interpretations of the Hicksite separation, see Bliss Forbush, *Elias Hicks: Quaker Liberal* (New York: Columbia University Press, 1956); Robert W. Doherty, *The Hicksite Separation: A Sociological Analysis of Religious Schism in Early Nineteenth-Century America* (New Brunswick: Rutgers University Press, 1967); and H. Larry Ingle, *Quakers in Conflict: The Hicksite Reformation* (Knoxville: University of Ten-

nessee Press, 1986). The study of Quaker groups outside the Northeast was long the preserve of antiquarians, some pedestrian, some inspired. During the last twenty years several dissertations have dealt with western and southern Quakers, including James H. Norton, "Quakers West of the Alleghenies and in Ohio to 1861" (Ph.D. diss., Case Western Reserve University, 1965); David C. LeShana, *Quakers in California: A Study of the Effect of Nineteenth-Century Revivalism upon Western Quakerism* (Newberg, Ore.: Barclay Press, 1969); John William Buys, "Quakers in Indiana in the Nineteenth Century" (Ph.D. diss., University of Florida, 1973); Richard Eugene Wood, "Evangelical Quakers in the Mississippi Valley, 1854–1894" (Ph.D. diss., University of Minnesota, 1985); the work in progress by Damon D. Hickey at the University of South Carolina on North Carolina Friends from 1865 to 1920; and several theses by students of Hugh Barbour at the Earlham School of Religion—for example, B. Eugene Fisher, "A Study of Toleration among Midwest Quakers, 1850–1900" (M.A. thesis, Earlham School of Religion, 1972); Mark E. Minear, "The Richmond Conference of 1887" (M.A. thesis, Earlham School of Religion, 1984); and Richard C. Sartwell, "The Influence of Leading Friends in Ohio Yearly Meeting of Friends, Evangelical, 1854–1919" (M.A. thesis, Earlham School of Religion, 1974). The model study of any regional Quaker group remains, however, Philip S. Benjamin, *The Philadelphia Quakers in the Industrial Age, 1865–1920* (Philadelphia: Temple University Press, 1976). Among the few useful studies of nineteenth-century Orthodox Friends other than Whittier are Donald G. Good, "Elisha Bates: American Quaker Evangelical in the Early Nineteenth Century" (Ph.D. diss., University of Iowa, 1967); Myron Dee Goldsmith, "William Hobson and the Founding of Quakerism in the Pacific Northwest" (Ph.D. diss., Boston University, 1962); J. Brent Bill, *David B. Updegraff: Quaker Holiness Preacher* (Richmond, Ind.: Friends United Press, 1983); and Ronald Eugene Selleck, "I Shall Not Pass This Way Again: A Study of Stephen Grellet's Life and Thought" (Ph.D. diss., University of Chicago, 1985).

5. The literature on these subjects is vast. An excellent treatment is R. Laurence Moore, *Religious Outsiders and the Making of Americans* (New York: Oxford University Press, 1986), esp. 3–21. See also Robert T. Handy, *A History of the Churches in the United States and Canada* (New York: Oxford University Press, 1976), 162–227; and Sydney E. Ahlstrom, *A Religious History of the American People* (New Haven: Yale University Press, 1972), 388–501.

6. For an excellent discussion of these topics, see Willard C. Heiss, ed., *Abstracts of the Records of the Society of Friends in Indiana* (7 vols., Indianapolis: Indiana Historical Society, 1962–1977), I, xiii–xv.

I   THE QUAKER VISION OF RELIGIOUS
LIFE, 1800–1860

1. B. C. Hobbs, ed., *Autobiography of William Hobbs* (Indianapolis: John Woolman Press, 1962); *Memoirs of Rev. Charles G. Finney* (New York: A. S. Barnes, 1876); Barbara M. Cross, ed., *The Autobiography of Lyman Beecher* (Cambridge, Mass.: Belknap, 1961).

2. Donald G. Mathews, *Religion in the Old South* (Chicago: University of Chicago Press, 1977), xvi–xvii; Philip Greven, *The Protestant Temperament: Patterns of Child-Rearing, Religious Experience, and the Self in Early America* (New York: Knopf, 1977), 62–65. Although the literature on antebellum evangelicalism is enormous, the best introduction is Perry Miller, *The Life of the Mind in America from the Revolution to the Civil War* (New York: Harcourt Brace Jovanovich, 1965), 3–95.

3. Rufus M. Jones, *The Later Periods of Quakerism* (2 vols., London: Macmillan, 1921), I, 32–103; Elbert Russell, *The History of Quakerism* (New York: Macmillan, 1942), 229–40.

4. *The Works of George Fox* (8 vols., Philadelphia: Marcus T. C. Gould, 1831), I, 71; J. William Frost, *The Quaker Family in Colonial America: A Portrait of the Society of Friends* (New York: St. Martin's, 1973), 25–26; Thomas Arnett, "A Solemn Address to Youth" [1823], in Thomas Arnett, *Address to the Christian Traveler in Every Evangelical Denomination, and to Others; Containing Devout Meditations and Remarks on Various Subjects; with Occasional Religious Exercises* (Cincinnati: Achilles Pugh, 1872), 24; *Journal of That Faithful Servant of Christ, Charles Osborn, Containing an Account of Many of His Travels and Labors in the Ministry, and His Trials and Exercises in the Service of the Lord, and in Defense of the Truth, as It Is in Jesus* (Cincinnati: Achilles Pugh, 1854), 76.

5. William Hodgson, *Selections of the Letters of Thomas B. Gould, a Minister in the Society of Friends, with Memoirs of His Life* (Philadelphia: C. Sherman and Son, 1860), 45; *A Brief Memoir of Nathan Hunt, Chiefly Extracted from His Journal and Letters* (Philadelphia: Uriah Hunt, 1858), 76–77; William Hobson Journal, 1868, p. 23, William Hobson Papers (Friends Historical Library, Swarthmore College, Swarthmore, Pa.); Howard Brinton, "Stages in Spiritual Development as Reflected in Quaker Journals," in *Children of Light: In Honor of Rufus M. Jones*, ed. Howard Brinton (New York: Macmillan, 1938), 381–406; [Josiah Butler et al.], *John Butler: A Sketch of His Life* (Columbus: William G. Hubbard, 1890), 48; Miriam Cox to Rachel P. Green, 9th Mo. 25, 1850, Reuben Green Papers (Indiana Historical Society Library, Indianapolis); John Cox to Elizabeth Barton, 7th Mo. 17, 1822, box 1, Charles Evans Papers (Quaker Collection, Haverford College, Haverford, Pa.); O. T. Conger, ed., *Autobiography of a Pioneer: The Nativity, Experiences, Travels, and Ministerial Labors of Rev. Samuel Pickard, the "Converted Quaker," Containing Stirring Incidents and Practical Thoughts* (Chicago: Church and Goodman, 1866), 25–26.

6. Benjamin Seebohm, ed., *Memoirs of the Life and Gospel Labours of Stephen Grellet* (2 vols., Philadelphia: Henry Longstreth, 1860), I, 23–25; "Memorial of Muncy Monthly Meeting regarding Mercy Ellis," *Friends' Review*, 11th Mo. 30, 1850, pp. 161–62; Hobbs, ed., *Autobiography of William Hobbs*, 2–5. Howard Brinton argues that Friends routinely underwent an experience that he labels "conversion." They, however, did not refer to this stage of their spiritual life as "conversion," and they did not see themselves as saved because of it. See Brinton, "Stages in Spiritual Development," 381–82. Cf. evangelical conversion narratives in Robert H. Abzug, *Passionate Liberator: Theodore Dwight Weld and the Dilemma of Reform* (New York: Oxford University Press, 1980), 47–51; Charles G. Finney, *Lectures on Revivals of Religion* (New York: Goodrich, 1868), 322; and Charles L. Wallis, ed., *Autobiography of Peter Cartwright* (Nashville: Abingdon, 1956), 36–42.

7. "Anna Lindley," in *Memorials of Deceased Friends Who Were Members of Indiana Yearly Meeting* (Cincinnati: E. Morgan, 1857), 35; *Memoir of the Life and Religious Labours of Henry Hull, a Minister of the Gospel in the Society of Friends, Late of Stanford, in the State of New York* (Philadelphia: Friends' Book Store, 1864), 12; *Extracts from the Memorandums of Jane Bettle, with a Short Memoir concerning Her* (Philadelphia: Joseph and William Kite, 1843), 58–59; Obituary of Dougan Clark, Sr., "Deaths," *Friends' Review*, 9th Mo. 8, 1855, p. 824; Katherine Macy Noyes, ed., *Jesse Macy: An Autobiography* (Springfield, Ill.: Charles C. Thomas, 1933), 22.

8. Hodgson, *Selection of the Letters of Thomas B. Gould*, 34–36, 55; Arnett,

Advice to the Christian Traveler, 51–58; Indiana Yearly Meeting, *Testimony and Epistle of Advice* (n.p., 1827), 2–3; Elisha Bates, *The Doctrines of Friends; or, Principles of the Christian Religion, as Held by the Society of Friends—Commonly Called Quakers* (Mount Pleasant, Ohio, 1868), 3, 34–35. Bates's work first appeared in 1825.

9. Philadelphia Yearly Meeting, *The Ancient Testimony of the Religious Society of Friends, Commonly Called Quakers, Respecting Some of Their Christian Doctrines and Practices* (Philadelphia: Joseph Rakestraw, 1843), 58–59; Russell, *History of Quakerism,* 49–50.

10. "Memorial of Stephen Grellet," in *Memorials concerning Deceased Friends: Members of Philadelphia Yearly Meeting* (Philadelphia: Friends' Book Store, 1875), 39; Arnett, *Advice to the Christian Traveler,* 205–6; *Memoirs of Joseph Tallcot* (Auburn, N.Y.: Miller, Orton, and Milligan, 1855), 19–20; Margaret White to Marcia White, [ca. 1834], box 5, Furnas Family Papers (Friends Historical Library, Swarthmore); John Cox to Elizabeth Barton, 7th Mo. 17, 1822, box 1, Evans Papers; Caleb McComber to Joseph Tallcot, 3rd Mo. 23, 1808, box 3, Tallcot Family Papers (Quaker Collection, Haverford).

11. *Journal of the Life of John Wilbur, a Minister of the Gospel in the Society of Friends; with Selections from His Correspondence* (Providence: George H. Whitney, 1859), 35; "Vision of John Beals," ca. 1797, John Beals Collection (Friends Historical Collection, Guilford College, Greensboro, N.C.).

12. John Cox to Elizabeth Barton, 4th Mo. 2, 1823, box 1, Evans Papers; Margaret Jones Diary, 7th Mo. 6, 1856, typescript (in Willard C. Heiss's possession Indianapolis); Isom Cox to Mary Beeson, 7th Mo. 11, 1841, box 1, Isaac W. and Benjamin B. Beeson Papers (Indiana Division, Indiana State Library, Indianapolis); Walt Whitman, "Notes (Such as They Are) Founded on Elias Hicks," in *The Complete Prose Works of Walt Whitman,* ed. Richard Maurice Burke et al. (10 vols., New York: G. H. Putnam and Sons, 1902), VI, 257–58; Rhys Isaac, *The Transformation of Virginia, 1740–1790* (Chapel Hill: University of North Carolina Press, 1982), 164. Cf. Finney, *Lectures,* 323–24.

13. Arnett, "Solemn Address," 24–25; *Journal of That Faithful Servant of Christ, Charles Osborn,* 146; Joseph Edgerton, *Address to the Members of the Society of Friends* (n.p., 1841), 11; "Memoir of David Sands," *Friends' Review,* 8th Mo. 4, 1860, p. 753; Bates, *Doctrines of Friends,* 125; *Journal of the Life and Religious Services of William Evans, a Minister of the Gospel in the Society of Friends* (Philadelphia: Friends' Book Store, 1870), 146; Lydia Bond Wasson Diary, 2nd Mo. 1820, typescript (in Heiss's possession); Rebecca Grellet to Mildred Ratcliff, 11th Mo. 6, 1812, box 2, Evans Papers.

14. *Journal of the Life and Religious Services of William Evans,* 244–45; Arnett, "Solemn Address," 13; Jones Diary, 4th Mo. 6, 1849; Edgerton, *Address,* 5; Aaron White to Mary White, 5th Mo. 7, 1826, box 2, Furnas Papers; *Extracts from the Memorandums of Jane Bettle,* 54; "A Memoir of the Late Dr. Samuel Emlen, Jr.," *Friend,* 11th Mo. 1, 1828, p. 18; *The Memoirs and Letters of Thomas Kite, a Minister of the Gospel of the Society of Friends* (Philadelphia: Friends' Book Store, 1883), 12.

15. *Journal of Ann Branson, a Minister of the Gospel in the Society of Friends* (Philadelphia: William H. Pile's Sons, 1892), 21–22; "On Giving Alms," *Friend,* 1st Mo. 27, 1838, pp. 132–33; *Discipline of the Society of Friends of Ohio Yearly Meeting* (Mount Pleasant, Ohio: Elisha Bates, 1819), 70; *Journal of That Faithful Servant of Christ, Charles Osborn,* 142; *Indiana Yearly Meeting Minutes,* 1826, p. 18.

16. "An Examination of the Tendency of Fictitious Writings," *Friend,* 10th Mo.

28, 1837, p. 25; *Journal of That Faithful Servant of Christ, Charles Osborn,* 31; Bates, *Doctrines of Friends,* 266–67.

17. William Penn, *No Cross, No Crown: A Discourse Showing the Nature and Discipline of the Holy Cross of Christ, and Denial of Self, and Daily Bearing of Christ's Cross, Is the Way Alone to the Rest and Kingdom of God* (London: Benjamin Clark, 1682); "Memoir of David Sands," 753; Arnett, *Advice to the Christian Traveler,* 227–29; Edgerton, *Address,* 5; "The Doctrine of the Cross," *Friend,* 4th Mo. 14, 1838, pp. 223–24; Hannah Gibbons to Middleton Monthly Meeting, 7th Mo. 31, 1850, box 1, Stratton Papers (Friends Historical Library, Swarthmore).

18. Philadelphia Yearly Meeting, *An Appeal for the Ancient Doctrines of the Society of Friends* (Philadelphia: Joseph Kite, 1847), 32–33; *Brief Memoir of Nathan Hunt,* 103; Editorial, *Friends' Review,* 10th Mo. 5, 1850, p. 40; *Memoirs and Letters of Thomas Kite,* 106; *Journal of the Life of John Wilbur,* 48; "Practical Christianity," *Friend,* 12th Mo. 23, 1837, pp. 93–94; D. H., "Some Lines Intended Principally for the Youth of the Society of Friends," ibid., 2nd Mo. 13, 1841, p. 157. For the Wesleyan and Finneyite formulations of holiness, see Timothy L. Smith, *Revivalism and Social Reform: American Protestantism on the Eve of the Civil War* (New York: Harper and Row, 1965), 103–47. Wesleyans saw sanctification as perfection; those in the Reformed tradition viewed it as empowerment. Friends were thus closer to the Wesleyan formulation.

19. Bates, *Doctrines of Friends,* 187–95.

20. *Memoirs of Joseph Tallcot,* 94; Arnett, *Advice to the Christian Traveler,* 243; "On Silent Worship," *Friends' Review,* 3rd Mo. 15, 1851, pp. 402–3. For an account of a Quaker meeting for worship about 1800, see John Belton O'Neall, *The Annals of Newberry, Historical, Biographical, and Anecdotal* (Charleston, S. C.: S. G. Courtenay, 1859), 32–37.

21. *Journal of the Life of John Wilbur,* 26–27; *Memoirs of Joseph Tallcot,* 103–5; *Journal of That Faithful Servant of Christ, Charles Osborn,* 18; Bates, *Doctrines of Friends,* 196–219; *Memoir of the Life and Religious Labours of Henry Hull,* 103.

22. Bates, *Doctrines of Friends,* 199–202; *Memoirs of Joseph Tallcot,* 79–80, 259, 289; Philadelphia Yearly Meeting, *Ancient Doctrines,* 64–66; Jacob Baker, *Incidents of My Life and Work of 84 Years* (Richmond, Ind.: Nicholson, 1911), 33–34; *Journal of the Life and Religious Services of William Evans,* 146; Henry W. Painter, "History of Spiceland Quarterly Meeting," 1921, p. 14, Spiceland Township file, Local History Collection (Henry County Historical Society, New Castle, Ind.); [James Baldwin], *In My Youth: From the Posthumous Papers of Robert Dudley* (Indianapolis: Bobbs-Merrill, 1914), 12–24.

23. Russell, *History of Quakerism,* 236–37; Kenneth L. Carroll, "Singing in the Spirit in Early Quakerism," *Quaker History,* 73 (Spring 1984), 10–13; Christopher Densmore, "Quaker Publishing in New York State, 1784–1860," ibid., 74 (Fall 1985), 51; "Habits of Ministers," *Friends' Review,* 11th Mo. 3, 1860, pp. 135–36; *Journal of the Life, Travels, and Gospel Labours of William Williams, Dec.; A Minister of the Society of Friends Late of White-Water, Indiana* (Cincinnati: Lodge, L'Hommedieu, and Hammond, 1828), 100.

24. *Journal of the Life of John Wilbur,* 19, 30–31, 36–39, 570; *Journal of Ann Branson,* 74; *Memoirs of Joseph Tallcot,* 39; Hobbs, ed., *Autobiography of William Hobbs,* 1–2; Seebohm, ed., *Memoirs of the Life and Gospel Labours of Stephen Grellet,* I, 37–38; Charles F. Coffin, "Personal Recollections of Jeremiah Hubbard," Dec. 1909, Jeremiah Hubbard folder, Charles F. and Rhoda M. Coffin Papers (Archives, Earlham College, Richmond, Ind.); *Memoir of Christopher Healy, Taken Chiefly from His Own Memoranda* (Philadelphia: Friends' Book Store, 1886), 1–2, 69, 83; *Journal of That Faithful Servant of Christ, Charles Osborn,* viii, 192; "Faithfulness and Consistency in Supporting Religious Testimonies," *Friend,* 7th

Mo. 7, 1838, p. 318; Rebecca Collins to Joseph Tallcot, 9th Mo. 6, 1835, box 1, Tallcot Papers.

25. "Faithfulness and Consistency," 317–18; Arnett, *Advice to the Christian Traveler*, 220; *Memoirs of Joseph Tallcot*, 141, 260–61; Philadelphia Yearly Meeting, *Ancient Testimony*, 36; Jones, *Later Periods of Quakerism*, II, 921; *Memorandums of Jane Bettle*, 97–98.

26. [Baldwin], *In My Youth*, 100; *Discipline of the Society of Friends of Ohio Yearly Meeting*, 19, 34–35; Isaac W. Beeson to Joshua Stanley, 2nd Mo. 26, 1841, box 1, Beeson Papers; Jack D. Marietta, *The Reformation of American Quakerism, 1748–1783* (Philadelphia: University of Pennsylvania Press, 1984), 3–128. For some typical disciplines besides that of Ohio, see *Discipline of the Society of Friends of Indiana Yearly Meeting* (Cincinnati: Achilles Pugh, 1839); *Rules of Discipline of the Yearly Meeting of Friends Held in Philadelphia* (Philadelphia: J. Mortimer, 1828); and *Discipline of the Yearly Meeting of Friends Held in New-York for the State of New-York and Parts Adjacent as Revised and Adopted, in the Sixth Month, 1810* (New York: Mahlon Day, 1836). For an evocation of a life lived under these regulations during the 1840s and 1850s, see Hannah Whitall Smith, *The Unselfishness of God and How I Discovered It: A Spiritual Autobiography* (New York: Revell, 1903).

27. [Baldwin], *In My Youth*, 147; *Journal of the Life, Travels, and Gospel Labours of William Williams*, 45; Bernhard Knollenberg, *Pioneer Sketches of the Upper Whitewater Valley: Quaker Stronghold of the West* (Indianapolis: Indiana Historical Society, 1945), 90–96; Marjorie Horsepian Dobkin, ed., *The Making of a Feminist: Early Journals and Letters of M. Carey Thomas* (Kent, Ohio: Kent State University Press, 1979), 290; *Discipline of the Society of Friends of Ohio Yearly Meeting*, 43–45; James H. Norton, "Quakerism West of the Alleghenies and in Ohio to 1861" (Ph.D. diss., Case Western Reserve University, 1965), 72, 91, 123–26; William Wade Hinshaw, ed., *Encyclopedia of American Quaker Genealogy* (6 vols., Ann Arbor: Edwards Brothers, 1936–1950), I, xiii, 959; *Memoirs of Joseph Tallcot*, 47; Noyes, ed., *Autobiography of Jesse Macy*, 10; Conger, ed., *Autobiography of a Pioneer*, 18–19; Lost Creek Monthly Meeting Men's Minutes, 7th Mo. 26, 1806, 9th Mo. 27, 1806 (Friends Historical Collection, Guilford). For the intricacy of Quaker family connections, see, for example, Alpheus H. Harlan, *History and Genealogy of the Harlan Family, and Particularly of the Descendants of George and Michael Harlan, Who Settled in Chester County, Pennsylvania, 1687* (Baltimore, 1914); and Gilbert S. Cope, *Genealogy of the Sharpless Family, Descended from John and Jane Sharpless, Settlers Near Chester, Pa., 1682* (Philadelphia, 1887).

28. "Benevolence," *Friends' Review*, 3rd Mo. 2, 1850, pp. 370–72; Sydney V. James, *A People among Peoples: Quaker Benevolence in Eighteenth-Century America* (Cambridge: Harvard University Press, 1963); Arnett, *Advice to the Christian Traveler*, 112–13; *Memoirs of Joseph Tallcot*, 107; David Brion Davis, *The Problem of Slavery in the Age of Revolution, 1770–1823* (Ithaca: Cornell University Press, 1975), 251, 254; Russell, *History of Quakerism*, 262.

II   THE BREAKDOWN OF THE OLDER VISION, 1800–1850

1. William Hodgson, *The Society of Friends in the Nineteenth Century: A Historical View of the Successive Convulsions and Schisms Therein during That Period* (2 vols., Philadelphia, 1875–1876).

2. See, for example, Errol T. Elliott, *Quakers on the American Frontier* (Richmond, Ind.: Friends United Press, 1969); and Myron Dee Goldsmith, "William Hobson and the Founding of Quakerism in the Pacific Northwest" (Ph.D. diss., Boston University, 1963), 112–51.

3. Stephen B. Weeks, *Southern Quakers and Slavery: A Study in Institutional History* (Baltimore: Johns Hopkins University Press, 1896), 245–307; Rufus M. Jones, *The Later Periods of Quakerism* (2 vols., London: Macmillan, 1921), I, 377–434; Amos and Matilda Stuart to Rachel P. Wilson, Sept. 18, 1831, Reuben Green Papers (Indiana Historical Society Library, Indianapolis); Larry Dale Gragg, *Migration in Early America: The Virginia Quaker Experience* (Ann Arbor: UMI Press, 1980); *Memoirs and Letters of Thomas Kite, a Minister of the Gospel of the Society of Friends* (Philadelphia: Friends' Book Store, 1883), 305.

4. Weeks, *Southern Quakers and Slavery*, 269; "Journal of John Hunt," in *Friends Miscellany*, ed. John Comly and Isaac Comly (13 vols., Philadelphia, 1831–1839), X, 353; Elbert Russell, *The History of Quakerism* (New York: Macmillan, 1942), 275–76, 434.

5. "Excerpts from a Letter of Borden Stanton to Friends of Wrightsborough Monthly Meeting," *Friends Miscellany*, XII, 216–17; George Carter letter, *Christian Worker*, 12th Mo. 1, 1874, pp. 362–63; *Discipline of the Society of Friends of Ohio Yearly Meeting* (St. Clairsville, Ohio: Elisha Bates, 1819), 19; Alexander H. Hay, "The Rise of the Pastoral System in the Society of Friends" (M.A. thesis, Haverford College, 1938), 17.

6. Editorial, *Friends' Review*, 10th Mo. 30, 1847, p. 89; [James Baldwin], *In My Youth: From the Posthumous Papers of Robert Dudley* (Indianapolis: Bobbs-Merrill, 1914), 146; *Discipline of the Society of Friends of Ohio Yearly Meeting; Discipline of the Society of Friends of Indiana Yearly Meeting* (Cincinnati: Achilles Pugh, 1839); "Circular, Friends Boarding School, Near Richmond, Indiana," *Western Friend*, 1st Mo. 6, 1848, p. 67; Jones, *Later Periods of Quakerism*, I, 427–29; Russell, *History of Quakerism*, 400.

7. *A Journal of the Life, Travels, Religious Exercises, and Labours in the Work of the Ministry of Joshua Evans, Late of Newton Township, Gloucester County, New Jersey* (Byberry, Pa.: John Comly, 1837), 160; Benjamin Seebohm, ed., *Memoirs of William Forster* (2 vols., London: Alfred W. Bennett, 1865), I, 333, 342–43; Benjamin Seebohm, ed., *Memoirs of the Life and Gospel Labours of Stephen Grellet* (2 vols., Philadelphia: Henry Longstreth, 1860), I, 166; Jones, *Later Periods of Quakerism*, I, 415. Records examined include the earliest volumes of men's and women's minutes to circa 1850 of New Garden, White River, Duck Creek, Springfield, and Whitewater monthly meetings in Indiana (Archives, Earlham College, Richmond, Ind.); West Branch Monthly Meeting in Ohio (ibid.); Center and Caesar's Creek monthly meetings in Ohio (Wilmington Yearly Meeting Archives, Wilmington College, Wilmington, Ohio); Adrian Monthly Meeting in Michigan and Goshen Monthly Meeting in Ohio (Archives, Malone College, Canton, Ohio); and Lost Creek Monthly Meeting in Tennessee (Friends Historical Collection, Guilford College, Greensboro, N.C.). See also Chap. 3, tables 1, 2, and 3.

8. The best guide to the controversies of this period is Jones, *Later Periods of Quakerism*, I, 435–537.

9. For Elias Hicks, see Bliss Forbush, *Elias Hicks: Quaker Liberal* (New York: Columbia University Press, 1956). The standard interpretation of the Hicksite separation is Robert W. Doherty, *The Hicksite Separation: A Sociological Analysis of Religious Schism in Early Nineteenth-Century America* (New Brunswick: Rutgers University Press, 1967).

10. Jones, *Later Periods of Quakerism*, I, 443–44; Forbush, *Elias Hicks*, 191–98, 218–19; Doherty, *Hicksite Separation*, 28. The theme of the Hicksites as advocates of a Quaker reformation is developed in H. Larry Ingle, *Quakers in Conflict: The Hicksite Reformation* (Knoxville: University of Tennessee Press, 1986), 38–61.

11. Doherty, *Hicksite Separation*, 25–28; Jones, *Later Periods of Quakerism*, I, 439–58.

12. Doherty, *Hicksite Separation*, 26–27, 30; *Letters of Elias Hicks* (Philadelphia: T. Ellwood Zell, 1861), 23–27, 43–57, 76–77.

13. Doherty, *Hicksite Separation*, 33–89, esp. 67–76. For the Hicksites as liberals, see Samuel M. Janney, *An Examination of the Causes Which Led to the Separation of the Religious Society of Friends in America in 1827–28* (Philadelphia: T. Ellwood Zell 1868); and Russell, *History of Quakerism*, 282–83.

14. Jones, *Later Periods of Quakerism*, I, 480; *Extracts from the Journals and Letters of Hannah Chapman Backhouse* (London: Richard Barrett, 1858), 282–83; Nathan Mendenhall to Asa Folger, 7th Mo. 16, 1826, Meeting for Sufferings Papers (Friends Historical Collection, Guilford); Richard Mendenhall to George C. Mendenhall, 12th Mo. 22, 1828, box 2, Hobbs-Mendenhall Papers (Southern Historical Collection, University of North Carolina, Chapel Hill); Richard D. Brown, *Modernization: The Transformation of American Life, 1607–1865* (New York: Hill and Wang, 1976), 124–27. Some historians have argued that the "New Light" movement in New England during the 1810s and 1820s was a forerunner of the Hicksite separation and that the New England New Light Quakers "logically would have followed the Liberal prophet." There is considerable evidence to support such a position. The New Lights spoke in much the same language as Hicks, emphasizing the guidance of the Inner Light over that of the Bible, deemphasizing the divinity of Christ, and speaking in terms of progressive revelation. They suffered the same fate of disownment as did the Hicksites. Here the similarities break down. The New Lights, concentrated in Lynn and New Bedford, Massachusetts, were not struggling farmers and small merchants. In New Bedford, at least, they were, in the words of Frederick B. Tolles, "to be found among the wealthiest families in the city, families prominently engaged in whaling and other mercantile and manufacturing pursuits; at least eight of the most conspicuous were later listed among the richest men in the state." Thus in New England, at least, economic advance led, not toward evangelical Quakerism, but toward a variation of the Hicksite position. See Forbush, *Elias Hicks*, 208–10, 283; and Frederick B. Tolles, "The New Light Quakers of Lynn and New Bedford," *New England Quarterly*, 32 (Sept. 1959), 291–319. No study of the Hicksite separation in Ohio has ever been undertaken, at least not of its social and economic ramifications. The surviving records of Hicksite meetings in Indiana suggest that a disproportionate number of Hicksites there had Pennsylvania, New Jersey, or Maryland roots. See Willard C. Heiss, ed., *Abstracts of the Records of the Society of Friends in Indiana* (7 vols., Indianapolis: Indiana Historical Society, 1962–1977), I, 193–236, II, 427–31, III, 539–53, IV, 97–151, V, 123–42, 199–202.

15. *A Testimony and Epistle of Advice Issued by Indiana Yearly Meeting* (n.p., 1827), 2; *The Testimony of the Society of Friends on the Continent of North America* (Philadelphia: Friends' Book Store, 1830), 7, 13, 20–21; *Epistles and Testimonies Issued by the Yearly Meetings of Friends in North America Setting Forth Their Belief in the Holy Scriptures and in the Divinity and Offices of Our Lord and Saviour Jesus Christ* (Philadelphia: n.p., 1828); Philadelphia Yearly Meeting, *The Ancient Testimony of the Religious Society of Friends, Commonly Called Quakers, Respecting Some of Their Christian Doctrines and Practices* (Philadelphia: Joseph Rakestraw, 1843), 36–41. For similar controversy among other Protestants, see Stuart C. Henry, *Unvanquished Puritan: A Portrait of Lyman Beecher* (Grand Rapids: Eerdmans, 1973), 117–26.

16. The problems that diverse perceptions of the Inner Light posed for later generations of Friends are treated in chap. 6.

17. *Memoirs of Joseph Tallcot* (Auburn, N.Y.: Miller, Orten, and Milligan, 1855),

209; Donald Good, "Elisha Bates: American Quaker Evangelical in the Early Nineteenth Century" (Ph.D. diss., University of Iowa, 1967), 137–38; *Christianity and Infidelity Compared* (Philadelphia: Thomas Kite, 1824); "Anarchy of Hicksism," *Friend*, 1st Mo. 16, 1830, pp. 110–11; "Deism," ibid., 8th Mo. 8, 1830, pp. 341–42; "German Rationalists," ibid., 10th Mo. 25, 1828, pp. 14–15; editorial, ibid., 3rd Mo. 12, 1830, p. 172.

18. *Journal of the Life, Travels, and Gospel Labors of Thomas Arnett* (Chicago: Publishing Association of Friends, 1884), 69; *Journal of That Faithful Servant of Christ, Charles Osborn, Containing an Account of Many of His Travels and Labors in the Ministry, and His Trials and Exercises in the Service of the Lord, and in Defense of the Truth, as It Is in Jesus* (Cincinnati: Achilles Pugh, 1854), 204–7, 210–14; *Journal of the Life and Religious Labors of William Evans, a Minister of the Gospel in the Society of Friends* (Philadelphia: Friends' Book Store, 1870), 106; "Orthodox Disownments," *Miscellaneous Repository*, 1 (9th Mo. 1828), 363–71.

19. Jones, *Later Periods of Quakerism*, I, 465–81; James H. Norton, "Quakers West of the Alleghenies and in Ohio to 1861" (Ph.D. diss., Case Western Reserve University, 1965), 147–56. In Indiana, for example, one Friend stormed out of his monthly meeting averring that "Elias Hicks is as good a man as Jesus Christ and that a certain approved minister aught [sic] to be killed off." Duck Creek Monthly Meeting Men's Minutes, 4th Mo. 28, 1828.

20. *Extracts from the Journals and Letters of Hannah Chapman Backhouse*, 83, 87, 92; Samuel Parsons to North Carolina Yearly Meeting for Sufferings, 10th Mo. 6, 1828, Meeting for Sufferings Papers; "Communication," *Friend*, 10th Mo. 27, 1827, p. 15; Charles Fisher to Elijah Coffin, 12th Mo. 3, 1828, box 1, Coffin Family Papers (Friends Historical Library, Swarthmore College, Swarthmore, Pa.); Mary Coffin Johnson and Percival Brooks Coffin, *Charles F. Coffin: A Quaker Pioneer* (Richmond, Ind.: Nicholson, 1923), 72–73; Jonathan Evans to Hannah Evans, 9th Mo. 5, 1828, box 1, Charles Evans Papers (Quaker Collection, Haverford College, Haverford, Pa.).

21. Arthur J. Mekeel, *Quakerism and a Creed* (Philadelphia: Friends' Book Store, 1936), 59–67; Good, "Elisha Bates," 124–27; *Testimony of the Society of Friends*; Jones, *Later Periods of Quakerism*, I, 481.

22. Good, "Elisha Bates," 279; Johnson and Coffin, *Charles F. Coffin*, 73; Henry Hoover, *Sketches and Incidents, Embracing a Period of Fifty Years* (Indianapolis: John Woolman Press, 1962), 3–4, 19; "Compromise," *Friend*, 10th Mo. 10, 1831, pp. 15–16; "The Hicksite Yearly Meeting," ibid., 9th Mo. 18, 1830, p. 392; Thomas Evans to Henry Cope, 6th Mo. 21, 1829, box 1, Evans Papers; Elijah Coffin to Samuel Boyd Tobey, 7th Mo. 25, 1845, Miscellaneous Letters (Quaker Collection, Haverford).

23. *Extracts from the Journals and Letters of Hannah Chapman Backhouse*, 100; Jones, *Later Periods of Quakerism*, I, 473; William Tallack, *Friendly Sketches in America* (London: A. W. Bennett, 1861), 87–88; "Excellence of Unity," *Friend*, 2nd Mo. 20, 1829, pp. 134–35.

24. Cf. Forbush, *Elias Hicks*, 217–27; and Ronald Eugene Selleck, "I Shall Not Pass This Way Again: A Study of Stephen Grellet's Life and Thought" (Ph.D. diss., University of Chicago, 1985).

25. The standard biography of Gurney is David E. Swift, *Joseph John Gurney: Banker, Reformer, and Quaker* (Middletown, Conn.: Wesleyan University Press, 1962). See also Joseph Bevan Braithwaite, ed., *Memoirs of Joseph John Gurney; With Selections from His Journal and Correspondence* (2 vols., Philadelphia: Lippincott and Grambo, 1855).

26. Swift, *Joseph John Gurney*, 114–18; Joseph John Gurney, *Observations on the*

Distinguishing Views and Practices of the Society of Friends (New York: Mahlon Day, 1840).

27. Swift, *Joseph John Gurney*, 175–80.

28. Ibid., 175; Gurney, *Observations*, 45–46; Jones, *Later Periods of Quakerism*, I, 504–5.

29. Jones, *Later Periods of Quakerism*, I, 503–4; Arthur Owen Roberts, "The Concepts of Perfection in the History of the Quaker Movement" (B.D. thesis, Nazarene Theological Seminary, 1951), 94–95, 100; Joseph John Gurney, *Essays on the Doctrines, Evidences, and Practical Operation of Christianity* (Philadelphia: Longstreth, 1884), 625–27, 630–31.

30. Wells, *Joseph John Gurney*, 48–68, 89–113; David Brion Davis, *The Problem of Slavery in the Age of Revolution, 1770–1823* (Ithaca: Cornell University Press, 1975), 246–47.

31. Braithwaite, ed., *Memoirs of Joseph John Gurney*, II, 111, 118–20, 143–47, 149–50; Jones, *Later Periods of Quakerism*, I, 520; Johnson and Coffin, *Charles F. Coffin*, 101; William Hodgson, *Selections from the Letters of Thomas B. Gould, a Minister of the Gospel in the Society of Friends, with Memoirs of His Life* (Philadelphia: C. Sherman and Son, 1860), 90–95; *Memoirs of Nathan Hunt, Taken Chiefly from His Journal and Letters* (Philadelphia: Uriah Hunt, 1858), 115–16. For an account of the humanitarian aspects of Gurney's journey, see James A. Rawley, "Joseph John Gurney's Mission to America, 1837–1840," *Mississippi Valley Historical Review*, 49 (March 1963), 653–74.

32. Russell, *History of Quakerism*, 341, 392.

33. Susanna and Lydia Hockett verses, n.d., Miscellaneous Manuscripts (Friends Historical Library, Swarthmore); Isaac W. Beeson account book, 1839–1861, pp. 29, 31–32, box 1, Isaac W. and Benjamin B. Beeson Papers (Indiana Division, Indiana State Library, Indianapolis); Ann Williams Hunt commonplace book, Individual Friends Collection (Archives, Earlham); Elijah Coffin scrapbook, Scrapbook Collection (Henry County Historical Society Museum, New Castle, Ind.); L. H. Eddy, "Extracts from an Essay 'On the Exertions of Pious Ladies,' by Hannah More," 1833, box 2, Tallcot Family Papers (Quaker Collection, Haverford).

34. Norton, "Quakers West of the Alleghenies," 316–18; Ann Taylor Updegraff Diary, 10th Mo. 24, 1842, 5th Mo. 30, 1843, 2nd Mo. 8, 1844, 5th Mo. 10, 1844, 12th Mo. 2, 1843, 3rd Mo. 9, 1845, box 1, Updegraff Family Papers (Quaker Collection, Haverford); J. Brent Bill, *David B. Updegraff: Quaker Holiness Preacher* (Richmond, Ind.: Friends United Press, 1983), 13.

35. Joseph Tallcot, "Circular," [ca. 1849], box 4, Tallcot Papers; Synod of Geneva to Tallcot, Feb. 19, 1819, box 2, ibid.; *Memoirs of Joseph Tallcot*, 116–17; Joseph Tallcot, *The Friendly Visitant for Parents and Children* (2 vols., Philadelphia: Longstreth, n.d.), II, iv, 5–14, 99–102, 107, 172–76, 188–96, 248. Although Tallcot issued the *Friendly Visitant* as a periodical, he apparently also sold collected numbers in book form.

36. Silas Cornell to Joseph Tallcot, 12th Mo. 18, 1837, box 1, Tallcot Papers; Richard Mott to Tallcot, 8th Mo. 9, 1844, box 3, ibid.; Ann Taylor Updegraff Diary, 10th Mo. 7, 1844; Tallcot, *Friendly Visitant*, 97–99; Thomas E. Drake, *Quakers and Slavery in America* (New Haven: Yale University Press, 1950), 133–66; Centerville, Ind. *Wayne County Record*, Aug. 28, 1841, p. 1; Russell, *History of Quakerism*, 394–97; Thomas Arnett, *Address to the Christian Traveler in Every Evangelical Denomination, and to Others; Containing Devout Meditations and Remarks on Various Subjects; with Occasional Religious Exercises* (Cincinnati: Achilles Pugh, 1872), 97; Randolph County, Indiana, Temperance Society Records, 1839–1845 (in Willard C. Heiss's possession, Indianapolis). The literature on evangelicalism and

reform is immense. A good survey is Ronald G. Walters, *American Reformers, 1815–1860* (New York: Hill and Wang, 1978). For a vivid reminiscence by a Friend in the "Burned-Over District" of New York, see Alex. M. Purdy, "Reminiscences of 1848–50," *American Friend*, 10th Mo. 16, 1902, pp. 807–8.

37. "First Day Schools," *Friend*, 8th Mo. 21, 1830, p. 359; *Memoirs of Joseph Tallcot*, 275; Joseph Tallcot, "Address to Young Parents," n.d., box 4, Tallcot Papers; Isaac Collins to Tallcot, 11th Mo. 20, 1833, box 1, ibid.; [Frederic W. Seebohm et al., comps.], *Private Memoirs of B. and E. Seebohm* (London: Provest, 1873), 281–82.

38. "To the Bible Association of Friends in America," *Friend*, 6th Mo. 2, 1832, pp. 266–67; Editorial, ibid., 2nd Mo. 13, 1830, p. 144; *Extracts from the Journals and Letters of Hannah Chapman Backhouse*, 155; *Memoir of Joseph Tallcot*, 201, 279; *Eleventh Annual Report of the Bible Association of Friends in America* (Philadelphia: The Association, 1840), 6; Records of the Spiceland Auxiliary to the Bible Association of Friends in America, 1837–1851, 8th Mo. 17, 1838, 2nd Mo. 18, 1840 (Henry County Historical Society). For similar activities among non-Quaker evangelicals, see Mark A. Noll, "The Image of the United States as a Biblical Nation, 1776–1865," in *The Bible in America: Essays in Cultural History*, ed. Nathan O. Hatch and Mark A. Noll (New York: Oxford University Press, 1982), 39.

39. *Memoirs of Joseph Tallcot*, 201, 279, 220–22; "Remarks on Domestic Piety and Social Converse among Friends," *Friends' Review*, 10th Mo. 30, 1847, p. 84; "Indiana Yearly Meeting," ibid., 12th Mo. 1, 1849, pp. 170–71; Joseph John Gurney, *A Letter to the Friends of the Monthly Meeting of Adrian, Michigan* (New York: Mahlon Day, 1839), 14.

40. "First Day Schools," *Friend*, 8th Mo. 7, 1830, p. 344; "First Day Schools," ibid., 2nd Mo. 10, 1838, p. 152; *Memoirs of Joseph Tallcot*, 140–41; *Extracts from the Journals and Letters of Hannah Chapman Backhouse*, 133–44. The Tallcot Papers at Haverford are especially rich in material on First Day schools. See, for example, David Lindley to Tallcot, 9th Mo. 22, 1834, box 2; William Bassett to Tallcot, 2nd Mo. 7, 1837, box 1; and Stephen Wood to Tallcot, 8th Mo. 3, 1834, box 5.

41. *Extracts from the Journals and Letters of Hannah Chapman Backhouse*, 133. For the books recommended for use in First Day schools, see Stephen Wood to Tallcot, 8th Mo. 3, 1834, box 5, Tallcot Papers; and printed circular attached to Thomas Cock to Tallcot, 9th Mo. 12, 1836, box 1, ibid. For the similarity of First Day schools to evangelical Sunday schools, see Paul E. Johnson, *A Shopkeeper's Millennium: Society and Revivals in Rochester, 1815–1837* (New York: Hill and Wang, 1978), 111.

42. Norton, "Quakers West of the Alleghenies," 289; Bernhard Knollenberg, *Pioneer Sketches of the Upper Whitewater Valley: Quaker Stronghold of the West* (Indianapolis: Indiana Historical Society, 1945), 28–29; Ebenezer C. Tucker, *History of Randolph County, Indiana* (Chicago: Interstate, 1882), 53. From 1816 to 1851 a Friend sought legislative office in almost every election in Indiana. See Dorothy Riker and Gayle Thornbrough, *Indiana Election Returns, 1816–1851* (Indianapolis: Indiana Historical Bureau, 1960).

43. Robert Kelley, *The Cultural Pattern in American Politics: The First Century* (New York: Knopf, 1979), 167; Daniel Walker Howe, *The Political Culture of the American Whigs* (Chicago: University of Chicago Press, 1979), 167; Ronald P. Formisano, *The Birth of Mass Political Parties: Michigan, 1837–1861* (Princeton: Princeton University Press, 1971), 149–50; L. Branson to Isaac W. and Mary Beeson, 8th Mo. 3, 1840, box 1, Beeson Papers; Walter Edgerton, *A History of the Separation in Indiana Yearly Meeting of Friends in the Winter of 1842 and 1843 on the Anti-*

Slavery Question (Cincinnati: Achilles Pugh, 1856), 84–86, 139–41, 224; Knollenberg, *Pioneer Sketches*, 74–82. The account of George Evans is in a reminiscence by Martin L. Bundy, another Whig with Quaker antecedents, in the *New Castle* (Ind.) *Courier*, Dec. 14, 1883, p. 12. Interestingly, when Evans lost his position as assistant clerk, he had bolted the Whigs and was running for state senator as a Free Soil Democrat. Oliver Albertson Journal, 10th Mo. 6, 1848 (in Heiss's possession).

44. *Memoirs of Joseph Tallcot*, 329. The literature on antebellum evangelicalism is extensive. Illuminating summaries include Perry Miller, *The Life of the Mind in America from the Revolution to the Civil War* (New York: Harcourt Brace Jovanovich, 1965), 3–95; Robert T. Handy, *A Christian America: Protestant Hopes and Historical Realities* (New York: Oxford University Press, 1971), 27–64; and Sydney E. Ahlstrom, *A Religious History of the American People* (New Haven: Yale University Press, 1972), 469–71.

45. John Wilbur, *Letters to a Friend on Some of the Primitive Doctrines of Christianity* (London: Harvey and Darton, 1832); Jones, *Later Periods of Quakerism*, I, 511–15; Tallack, *Friendly Sketches*, 9–12; "New England Quakerieties," *Western Work*, 5 (Oct. 1901), 3; John Wilbur, *A Narrative and Exposition of the Late Proceedings of New England Yearly Meeting, with Some of Its Subordinate Meetings and Their Committee, in Relation to the Doctrinal Controversy Now Existing in the Society of Friends* (New York: Piercy and Reed, 1845), 68–69.

46. Jones, *Later Periods of Quakerism*, I, 521–26; Wilbur, *Narrative*, 140–56. Wilbur was not the only Friend to snipe at Gurney. Gurney had been liberated to travel in the United States only after extended debate in London Yearly Meeting and had crossed the Atlantic pursued by letters warning American Friends against his "unsoundness." See Jones, *Later Periods of Quakerism*, I, 516–18. For one of the letters, see "Joseph John Gurney's Proposal to Go to America," 1837, box 2, Evans Papers.

47. There is no modern analysis of Wilburism. For a relatively balanced sketch by an English Friend, see Tallack, *Friendly Sketches*, 88–107, 118–31.

48. Jones, *Later Periods of Quakerism*, I, 531; Russell, *History of Quakerism*, 351–52.

49. Wilbur, *Narrative*, 20–21, 27–28, 224–25; *Journal of That Faithful Servant of Christ, Charles Osborn*, 392–401; Rhode Island letter, *Friend*, 3rd Mo. 24, 1838, p. 199; "The First Friends: Plea on Behalf of the Early Friends," ibid., 10th Mo. 7, 1837, p. 5; John L. Kite, *Separation from the Religious Society of Friends* (Philadelphia: n.p., 1859), 5.

50. Philadelphia Yearly Meeting, *An Appeal for the Ancient Doctrines of the Society of Friends* (Philadelphia: Joseph Kite, 1847), 16; Eunice Thomasson, comp., *Some Account of the Life and Religious Services of Joseph Edgerton, a Minister of the Gospel in the Society of Friends, with Extracts from His Correspondence* (Philadelphia: William H. Pile, 1885), 55; Hodgson, *Society of Friends in the Nineteenth Century*, I, 304–5.

51. *Journal of the Life of John Wilbur*, 394; Philadelphia Yearly Meeting, *Appeal*, 6–7; *Memoirs of Joseph Tallcot*, 279; Hodgson, *Society of Friends in the Nineteenth Century*, I, 232–33; Mildred Ratcliff to Jonathan Evans, 1st Mo. 23, 1835, box 2, Evans Papers.

52. Wilbur, *Narrative*, 14–15, 30; Philadelphia Yearly Meeting, *Appeal*, 9, 32–33; Thomas Lamborn, *Mystery Babylon Somewhat Exposed: The Standing of the Church Referred To and the True Seed Encouraged* (New Garden, Pa., 1858), 5.

53. Wilbur, *Narrative*, 29, 345; Joshua Maule, *Transactions and Changes in the Society of Friends, and Incidents in the Life and Experience of Joshua Maule*

(Philadelphia: J. B. Lippincott, 1886), 55–56; *Journal of That Faithful Servant of Christ, Charles Osborn*, 409–10; *Address to the Society of Friends* (n.p., 1855).

54. Hodgson, *Selections from the Letters of Thomas B. Gould*, 109; *Journal of Ann Branson, a Minister of the Gospel in the Society of Friends* (Philadelphia: Wm. H. Pile's Sons, 1892), 75; Thomasson, comp., *Some Account of the Life and Religious Services of Joseph Edgerton*, 133, 240–41; *Journal of That Faithful Servant of Christ, Charles Osborn*, 344.

55. Tucker, *History of Randolph County, Indiana*, 172; White River Monthly Meeting Men's Minutes, 5th Mo. 14, 1836, 6th Mo. 11, 1836; Duck Creek Monthly Meeting Men's Minutes, 3rd Mo. 23, 1837, 8th Mo. 24, 1837; "Journal of Benjamin Cox," 3rd Mo. 1836, p. 37, typescript (in Heiss's possession); Braithwaite, ed., *Memoirs of Joseph John Gurney*, II, 104–5; Nathan Hunt Ballenger, "Quakers in Henry County," *New Castle* (Ind.) *Courier*, July 11, 1890, p. 1; Good, "Elisha Bates," 201–26, 255–56, 262–70, 277–300; Elisha Bates, *An Examination of Certain Proceedings and Principles of the Society of Friends, Called Quakers* (St. Clairsville, Ohio, 1837), viii–ix, 86–96, 116–17, 122–23; "Letters from George Evans to His Family and Friends at Spiceland, Indiana," 1839–1840, typescript, pp. 14–16 (Indiana Division); Laura S. Haviland, *A Woman's Life-Work: Labors and Experiences* (Chicago: C. V. Waite, 1887), 32–34.

56. Jones, *Later Periods of Quakerism*, 526, 532. For typical presentations of the Wilburite position, see Wilbur, *Narrative*; Philadelphia Yearly Meeting, *Appeal*; [Charles Evans], *Considerations Addressed to the Members of the Yearly Meeting of Philadelphia* (Philadelphia: John Penington, 1846); Joseph E. Maule, *Some Extracts and Remarks on Acknowledging Meetings of Separatists as Though They Were Meetings of Friends* (Philadelphia: William S. Young, 1859); Philadelphia Yearly Meeting, *Report in Relation to the Facts and Causes of the Division Which Occurred in New England Yearly Meeting in the Year 1845* (Philadelphia: The Yearly Meeting, 1847); and William Hodgson, Jr., *An Examination of the Memoirs and Writings of Joseph John Gurney* (Philadelphia, 1856). For the Gurneyite position, see *Narrative of the Facts and Circumstances That Have Tended to Produce a Secession from the Society of Friends in New England Yearly Meeting* (Providence: Knowles and Vose, 1845); *A Declaration of New-England Yearly Meeting of Friends upon Various Christian Subjects* (Providence: Knowles and Vose, 1845); New England Yearly Meeting for Sufferings, *A Vindication of the Disciplinary Proceedings of New England Yearly Meeting of Friends* (Boston: Damrell and Moore, 1852); *Action of the Several Yearly Meetings of Friends, relative to the Secession from New England Yearly Meeting* (Philadelphia: n.p., 1846); and the Gurney letter in William Bacon Evans, *Jonathan Evans and His Time, 1759–1839; A Bi-Centennial Biography* (Boston: Christopher Publishing, 1959), 139–40.

57. No adequate modern study of the Anti-Slavery separation in Indiana Yearly Meeting exists. An indispensable contemporary guide, although biased in favor of the seceders, is Edgerton, *History of the Separation*. See also Ruth Anna Ketring, *Charles Osborn in the Anti-Slavery Movement* (Columbus: Ohio State Archaeological and Historical Society, 1937); and Harold Lee Gray, "An Investigation of the Causes of Separation in Indiana Yearly Meeting of Friends in 1843" (M.A. thesis, Indiana Central College, 1970).

58. Edgerton, *History of the Separation*, 27, 39; *Journal of That Faithful Servant of Christ, Charles Osborn*, xii, 409–11; "A Tribute to the Memory of Walter Edgerton," *Western Friend*, 2 (9th Mo. 1880), 79–80; "Discipline of Indiana Yearly Meeting of Anti-Slavery Friends," n.d., box 1, Beeson Papers; Bates, *Examination*, 81–82.

59. Hodgson, *Selections from the Letters of Thomas B. Gould*, 176–77; Elijah Coffin to North Carolina Yearly Meeting, 3rd Mo. 6, 1843, Meeting for Sufferings Papers; Coffin to George W. Taylor, 1st Mo. 6, 1847, letterbook 1, box 1, Coffin Papers.

60. *Private Memoirs of B. and E. Seebohm*, 213; Hodgson, *Selections from the Letters of Thomas B. Gould*, 354, 359, 362–63, 368; "Ohio Yearly Meeting, 1847," *Western Friend*, 11th Mo. 11, 1847, p. 6; Ohio Yearly Meeting (Gurneyite) Meeting for Sufferings Minutes, 9th Mo. 8, 1854, 2nd Mo. 16, 1855 (Archives, Malone); Enoch Lewis, *A Brief Review of the Division in the Yearly Meeting of Ohio* (Philadelphia: n.p., 1855); Norton, "Quakers West of the Alleghenies," 243–57; Joshua Maule, *A Plea for the Unchangeable Truth Addressed to Friends* (Colerain, Ohio: n.p., 1860), 5.

61. Jones, *Later Periods of Quakerism*, I, 532–33; Thomas Evans to Joseph Tallcot, 7th Mo. 29, 1846, box 2, Tallcot Papers.

62. Jones, *Later Periods of Quakerism*, I, 532–33; Tallack, *Friendly Sketches*, 89.

63. Jones, *Later Periods of Quakerism*, I, 535–37; Hodgson, *Society of Friends in the Nineteenth Century*, II, 118–25, 212–18, 240–44; William Evans to Elizabeth Evans, 10th Mo. 4, 1851, box 1, Evans Papers; *Document Issued by the Conference of Friends, Held in Baltimore, 7th Mo. 1849. With Some Remarks Thereon* (Philadelphia: John Penington, 1850); *An Address to Friends, Prepared by the Committees of New York, New England, Baltimore, North Carolina, and Indiana, at Baltimore in the Fifth Month 1851* (New York: James Egbert, 1852).

64. This analysis is based on a comparison of information in the 1850 and 1860 federal censuses for members of three monthly meetings: Stillwater in Belmont County, the Wilburite stronghold; Smithfield in Jefferson County, which was almost entirely Gurneyite; and Salem in Columbiana County, which was badly split. Membership records are taken from William Wade Hinshaw, ed., *Encyclopedia of American Quaker Genealogy* (6 vols., Ann Arbor: Edwards Brothers, 1936–1950), IV, 361–501, 669–793.

III   THE RENEWAL MOVEMENT, 1850–1870

1. George Chittenden to Amanda Chittenden, [July 1861], George Chittenden Papers (Indiana Division, Indiana State Library, Indianapolis).

2. Rufus M. Jones, *The Later Periods of Quakerism* (2 vols., London: Macmillan, 1921), II, 868–908; Elbert Russell, *The History of Quakerism* (New York: Macmillan, 1942), 421–34; Walter R. Williams, *The Rich Heritage of Quakerism* (Grand Rapids: Eerdmans, 1962), 192–201; Myron Dee Goldsmith, "William Hobson and the Founding of Quakerism in the Pacific Northwest" (Ph.D. diss., Boston University, 1962), 205–6; Richard E. Wood, "The Rise of Semi-Structured Worship and Paid Pastoral Leadership among 'Gurneyite' Friends, 1850–1900," in *Quaker Worship in North America*, ed. Francis B. Hall (Richmond, Ind.: Friends United Press, n.d.), 53–57; Arthur J. Mekeel, *Quakerism and a Creed* (Philadelphia: Friends' Book Store, 1936), 83; Arthur Owen Roberts, "The Concepts of Perfection in the History of the Quaker Movement" (B.D. thesis, Nazarene Theological Seminary, 1951), 106; David C. LeShana, *Quakers in California: The Impact of 19th-Century Revivalism on Western Quakerism* (Newberg, Ore.: Barclay, 1969), 34–39.

3. Thomas L. Haskell, *The Emergence of Professional Social Science: The American Social Science Association and the Nineteenth-Century Crisis of Authority* (Urbana: University of Illinois Press, 1977), 30–39. See also Richard D. Brown,

Modernization: The Transformation of American Life, 1607–1865 (New York: Hill and Wang, 1976), 164–70.

4. William Tallack, *Friendly Sketches in America* (London: A. W. Bennett, 1861), 27–29.

5. Ibid., 31–32. An Indiana Friend remembered a similar situation: "During the time from 1856 to 1860, there was great unrest in every part of social, political, religious and domestic life. New thoughts seemed suddenly to come into the minds of every one." Addison Coffin, *Life and Travels of Addison Coffin* (Cleveland: William G. Hubbard, 1897), 115.

6. Bernhard Knollenberg, *Pioneer Sketches of the Upper Whitewater Valley: Quaker Stronghold of the West* (Indianapolis: Indiana Historical Society, 1945), 138; T. B. Deem, *Olden Spiceland* (n.p., 1934); manuscript population schedules, 1850 and 1860 federal censuses, Spiceland Township, Henry County, Indiana; James M. McPherson, *Ordeal by Fire* (New York: Knopf, 1982), 7; Richard P. Ratcliff, *The Quakers of Spiceland, Henry County, Indiana: A History of Spiceland Friends Meeting, 1828–1968* (New Castle, Ind.: Community Printing, 1968), 65–70; George Evans to Eli and Mahalah Jay, 7th Mo. 23, 1860, 7th Mo. 23, 1861, Eli and Mahalah Jay Family Papers (Archives, Earlham College, Richmond, Ind.); Jesse Bond to Eli and Mahalah Jay, 8th Mo. 27, 1861, ibid.

7. Errol T. Elliott, *Quakers on the American Frontier* (Richmond, Ind.: Friends United Press, 1969); Elijah Coffin to Thomas Kimber, 12th Mo. 2, 1857, Coffin-Kimber folder, Charles F. and Rhoda M. Coffin Papers (Archives, Earlham); James A. Henretta, "Families and Farms: *Mentalité* in Pre-Industrial America," *William and Mary Quarterly*, 3d ser., 35 (Jan. 1978), 3–32; Goldsmith, "William Hobson," 205–6. For the lack of organized reform activities in another frontier society, see Kathleen Smith Kutolowski, "Antimasonry Reconsidered: Social Bases of the Grass-Roots Party," *Journal of American History*, 71 (Sept. 1984), 280.

8. John Griffith to Samuel Bettle, Jr., 9th Mo. 24, 1853, box 1, Bettle Family Papers (Friends Historical Library, Swarthmore College, Swarthmore, Pa.); "Index Rerum," box 4, Hobbs-Mendenhall Papers (Southern Historical Collection, University of North Carolina, Chapel Hill); D. E. Mendenhall to James R. Mendenhall, 6th Mo. 29, 1850, box 1, ibid.; Rebecca Russell Diary, 4th Mo. 24, 1861, 5th Mo. 21, 1861, typescript (Indiana Historical Society Library, Indianapolis); Martha White Talbert Diary, Aug. 31, 1849, June 17, 1852, Dec. [?], 1855 (ibid.); Joel Bean Diary, 3rd Mo. 6, 1858, box 1, Joel Bean Papers (Friends Historical Library, Swarthmore); untitled essay on silence, [ca. 1850], box 1, Tallcot Family Papers (Quaker Collection, Haverford College, Haverford, Pa.); H. and Mary M. Collins to Joseph Tallcot, 9th Mo. 14, 1853, ibid.; Joseph Tallcot to Meeting for Sufferings, n.d., box 4, ibid.; *Indiana Yearly Meeting Minutes, 1859*, p. 9; Mary Coffin Johnson, ed., *Rhoda M. Coffin: Her Reminiscences, Addresses, Papers, and Ancestry* (New York: Grafton, 1910), 71–72; Darius B. Cook, *History of Quaker Divide* (Dexter, Iowa: Dexter Sentinel, 1914), 172–80; editorial, *American Friend*, 2 (12th Mo. 1868), 292.

9. Elbert Russell, "Friends Secondary Schools," *Quaker*, 11th Mo. 12, 1921, pp. 171–72. For an account of the founding of one Quaker secondary school, see William Philips Bickley, "Education as Reformation: An Examination of Orthodox Quakers' Formation of the Haverford School Association and Founding of Haverford School, 1815–1840" (Ed.D. diss., Harvard University, 1983). For education as a factor in social and cultural change, see Lawrence A. Cremin, *American Education: The National Experience, 1783–1876* (New York: Harper and Row, 1980), 490–506.

10. Rufus M. Jones, *Haverford College: A History and an Interpretation* (New York: Macmillan, 1933), 2–4, 31–33; Tallack, *Friendly Sketches*, 157; *Autobiography*

of Allen Jay, Born 1831, Died 1910 (Philadelphia: John C. Winston, 1910), 57–58, 73; *History of Wayne County, Indiana* (2 vols., Chicago: Interstate, 1884), II, 607; Charles W. Osborn to William and Caroline Edgerton, 9th Mo. 14, 1856, Osborn Genealogical file (Henry County Historical Society Museum, New Castle, Ind.); Elijah Coffin to Joseph Moore, 12th Mo. 16, 1859, photostat, Joseph Moore Papers (Archives, Earlham); John D. Carter, "Autobiography," [ca. 1900], typescript (in author's possession); Opal Thornburg, *Earlham: The Story of the College, 1847–1962* (Richmond, Ind.: Earlham College Press, 1963), 77–79.

11. Tallack, *Friendly Sketches*, 27–28; Dorothy Lloyd Gilbert, *Guilford: A Quaker College* (Greensboro, N.C.: Guilford College, 1937), 57, 63; Solomon B. Woodard, *Story of a Life of Ninety Years: Biographical and Descriptive* (Richmond, Ind.: Nicholson, 1928), 13–14; Delphina E. Mendenhall to Joshua L. Baily, 6th Mo. 21, 1859, box 2, Joshua L. Baily Papers (Quaker Collection, Haverford). In Indiana Yearly Meeting in 1859, for example, only 1,629 children were in meeting schools, but another 2,215 were in public schools and were taught by Friends. There were 2,336 in public schools not taught by Friends. In Western Yearly Meeting the same year, of 3,006 children, 1,501 were in meeting schools, 789 were in public schools taught by Friends, and only 466 were in public schools not taught by Friends. *Indiana Yearly Meeting Minutes*, 1859, p. 37; *Western Yearly Meeting Minutes, 1859*, p. 18. For Philadelphia, see *Report of the Committee on Education to the Yearly Meeting* (n.p., 1844), 5–11. The proportion of Quaker children in public schools did increase steadily after 1860. See Richard Eugene Wood, "Evangelical Quakers in the Mississippi Valley, 1854–1894" (Ph.D. diss., University of Minnesota, 1985), 88–89.

12. John M. Macy to Aaron White, 12th Mo. 30, 1847, box 2, Furnas Family Papers (Friends Historical Library, Swarthmore); Ethel Hittle McDaniel, *The Contribution of the Society of Friends to Education in Indiana* (Indianapolis: Indiana Historical Society, 1939), 33–34; B. C. Hobbs, *School Friend, Fourth Book: Reading Exercises for the Use of Schools* (Cincinnati: n.p., 1854), 5–6, 35–38, 70–73, 77–79, 97–99, 129–37, 150–52, 162–67, 202–4; John H. Westerhoff III, *McGuffey and His Readers: Piety, Morality, and Education in Nineteenth-Century America* (Nashville: Abingdon, 1977).

13. [James Baldwin], *In My Youth: From the Posthumous Papers of Robert Dudley* (Indianapolis: Bobbs-Merrill, 1914), 147, 239, 371, 379–80, 386–88, 404, 409–10.

14. Biographical data on all of these Friends is from William Bacon Evans et al., comps., "Dictionary of Quaker Biography" (Quaker Collection, Haverford).

15. Elizabeth H. Emerson, "Barnabas C. Hobbs: Midwestern Quaker Minister and Educator," *Bulletin of Friends Historical Association*, 49 (Spring 1960), 21–35; Minnie B. Clark, "Barnabas Coffin Hobbs," *Indiana Magazine of History*, 19 (Sept. 1923), 282–90; [Baldwin], *In My Youth*, 139–40.

16. Mary Coffin Johnson and Percival Brooks Coffin, *Charles F. Coffin: A Quaker Pioneer* (Richmond, Ind: Nicholson, 1923); Charles F. Coffin, "Autobiography," typescript, n.d., Autobiography folder, Charles F. and Rhoda M. Coffin Papers.

17. Johnson, ed., *Rhoda M. Coffin*. For nineteenth-century evangelical women and reform, see Barbara Berg, *The Remembered Gate: Origins of American Feminism: The Woman and the City, 1800–1860* (New York: Oxford University Press, 1978); and Barbara Leslie Epstein, *The Politics of Domesticity: Women, Evangelism, and Temperance in Nineteenth-Century America* (Middletown, Conn.: Wesleyan University Press, 1981).

18. *Autobiography of Allen Jay*, 89–90; W. Rufus Kersey, comp., "Some Docu-

ments Dealing with the Life and Career of John Henry Douglas, Quaker Evangelist, 1832–1919" (Divinity School Library, Duke University).

19. Coffin, "Autobiography," 19; Elliott, *Quakers on the American Frontier,* 389–91; Walter C. Woodward, *Timothy Nicholson: Master Quaker* (Richmond, Ind.: Nicholson, 1927), 54–55; Errol T. Elliott, *Quaker Profiles from the American West* (Richmond, Ind.: Friends United Press, 1972), 1–46. See also Evans et al., comps., "Dictionary."

20. Jones, *Later Periods of Quakerism,* I, 532–33, II, 690–94, 913–15; Samuel Rhoads to William Wood, 2nd Mo. 10, 1856, Wood Family Papers (Friends Historical Library, Swarthmore); "Philadelphia Yearly Meeting," *Friends' Review,* 4th Mo. 21, 1855, pp. 505–6; Thomas Kimber, Jr., "Philadelphia Yearly Meeting," *Christian Worker,* 6th Mo. 15, 1873, pp. 185–86; Henry Hartshorne to William L. Edwards, 9th Mo. 4, 1874, box 4, Hartshorne Family Papers (Quaker Collection, Haverford); Philip S. Benjamin, *The Philadelphia Quakers in the Industrial Age, 1865–1920* (Philadelphia: Temple University Press, 1976), 15–17, 41–43; Tallack, *Friendly Sketches,* 99–100.

21. See, for example, "Prospectus," *Friends' Review,* 9th Mo. 4, 1847, pp. 1–2; "Joseph John Gurney and His Accusers," ibid., 7th Mo. 21, 1855, pp. 709–10; editorial, ibid., 8th Mo. 4, 1855, pp. 746–49; "Theologic Study," ibid., 5th Mo. 15, 1869, p. 596.

22. *Memoir of Elizabeth T. King, with Extracts from Her Letters and Journal* (Baltimore: Armstrong and Berry, 1859), 113–14; Joshua Maule, *Transactions and Changes in the Society of Friends, and Incidents in the Life and Experience of Joshua Maule* (Philadelphia: Lippincott, 1886), 113–14; Talbert Diary, Dec. 21, 1858; "A Testimony of Norwich Monthly Meeting, concerning Joseph John Gurney, Deceased," *Friends' Review,* 10th Mo. 23, 1847, pp. 68–70; William F. Mott to Joseph Tallcot, 3rd Mo. 11, 1847, box 3, Tallcot Papers.

23. *Memoir of Elizabeth T. King,* 12; "Minute of Indiana Yearly Meeting on the State of Society," *Friends' Review,* 12th Mo. 1, 1860, p. 193; Mekeel, *Quakerism and a Creed,* 78.

24. "The Biennial Conference," *Christian Worker,* 12th Mo. 12, 1871, pp. 208–9; "Cedar Creek Monthly Meeting, Iowa," ibid., 9th Mo. 15, 1871, p. 157; *Indiana Yearly Meeting Minutes, 1859,* 9; *Autobiography of Allen Jay,* 24–26; "First Day Schools," *Friends' Review,* 2nd Mo. 19, 1859, p. 378; "Report of the Cincinnati Conference on First Day Schools," ibid., 3rd Mo. 1, 1862, p. 403; [Ruth S. Murray], *Under His Wings: A Sketch of the Life of Robert Lindley Murray* (New York: Anson D. F. Randolph, 1876), 97; Elijah Coffin to Thomas Kimber, 7th Mo. 11, 1854, 2nd Mo. 19, 1860, Kimber-Coffin folder, Charles F. and Rhoda M. Coffin Papers; Charles F. Coffin to Isaac and Hannah M. Parker, 12th Mo. 21, 1854, Coffin-Parker folder, ibid.; Mary H. Thomas to Joseph Tallcot, 11th Mo. 13, 1851, box 5, Tallcot Papers.

25. *Journal of the Life, Travels, and Gospel Labors of Thomas Arnett* (Chicago: Publishing Association of Friends, 1884), 305; *Western Yearly Meeting Minutes, 1868,* pp. 25–26; *Concise Statement of the Christian Doctrines of the Society of Friends* (Richmond, Ind.: Central Book and Tract Committee, 1855); Indiana Yearly Meeting of Ministers and Elders Minutes, 10th Mo. 1, 1859 (Archives, Earlham); Marjorie Horsepian Dobkin, ed., *The Making of a Feminist: Early Journals and Letters of M. Carey Thomas* (Kent, Ohio: Kent State University Press, 1979), 308.

26. Dougan Clark, Jr., *Address by Dr. Dougan Clark* (n.p., 1858), 4; William Nicholson letter, *Friends' Review,* 3rd Mo. 2, 1867, pp. 428–29.

27. Francis Charles Anscombe, "The Contribution of the Quakers to the Reconstruction of the Southern States" (Ph.D. diss., University of North Carolina,

1926), 94–104; Johnson, ed., *Rhoda M. Coffin*, 141, 154–57; Dougan Clark, Jr., to Joel Bean, 4th Mo. 20, 1850, box 3, Bean Papers; [Murray], *Under His Wings*, 18, 47–48, 88, 97; Mary C. Johnson, ed., *Life of Elijah Coffin* (Cincinnati: E. Morgan and Sons, 1863), 106–8, 132, 254–55, 269, 272–73; editorial, *Friends' Review*, 10th Mo. 10, 1863, pp. 82–84; "Friends in Kansas," ibid., 3rd Mo. 20, 1858, p. 436; "Report of Fowell Buxton Sabbath School," *American Friend*, 1 (6th Mo. 1867), 157; Mary H. Thomas to Mary S. Wood, 11th Mo. 30, 1867, Wood Family Papers; Elizabeth L. Comstock letter, *Herald of Peace*, 2nd Mo. 29, 1868, p. 40.

28. "C. H. Spurgeon Harmonizing with Friends," *Friends' Review*, 9th Mo. 3, 1864, pp. 5–6; "Religious Awakening," ibid., 5th Mo. 1, 1858, pp. 532–33; B. A. Marshall, "In Essentials, Unity; In Non-Essentials, Liberty; In All Things, Charity," ibid., 5th Mo. 29, 1858, p. 593.

29. Edward D. Snyder, "Whittier and the Unitarians," *Bulletin of Friends Historical Association*, 49 (Fall 1960), 111–16; "Peace Conference," *American Friend*, 1 (4th Mo. 1867), 93–94; "Correspondence," ibid., (9th Mo. 1867), 233–36; "Orthodox versus Hicksite," *Herald of Peace*, 6th Mo. 1, 1868, p. 136; Tallack, *Friendly Sketches*, 116.

30. Caroline Hare, comp., *Life and Letters of Elizabeth L. Comstock* (London: Headley Brothers, 1895), 85; Tallack, *Friendly Sketches*, 15–16; "Peace Conference," 93–94, 97.

31. Nereus Mendenhall Diary, April 7, 1851, April 22, 1851, box 4, Hobbs-Mendenhall Papers; Elijah Coffin to David Buffum, 3rd Mo. 25, 1857, 1851–1862 letterbook, box 1, Coffin Family Papers (Friends Historical Library, Swarthmore); Elijah Coffin to Joseph Doan, 12th Mo. 22, 1856, ibid.; *Discipline of the Society of Friends of New-York Yearly Meeting* (New York: Samuel S. and William Wood, 1859), 65–66; "Indiana Yearly Meeting," *Friends' Review*, 10th Mo. 18, 1856, p. 88; "The Marriage Question," ibid., 1st Mo. 16, 1864, pp. 312–13; "Marriage," ibid., 3rd Mo. 9, 1867, p. 443.

32. Clark, *Address*, 13–14; Bean Diary, 2nd Mo. 6, 1857, box 1, Bean Papers; Jacob Baker, *Incidents of My Life and Life Work of 84 Years* (Richmond, Ind.: Nicholson, 1911), 17; "These Ought Ye Have Done," *Friends' Review*, 11th Mo. 19, 1864, pp. 180–81; P. A. W., "Dress," ibid., 2nd Mo. 6, 1864, p. 364; "War and Worldly Fashions," ibid., 1st Mo. 9, 1864, pp. 296–97; "Plainness of Apparel," ibid., 6th Mo. 8, 1867, pp. 648–49; Tallack, *Friendly Sketches*, 18–23; editorial, *Herald of Peace*, 4th Mo. 15, 1868, p. 86; Amy Ann Sanders to Louzena Sanders, Feb. 19, 1867, Earlham Students Collection (Archives, Earlham); Karen S. Halttunen, *Confidence Men and Painted Women: A Study of Middle-Class Culture in America, 1830–1870* (New Haven: Yale University Press, 1982), 63–64.

33. *Western Yearly Meeting Minutes*, 1865, p. 29; "Sound Words," *Friends' Review*, 11th Mo. 12, 1864, pp. 168–69; "Disownments," ibid., 5th Mo. 12, 1860, pp. 568–69; "Acknowledgements," ibid., 9th Mo. 1, 1860, p. 824; "Indiana Yearly Meeting," ibid., 10th Mo. 19, 1861, p. 104. Rich resources for the study of mores and the exercise of the discipline among Quakers are the records of the various monthly meetings throughout the United States in William Wade Hinshaw, ed., *Encyclopedia of American Quaker Genealogy* (6 vols., Ann Arbor: Edwards Brothers, 1936–1950); the William Wade Hinshaw Collection (Friends Historical Library, Swarthmore); and Willard C. Heiss, ed., *Abstracts of the Records of the Society of Friends in Indiana* (7 vols., Indianapolis: Indiana Historical Society, 1962–1977).

34. Elmina Foster Wilson, "Reminiscences of New Garden Boarding School," n.d., Elmina Foster Wilson Papers (Friends Historical Collection, Guilford College, Greensboro, N.C.); Russell, *History of Quakerism*, 435–40; "Louis and Sarah Street," *American Friend*, 1 (1st Mo. 1867), 65–66; David Tatum, "Pioneer Mission-

ary Work among Friends," ibid., 2nd Mo. 12, 1903, pp. 111–12; "Joel Bean in the Sandwich Islands," *Friends' Review*, 12th Mo. 28, 1861, p. 269; "Faithfulness in Our Profession," ibid., 5th Mo. 8, 1858, p. 549; Rufus M. Jones, *Eli and Sybil Jones and Their Work* (Philadelphia: John C. Winston, 1889), 185–98. For a discussion of the role of Friends in the "Peace Policy," see Robert H. Keller, Jr., *American Protestantism and United States Indian Policy, 1869–1882* (Lincoln: University of Nebraska Press, 1983), 47–49, 126–48, 17–30.

35. Rhoda M. Coffin, "The Home Mission Association of Women of Indiana Yearly Meeting of Friends," *American Friend*, 11th Mo. 5, 1903, pp. 752–54; Hare, comp., *Life and Letters of Elizabeth L. Comstock*, 253–55; *Memoir of Elizabeth T. King*, 91–92; "Murray Shipley," *American Friend*, 2nd Mo. 2, 1899, p. 107; Johnson, ed., *Rhoda M. Coffin*, 215–21; John William Buys, "Quakers in Indiana in the Nineteenth Century" (Ph.D. diss., University of Florida, 1973), 218–20; Tallack, *Friendly Sketches*, 45; *Indiana Yearly Meeting Minutes, 1865*, p. 18.

36. Indiana Yearly Meeting of Ministers and Elders Minutes, 10th Mo. 1, 1859; David Hunt, "Silent Worship," *Friends' Review*, 1st Mo. 25, 1862, p. 326; "Silent Worship—Gospel Ministry," ibid., 9th Mo. 20, 1856, p. 25; Francis W. Thomas, *An Address to the Society of Friends* (Richmond, Ind.: Central Book and Tract Committee, 1863), 10–11; Johnson and Coffin, *Charles F. Coffin*, 115–17; Tallack, *Friendly Sketches*, 45; *Autobiography of Allen Jay*, 82. For fears about speaking in meeting, see Eleazer Bales Diary, 7th Mo. 16, 1859, Eleazer Bales Collection (Indiana Historical Society Library); and "Notes on Memoirs of Rodema Newlin," in Darius B. Cook, "History of the Cook and Bowles Families," typescript, n.d., p. 227 (in Willard C. Heiss's possession, Indianapolis).

37. "Tones and Gestures in Preaching," *Friends' Review*, 6th Mo. 7, 1856, pp. 616–17; "Colleges and the Ministry," ibid., 3rd Mo. 31, 1860, pp. 472–73; editorial, ibid., 12th Mo. 26, 1868, pp. 280–81; "Friends Books," ibid., 9th Mo. 10, 1864, p. 26; Mary S. Wood to Mary Gough, [ca. 1862], Wood Family Papers; Indiana Yearly Meeting of Ministers and Elders Minutes, 9th Mo. 28, 1858, 10th Mo. 6, 1863.

38. "Reading Circle at Springwater, Iowa," *Friends' Review*, 3rd Mo. 18, 1865, p. 451; L. N. H., "Social Religious Meetings," *Christian Worker*, 1st Mo. 15, 1872, pp. 14–16; "General Meeting of Friends in Chicago," *Herald of Peace*, 5th Mo. 1, 1869, p. 82; "Too Fast! Too Slow!" ibid., 5th Mo. 15, 1868, p. 120; Minutes of Mill Creek Social Circle, 4th Mo. 29, 1865, 5th Mo. 6, 1865, 3rd Mo. 3, 1865, 12th Mo. 17, 1865, Society of Friends section, Church History Collection (Indiana Division, Indiana State Library, Indianapolis).

39. Johnson, ed., *Rhoda M. Coffin*, 79–82; Coffin and Johnson, *Charles F. Coffin*, 115–17; Tallack, *Friendly Sketches*, 269–70. Fears about the meeting are chronicled in John M. Macy to Lydia B. Macy, 6th Mo. 2, 1862 (in George F. Parker's possession, Bakersfield, Calif.).

40. William Hodgson, *The Society of Friends in the Nineteenth Century: A Historical View of the Successive Convulsions and Schisms Therein during That Period* (2 vols., Philadelphia, 1875–1876), II, 46–48; Thomas E. Drake, *Quakers and Slavery in America* (New Haven: Yale University Press, 1950), 167.

41. Drake, *Quakers and Slavery in America*, 167; J. William Frost, "Years of Crisis and Separation: Philadelphia Yearly Meeting, 1790–1860," in *Friends in the Delaware Valley: Philadelphia Yearly Meeting, 1681–1981*, ed. John M. Moore (Haverford, Pa.: Friends Historical Association, 1981), 96–99; Jones, *Later Periods of Quakerism*, I, 373–74; Buys, "Indiana Quakers," 75–77, 236; "Testimony of Piney Woods Monthly Meeting, North Carolina, concerning David White," *Friends' Review*, 1st Mo. 7, 1865, pp. 289–90; Hare, comp., *Life and Letters of Elizabeth L. Comstock*, 340. For the larger temperance movement, see Ian R. Tyrrell, *Sobering*

Up: From Temperance to Prohibition in Antebellum America, 1800–1860 (Westport, Conn.: Greenwood, 1979).

42. "The Importance of One Vote," *Herald of Peace*, 11th Mo. 1, 1868, p. 97; Maule, *Transactions and Changes*, 266–67; Hare, comp., *Life and Letters of Elizabeth L. Comstock*, 169–71; Louis Thomas Jones, *The Quakers of Iowa* (Iowa City: Clio, 1914), 314; Jones, *Later Periods of Quakerism*, II, 729; Emerson, "Barnabas C. Hobbs," 29; Grace Julian Clarke, *George W. Julian* (Indianapolis: Indiana Historical Commission, 1923), 244; Melvyn Hammarburg, "Indiana Farmers and the Group Basis of the Late Nineteenth-Century Political Parties," *Journal of American History*, 61 (June 1974), 102; "The Presidential Election," *Friends' Review*, 11th Mo. 5, 1864, pp. 156–57; Eric Foner, *Free Soil, Free Labor, Free Men: The Ideology of the Republican Party before the Civil War* (New York: Oxford University Press, 1970), 237–42. For the attraction of other northern evangelicals to the Republican party, see Paul Kleppner, *The Cross of Culture: A Social Analysis of Midwestern Politics, 1850–1900* (New York: Free Press, 1970).

43. Clark, *Address*, 12–13; "Reflections of the Nature and Effects of God's Love for Man," *Friends' Review*, 4th Mo. 14, 1865, pp. 516–17. For the similarity of Clark's view of holiness and the millennium to that of contemporary evangelicals, see Timothy L. Smith, "Righteousness and Hope: Christian Holiness and the Millennial Vision in America, 1800–1900," *American Quarterly*, 31 (Spring 1979), 21–45.

44. Anscombe, "Contribution of the Quakers," 95; Edwin B. Bronner, ed., *An English View of American Quakerism: The Journal of Walter Robson* (Philadelphia: American Philosophical Society, 1970), 93; *Cincinnati Enquirer* clipping on Charles F. Coffin, [ca. 1886], Eli and Mahalah Jay Family Papers (Archives, Earlham); "The Late Thomas Kimber, Minister in the Society of Friends," *Friends' Review*, 4th Mo. 23, 1891, pp. 612–13.

45. Of these ministers, only Grellet has been the subject of an adequate modern study. See Ronald Eugene Selleck, "I Shall Not Pass This Way Again: A Study of Stephen Grellet's Life and Thought" (Ph.D. diss., University of Chicago, 1985). For Jeremiah Hubbard, see "Personal Recollections of Jeremiah Hubbard," Dec. 1909, Jeremiah Hubbard folder, Charles F. and Rhoda M. Coffin Papers; Francis W. Thomas to Charles F. Coffin, 5th Mo. 30, 1897, Family Letters folder, ibid.; Jeremiah Hubbard, *An Exhortation to the Families, and More Particularly to the Heads of Families That Constitute North Carolina Yearly Meeting of Friends* (Greensboro, N.C.: William Swaim, 1833); and *Memorials of Deceased Friends Who Were Members of Indiana Yearly Meeting* (Cincinnati: E. Morgan, 1857), 147–54. For Arnett, see *Journal of the Life, Travels, and Gospel Labors of Thomas Arnett.* For Pray, see *Western Yearly Meeting Minutes, 1877*, pp. 86–89; Thomas to Charles F. Coffin, 5th Mo. 30, 1897, Family Letters folder, Charles F. and Rhoda M. Coffin Papers; Hare, comp., *Life and Letters of Elizabeth L. Comstock*, 90; and L. Frank Bedell, *Quaker Heritage: Friends Coming into the Heart of America: A Story of Iowa Conservative Yearly Meeting* (Cedar Rapids, Iowa, 1966), 232. For Sybil Jones, see Jones, *Eli and Sybil Jones.*

46. H. J. Bailey, *Memoirs of a Christian Life* (Portland, Me.: Hoyt, Fogg, and Donham, 1885), 89–90, 95; Hare, comp., *Life and Letters of Elizabeth L. Comstock*, 89–90; "Iowa Yearly Meeting," *Friends' Review*, 10th Mo. 3, 1863, pp. 71–72; *New Castle* (Ind.) *Courier*, Oct. 10, 1867, p. 2.

47. "Memorial of Whitewater Monthly Meeting, Indiana, concerning Nathan C. Hoag," *Friends' Review*, 11th Mo. 21, 1857, p. 161; *Memoir of Martha C. Thomas, Late of Baltimore Maryland* (Richmond, Ind.: Central Book and Tract Committee, n.d.). For some conversion experiences, see Woodard, *Story*, 28–30; *Autobiography*

of Allen Jay, 22–24; and John Y. Hoover, "A Sketch of Life," *Evangelical Friend*, July 12, 1906, p. 441.

48. *Indiana Yearly Meeting Minutes, 1864*, p. 8; *The Discipline of the Society of Friends of Iowa Yearly Meeting* (Chicago: n.p., 1865), 38–39; Elijah Coffin, *The Mother's Catechism of Christian Doctrine and Practice* (Richmond, Ind.: Central Book and Tract Committee, 1859), 10–11; "Repentance and Faith," *Friends' Review*, 11th Mo. 28, 1863, pp. 195–97; "Baltimore Monthly Meeting Epistle," ibid., 6th Mo. 9, 1866, pp. 646–47; "Letters to a Young Man," *Southern Friend*, 3rd Mo. 15, 1865, pp. 90–92; *The Experience of J. H. Merle D'Aubigne in the Work of Conversion* (Richmond, Ind.: Central Book and Tract Committee, 1861).

49. *Reminiscences of Nathan T. Frame and Esther G. Frame* (Cleveland: Britton, 1907), 60–62; "Editorial Notes," *Herald of Peace*, 6th Mo. 1, 1869, p. 113; "Missionary Work," ibid., 11th Mo. 15, 1868, p. 128; "A Glorious Harvest," ibid., 5th Mo. 1, 1869, p. 82; Hare, comp., *Life and Letters of Elizabeth L. Comstock*, 253–56. See also the membership statistics in Ch. 3, table 4, and those in Indiana Yearly Meeting for this period.

50. W. Y. Brown to Newton D. Woody, [ca. Feb.–March 1866], box 4, Robert and Newton D. Woody Papers (Manuscripts Department, Duke University Library, Durham, N.C.); "General Meeting of Friends in Chicago," *Herald of Peace*, 1st Mo. 31, 1868, p. 7; "Too Fast! Too Slow!" ibid., 5th Mo. 15, 1868, p. 120; "Differences of Opinion," ibid., 8th Mo. 15, 1869, p. 19; Thomas, *Address*, 7; Joel Bean letter, 6th Mo. 20, 1870, *Friends' Review*, 7th Mo. 9, 1870, pp. 730–31; H. D. Williams, "Friends' Meetings in Iowa," *Christian Worker*, 6th Mo. 26, 1884, p. 417; E. B. Mendenhall, "When and Where the Revival Flame Was First Kindled," ibid., 12th Mo. 15, 1887, p. 591; Howard H. Brinton, ed., "The Revival Movement in Iowa: A Letter from Joel Bean to Rufus M. Jones," *Bulletin of Friends Historical Association*, 50 (Fall 1961), 106.

51. See, for example, Mary S. Wood, "An Account of the Opening of Western Yearly Meeting," *Semi-Centennial Anniversary of Western Yearly Meeting of Friends Church, Plainfield, Indiana, Ninth Month 23, 1908* (Plainfield, Ind.: Publishing Association of Friends, 1908), 232–45; *Thoughts on Growth in Grace* (Richmond, Ind.: Central Book and Tract Committee, n.d.); [Josiah Butler et al.], *John Butler: A Sketch of His Life* (Columbus: William G. Hubbard, 1890), 175; and *Iowa Yearly Meeting Minutes, 1866*, p. 32. Particularly revealing are obituaries from this period. For a striking contrast of the older emphasis on growth into holiness with the new emphasis on an instantaneous conversion experience, cf. the obituaries of Edward D. Gummere, Jesse Kenworthy, Sarah Picket, Mary N. Smith, and William Stubbs with those of Hugh Balderston, Alfred R. Dorland, Jesse D. Hiatt, Margaret Ann Morris, and Richard Thomas in *The American Annual Monitor for 1861; or, Obituary of the Members of the Society of Friends in America for the Year 1860* (New York: Samuel S. and William Wood, 1861), 5–6, 34–36, 51–60, 76–78, 95–98, 115–19, 138–39, 155–56, 161–62, 164–77.

52. Joseph Moore Diary, 8th Mo. 30, 1856, Moore Papers (Archives, Earlham); "Vision of Joseph Hoag," n.d., attached to Nicholas Barker to Mary Mendenhall, 1st Mo. 11, 1861, box 1, Hobbs-Mendenhall Papers; Russell Diary, 1st Mo. 18, 1861; untitled manuscript on war, n.d., Griffith Family Papers (Friends Historical Library, Swarthmore).

53. Daniel H. Martin to Jesse Dobbins, 4th Mo. 23, 1863, Jesse Dobbins family letters, Genealogical Collection (Yadkin County Public Library, Yadkinville, N.C.); Francis T. King to William Wood, 5th Mo. 31, 1861, 6th Mo. 2, 1861, Wood Family Papers; "Presidential Election," 152–53.

54. Fernando G. Cartland, *Southern Heroes; or, the Friends in Wartime* (Cambridge, Mass.: Riverside, 1895); Richard L. Zuber, "Conscientious Objectors in the Confederacy: The Quakers of North Carolina," *Quaker History*, 67 (Spring 1978), 1–19; Peter Brock, *Pacifism in the United States from the Colonial Era to the First World War* (Princeton: Princeton University Press, 1968), 744. For the reaction of Edwin M. Stanton's Quaker relatives to his activities during the war, see William Henry Stanton, *A Book Called Our Ancestors the Stantons* (Philadelphia: n.p., 1922), 154.

55. Brock, *Pacifism in the United States*, 713–64.

56. Ibid., 719; Indiana Yearly Meeting, *An Appeal for the Rights of Conscience* (Richmond, Ind.: n.p., 1863), 7.

57. Brock, *Pacifism in the United States*, 716; Hare, comp., *Life and Letters of Elizabeth L. Comstock*, 96–97.

58. Brock, *Pacifism in the United States*, 726–27; Daniel Newby, "Memoranda of Old Rich Square," Franklin Township file (Henry County Historical Society); Jacquelyn S. Nelson, "The Military Response of the Society of Friends in Indiana to the Civil War," *Indiana Magazine of History*, 81 (June 1985), 101–30; Joseph Moore to John Hodgkin, 6th Mo. 3, 1862, Miscellaneous Correspondence folder, Moore Papers; *Western Yearly Meeting Minutes, 1862*, pp. 5–6; Hare, comp., *Life and Letters of Elizabeth L. Comstock*, 109; *Journal of the Life, Travels, and Gospel Labors of Thomas Arnett*, 400–401; "The Peace Conference at Baltimore," *American Friend*, 1 (2nd Mo. 1867), 8. For James Parnell Jones, the son of Eli and Sybil Jones, see Peter H. Curtis, "A Quaker and the Civil War: The Life of James Parnell Jones," *Quaker History*, 67 (Spring 1978), 35–41.

59. "Words of Cheer and Caution," *Friends' Review*, 3rd Mo. 2, 1861, p. 408.

60. "Peace Conference at Baltimore," 5–10; "Peace Conference," 88–97; Brock, *Pacifism in the United States*, 872–73.

61. "What Things Are Caesar's?" *American Friend*, 1 (2nd Mo. 1867), 33–36; "General Meeting on Peace at Spiceland, Indiana," ibid., 2 (2nd Mo. 1868), 27–30; Amy Ann Sanders to Louzena Sanders, Feb. 19, 1867, Earlham Students Collection; Deem, *Olden Spiceland*, 5; Keller, *American Protestantism*, 126–48.

62. Talbert Diary, Sept. 1, 1863; Hare, comp., *Life and Letters of Elizabeth L. Comstock*, 237–38. For dated but useful treatment of Friends and the freedmen in a Dunningesque vein, see Anscombe, "Contributions of the Quakers," 116–272. The efforts of Philadelphia Friends are described in Benjamin, *Philadelphia Quakers*, 128–36. See also Thomas H. Smith, "Ohio Quakers and the Mississippi Freedmen: 'A Field to Labor,' " *Ohio History*, 78 (Summer 1969), 159–71.

63. Anscombe, "Contribution of the Quakers," 166–67, 172, 197, 213, 247, 250; [Murray], *Under His Wings*, 81; J. H. Douglas, "Thoughts and Suggestions about the Freed-People," *Friends' Review*, 3rd Mo. 3, 1866, pp. 425–26. The most frequent lead feature in the *American Friend* in 1867 and 1868 was an article on the freedmen.

64. Anscombe, "Contribution of the Quakers," 191–92; *Western Yearly Meeting Minutes*, 1865, pp. 40–41; Tallack, *Friendly Sketches*, 51–52; Stafford Allen Warner, *Yardley Warner: The Freedman's Friend: His Life and Times* (Didcot, Eng.: Wessex, n.d.), 81; *North Carolina Yearly Meeting Minutes, 1869*, pp. 5, 19; Ohio Yearly Meeting for Sufferings Minutes, 5th Mo. 14, 1866. Friends treated American Indians in a similar manner. See Keller, *American Protestantism*, 49.

65. Anscombe, "Contribution of the Quakers," 191–93, 213–16; D. C. letter, *Freedmen's Record*, 9th Mo. 1866, p. 11; "Letter from John Henry Douglas," ibid., 2nd Mo. 1865, p. 5; "Letter from Elkanah Beard," *Friends' Review*, 12th Mo. 2, 1865, pp. 218–19; Thomas C. Kennedy, "Southland College: The Society of Friends

and Black Education in Arkansas," *Arkansas Historical Quarterly*, 42 (Autumn 1983), 207–38.

66. [Butler et al.], *John Butler*, 142. For the involvement of other revival Friends, see Anscombe, "Contribution of the Quakers," 166–67, 172, 197, 213, 247, 250.

67. *Autobiography of Allen Jay*, 45–46; *New Castle* (Ind.) *Courier*, Oct. 17, 1867, p. 2; ibid., Oct. 31, 1867, p. 2; Benjamin Pickett to Joseph Pickett, 2nd Mo. 19, 1869, in Willard C. Heiss, comp., "Pickett-Allen Family Letters," typescript, 1954, item 4 (Indiana Historical Society Library).

68. William Nicholson, "Serious Thoughts for Serious Friends," *Christian Worker*, 4th Mo. 15, 1880, pp. 183–84; Johnson and Coffin, *Charles F. Coffin*, 109; "Indiana Yearly Meeting," *American Friend*, 1 (11th Mo. 1867), 266–67.

69. For accounts of some early general meetings, see "The General Meeting of Friends in Chicago," *American Friend*, 2 (1st Mo. 1868), 5–11; and "General Meeting of Friends in Kansas," *Herald of Peace*, 7th Mo. 15, 1869, pp. 155–56.

70. See ibid.; Nicholson, "Serious Thoughts," 183; and Johnson and Coffin, *Charles F. Coffin*, 109.

71. Nicholson, "Serious Thoughts," 183–85; "General Meetings," *Christian Worker*, 2nd Mo. 15, 1871, pp. 32–33; "Protracted Meetings," *ibid.*, pp. 11–12.

IV   THE REVIVAL, 1867–1880

1. *Christian Standard*, Oct. 16, 1875, reprinted in editorial, *Western Friend*, 2 (4th Mo. 1881), 32.

2. For the use of "revival," cf. William Tallack, *Friendly Sketches in America* (London: A. W. Bennett, 1861), 269–70; "The British Friend on Revivals," *Friends' Review*, 9th Mo. 25, 1869, pp. 73–74; and Joel Bean, "The Issue," *British Friend*, 3rd Mo. 1, 1881, p. 49; with D. B. Updegraff, *Open Letters for Interested Readers* (Philadelphia: n.p., 1880), 13; and Thomas Arnett, "On Revivals," *Christian Worker*, 10th Mo. 15, 1871, pp. 161–62.

3. Darius B. Cook, *History of Quaker Divide* (Dexter, Iowa: Dexter Sentinel, 1914), 67–68.

4. Daniel Clark, "From Walnut Ridge," *American Friend*, 1 (12th Mo. 1867), 302–4; Walter Edgerton, *Modern Quakerism Examined and Contrasted with That of the Ancient Type* (Indianapolis: Printing and Publishing House Press, 1876), 8–9; Luke Woodard, *Sketches of a Life of 75 in Three Parts: Biographical, Historical, and Descriptive* (Richmond, Ind.: Nicholson, 1907), 23–24; Gurney Binford, *As I Remember It: 43 Years in Japan* (n.p., 1950), 16–18. For a discussion of the Spiceland revival, see Thomas D. Hamm, "The Transformation of American Quakerism, 1800–1910" (Ph.D. diss., Indiana University, 1985), 181.

5. Rufus M. Jones, *The Later Periods of Quakerism* (2 vols., London: Macmillan, 1921), II, 900; *Reminiscences of Nathan T. Frame and Esther G. Frame* (Cleveland: Britton, 1907), 60–63. Richard E. Wood has found at least eight such outbreaks among American Friends from 1868 to 1870. Richard Eugene Wood, "Evangelical Quakers in the Mississippi Valley, 1854–1894" (Ph.D. diss., University of Minnesota, 1985), 62. For a different view of these incidents, see Hamm, "Transformation of American Quakerism," 143–48, 181.

6. Joel Bean letter, *Friends' Review*, 7th Mo. 9, 1870, p. 731; "Edith Griffith," *British Friend*, 10th Mo. 2, 1876, p. 271.

7. "A Practical Ministry the Need of the Society of Friends," *Herald of Peace*, 7th Mo. 1, 1869, p. 144.

8. Timothy L. Smith, *Revivalism and Social Reform: American Protestantism on the Eve of the Civil War* (New York: Harper and Row, 1965), 103–47. Wesleyan holiness theorists saw sanctification as entailing holiness. For those in the Reformed tradition, it meant consecration and empowerment. For a longer discussion of these topics, see pp. 000–00. For most nineteenth-century holiness writers and evangelists, the terms "sanctification," "holiness," "perfect love," and "higher Christian life" were interchangeable.

9. Melvin Easterday Dieter, *The Holiness Revival of the Nineteenth Century* (Metuchen, N.J.: Scarecrow, 1980), 96–156.

10. Dougan Clark and Joseph H. Smith, *David B. Updegraff and His Work* (Cincinnati: M. W. Knapp, 1895), 9–12; Erving E. Beauregard, *Old Franklin: The Eternal Touch: A History of Franklin College, New Athens, Harrison County, Ohio* (Lanham, Md.: University Press of America, 1983), 46; Joseph Conforti, "Jonathan Edwards' Most Popular Work: 'The Life of David Brainerd' and Nineteenth-Century Evangelical Culture," *Church History*, 54 (June 1985), 188–203; Joshua Maule, *Transactions and Changes in the Society of Friends, and Incidents in the Life and Experience of Joshua Maule* (Philadelphia: J. B. Lippincott, 1886), 42–43; Jonathan T. Updegraff to David and Rebecca Updegraff, 7th Mo. 15, 1841, box 1, Updegraff Family Papers (Quaker Collection, Haverford College, Haverford, Pa.); Donald G. Good, "Elisha Bates: American Quaker Evangelical in the Early Nineteenth Century" (Ph.D. diss., University of Iowa, 1967), 303–5. Jonathan T. Updegraff later served as a surgeon in the Union army and as a Republican congressman from Ohio. Beauregard, *Old Franklin*, 46. For a discussion of David B. Updegraff's sister Ann, see chap. 2.

11. J. Brent Bill, *David B. Updegraff: Quaker Holiness Preacher* (Richmond, Ind.: Friends United Press, 1983), 14–16; Caroline Hare, comp., *Life and Letters of Elizabeth L. Comstock* (London: Headley Brothers, 1895), 400. Bill states that David B. Updegraff went with the Wilburites in the Ohio separation of 1854, citing Updegraff's disownment by the Wilburite Short Creek Monthly Meeting in 1865 for joining the Gurneyites. The intricacies of Ohio Yearly Meeting politics have misled Bill. In the 1860s several Ohio Wilburite monthly meetings decided that, since they were the legitimate Society of Friends, members of the corresponding Gurneyite meetings had to be disowned as separatists. This is the course that the Short Creek Wilburites took with Updegraff. Joshua Maule, a leading Ohio Wilburite, recorded that the whole Updegraff family, along with the grandmother Ann Taylor, were Gurneyites, as does a reminiscence by Allen Jay of a visit to the Gurneyite Ohio Yearly Meeting in 1859. Bill, *David B. Updegraff*, 16–17; Maule, *Transactions and Changes*, 42–43; *Autobiography of Allen Jay, Born 1831, Died 1910* (Philadelphia: John C. Winston, 1910), 84–85. The long obituaries in the *Friends' Review* of David and Rebecca Updegraff, David B.'s parents, indicate that they had to be Gurneyites. David Updegraff obituary, *Friends' Review*, 3rd Mo. 18, 1865, p. 458; "Memorial of Short Creek Monthly Meeting concerning Our Dear Friend, Rebecca Updegraff," ibid., 5th Mo. 2, 1870, pp. 579–82. For the Wilburite disownment of Gurneyites, see Maule, *Transactions and Changes*, 211–12; and "Separation in Philadelphia Yearly Meeting," *Friends' Review*, 11th Mo. 16, 1861, p. 169.

12. Bill, *David B. Updegraff*, 17–18.

13. Woodard, *Sketches*, 9–11; "Ohio Yearly Meeting," *American Friend*, 9th Mo. 6, 1894, p. 185; M. M. Binford, "Dr. Dougan Clark," ibid., 10th Mo. 22, 1896, p. 1026; Jacob Baker, *Incidents of My Life and Work of 84 Years* (Richmond, Ind.: Nicholson, 1911), 36.

14. Binford, "Dr. Dougan Clark," 1025–26.

15. "Field Notes," *Friends' Expositor*, 2 (Oct. 1888), 208; ibid., 6 (Oct. 1892), 718;

Dougan Clark, *Address by Dr. Dougan Clark* (n.p., 1858); D. C., "Without Holiness No Man Shall See the Lord," *American Friend*, 2 (8th Mo. 1868), 195; Dougan Clark to Joel Bean, 12th Mo. 30, 1848, 12th Mo. 22, 1849, 6th Mo. 2, 1852, box 3, Joel Bean Papers (Friends Historical Library, Swarthmore College, Swarthmore, Pa.); Clark to Rhoda M. Coffin, 4th Mo. 12, 1872, box 1, Coffin Family Papers (ibid.)

16. Douglas lacks an easily accessible biography. The best sources for his life are W. Rufus Kersey, comp., "Documents Dealing with the Life and Work of John Henry Douglas, Quaker Evangelist, 1832–1919" (Manuscripts Department, Duke University, Durham, N.C.); Louis Thomas Jones, *The Quakers of Iowa* (Iowa City: Clio, 1914), 118–19; and John Henry Douglas, "Personal Testimony," *Christian Worker*, 6th Mo. 23, 1887, pp. 289–90.

17. Douglas, "Personal Testimony," 289–90.

18. David Marshall, *Justification and Sanctification Inseparable in the Work of Redemption* (Carthage, Ind.: n.p., 1881), 2; Charles F. Coffin, "Tribute to the Memory of My Mother, Naomi Coffin," Naomi Coffin folder, Charles F. and Rhoda M. Coffin Papers (Archives, Earlham College, Richmond, Ind.); Mary H. Rogers, "My Experience," *Friends' Expositor*, 1 (April 1887), 52; J. Y. Hoover, "Sketches from Life," *Evangelical Friend*, Aug. 8, 1907, p. 501; *Reminiscences of Nathan T. Frame*, 44. Both Marshall and Coffin state that the subject of second-experience holiness was first agitated among Quakers during the mid-1860s.

19. *Iowa Yearly Meeting Minutes, 1901*, p. 72; Lydia M. Cammack-Williams and Truman C. Kenworthy, *Life and Works of Amos M. Kenworthy* (Richmond, Ind.: Nicholson, 1919), 3–4. Lawrie Tatum's sanctification followed closely on the heels of his resignation as United States Indian agent for the Kiowa and Comanche tribes. Tatum had called on the army to put down a Kiowa uprising. His use of force brought him impassioned criticism from a number of Gurneyite Friends. Tatum gave up his agency, telling his critics to turn it over to any Friend they could find who could abide by peace principles and control Comanches at the same time. Robert H. Keller, Jr., *American Protestantism and United States Indian Policy, 1869–82* (Lincoln: University of Nebraska Press, 1983), 132–38. It is tempting to see Tatum's subsequent career as a response to the attacks that leading moderate Gurneyites had made on him. For Francis W. Thomas's opposition to second-experience sanctification, see Francis W. Thomas, "Joseph Cox," *Friends' Review*, 3rd Mo. 8, 1873, p. 458; and Carrie T. [Johnson] to Allen Jay, Nov. 18, 1892, miscellaneous folder, M-R box, Allen Jay Papers (Archives, Earlham). Jay's works are silent on the subject of holiness.

I have not included Hannah Whitall Smith in this list of holiness Quaker revivalists. She was unquestionably the most famous of all holiness Friends; her *Christian's Secret of a Happy Life* (1875) has gone through numerous editions and is still in print. Smith and her husband had left the society in Philadelphia by 1872, however, and had moved to England, so neither played an important role in the revival. Once overseas Smith moved in a world very different from that of Updegraff, whose methods she questioned. She became a militant suffragette and socialist; she repudiated many revival methods; and, most interesting of all, became the mother-in-law of both Bernard Berenson and Bertrand Russell and the grandmother of Karin Stephen, one of the first English psychoanalysts. Logan Pearsall Smith, ed., *Philadelphia Quaker: The Letters of Hannah Whitall Smith* (New York: Harcourt, Brace, 1950), 69; Barbara Strachey, *Remarkable Relations: The Story of the Pearsall Smith Women* (London: Gollancz, 1980), 9, 23–26, 33–36, 236.

20. Elbert Russell, *The History of Quakerism* (New York: Macmillan, 1942), 424–26; Jones, *Quakers of Iowa*, 118–19; *Minutes of North Carolina Yearly Meeting, 1856*, p. 11; *Autobiography of Allen Jay*, 121–22; John Y. Hoover, "A Sketch of Life,"

Evangelical Friend, July 12, 1906, p. 441. Some of the conditions of Mary H. Rogers's girlhood can be glimpsed in the memorial of her father, Joseph B. Hunt, in *Memorials of Deceased Friends, Who Were Members of Indiana Yearly Meeting* (Cincinnati: E. Morgan, 1857), 62–72.

21. Edgerton, *Modern Quakerism*, 7; D. H. P., "Spiceland General Meeting," *Christian Worker*, 2nd Mo. 15, 1874, p. 60.

22. George Cobb, "Ohio Yearly Meeting," *Christian Worker*, 2nd Mo. 15, 1874, p. 74.

23. Cook, *History of Quaker Divide*, 70–71.

24. Timothy Harrison to "Sister Elizabeth," 11th Mo. 6, 1873, Timothy Harrison letterbook, p. 94, Merritt Harrison Papers (Indiana Division, Indiana State Library, Indianapolis); "Brooklyn General Meeting," *Friends' Review*, 12th Mo. 16, 1871, pp. 257–58; Luke Woodard, *The Morning Star! A Treatise on the Nature, Office, and Works of the Lord Jesus Christ* (New Vienna, Ohio: Friends Publishing House, 1875), 271–73.

25. E. G. "Reminiscences," *Christian Worker*, 10th Mo. 1, 1876, pp. 312–13; L[uke] W[oodard], "Philadelphia Yearly Meeting," ibid., 6th Mo. 1, 1876, pp. 169–70; Cobb, "Ohio Yearly Meeting," 74.

26. William Nicholson to Timothy Nicholson, 11th Mo. 2, 1881, Timothy Nicholson Papers (Archives, Earlham); Williams-Cammack and Kenworthy, *Life and Works of Amos M. Kenworthy*, 214; S. Lindley Stanley, "A History of the Quaker Settlement at Hesper, Kansas" (M.S. thesis, Kansas State Teachers College, 1937), 19.

27. Williams-Cammack and Kenworthy, *Life and Works of Amos M. Kenworthy*, 61–62; Baker, *Incidents of My Life*, 70–71; David B. Updegraff notebook, n.d., unpaged, box 2, Updegraff Papers; "Proceedings of the Sixth Biennial Conference of Teachers and Delegates from Friends' First Day Schools," *Christian Worker*, 2nd Mo. 15, 1872, p. 22; "Why Do Not Friends Sing in Their Religious Meetings?" ibid., 6th Mo. 15, 1873, p. 187; [Ruth S. Murray], *Under His Wings: A Sketch of the Life of Robert Lindley Murray* (New York: Anson D. F. Randolph, 1876), 139–41; J. and E. G. Hadley to David Huddleston, 12th Mo. 8, 1883, David Huddleston Papers (Archives, Earlham).

28. Seth C. Rees, "Experience," *Friends' Expositor*, 1 (April 1887), 34; Updegraff, *Open Letters*, 22.

29. Mariana Wilson, "An Essay on Sectarianism," *Christian Worker*, 7th Mo. 15, 1875, p. 214; Woodard, *Morning Star!* 377–81; "She Hath Done What She Could," *Friends' Review*, 5th Mo. 15, 1875, p. 617; Dougan Clark, *The Offices of the Holy Spirit* (Philadelphia: National Publishing Association for the Promotion of Holiness, n.d.), 223–24.

30. David B. Updegraff, *Old Corn; or, Sermons on the Spiritual Life* (Boston: McDonald and Gill, 1892), 284–85; Clark, *Offices of the Holy Spirit*, 80, 94–95; "Then and Now," *Christian Worker*, 4th Mo. 12, 1877, pp. 233–39; "From Farmington, N.Y.," ibid., 12th Mo. 30, 1871, p. 235. For the controversies of Richard Baxter and John Bunyan with the early Friends, see Hugh Barbour and Arthur O. Roberts, eds., *Early Quaker Writings, 1650–1700* (Grand Rapids: Eerdmans, 1973), 262–98; and Hugh Barbour, *The Quakers in Puritan England* (New Haven: Yale University Press, 1964), 136–37.

31. Ann T. Updegraff to Rebecca Cattell, 2nd Mo. 5, [1841], box 1, Updegraff Papers; Hare, comp., *Life and Letters of Elizabeth L. Comstock*, 305.

32. H[annah] W[hitall] S[mith], "Diversities of Gifts and the Unity of the Spirit," *Christian Worker*, 6th Mo. 10, 1880, p. 283.

33. Aaron L. Benedict to Aaron Pleas, 5th Mo. 27, 1855, Susan B. Unthank Papers (Indiana Division, Indiana State Library); J. T., "Why Are We a Small

Denomination?" *Christian Worker*, 1st Mo. 29, 1880, p. 55; C. W. Osborn letter, *Herald of Peace*, 3rd Mo. 29, 1868, p. 71.

34. "Meetings for Discipline," *Christian Worker*, 5th Mo. 15, 1871, p. 74; "Our Fathers," ibid., 11th Mo. 15, 1875, p. 348; "Conservatism," ibid.; W. E. Hathaway, "An Idea," ibid., 1st Mo. 15, 1874, p. 29; John D. Miles to Allen Jay, 2nd Mo. 14, 1908, A-F box, Jay Papers; E. Updegraff to "Dear Sister," March 10, 1873, box 1, Updegraff Papers.

35. For sanctification as the baptism of the Holy Ghost, see, for example, "Friends General Meeting," *Christian Worker*, 12th Mo. 12, 1871, p. 203; Woodard, *Morning Star!* 302–5; and, generally, Clark, *Offices of the Holy Spirit*. For the leadings of the spirit and the ministry, see the letters from David B. Updegraff and Thomas W. Ladd in "Correspondence," *Friends' Review*, 12th Mo. 1, 1877, p. 250.

36. "General Meeting at Salem, Union County, Indiana," *Christian Worker*, 2nd Mo. 15, 1871, pp. 16–17; "General Meeting at West Milton, Ohio," ibid., pp. 1–3; "General Meetings," ibid., pp. 11–12; "The General Meeting at Waynesville, Ohio," ibid., 4th Mo. 15, 1871, p. 48; Harrison to "Dear Brother," 11th Mo. 13, 1871, letterbook, Harrison Papers; *Indiana Radical* quoted in editorial, *Friend*, 12th Mo. 2, 1871, p. 119; J. Hill letter, ibid. The memoirs of Nathan and Esther Frame, which consist largely of detailed chronological accounts of their evangelistic campaigns, are revealing. Before 1872 they emphasize the absence of singing, altar calls, and demonstrations of extreme emotionalism in their meetings. After 1872 such restraint is missing. *Reminiscences of Nathan T. Frame*, 120–40.

37. Hare, comp., *Life and Letters of Elizabeth L. Comstock*, 297; editorial, *Christian Worker*, 11th Mo. 15, 1871, p. 191; Alexander H. Hay, "The Rise of the Pastoral System in the Society of Friends, 1850–1900" (M.A. thesis, Haverford College, 1938), 53–54; Cook, *History of Quaker Divide*, 67–68. For the acquiescence of conservative Friends, see *Western Yearly Meeting Minutes, 1872*, p. 10; and *Memorial of Plainfield Monthly Meeting of Friends, concerning Our Dear Friend, Eleazer Bales, Deceased* (n.p., 1887), 4.

38. "Brooklyn General Meeting," 274–77; "Union Meetings," *Christian Worker*, 4th Mo. 15, 1871, pp. 45–46; "Friends General Meeting," ibid., 9th Mo. 15, 1871, pp. 141–48; *Providence* (R.I.) *Daily Journal*, Dec. 23, 1871, reprinted in editorial, *Friend*, 1st Mo. 6, 1872, p. 157.

39. No one general meeting constituted a decisive break with the others. Instead, the revival crescendo rose gradually as the power of the holiness ministers increased. For a sense of the change, see "General Meeting at Jericho, Indiana," *Christian Worker*, 1st Mo. 15, 1872, p. 11; "A Protracted Meeting," ibid., 5th Mo. 15, 1872, p. 92; letter from "An Old Member of Ohio Yearly Meeting," *Friends' Review*, 3rd Mo. 15, 1873, pp. 475–77; David B. Updegraff to "Darling Daughter," June 10, 1873, box 1, Updegraff Papers; Harrison to Louisa Coffin, 11th Mo. 11, 1873, letterbook, pp. 97–98, Harrison Papers; "Indiana Yearly Meeting," *Christian Worker*, 2nd Mo. 15, 1874, p. 75; "Iowa Yearly Meeting," ibid., 78: Joseph H. Pratt, "Ohio Yearly Meeting," ibid., 1st Mo. 1, 1875, p. 2; "New England Yearly Meeting," ibid., 12th Mo. 1, 1875, p. 355; Woodard, *Sketches*, 27–61; and *Autobiography of Allen Jay*, 205–14.

40. Howard H. Brinton, ed., "The Revival Movement in Iowa: A Letter from Joel Bean to Rufus M. Jones," *Bulletin of Friends Historical Association*, 50 (Fall 1961), 108; C. W. Harvey to Herman Newman, 11th Mo. 2, 1906, Herman Newman Collection (Manuscripts Department, Kansas State Historical Society, Topeka); Henry Stanley Newman, *Memories of Stanley Pumphrey* (New York: Friends Book and Tract Committee, 1883), 245–46; "London Yearly Meeting," *British Friend*, 6th Mo. 1, 1878, p. 140. For another account of the coming of the revival to a Quaker

community, this one in Indiana, see David Huddleston Diary, 3rd Mo. 9, 10, 12, 1874, Huddleston Papers.

41. *Autobiography of Allen Jay*, 205–14; Allen Jay to Martha Jay, 1st Mo. 28, 1875, G-L box, Jay Papers. Jay's success is all the more remarkable in view of a speech impediment caused by a cleft palate, leaving him with a speech "like nothing else in the world." Levi T. Pennington, *Rambling Recollections of Ninety Happy Years* (Portland, Ore.: Metropolitan Press, 1967), 127.

42. Cf. *The Discipline of the Society of Friends of Ohio Yearly Meeting, Revised by the Meeting Held at Mt. Pleasant, in the Year 1859* (Cincinnati: Achilles Pugh, 1860), 83–89; with *The Discipline of Ohio Yearly Meeting of the Society of Friends* (New Vienna, Ohio: Friends Publishing House, 1876), 78–79. For the unity in Ohio in favor of revision, see Joseph W. Taylor to "Dear Sister," 9th Mo. 1, 1876, box 10, Taylor Family Papers (Quaker Collection, Haverford).

43. "Religious Statistics," *Christian Worker*, 7th Mo. 15, 1873, pp. 216–17; "Question Drawer," ibid., 11th Mo. 15, 1876, p. 365; "Marriage with Non Members," *Friends' Review*, 7th Mo. 12, 1879, p. 758. When two elderly Friends in Spiceland, Indiana, were united by the traditional Quaker ceremony in 1896, a local newspaper commented that it was "the first marriage here for years conducted according to the ceremonies of the church these people are members of." *New Castle* (Ind.) *Courier*, May 7, 1896, p. 8.

44. See, for example, *Discipline of Ohio Yearly Meeting*, 75–76, 78, 84–85. For rural morality, see Lewis Atherton, *Main Street on the Middle Border* (Bloomington: Indiana University Press, 1954), 67–75.

45. Clark and Smith, *David B. Updegraff*, 195; [William Nicholson], "The Eldership in the Society of Friends," *Friends' Review*, 7th Mo. 25, 1868, pp. 753–55; "Ministers and Elders," ibid., 1st Mo. 29, 1876, p. 376; William Scarnell Leon, "The Oversight of the Ministry," *Christian Worker*, 1st Mo. 25, 1877, p. 53; David Hunt, "Church Government, Officers, and Helps," ibid., 12th Mo. 1, 1873, pp. 354–55.

46. "Priesthood and Clergy," *Friends' Review*, 11th Mo. 7, 1874, p. 184; "Conference of Ministers and Elders in New York," ibid., 6th Mo. 26, 1875, p. 713; "Western Yearly Meeting," *Christian Worker*, 3rd Mo. 20, 1878, p. 134; T. W. Ladd, "Fundamentals of the Christian Faith," ibid., 12th Mo. 4, 1879, pp. 583–84; *New York Yearly Meeting Minutes, 1874*, p. 24; "To Ministers of the Gospel and Friends Generally," n.d., file 1, Joseph Moore Papers (Archives, Earlham). At the opposite end of the spectrum were a few revival enthusiasts who wanted to abolish all distinctions and to let all labor as they felt called, without any direction save that of God. Hathaway, "An Idea," 29.

47. Jones, *Later Periods of Quakerism*, II, 915–16; "Indiana Yearly Meeting," *Friends' Review*, 10th Mo. 13, 1877, p. 138; William Nicholson, "Serious Thoughts for Serious Friends," *Christian Worker*, 3rd Mo. 25, 1880, p. 148. In 1873 there were about sixty thousand Gurneyite Friends in America. By 1896 this number had increased to about eighty thousand, about the number of Orthodox Friends in America in 1843. Russell, *History of Quakerism*, 434.

48. Edwin B. Bronner, ed., *An English View of American Quakerism: The Journal of Walter Robson* (Philadelphia: American Philosophical Society, 1970), 67–69; [Anna B. Thomas], *J. Bevan Braithwaite: A Friend of the Nineteenth Century* (London: Hodder and Stoughton, 1909), 240; Addison Coffin, *Life and Travels of Addison Coffin* (Cleveland: William G. Hubbard, 1897), 132, 156; "Western Yearly Meeting," *Christian Worker*, 5th Mo. 15, 1875, p. 155; ibid., 9th Mo. 27, 1877, p. 611; *Memorial of Plainfield Monthly Meeting, concerning Our Dear Friend, Eleazer Bales*, 4; "Some Information on the Recent Division in Western Yearly Meeting of Friends," *British Friend*, 5th Mo. 1, 1878, pp. 106–8; Joseph W. Taylor to "Dear

Sister," 9th Mo. 25, 1876, box 10, Taylor Papers; Taylor to "Home," 9th Mo. 20, 1876, ibid.; Edward Grubb, *Separations, Their Causes and Effects: Studies in Nineteenth-Century Quakerism* (London: Headley Brothers, 1914), 150–52. A concise history of the Conservative group is Willard Heiss, *A Brief History of Western Yearly Meeting of Conservative Friends and the Separation of 1877* (Indianapolis: John Woolman Press, 1963).

49. "Separation and Compromise," *Western Friend*, 1 (11th Mo. 1879), 4; "The Division in Kansas Yearly Meeting," ibid. (12th Mo. 1879), 10; William Nicholson to Timothy Nicholson, 10th Mo. 24, 1877, Nicholson Papers; Bronner, ed., *English View*, 57–59; Heiss, *Brief History*, 17–28; Joseph Bevan Braithwaite to Taylor, 10th Mo. 20, 1878, box 1, Taylor Papers.

50. Bronner, ed., *English View*, 15–16; editorial, *Friend*, 9th Mo. 8, 1877, p. 31; William Nicholson to Timothy Nicholson, 10th Mo. 24, 1877, Nicholson Papers.

51. Edgerton, *Modern Quakerism*; Walter Edgerton, *Walter Edgerton's Disownment by Spiceland Monthly Meeting* (n.p., 1877); David Hunt, "Fault Finding and Accusing the Brethren," *Christian Worker*, 7th Mo. 15, 1876, p. 219; "A Tribute to the Memory of Walter Edgerton," *Western Friend*, 2 (9th Mo. 1880), 79–80; Thomas D. Hamm, *The Anti-Slavery Movement in Henry County, Indiana* (New Castle, Ind.: Henry County Historical Society, 1975), 17–18; T. B. Deem, *Olden Spiceland* (n.p., 1934), 3.

52. J. B., "The English Deputation," *Friends' Review*, 7th Mo. 27, 1878, pp. 387–88; Cammack-Williams and Kenworthy, *Life and Work of Amos M. Kenworthy*, 37–39. James Baldwin paints an attractive portrait of Levi T. Pennington (1812–1896) as the character Levi T. Jay in [James Baldwin], *In My Youth: From the Posthumous Papers of Robert Dudley* (Indianapolis: Bobbs-Merrill, 1914), 100, 172–76. Pennington was the grandfather and namesake of George Fox College president Levi T. Pennington, well known to twentieth-century Quakers.

53. Bean, "The Issue," 49; Joel Bean, "The First Day School Conference," *Friends' Review*, 12th Mo. 23, 1871, p. 273.

54. "American Friends on the Philadelphia Address," *British Friend*, 8th Mo. 1, 1883, p. 204; John G. Whittier to [Walter Edgerton], 2nd Mo. 14, 1872, John Greenleaf Whittier Collection (Friends Historical Library, Swarthmore); Nereus Mendenhall to "Dear Friend," 1st Mo. 13, 1874, 11th Mo. 10, 1874, box 1, Hobbs-Mendenhall Papers (Southern Historical Collection, University of North Carolina, Chapel Hill); Mendenhall to Richard Randolph, 11th Mo. 27, 1881, box 2, Hobbs-Mendenhall Papers (Friends Historical Collection, Guilford College, Greensboro, N.C.); William Nicholson to Timothy Nicholson, 10th Mo. 24, 1877, Nicholson Papers; Timothy Nicholson to Joel and Hannah E. Bean, 5th Mo. 2, 1880, 11th Mo. 13, 1883, box 4, Bean Papers; "Critical Interrogatories by Charles F. Coffin," *Western Friend*, 3 (12th Mo. 1882), 96; editorial, ibid., 4 (8th Mo. 1883), 63; "Settling Back," ibid., 1 (10th Mo. 1880), 88; [Josiah Butler et al.], *John Butler: A Sketch of His Life* (Columbus: William G. Hubbard, 1890), 168–69; Errol T. Elliott, *Quaker Profiles from the American West* (Richmond, Ind.: Friends United Press, 1972), 100–103; Charles F. Coffin to Joseph Bevan Braithwaite, 6th Mo. 15, 1878, box 1, Taylor Papers; Indiana Yearly Meeting of Ministers and Elders Minutes, 9th Mo. 28, 1875, 10th Mo. 2, 1875, 10th Mo. 2, 1877 (Archives, Earlham). For a somewhat different breakdown of this group, see Mark E. Minear, "The Richmond Conference of 1887" (M.A. thesis, Earlham School of Religion, 1984), 43.

55. "General Meetings," *Friends' Review*, 11th Mo. 11, 1871, pp. 184–85; "Moderation in All Things," ibid., 1st Mo. 13, 1872, pp. 328–29; "Not a Platform, But the Rock," ibid., 11th Mo. 20, 1875, pp. 216–17; "The Philadelphia Yearly Meeting Epistle," ibid., 6th Mo. 10, 1876, pp. 681–82; "The Standard," ibid., 10th Mo. 19,

1878, p. 753; Henry Hartshorne to William L. Edwards, 8th Mo. 4, 1874, box 4, Hartshorne Family Papers (Quaker Collection, Haverford); Hartshorne to Rachel H. Hopkins, 9th Mo. 14, 1884, ibid.; Hartshorne to David B. Updegraff, 10th Mo. 9, 1875, ibid.; editorial, *Western Friend*, 4 (6th Mo. 1883), 48; Philip S. Benjamin, *The Philadelphia Quakers in the Industrial Age, 1865–1920* (Philadelphia: Temple University Press, 1976), 15–16.

56. Woodard, *Sketches*, 14–37; *Reminiscences of Nathan T. Frame*, 50–102; Brinton, ed., "Revival Movement in Iowa," 106–9; Updegraff, *Open Letters*, 22; Nicholson, "Serious Thoughts," 183–84; [Butler et al.], *John Butler*, 173–74.

57. See, for example, Arthur Owen Roberts, "The Concepts of Perfection in the History of the Quaker Movement" (B. D. thesis, Nazarene Theological Seminary, 1951), 117; Walter R. Williams, *The Rich Heritage of Quakerism* (Grand Rapids: Eerdmans, 1962), 192–201; and Richard E. Wood, "The Emergence of Revivalistic, Pastoral Quakerism in Midwestern America, 1850–1890: Creative Response or Tragic Accommodation?" 1976, pp. 20–21 (in author's possession).

58. "Friends in America," *London Friend*, 3rd Mo. 1, 1872, p. 47; "Friends in 1900," *American Friend*, 1st Mo. 3, 1901, p. 3; "A Series of Meetings," *Friends' Review*, 4th Mo. 5, 1879, pp. 538–39; [Anna B. Thomas], *Richard H. Thomas, M.D.: Life and Letters* (London: Headley Brothers, 1905), 40, 83–85, 166–67, 172–74, 187–88, 192–97; Charles C. Hendricks, "The Influence of Joseph Moore and the Baltimore Association on North Carolina Quakers," *Southern Friend*, 2 (Autumn 1980), 71–83; *Discipline of the Yearly Meeting of Friends Held in Baltimore, for the Western Shore of Maryland, Virginia, and the Adjacent Parts of Pennsylvania, as Revised and Adopted in 1876* (Baltimore: Wm. K. Boyle, 1877); Bliss Forbush, *A History of Baltimore Yearly Meeting of Friends: Three Hundred Years of Quakerism in Maryland, Virginia, the District of Columbia, and Central Pennsylvania* (Baltimore: Baltimore Yearly Meeting, 1972), 93–96.

V   THE REALIGNMENT OF AMERICAN QUAKERISM, 1875–1890

1. John Nicholson to Timothy Nicholson, Sept. 14, 1885, Timothy Nicholson Papers (Archives, Earlham College, Richmond, Ind.).

2. [Ezra Barker] to Simeon Barker, 10th Mo. 7, 1883, Simeon Barker Papers (Manuscripts Division, Duke University Library, Durham, N.C.).

3. "The 'Smaller Bodies' of Friends in America," *Friends' Review*, 12th Mo. 9, 1886, p. 292; Philip S. Benjamin, *The Philadelphia Quakers in the Industrial Age, 1865–1920* (Philadelphia: Temple University Press, 1976), 15–17; William Hodgson, *The Society of Friends in the Nineteenth Century: A Historical View of the Successive Convulsions and Schisms Therein during That Period* (2 vols., Philadelphia, 1875–1876), II, 168–90, 203–12, 250–63, 281–344; A. Day Bradley, "New York Yearly Meeting at Poplar Ridge and the Primitive Friends," *Quaker History*, 68 (Autumn 1979), 75–82; William P. Taber, Jr., *The Eye of Faith: A History of Ohio Yearly Meeting, Conservative* (Barnesville, Ohio: Ohio Yearly Meeting, 1985), 78–101; Joseph E. Maule, *An Earnest Appeal to All Those Who Desire the Maintenance of the Ancient Doctrines and Testimonies of the Gospel as Held by the Primitive Friends* (Philadelphia: n.p., 1872). Small communities of Primitive Friends still exist in Pennsylvania and Virginia; they are the only Quakers who still hold to the uncompromising plain life.

4. Taber, *Eye of Faith*, 107–9; Elbert Russell, *The History of Quakerism* (New York: Macmillan, 1942), 430–31. Conservative Friends in North Carolina did not

separate until 1904. They subsequently joined the network of Conservative yearly meetings. See Damon D. Hickey, "Progressives and Conservatives Search for Order: The Division of North Carolina Quakers," *Southern Friend*, 6 (Spring 1984), 17–35.

5. Western Yearly Meeting for Sufferings [Conservative], *A Salutation of Love, to All True Friends* (n.p., 1878), 2; Jesse Edgerton, *Why Am I a Friend?* (n.p., 1893); editorial, *Western Friend*, 10 (5th Mo. 1889), 39.

6. Benjamin, *Philadelphia Quakers*, 15–16; "Philadelphia Yearly Meeting," *Friends' Review*, 4th Mo. 26, 1879, p. 587; ibid., 5th Mo. 3, 1879, p. 602; editorial, *Friend*, 9th Mo. 8, 1877, p. 31; Samuel Emlen letter, ibid., 5th Mo. 22, 1886, pp. 331–32; *An Address to Its Own Members and to the Members of Our Society Elsewhere, Issued by the Yearly Meeting of Friends in Philadelphia, Fourth Month 18, 1883* (Philadelphia: Friends' Book Store, 1883), 30–34; James Henley to Henry Hartshorne, 1st Mo. 12, 1893, box 10, Hartshorne Family Papers (Quaker Collection, Haverford College, Haverford, Pa.); editorial, *Western Friend*, 4 (6th Mo. 1883), 46–47.

7. [Julianna Harvey], *Memorial of Cyrus W. Harvey* (Philadelphia: Friends' Book Store, 1920), 1–10; Kathaleen J. Carter to Thomas D. Hamm, Sept. 20, 1984 (in author's possession); "Cheering Words," *Western Friend*, 1 (3rd Mo. 1880), 33. Kathaleen J. Carter is Cyrus W. Harvey's granddaughter.

8. Harvey published the *Western Friend* from 1879 to 1890. The issue for Sixth Month 1883 is typical. Within three pages it praises Philadelphia Yearly Meeting, blasts the revivalist journals *Gospel Expositor* and *Christian Worker* and all revival methods, asserts that such moderates as William Nicholson were turning against the revival, denounces Charles F. Coffin for temporizing, and predicts that David B. Updegraff's days as a Friend are numbered (see pp. 46–48). For a typical account of a revival, see editorial, *Western Friend*, 4 (10th Mo. 1883), 79.

9. Joshua Maule, *Transactions and Changes in the Society of Friends, and Incidents in the Life and Experience of Joshua Maule* (Philadelphia: J. B. Lippincott, 1886), 43–44, 80–81, 192–97, 67–68, 317, 372–73; Charles P. Morlan, comp., *A Brief History of Ohio Yearly Meeting of the Religious Society of Friends (Conservative)* (n.p., 1959), 54, 57, 154–57; Benjamin, *Philadelphia Quakers*, 8, 24–25; L. Frank Bedell, *Quaker Heritage: Friends Coming into the Heart of America: A Story of Iowa Conservative Yearly Meeting* (Cedar Rapids, Iowa, 1966), 204; Willard Heiss, *A Brief History of Western Yearly Meeting of Conservative Friends and the Separation of 1877* (Indianapolis: John Woolman Press, 1963), 9–10, 13, 17, 20, 23, 25; Taber, *Eye of Faith*, 116–18.

10. William P. Taber, Jr., "The Expanding World of Ohio Wilburites in the Latter Part of the Nineteenth Century," *Quaker History*, 56 (Spring 1967), 18–33; "Philadelphia Yearly Meeting," *Friends' Review*, 5th Mo. 4, 1893, p. 647; "First Day Schools," *Western Friend*, 1 (11th Mo. 1879), 2; editorial, ibid., 9 (7th Mo. 1888), 56; ibid. (10th Mo. 1888), 79–80; Taber, *Eye of Faith*, 105–63.

11. "Smaller Bodies of Friends," 292; Benjamin, *Philadelphia Quakers*, 20–21; *Journal of Ann Branson, a Minister of the Gospel in the Society of Friends* (Philadelphia: William H. Pile's Sons, 1892), 332–33; Edgerton, *Why Am I a Friend?* 8; Ann W. Fry to Jesse Edgerton, 8th Mo. 30, 1894, box 5, Stratton Papers (Friends Historical Library, Swarthmore College, Swarthmore, Pa.).

12. For biographical data on these men and women, see William Bacon Evans et al., comps., "Dictionary of Quaker Biography" (Quaker Collection, Haverford).

13. Henry J. Cadbury, "Negro Membership in the Society of Friends," *Journal of Negro History*, 21 (April 1936), 206–8; H. W. Jones to Allen Jay, 1st Mo. 5, 1891, 1st Mo. 10, 1893, G-L box, Allen Jay Papers (Archives, Earlham); "From the Field," *Christian Worker*, 4th Mo. 4, 1889, p. 214; O. L. Olds, "A Look from Without,"

ibid., 2nd Mo. 13, 1878, p. 77; James Grandstaff letter, ibid., 3rd Mo. 16, 1882, p. 125; "From the Field," ibid., 1st Mo. 18, 1883, p. 25; Alex M. Purdy letter, *Friends' Review*, 9th Mo. 23, 1886, p. 126; "Memorial of David Sampson," 1916 (Friends Historical Collection, Guilford College, Greensboro, N.C.); *Word and Work of David J. Lewis* (Cincinnati: M. W. Knapp, 1900), 27–28.

14. Editorial, *Christian Worker*, 4th Mo. 26, 1883, p. 199; "Valedictory," ibid., 198; "The Christian Worker and Gospel Expositor," ibid., 12th Mo. 4, 1884, p. 770; "The Mission of the Society of Friends," ibid., 5th Mo. 17, 1883, p. 237. Cyrus W. Harvey asserted that a "Fast Quaker conspiracy" outmaneuvered Charles F. Coffin and other moderates and forced Hill from the editor's post. "Inside the Ring or a Bit of Secret History," *Western Friend*, 7 (9th Mo. 1886), 70–71.

15. *Indiana Yearly Meeting Minutes, 1882*, p. 23.

16. "From the Field," *Christian Worker*, 2nd Mo. 21, 1884, p. 123.

17. "Friends: Are They Arminians or Calvinists?" *Christian Worker*, 7th Mo. 21, 1887, p. 342; George M. Marsden, *Fundamentalism and American Culture: The Shaping of Twentieth-Century Evangelicalism, 1870–1925* (New York: Oxford University Press, 1980), 72–80.

18. Thomas Kimber, "The Truth as It Is in Jesus," *Friends' Review*, 1st Mo. 10, 1885, pp. 353–54; "Editorial Notes," *Friends' Expositor*, 5 (April 1891), 525; Dougan Clark, *The Holy Ghost Dispensation* (Chicago: Publishing Association of Friends, 1892), 22–23.

19. N. D. Baldwin report in "From the Field," *Christian Worker*, 2nd Mo. 7, 1884, p. 91; M. F. Moorman, "Gradual Conversion," ibid., 6th Mo. 21, 1883, p. 329; G. D. Watson, "Entire Sanctification a Necessity," ibid., 1st Mo. 8, 1885, p. 20; A. H. Hussey, "Sin and Trespass Offerings," ibid., 11th Mo. 6, 1884, p. 708; Elwood Scott, "Sanctification Completed," ibid., 1st Mo. 10, 1884, pp. 18–19.

20. "Our Holiness Exchanges," *Gospel Expositor*, Jan. 26, 1883, p. 2; Luke Woodard, "The Consistency and Unity of Truth," *Christian Worker*, 8th Mo. 25, 1887, pp. 406–7; "Christian Economics," *Friends' Expositor*, 2 (July 1888), 159; editorial, *Western Friend*, 4 (7th Mo. 1883), 54; Timothy Nicholson to Joel Bean, 11th Mo. 13, 1883, box 4, Joel Bean Papers (Friends Historical Library, Swarthmore); Dougan Clark and Joseph H. Smith, *David B. Updegraff and His Work* (Cincinnati: M. W. Knapp, 1895), 98–99.

21. Dougan Clark, *The Offices of the Holy Spirit* (Philadelphia: National Association for the Promotion of Holiness, n.d.), 223–24; A. H. Hussey, "Holiness Convention," *Christian Worker*, 5th Mo. 7, 1885, p. 240; Clark and Smith, *David B. Updegraff*, 161–80; "Sectarian Bigotry," *Friends' Expositor*, 1 (April 1887), 37; "Notes by the Way," ibid., 3 (April 1889), 260; "The Glen's Falls Revival," ibid., 258–59; "Field Notes," ibid., (Oct. 1889), 327–32; Jacob Baker, *Incidents of My Life and Work of 84 Years* (Richmond, Ind.: Nicholson, 1911), 109.

22. W. G. H[ubbard], "Wonders of Faith: The Days of Miracles Revived," *Christian Worker*, 1st Mo. 10, 1884, pp. 20–21; H. H. Mills, "Facts and Faith," ibid., 2nd Mo. 14, 1884, p. 103; David B. Updegraff, 1880 notebook, pp. 107–8, box 2, Updegraff Family Papers (Quaker Collection, Haverford); Sydney E. Ahlstrom, *A Religious History of the American People* (New Haven: Yale University Press, 1972), 818.

23. Lydia M. Williams-Cammack and Truman C. Kenworthy, *Life and Works of Amos M. Kenworthy* (Richmond, Ind.: Nicholson, 1918), 45–46, 54, 57–58, 110–11, 113; "Ohio Yearly Meeting," *Christian Worker*, 9th Mo. 11, 1890, pp. 586–87; Calvin W. Pritchard, "A Testimony to Divine Healing," ibid., 580–81; A. H. Hussey, "A Case of Divine Healing," ibid., 2nd Mo. 4, 1886, p. 53; Nathan T. Frame, "Healing the Sick," 8th Mo. 16, 1883, p. 467. Holiness Friends did urge believers to consult

physicians. Clark and Smith, *David B. Updegraff*, 190–91. Amos M. Kenworthy, who claimed special gifts as a healer, underwent a hernia operation in 1893. A. M. Kenworthy to Allen Jay, 3rd Mo. 28, 1893, G-L box, Jay Papers.

24. For the permeation of pre–Civil War America with postmillennial views, see Ernest Lee Tuveson, *Redeemer Nation: The Idea of America's Millennial Role* (Chicago: University of Chicago Press, 1968). For the rise of premillennialism, see Timothy P. Weber, *Living in the Shadow of the Second Coming: American Premillennialism, 1875–1925* (New York: Oxford University Press, 1979); and Marsden, *Fundamentalism and American Culture*, 48–55. A somewhat revisionist perspective is provided by James A. Moorhead, "Between Progress and Apocalypse: A Reassessment of Millennialism in American Religious Thought, 1800–1880," *Journal of American History*, 71 (Dec. 1984), 524–42; and Grant Wacker, "The Holy Spirit and the Spirit of the Age in American Protestantism, 1880–1910," ibid., 72 (June 1985), 45–62.

25. D. B. Updegraff, "The Second Advent," *Christian Worker*, 12th Mo. 26, 1878, pp. 615–16; *In the Court of Appeal. Appeal from the Chancery Division of the High Court of Justice. Between John T. Dorland and Others Plaintiffs (Appellants) and Gilbert Jones and Others, Defendants (Respondents). Appeal Book* (Belleville, Ont.: Ontario Steam Press Printing, 1884), 318–21, 325–26; William Nicholson to Cyrus Beede, 2nd Mo. 21, 1883, Watson-Nicholson Papers (Southern Historical Collection, University of North Carolina, Chapel Hill); "Dr. Dougan Clark on Temperance," *Christian Worker*, 7th Mo. 24, 1879, pp. 354–55; Marsden, *Fundamentalism and American Culture*, 55–71. For a somewhat different interpretation of Quaker premillennialism, see Richard Eugene Wood, "Evangelical Quakers in the Mississippi Valley, 1854–1894" (Ph.D. diss., University of Minnesota, 1985), 202–11.

26. "Is the World Growing Better?" *Friends' Expositor*, 1 (Oct. 1887), 72–74; Clark and Smith, *David B. Updegraff*, 187–89; W. J. Thornberry sermon reported in "The Church at Work," *Christian Worker*, 10th Mo. 24, 1878, p. 505; Updegraff 1880 notebook, p. 124, box 2, Updegraff Papers.

27. "Dr. Dougan Clark on Temperance," 354; Clark and Smith, *David B. Updegraff*, 189–90. Many holiness Friends were, however, committed Prohibitionists. See, for example, E. B. Tuttle, "Prohibition Amendment," *Gospel Expositor*, Feb. 2, 1883, p. 4. For Wilburite views on reform, see chap. 2.

28. For this problem in Ohio Yearly Meeting, the holiness bastion, see Richard C. Sartwell, "The Influence of Leading Friends in Ohio Yearly Meeting of Friends, Evangelical, 1854–1919" (M.A. thesis, Earlham School of Religion, 1974), 27–30. For a different interpretation of the relationship of holiness theology to pacifism, see Wood, "Evangelical Quakers in the Mississippi Valley," 203–7.

29. D. B. Updegraff letter, *Christian Worker*, 4th Mo. 17, 1878, p. 187; ibid., 5th Mo. 8, 1878, p. 221; Luke Woodard letter, ibid., 10th Mo. 31, 1878, pp. 522–23; "Christianity and War," ibid., 5th Mo. 30, 1878, p. 248; E. J. Farmer, "A New War Advocate," ibid., 255–56; W. F. Mitchell, "Thus We Find Undoubted Christians Are at Times Engaged in War," ibid., 7th Mo. 11, 1878, p. 332; "D. B. U. Again," ibid., 7th Mo. 18, 1878, p. 342; D. B. Updegraff, "Explanatory," ibid., 7th Mo. 11, 1878, pp. 327–29. Joseph Bevan Braithwaite asserted that Updegraff had tried to undermine peace efforts long before 1878. Braithwaite to Joseph W. Taylor, 8th Mo. 29, 1878, box 1, Taylor Family Papers (Quaker Collection, Haverford).

30. Nereus Mendenhall to "Dear Friend," 7th Mo. 5, 1893, box 2, Hobbs-Mendenhall Papers (Southern Historical Collection); J. H. Douglas, "The Peace Association of Friends," *Herald of Peace*, 12th Mo. 1, 1868, p. 134; *Ohio Yearly Meeting Minutes, 1880*, p. 36; *Kansas Yearly Meeting Minutes, 1879*, p. 32; *Indiana*

Yearly Meeting Minutes, 1885, p. 111; *Iowa Yearly Meeting Minutes, 1884,* p. 15. For the peace activities of such revivalists as Nathan T. Frame and Robert W. Douglas, see *Indiana Yearly Meeting Minutes, 1886,* p. 11; and "Indiana Yearly Meeting," *Friends' Review,* 10th Mo. 25, 1879, p. 172. In 1876, when a number of prominent Friends called for a peace conference of evangelical denominations, not a single holiness Friend signed the document calling for it. "Call for a Conference of Churches," *ibid.,* 10th Mo. 7, 1876, pp. 123–24.

31. H. C. Bundy, "Witnessing for Christ," *Christian Worker,* 5th Mo. 12, 1881, p. 220; "Our Letter from England," ibid., 4th Mo. 2, 1885, p. 177; *David B. Updegraff on the Ordinances: An Interview* (Richmond, Ind.: n.p., 1886), 8; C. W. Pritchard to Allen Jay, 10th Mo. 24, 1886, M-R box, Jay Papers; David B. Updegraff, *Old Corn; or, Sermons on the Spiritual Life* (Boston: McDonald and Gill, 1892), xiii; Marsden, *Fundamentalism and American Culture,* 17.

32. A. H. Hussey, "Antichrist," *Christian Worker,* 7th Mo. 15, 1886, p. 326; editorial, ibid., 9th Mo. 23, 1886, p. 450; "Iowa Yearly Meeting," ibid., 451; Lewis Perry, *Intellectual Life in America: A History* (New York: Franklin Watts, 1984), 292.

33. Robert Mapes Anderson, *Vision of the Disinherited: The Making of American Pentecostalism* (New York: Oxford University Press, 1979), 30–33; Melvin Easterday Dieter, *The Holiness Revival of the Nineteenth Century* (Metuchen, N.J.: Scarecrow, 1980), 204–25; editorial, *Christian Worker,* 5th Mo. 19, 1887, p. 234.

34. Dougan Clark, "The Society of Friends and Holiness," *Christian Worker,* 1st Mo. 14, 1886, pp. 13–14; D. B. Updegraff, "Law and Gospel in Canada," ibid., 2nd Mo. 7, 1884, pp. 82–84; David Hunt, "Speak Evil of No Man," ibid., 2nd Mo. 15, 1883, p. 77.

35. "Week-Day Meetings," *Christian Worker,* 1st Mo. 20, 1887, p. 31; "The Reasons Why," ibid., 3rd Mo. 5, 1885, p. 135; M. F. Moorman, "The Prayer Meeting," ibid., 8th Mo. 4, 1887, p. 363; "Church Work," ibid., 8th Mo. 25, 1881, p. 397; "Iowa Yearly Meeting," *Friends' Review,* 9th Mo. 22, 1877, p. 90; "Kansas Yearly Meeting," ibid., 12th Mo. 30, 1882, p. 326; *Kansas Yearly Meeting Minutes, 1884,* pp. 23–24. For a convenient summary of statistics on conversions, renewals, and sanctifications from one yearly meeting, see Sheldon Glenn Jackson, *A Short History of Kansas Yearly Meeting of Friends* (Wichita: Day's Print Shop, 1946), 66.

36. Among the most important moderates were Charles F. and Rhoda M. Coffin, Timothy Nicholson, Allen and Eli Jay, and Clarkson Davis in Indiana; William Nicholson in Kansas; Joseph and Gertrude Cartland and Augustine Jones in New England; Barnabas C. Hobbs in Western Yearly Meeting; Joseph Moore and Nereus Mendenhall in North Carolina; Thomas Kimber in New York; Elizabeth L. Comstock and John Butler in Ohio; and Lindley M. Hoag and Joel and Hannah Bean in Iowa Yearly Meeting. My identification of these Friends is based on sources too numerous to list in detail. They include all of the periodicals, especially the *Friends' Review.* Manuscript collections whose accumulations of correspondence give a sense of the mutuality and self-consciousness of these Friends include the Bean Papers at Swarthmore; the Timothy Nicholson Papers at Earlham; the Hartshorne Papers at Haverford; and the Hobbs-Mendenhall Papers at Chapel Hill and Guilford College. Biographical information on all of these figures is available in Evans et al., comps., "Dictionary of Quaker Biography."

37. In addition to Evans et al., "Dictionary," see, for James Wood, "Views of the Conference," *Christian Worker,* 11th Mo. 3, 1887, p. 520; for the Philadelphia group, Rufus M. Jones, *The Trail of Life in the Middle Years* (New York: Macmillan, 1934), 26–30; for the Thomases, [Anna B. Thomas], *Richard H. Thomas, M.D.: Life and Letters* (London: Headley Brothers, 1905); for Lewis and Mary Hobbs, Dorothy Lloyd Gilbert, *Guilford: A Quaker College* (Greensboro, N.C.: Guilford College,

1937), 164–68, 239–55; for Benjamin F. Trueblood, Charles E. Beals, *Benjamin F. Trueblood: Prophet of Peace* (n.p.: Mosher Fund, 1916); and for William L. Pearson, "Faculty of Penn College," *Western Work*, 3 (June 1899), 4.

38. Editorial, *Friends' Review*, 4th Mo. 26, 1884, p. 600; "Moderation," ibid., 12th Mo. 11, 1875, pp. 264–65; Henry Hartshorne to David B. Updegraff, 2nd Mo. 6, 1876, box 4, Hartshorne Papers; Hartshorne to Charles Rhoads, 5th Mo. 20, 1876, ibid.; "Middle Friends," *Western Friend*, 6 (9th Mo. 1885), 67.

39. Joel Bean to Timothy Nicholson, 9th Mo. 14, 1881, Timothy Nicholson Papers; William Nicholson letters to Timothy Nicholson, ibid.; J. H. Stuart, "The Outlook for the Society of Friends," *Friends' Review*, 8th Mo. 19, 1886, p. 33. The ability of Friends such as Hobbs, William Nicholson, and John Butler in Ohio to hold their positions in the face of revival opposition deserves further study. It may have stemmed from respect for their past services or it may be a tribute to their diplomatic skills. The moderates usually saved their worst fears and blasts for private letters.

40. Joel Bean Diary, 7th Mo. 15, 1880, box 1, Bean Papers; Joel Bean, "A Visit to Iowa in 8th and 9th Mos. 1895," ibid.; B. C. Hobbs, "Western Yearly Meeting and 'The Friend,'" *Friends' Review*, 8th Mo. 11, 1877, p. 821; editorial, ibid., 11th Mo. 17, 1892, p. 259; Hartshorne to Cyrus W. Harvey, 5th Mo. 3, 1883, box 5, Hartshorne Papers. If Harvey is to be believed, moderate Friends regularly supplied him with items to embarass the revivalists. A quarter of his subscribers, Harvey contended, were members of Gurneyite yearly meetings. Editorial, *Western Friend*, 5 (2nd Mo. 1884), 15.

41. Editorial, *Friends' Review*, 4th Mo. 8, 1882, p. 553; "Germany in Danger," ibid., 6th Mo. 21, 1879, pp. 707–8; B. C. Hobbs, *Earlham Lectures* (Richmond, Ind.: Nicholson, 1885), 20–23; Thomas Kimber, *The True Christian Theology of the Early Friends: An Essay Read before the Professors and Students of Earlham College, Fifth Month 15th, 1880* (New York: Central Tract Committee, 1880); Joel Bean, "Substance of Statement of Belief Made in Yearly Meeting of Ministers and Elders," 1879, box 1, Bean Papers.

42. E. Howard and Ruth E. Brown, *Young People's History of the Friends' Church* (Chicago: Publishing Association of Friends, 1899), 64; *Foreign Mission Work of American Friends: A Brief History of Their Work from the Beginning to the Year 1912* (n.p.: American Friends Board of Foreign Missions, 1912); Eliza Armstrong Cox, *Looking Back Over the Trail* (n.p., 1927).

43. Hobbs, *Earlham Lectures*, 26–27; David B. Updegraff, "Notes on B. C. Hobbs at Indiana Yearly Meeting, 1882," 1880 notebook, box 2, Updegraff Papers; Caroline Hare, comp., *Life and Letters of Elizabeth L. Comstock* (London: Headley Brothers, 1895), 468.

44. "Friends Ecumenical Conference," *Friends' Expositor*, 1 (Oct. 1887), 79; William Nicholson to Beede, 2nd Mo. 21, 1883, Watson-Nicholson Papers; Richard H. Thomas, *Penelve; or, Among the Quakers* (London: Headley Brothers, 1898), 151–52; Cyrus Lindley, "The Word of God," *Friends' Review*, 12th Mo. 8, 1877, p. 261; editorial, ibid., 12th Mo. 17, 1881, pp. 296–97.

45. Thomas, *Penelve*, 151; Augustine Jones to Rufus M. Jones, 8th Mo. 18, 1893, box 1, Rufus M. Jones Papers (Quaker Collection, Haverford); William L. Pearson, "Biblical Instruction in the Society of Friends," *Friends' Review*, 4th Mo. 15, 1886, p. 578.

46. "Evenings with the Bible," *Friends' Review*, 3rd Mo. 18, 1865, pp. 454–56; "Charles Darwin," ibid., 5th Mo. 13, 1882, pp. 628–29; J. J. T., "Evolution," ibid., 6th Mo. 24, 1886, p. 743; editorial, ibid., 9th Mo. 8, 1883, p. 72; editorial, ibid., 10th Mo. 28, 1886, p. 201; Henry Hartshorne to William C. Lawton, 3rd Mo. 28, 1882, box 4, Hartshorne Papers; Paul F. Boller, Jr., *American Thought in Transition: The*

Impact of Evolutionary Naturalism, 1865-1900 (Washington: University Press of America, 1983), 28-35; William Cooper, "Joseph Moore: Quaker Evolutionist," *Indiana Magazine of History,* 72 (June 1976), 123-27.

47. Editorial, *Friends' Review.* 3rd Mo. 10, 1883, p. 488.

48. Hartshorne to Luke Woodard, 5th Mo. 23, 1886, box 4, Hartshorne Papers; William Nicholson, *Christian Conversion: Its Nature and Results and Some of Its Relations to Certain Other Topics* (Richmond, Ind.: Nicholson, 1884); William Nicholson to Beede, 2nd Mo. 21, 1883, Watson-Nicholson Papers; Thomas, *Penelve,* 212; B. C. H[obbs], "When and How Is a Christian Baptized with the Spirit?" *Friends' Review,* 4th Mo. 10, 1875, pp. 529-30; "Experience—New Birth—Baptisms," *Christian Worker,* 1st Mo. 26, 1882, p. 44; Nereus Mendenhall, *The Clue of Faith; in Science and Life. An Address before the Alumni Association of Haverford College, 24th of 6th Month 1879* (n.p., n.d.), 8-10.

49. Hartshorne to John Y. Hoover, 3rd Mo. 2, 1886, box 4, Hartshorne Papers; Hartshorne to John Henry Douglas, 3rd Mo. 9, 1884, ibid.; Marcus Mote to Hartshorne, 10th Mo. 1, 1888, box 11, ibid.; Timothy Nicholson to Joel and Hannah E. Bean, 5th Mo. 2, 1881, box 4, Bean Papers; Joel Bean, "Statement to Quarterly Meeting of Ministers and Elders," 4th Mo. 30, 1880, box 1, ibid.; William Nicholson to Timothy Nicholson, 10th Mo. 20, 1875, 11th Mo. 1, 1889, Timothy Nicholson Papers; Joel Bean to Timothy Nicholson, 11th Mo. 24, 1883, ibid.; H. E., "Employment of Pastors," *Friends' Review,* 1st Mo. 13, 1887, p. 382.

50. William Nicholson to Timothy Nicholson, 11th Mo. 2, 1881, Timothy Nicholson Papers.

51. Errol T. Elliott, *Quaker Profiles from the American West* (Richmond, Ind.: Friends United Press, 1972), 26-30.

52. J. B., "The Former and the Latter Days," *Friends' Review,* 7th Mo. 16, 1870, p. 742; J. B., "The Marks of Holiness," ibid., 4th Mo. 29, 1876, p. 579; Joel Bean, "Words for the Hour," ibid., 2nd Mo. 2, 1878, pp. 585-87; J. B. letter, *Christian Worker,* 1st Mo. 1, 1874, pp. 6-7.

53. Joel Bean, "Notes on the Revival at West Branch," n.d., box 1, Bean Papers.

54. Joel Bean, "The Issue," *British Friend,* 3rd Mo. 1, 1881, pp. 49-51.

55. Howard H. Brinton, ed., "The Revival Movement in Iowa: A Letter from Joel Bean to Rufus M. Jones," *Bulletin of Friends Historical Association,* 50 (Fall 1961), 107-8; "Persecution of Joel and Hannah Bean," *Western Friend,* 4 (1st Mo. 1883), 4; Joel Bean, "The Issue," ibid., 2 (4th Mo. 1881), 29-30; Gertrude Cartland to Joel and Hannah Bean, 4th Mo. 18, 1881, box 3, Bean Papers.

56. "Enthusiasm," *Friends' Review,* 8th Mo. 17, 1878, p. 8; "Edifying," ibid., 10th Mo. 13, 1877, p. 136; editorial, ibid., 8th Mo. 26, 1882, p. 40; ibid., 3rd Mo. 28, 1885, p. 536; ibid., 5th Mo. 17, 1879, pp. 632-33.

57. Hartshorne to Rachel H. Hopkins, 9th Mo. 14, 1884, box 4, Hartshorne Papers; Timothy Harrison to Joel and Hannah Bean, 3rd Mo. 27, 1880, box 4, Bean Papers; Timothy Nicholson to Joel and Hannah E. Bean, 5th Mo. 2, 1880, ibid.; Murray Shipley to Joel and Hannah Bean, 5th Mo. 18, 1880, box 5, ibid.

58. "London Yearly Meeting, 1878," *British Friend,* 6th Mo. 1, 1878, p. 140; "Critical Interrogatories by Charles F. Coffin," *Western Friend,* 3 (12th Mo. 1882), 92-96.

59. Editorial, *Friends' Review,* 4th Mo. 26, 1884, p. 600.

60. "Correspondence," ibid., 10th Mo. 27, 1883, p. 189; *Kansas Yearly Meeting Minutes, 1884,* p. 59; Thomas Kimber, *Historical Essays on the Worship of God, and the Ministry of the Gospel of Our Lord and Savior* (New York: David S. Taber, 1889), 24-31.

61. Joel Bean to Timothy Nicholson, 11th Mo. 24, 1884, Timothy Nicholson

Papers; "Music amongst Friends," *Friends' Review*, 8th Mo. 6, 1881, pp. 817–19; "Instrumental Music in Singing," ibid., 8th Mo. 5, 1882, pp. 820–21; editorial, ibid., 9th Mo. 11, 1880, pp. 72–73.

62. William Nicholson to Beede, 2nd Mo. 21, 1883, Watson-Nicholson Papers; "Question," *Christian Worker*, 5th Mo. 20, 1880, p. 246; "The Kingdom of God Is within You," *Friends' Review*, 11th Mo. 23, 1878, pp. 233–34; *Minutes of the Ministerial Conference of Western Yearly Meeting of Friends Held at Bloomingdale, Ind., Eleventh Mo. 1880* (Indianapolis: Baker and Randolph, 1881), 64–76; B. C. Hobbs to Hartshorne, 1st Mo. 17, 1876, box 10, Hartshorne Papers.

63. Peter Brock, *Pacifism in the United States from the Colonial Era to the First World War* (Princeton: Princeton University Press, 1968), 869–88; Mary Coffin Johnson and Percival Brooks Coffin, *Charles F. Coffin: A Quaker Pioneer* (Richmond, Ind.: Nicholson, 1923), 137–61; Hare, comp., *Life and Letters of Elizabeth L. Comstock*, 407–36; John William Buys, "Quakers in Indiana in the Nineteenth Century" (Ph.D. diss., University of Florida, 1973), 180–85, 223–27; "Christianity and Social Problems," *Friends' Review*, 11th Mo. 17, 1877, pp. 216–17; Nereus Mendenhall to Hartshorne, 8th Mo. 26, 1882, box 11, Hartshorne Papers; Walter C. Woodward, *Timothy Nicholson: Master Quaker* (Richmond, Ind.: Nicholson, 1927), 83–163; Thomas, *Penelve*, 237; Joseph E. Illick, " 'Some of Our Best Indians Are Friends': Quaker Attitudes and Actions regarding Western Indians during the Grant Administration," *Western Historical Quarterly*, 2 (July 1971), 283–94; Wood, "Evangelical Quakers in the Mississippi Valley," 111–54.

VI   THE QUAKER SEARCH FOR ORDER, 1875–1895

1. Editorial, *Friends' Review*, 11th Mo. 10, 1892, p. 243. The Friend quoted is almost certainly William Nicholson.

2. Robert H. Wiebe, *The Search for Order, 1877–1920* (New York: Hill and Wang, 1967), 44–111; Jay P. Dolan, *Catholic Revivalism: The American Experience, 1830–1900* (Notre Dame: University of Notre Dame Press, 1978); Theron F. Schlabach, "The Humble Become 'Aggressive Workers': Mennonites Organize for Mission, 1880–1910," *Mennonite Quarterly Review*, 52 (April 1978), 91–112; Theron F. Schlabach, "Mennonites, Revivalism, Modernity—1683–1850," *Church History*, 48 (Dec. 1979), 398–415; Albert T. Rank, *History of the Brethren Church* (Ashland, Ohio: Brethren Publishing Company, 1968), 102–6, 125–67.

3. Hugh Barbour, *The Quakers in Puritan England* (New Haven: Yale University Press, 1964), 109–10, 130. Several scholars have pointed out that the term "Inner Light" was usually not used by seventeenth-century Friends; instead, they spoke of the "Light," the "Light Within," the "Inward Light," and so on. Although some may distinguish among these today, few nineteenth-century Friends did.

4. Aaron White to "Dear Sister," 5th Mo. 7, 1826, box 2, Furnas Family Papers (Friends Historical Library, Swarthmore College, Swarthmore, Pa.); Samuel Bettle to "Dear Daughter," 7th Mo. 29, 1850, box 1, Bettle Family Papers (ibid.); *Journal of the Life, Travels, and Gospel Labours of William Williams, Dec., a Minister of the Society of Friends, Late of White-Water, Indiana* (Cincinnati: Lodge, L'Hommedieu, and Hammond, 1828), 100; *Journal of That Faithful Servant of Christ, Charles Osborn, Containing an Account of His Travels and Labors in the Work of the Ministry, and His Trials and Exercises in the Service of the Lord, and in Defense of the Truth, as It Is in Jesus* (Cincinnati: Achilles Pugh, 1854), 205; *A Brief Memoir of Nathan Hunt: Chiefly Extracted from His Journal and Letters* (Philadelphia: Uriah Hunt, 1858), 10–11.

5. *Iowa Yearly Meeting Minutes, 1867*, p. 32; Dougan Clark, Jr., *Address by Dr. Dougan Clark* (n.p., 1858), 5; Elijah Coffin, *The Mother's Catechism of the Christian Doctrine and Practice: Designed for the Use of Families and Schools* (Richmond, Ind.: Central Book and Tract Committee, 1859), 7-8, 12.

6. "Justification by Faith," *Friends' Review*, 5th Mo. 11, 1872, pp. 598-600; Nereus Mendenhall to "Dear Friend," 11th Mo. 2, 1871, box 1, Hobbs-Mendenhall Papers (Southern Historical Collection, University of North Carolina, Chapel Hill); "The More Sure Word of Prophecy," *Christian Worker*, 2nd Mo. 15, 1875, pp. 54-55.

7. Luke Woodard, *The Morning Star! A Treatise on the Nature, Offices, and Works of the Lord Jesus Christ* (New Vienna, Ohio: Friends Publishing House, 1875), 253-54; David Hunt, *Essays on Religious Subjects: Including the Ordinances, Deity of Our Lord and Savior Jesus Christ, Resurrection of the Dead, Etc.* (New Vienna, Ohio, 1874), 73, 76; Dougan Clark, *The Offices of the Holy Spirit* (Philadelphia: National Association for the Promotion of Holiness, n.d.), 76-77.

8. Luke Woodard, "The Light Within," *Christian Worker*, 2nd Mo. 6, 1878, p. 65; M. S., "Misapplied Texts," ibid., 4th Mo. 5, 1877, p. 218; ibid., 4th Mo. 26, 1877, pp. 264-65; D. B. Updegraff, "The Light Within," *Friends' Review*, 4th Mo. 19, 1879, pp. 561-64.

9. *Ohio Yearly Meeting Minutes, 1879*, pp. 28-29. There is evidence that the controversial minute was passed by the yearly meeting without recognition of its full import. See William Cattell to Joel Bean, 3rd Mo. 4, 1879, box 3, Joel Bean Papers (Friends Historical Library, Swarthmore); and J. Bevan Braithwaite to Joseph W. Taylor, 8th Mo. 27, 1878, box 1, Taylor Family Papers (Quaker Collection, Haverford College, Haverford, Pa.).

10. Joel Bean, "Notes on Iowa Yearly Meeting and Other Notes, 1880-1881," box 1, Bean Papers; D. B. Updegraff letter to Steubenville *Herald*, reprinted in "Denials of the Inner Light," *Western Friend*, 4 (3rd Mo. 1883), 18.

11. *An Address to Its Own Members and to the Members of Our Society Elsewhere, Issued by the Yearly Meeting of Philadelphia, Fourth Month 18th, 1883* (Philadelphia: Friends' Book Store, 1883), 6-13; "The Confession of Non-Belief," *Western Friend*, 7 (3rd Mo. 1886), 17; "Ohio Yearly Meeting (Binns Body)," ibid., 3 (10th Mo. 1882), 77.

12. Bean, "Notes on Iowa Yearly Meeting," box 1, Bean Papers; William Nicholson to Timothy Nicholson, 2nd Mo. 15, 1883, Timothy Nicholson Papers (Archives, Earlham College, Richmond, Ind.); B. C. Hobbs, *Earlham Lectures* (Richmond, Ind.: Nicholson, 1885), 28-31; editorial, *Friends' Review*, 7th Mo. 11, 1885, pp. 776-77; Henry Hartshorne to Barnabas C. Hobbs, 7th Mo. 7, 1885, box 4, Hartshorne Family Papers (Quaker Collection, Haverford); Augustine Jones, *The Principles, Methods, and History of the Society of Friends* (Lynn, Mass.: George C. Herbert, 1874), 41-44.

13. "Extract from the Report of the Committee on the Ministry of Indiana Yearly Meeting," *Friends' Review*, 11th Mo. 15, 1888, p. 244; H. C., "Van Wert Monthly Meeting," *Christian Worker*, 2nd Mo. 26, 1880, p. 99; Allen Jay letter in "From the Field," ibid., 6th Mo. 6, 1889, p. 358; *Semi-Centennial Anniversary of Western Yearly Meeting of Friends Church, Plainfield, Indiana, Ninth Month 23, 1908* (Plainfield, Ind.: Publishing Association of Friends, 1908), 74-76; "Charles Brady's View of America," *Christian Worker*, 2nd Mo. 23, 1888, pp. 85-86. An analysis of the records of Duck Creek Monthly Meeting, an old, established monthly meeting in Henry County, Indiana, for the period 1875 to 1900 shows that it had a total of 949 members. Of these, 302 were birthright Friends and 547 were received by request. Duck Creek Monthly Meeting Membership Book (Archives, Earlham).

14. Clifton J. Phillips, ed., "Charles A. Beard's Recollections of Henry County, Indiana," *Indiana Magazine of History*, 55 (March 1959), 20–21; Rufus M. Jones, *The Later Periods of Quakerism* (2 vols., London: Macmillan, 1921), II, 915–16; "Increase of Friends in the West," *Friends' Review*, 6th Mo. 17, 1886, p. 729.

15. W. H. Ladd, "Reception into Membership in the Society of Friends," *Christian Worker*, 3rd Mo. 30, 1882, pp. 148–49; William Nicholson, "Serious Thoughts for Serious Friends," ibid., 3rd Mo. 25, 1880, p. 148; "Evangelistic Work," *Friends' Review*, 7th Mo. 16, 1881, p. 769; C[harles] F. C[offin], "Pastors," ibid., 3rd Mo. 25, 1882, pp. 515–16.

16. Luke Woodard, *Gathered Fragments* (Columbus, Ohio: Joseph H. Miller, 1883), 214; Elwood C. Siler, "The Pastoral Question," *Christian Worker*, 8th Mo. 25, 1887, p. 400; Thomas D. Hubbard, *Will the Friends' Church Starve Out Its Ministers?* quoted in editorial, *Friends' Review*, 12th Mo. 2, 1886, pp. 281–82.

17. Elizabeth L. Comstock to Mary S. Wood, 1st Mo. 30, 1870, Wood Family Papers (Friends Historical Library, Swarthmore); Ohio Yearly Meeting for Sufferings Minutes, 8th Mo. 31, 1867 (Archives, Malone College, Canton, Ohio); Henry Stanley Newman, *Memories of Stanley Pumphrey* (New York: Friends Book and Tract Committee, 1883), 238; editorial, *Christian Worker*, 4th Mo. 6, 1882, p. 175.

18. *Proceedings of the Conference of Friends of America, Held in Indianapolis, Indiana, 1892* (Richmond, Ind.: Nicholson, 1892), 187; "The Ministry of the Word," *Friends' Expositor*, 3 (July 1889), 286; Siler, "Pastoral Question," 400–401.

19. Siler, "Pastoral Question," 401; David Hunt, "The Church and the Preached Gospel," *Christian Worker*, 12th Mo. 27, 1883, pp. 750–52; S. A. Wood, "The Support of the Ministry," *Friends' Review*, 1st Mo. 2, 1886, p. 350.

20. Mead A. Kelsey to Allen Jay, May 19, 1892, G-L box, Allen Jay Papers (Archives, Earlham); A. B. Wasson, "Evangelists and Pastors," *Christian Worker*, 1st Mo. 1, 1885, p. 14; M. F. Moorman, "Pastoral Care," ibid., 9th Mo. 7, 1882, p. 442; Siler, "Pastoral Question," 400–401.

21. Richard E. Wood, "The Rise of Semi-Structured Worship and Pastoral Leadership among 'Gurneyite' Friends, 1850–1900," in *Quaker Worship in North America*, ed. Francis B. Hall (Richmond, Ind.: Friends United Press, n.d.), 68–69.

22. *Iowa Yearly Meeting Minutes, 1886*, pp. 13–14; Louis Thomas Jones, *The Quakers of Iowa* (Iowa City: Clio, 1914), 104–7; Wood, "Rise of Semi-Structured Worship," 69. For an excellent discussion of the adoption of the pastoral system in Iowa, Western, and New York yearly meetings, see Alexander H. Hay, "The Rise of the Pastoral System in the Society of Friends, 1850–1900" (M.A. thesis, Haverford College, 1938), 47–72.

23. *Proceedings . . . 1892*, pp. 56, 124–27; William Nicholson to Timothy Nicholson, 9th Mo. 13, 1892, Timothy Nicholson Papers; A. M. Purdie, "The Support of the Ministry," *Friends' Review*, 1st Mo. 16, 1886, p. 361; Thomas Kimber, "Pastorates in the Society of Friends," ibid., 9th Mo. 23, 1886, pp. 113–16; Timothy Nicholson letter, ibid., 11th Mo. 21, 1889, pp. 270–71; Henry Hartshorne to John Henry Douglas, 11th Mo. 17, 1888, box 4, Hartshorne Papers; B. C. Hobbs to Hartshorne, 1st Mo. 18, 1886, box 10, ibid.; Nereus Mendenhall to Hartshorne, 4th Mo. 8, 1887, box 11, ibid.; [Anna B. Thomas], *Richard H. Thomas, M.D.: Life and Letters* (London: Headley Brothers, 1905), 182–83.

24. Editorial, *Friends' Review*, 11th Mo. 17, 1892, p. 259.

25. [Thomas], *Richard H. Thomas*, 241–42.

26. *Proceedings . . . 1892*, pp. 124–25; "Priesthood of All Believers," *Friends' Review*, 7th Mo. 8, 1886, p. 776; editorial, ibid., 9th Mo. 12, 1889, pp. 704–6; "A Free Gospel Ministry," ibid., 2nd Mo. 25, 1889, p. 616; [Thomas], *Richard H. Thomas*, 183; James Carey Thomas to Charles F. Coffin, 7th Mo. 8, 1890, Letters to

and from Charles F. and Rhoda M. Coffin folder, Charles F. and Rhoda M. Coffin Papers (Archives, Earlham); Isaac P. Hazard to Allen Jay, 3rd Mo. 24, 1887, G-L box, Jay Papers.

27. "More about the Ministry," *Friends' Review*, 8th Mo. 19, 1886, pp. 40–41; "The Pastoral Question," *Christian Worker*, 12th Mo. 30, 1886, pp. 616–18; J. H. Stewart, "Some Phases of the Pastoral Question," ibid., 9th Mo. 30, 1886, p. 458; C. F. C[offin], "Are Ministers a Separate Class?" ibid., 9th Mo. 7, 1881, pp. 424–25.

28. Wood, "Rise of Semi-Structured Worship," 68; Allen C. Thomas and Richard H. Thomas, *A History of the Friends in America* (Philadelphia: John C. Winston, 1919), 200–201; Timothy Nicholson letter, 270–71.

29. Stephen Breed, "The Fruits of the Pastoral System—Do We Want Them?" *Christian Worker*, 3rd Mo. 17, 1887, p. 123; editorial, *Friends' Review*, 10th Mo. 9, 1890, p. 168; Amy Betts to Melissa Fellow, 3rd Mo. 14, 1891, G-L box, Jay Papers; Ann Gause to Allen Jay, 3rd Mo. 17, 1893, ibid.; Mead A. Kelsey to Jay, April 18, 1892, July 26, 1893, ibid,; E. O. Ellis to Jay, 3rd Mo. 17, 1893, A-F box, ibid.

30. D. H. Jay and Eliza A. West to Allen Jay, 11th Mo. 30, 1891, G-L box, Jay Papers; O. N. Huff, "Topics concerning the Society of Friends from the Standpoint of a Layman," *American Friend*, 10th Mo. 3, 1907, p. 638; Interview with Robert A. and Elsie (Davis) Peirce, June 18, 1983 (in author's possession); Wood, "Rise of Semi-Structured Worship," 69; "Proceedings of the Conference Held at Mooresville, Ind.," *Christian Worker*, 4th Mo. 24, 1877, pp. 194–95; *Indiana Yearly Meeting Minutes, 1887*, pp. 42–43. As had been the case for years, the power to record ministers remained with monthly meetings, subject to the approval of quarterly meetings. No formal education or training was required, although most supporters of pastorates thought it desirable.

31. Frank E. Smith to Allen Jay, July 11, 1892, S-Z box; Jay Papers; Rachel Chandler to Allen Jay, March 2, 1893, April 6, 1893, A-F box, ibid.; Mead A. Kelsey to Jay, April 17, 1893, G-L box, ibid.

32. See chap. 1.

33. "Sarah F. Smiley," *Christian Worker*, 7th Mo. 15, 1872, p. 130; Stacy E. Bevan manuscript on baptism, May 18, 1915 (in Ethel Bevan's possession, Haviland, Kans.); editorial, *Friend*, 12th Mo. 2, 1876, pp. 127–28.

34. Editorial, *Christian Worker*, 8th Mo. 7, 1879, p. 380; "Recall of Helen Balkwill," ibid., 9th Mo. 25, 1879, p. 461; "Helen Balkwill," *British Friend*, 9th Mo. 1, 1879, pp. 926–27.

35. "Recall of Helen Balkwill," 461; T. W. Ladd, "The Conference at Glen's Falls," *Christian Worker*, 10th Mo. 30, 1879, pp. 520–21; Dougan Clark letter, ibid., 12th Mo. 25, 1879, p. 617.

36. D. B. Updegraff, *Open Letters for Interested Readers* (Philadelphia: n.p., 1880), 18–31; D. B. Updegraff, "J. C. Rogers' 'Rigid Exegesis,' " *Christian Worker*, 4th Mo. 8, 1880, p. 173; D. B. Updegraff letter, ibid., 10th Mo. 30, 1879, p. 521; Timothy Nicholson to Joel and Hannah E. Bean, 5th Mo. 31, 1880, 5th Mo. 2, 1881, box 4, Bean Papers.

37. Thomas Kimber, "Spiritual Christianity," *Friends' Review*, 9th Mo. 13, 1879, pp. 67–68; Stanley Pumphrey, "D. B. Updegraff on the Position of the Early Friends as to Water Baptism and the Supper," *Christian Worker*, 10th Mo. 16, 1879, p. 498; Mary Whitall Thomas, "Was Water Baptism Commanded by the Lord Jesus Christ?" ibid., 10th Mo. 9, 1879, pp. 486–88; Timothy Nicholson to Joel and Hannah E. Bean, 5th Mo. 31, 1880, 5th Mo. 2, 1881, box 4, Bean Papers; New York Yearly Meeting (Orthodox) Representative Meeting Minutes, 4th Mo. 28, 1881, pp. 184–85 (Haviland Records Room, New York, N.Y.).

38. Timothy Nicholson to Joel and Hannah E. Bean, 5th Mo. 3, 1880, 10th Mo. 9, 1880, 5th Mo. 2, 1881, box 4, Bean Papers.

39. J. Brent Bill, *David B. Updegraff: Quaker Holiness Preacher* (Richmond, Ind.: Friends United Press, 1983), 21–24. For one of the Farnum meetings, see Joseph H. Smith, "A Unique Gathering," *Friends' Expositor*, 3 (July 1889), 279–80. There is no conclusive evidence as to the date of Updegraff's baptism. Bill puts it in 1882. Elbert Russell thinks that it must have taken place in 1884, which the timing of subsequent events makes more likely. Elbert Russell, *The History of Quakerism* (New York: Macmillan, 1942), 488.

40. John Henry Douglas to Henry Hartshorne, 5th Mo. 5, 1884, box 10, Hartshorne Papers; David Tatum to Allen Jay, 7th Mo. 6, 1887, S-Z box, Jay Papers; Eli Jay to Allen Jay, 6th Mo. 18, 1885, A-F box, ibid.; "Correspondence," *Friends' Review*, 5th Mo. 30, 1885, p. 685; Timothy Nicholson, "A Defence of Indiana Yearly Meeting and Others," ibid., 11th Mo. 21, 1885, pp. 253–54; Timothy Nicholson to Thomas Kimber, 7th Mo. 4, 1885, First National Bank folder, Coffin Papers; Francis T. King to Timothy Nicholson, 8th Mo. 9, 1885, Timothy Nicholson Papers; editorial, *Western Friend*, 6 (9th Mo. 1885), p. 71.

41. Jones, *Later Periods of Quakerism*, II, 929–30.

42. Henry Hartshorne to editors of *Christian Advocate and Witness*, 9th Mo. 10, 1885, box 4, Hartshorne Papers. Enforcement of these regulations was lax. In 1894 Calvin Pritchard asserted that at least twenty Quaker ministers had been baptized but that only one had been deposed. See clipping, Oct. 5, [1894?], folder 3, Nathan Hunt Clark Papers (Indiana Historical Society, Indianapolis).

43. The views of Updegraff, Woodard, Clark, and Hussey have been discussed earlier. For John Henry Douglas, see Douglas to Hartshorne, 5th Mo. 5, 1884, box 10, Hartshorne Papers. For Mary H. Rogers, see "My Experience," *Friends' Expositor*, 1 (April 1887), 52. For Jacob Baker, see Jacob Baker, *Incidents of My Life and Work of 84 Years* (Richmond, Ind.: Nicholson, 1911), 97–98. For the Reeses, see Paul S. Rees, *Seth Cook Rees: The Warrior Saint* (Indianapolis: Pilgrim Book Room, 1934), 21–22. For the Pritchards, see C. W. Pritchard to Allen Jay, 10th Mo. 24, 1886, A-F box, Jay Papers; and Allen Jay to Mahalah Jay, 11th Mo. 29, 1888, box 1, Eli and Mahalah Jay Family Papers (Archives, Earlham). For the holiness opponents of the ordinances, see William P. Pinkham to Rufus M. Jones, 10th Mo. 26, 1894, box 1, Rufus M. Jones Papers (Quaker Collection, Haverford); Nathan T. Frame, "Nonessentials," *Christian Worker*, 5th Mo. 3, 1880, p. 269; editorial, *Friends' Review*, 6th Mo. 17, 1886, p. 729; "Western Yearly Meeting," ibid., 10th Mo. 7, 1886, p. 153; and Errol T. Elliott, *Quakers on the American Frontier* (Richmond, Ind.: Friends United Press, 1969), 376–78.

44. David B. Updegraff, *An Address to Ohio Yearly Meeting on the Ordinances, and the Position of Friends Generally in Relation to Them* (Columbus: William G. Hubbard, 1885), 39–75; *David B. Updegraff on the Ordinances: An Interview* (Richmond, Ind.: n.p., 1886), 6–7; editorial, *Friends' Expositor*, 4 (Jan. 1890), 354, 357; "Editorial Notes," ibid., 2 (July 1888), 175; H. C. Aydelotte, "The Form of Sound Words," *Christian Worker*, 10th Mo. 3, 1889, pp. 629–30; W. H. Ladd, "Can Men Baptize with the Holy Ghost?" ibid., 9th Mo. 2, 1880, p. 423; W. L. Pearson, "Some Passages of Scripture in Connection with Ordinances," *Star and Crown*, March 15, 1885, pp. 84–85.

45. Updegraff, *Address to Ohio Yearly Meeting*, 22–32; Thomas Kimber, "The Early Friends and the Outward Ordinances," *Friends' Review*, 11th Mo. 21, 1885, pp. 241–43; Israel P. Hole, *A Discourse, Delivered in Ohio Yearly Meeting of Friends, 9th Mo. 1st, 1885, in Answer to Arguments by D. B. Updegraff, in Favor of the Ordinances* (Columbus: William G. Hubbard, 1885), 43.

46. *Proceedings . . . 1887*, pp. 102–3; John O. Smith, "Dangers of the Doctrine of the Ordinances," *Star and Crown*, 1st Mo. 12, 1887, p. 1; David Hunt, "Some Reasons Why We Object," *Friends' Review*, 1st Mo. 9, 1886, p. 354; "Carnal Ordinances," *Friends' Expositor*, 5 (Jan. 1891), 483–88.

47. Updegraff, *Address to Ohio Yearly Meeting*, 10; *David B. Updegraff on the Ordinances*, 2–4; "Christian Tolerance Necessary to the Church's Existence," *Friends' Expositor*, 1 (Jan. 1887), 8–10; "Mary and Logan Rogers," ibid., 2 (April 1888), 142–44; "Editorial Notes," ibid., 4 (April 1890), 390–91.

48. "Restoring Old Landmarks," *Friends' Expositor*, 1 (July 1887), 49; John P. Brooks, "A Fraternal Letter," ibid., 2 (July 1888), 60–61; Kelso Carter, "Quakers, Baptism, and Missions," ibid., 1 (Jan. 1887), 14–15.

49. J. W. Morgan to Timothy Nicholson, 9th Mo. 28, 1885, Timothy Nicholson Papers; "Employment of Pastors," *Friends' Review*, 1st Mo. 13, 1887, p. 382; D. B. Updegraff, "Recall of Helen Balkwill," *Christian Worker*, 9th Mo. 25, 1879, pp. 462–64; Updegraff, *Address to Ohio Yearly Meeting*, 27; C. W. Pritchard to Allen Jay, 10th Mo. 24, 1886, *Christian Worker* folder, A-F box, Jay Papers; J. J. Thomas to C. W. Allis, 4th Mo. 22, 1881, New York Yearly Meeting (Orthodox) Representative Meeting Papers.

50. Hannah E. Sleeper, "Keep to Soul Saving," *Christian Worker*, 3rd Mo. 3, 1887, p. 98; Barnabas C. Hobbs, "Church Government," ibid., 1st Mo. 28, 1886, p. 46; editorial, *Friends' Review*, 7th Mo. 4, 1885, pp. 760–61; ibid., 1st Mo. 9, 1886, p. 360; ibid., 1st Mo. 2, 1886, p. 344; ibid., 5th Mo. 30, 1889, p. 697; Francis T. King to Timothy Nicholson, 8th Mo. 9, 1885, Timothy Nicholson Papers; Hartshorne to Updegraff, 10th Mo. 16, 1885, box 4, Hartshorne Papers.

51. William Nicholson to Timothy Nicholson, 10th Mo. 21, 1885, Timothy Nicholson Papers; Timothy Nicholson to William Nicholson, 6th Mo. 9, 1886, ibid.; Allen Jay to Mahalah Jay, 11th Mo. 29, 1886, box 1, Eli and Mahalah Jay Family Papers; "Declaration of Views," *Christian Worker*, 10th Mo. 22, 1885, p. 530; "Reading Ministers' Credentials," ibid., 2nd Mo. 11, 1886, p. 78; "Annual Meeting of Stockholders," ibid., 11th Mo. 25, 1886, p. 560; Walter C. Woodward, *Timothy Nicholson: Master Quaker* (Richmond, Ind.: Nicholson, 1927), 186–88.

52. "Ohio Yearly Meeting," *Friends' Review*, 9th Mo. 9, 1886, pp. 90–92; Richard C. Sartwell, "The Influence of Leading Friends in Ohio Yearly Meeting of Friends, Evangelical, 1854–1919" (M.A. thesis, Earlham School of Religion, 1974), 11–21; Joseph W. Taylor to Sarah Taylor, 9th Mo. 1, 1876, box 10, Taylor Family Papers (Quaker Collection, Haverford); editorial, *Western Friend*, 6 (10th Mo. 1885), 78. The vote was a striking departure from traditional consensus decisions.

53. John Butler to Timothy Nicholson, 7th Mo. 19, 1887, Timothy Nicholson Papers; Hartshorne to Butler, 7th Mo. 21, 1887, 9th Mo. 14, 1887, box 4, Hartshorne Papers; Letter, *Friends' Review*, 8th Mo. 25, 1887, p. 62; editorial, ibid., 9th Mo. 15, 1887, p. 104; [Josiah Butler et al.], *John Butler: A Sketch of His Life* (Columbus: William G. Hubbard, 1890), 185.

54. For the earlier conferences, see chap. 2.

55. *Autobiography of Allen Jay, Born 1831, Died 1910* (Philadelphia: John C. Winston, 1910), 359–60; *Proceedings, Including the Declaration of Christian Doctrine, of the General Conference of Friends Held in Richmond, Ind., U.S.A., 1887* (Richmond, Ind.: Nicholson, 1887), 326–29. For an excellent analysis of the conference, see Mark E. Minear, "The Richmond Conference of 1887" (M.A. thesis, Earlham School of Religion, 1984).

56. See *Proceedings . . . 1887*, esp. 18–23.

57. Ibid., 18, 179–80; *Autobiography of Allen Jay*, 361–62.

58. Jones, *Later Periods of Quakerism*, II, 931; Newton A. Trueblood, "The Richmond Conference, 1887," *Christian Worker*, 5th Mo. 17, 1888, p. 233. The Richmond Declaration of Faith can be found in the disciplines of the yearly meetings that endorsed it.

59. [Thomas], *Richard H. Thomas*, 218–19; Arthur J. Mekeel, *Quakerism and a Creed* (Philadelphia: Friends Book Store, 1936), 102–9; editorial, *Western Friend*, 9 (6th Mo. 1888), 104–5; "The 'Declaration' Again," *Friends' Expositor*, 3 (July 1889), 289–90; *Proceedings . . . 1887*, pp. 281–82, 315.

60. *Proceedings . . . 1887*, pp. 264–65; William Nicholson to Timothy Nicholson, 9th Mo. 26, 1879, Timothy Nicholson Papers.

61. "Another Conference," *Friends' Expositor*, 3 (Oct. 1889), 316–17; Luke Woodard, "The Proposition to Hold Another Conference Considered," *Christian Worker*, 5th Mo. 30, 1889, pp. 339–40; "An Authoritative Conference," *Friends' Review*, 11th Mo. 28, 1889, pp. 277–78.

62. Cf. William R. Hutchison, *The Modernist Impulse in American Protestantism* (Cambridge: Harvard University Press, 1976), 48–68, 77.

63. Joel Bean to Timothy Nicholson, 8th Mo. 19, 1881, 9th Mo. 14, 1881, 12th Mo. 25, 1881, 1st Mo. 23, 1882, Timothy Nicholson Papers.

64. James Bean to Timothy Nicholson, 7th Mo. 31, 1882, ibid.; David C. LeShana, *Quakers in California: The Effects of 19th-Century Revivalism on Western Quakerism* (Newberg, Ore.: Barclay, 1969), 88–89. For David Hunt, see Hunt, *Essays on Religious Subjects;* and David Hunt, "On the Deity and Death of the Lord Jesus Christ," *Christian Worker*, 10th Mo. 22, 1885, pp. 525–27.

65. LeShana, *Quakers in California*, 88–90; James Bean to Timothy Nicholson, 7th Mo. 31, 1882, 9th Mo. 14, 1882, Timothy Nicholson Papers; Joel Bean, "San Jose, California," *Christian Worker*, 11th Mo. 12, 1885, p. 567–68.

66. Mahlon Stubbs, "From the Pacific Coast," *Christian Worker*, 2nd Mo. 5, 1885, p. 88; William Nicholson to Timothy Nicholson, 2nd Mo. 11, 1885, Timothy Nicholson Papers; Bean, "San Jose," 468; "San Jose Monthly Meeting," *Friend*, 9th Mo. 5, 1885, p. 35.

67. "An Inquisition and Its Result," *Friends' Review*, 9th Mo. 12, 1885, pp. 93–94; editorial, ibid., 11th Mo. 14, 1885, p. 233; LeShana, *Quakers in California*, 93.

68. "From the Field," *Christian Worker*, 2nd Mo. 14, 1889, p. 103; "Discussion on the Iowa Epistle in London Yearly Meeting," ibid., 8th Mo. 11, 1887, p. 381; James Bean, "An Important Question," *Friends' Review*, 4th Mo. 12, 1888, pp. 588–89; "Joel Bean and Iowa," *British Friend*, 12th Mo. 1894, p. 255; *Iowa Yearly Meeting and San Jose Monthly Meeting*, broadside, n.d., box 1, Jones Papers.

69. The entire correspondence is reprinted in "Joel Bean," *Friends' Review*, 10th Mo. 12, 1893, pp. 186–87.

70. Ibid.

71. "The American Declaration of Faith—A Result," *British Friend*, 11th Mo. 1893, pp. 305–7; Henry Stanley Newman to Allen Jay, 9th Mo. 11, 1893, A-F box, Jay Papers. The English Friends' letter was reprinted and circulated as a broadside. A copy is in box 4, Jones Papers.

72. Lawrie Tatum to Rufus M. Jones, 11th Mo. 27, 1893, box 1, Jones Papers; John Nicholson to William Nicholson, 9th Mo. 20, 1894, Timothy Nicholson Papers; Rufus M. Jones to Joel Bean, 10th Mo. 26, 1893, box 4, Bean Papers; Murray Shipley to Joel and Hannah Bean, 10th Mo. 22, 1893, box 5, ibid.; "Matters of Fact rather than Speculation," *Friends' Review*, 12th Mo. 21, 1893, p. 340; Richard Henry Thomas, "A New Precedent," ibid., 1st Mo. 11, 1894, p. 33; William P. Pinkham, "The Right of Private Opinion," ibid., 4th Mo. 5, 1894, pp. 321–22.

73. Paul A. Carter, *The Spiritual Crisis of the Gilded Age* (DeKalb: Northern Illinois University Press, 1971).

74. I use *fundamentalist* here in its broadest sense to denote the wide movement in American Protestantism characterized by premillennialism, biblical literalism, and antimodernism rather than in the narrow sense that sees fundamentalism as an outgrowth of Reformed theology based on dispensationalism.

VII   THE RISE OF MODERNIST QUAKERISM, 1895–1907

1. [Anna B. Thomas], *Richard H. Thomas, M.D.: Life and Letters* (London: Headley Brothers, 1905); Paul S. Rees, *Seth Cook Rees: The Warrior Saint* (Indianapolis: Pilgrim Book Room, 1934).

2. Richard H. Thomas, *Penelve; or, Among the Quakers* (London: Headley Brothers, 1898).

3. Seth C. Rees, *The Ideal Pentecostal Church* (Cincinnati: M. W. Knapp, 1897).

4. Information on all of these may be found in William Bacon Evans et al., comps., "Dictionary of Quaker Biography" (Quaker Collection, Haverford College, Haverford, Pa.). For Rees, see Rees, *Seth Cook Rees,* 54–55. Charles F. Coffin's bank failed in 1884. Subsequent investigation showed that while Coffin was outwardly a pillar of religion and morality, he had extended large, unsecured loans to his sons for speculative purposes, watered his bank's stock, misrepresented its assets, and embezzled funds from estates for which he was trustee. Coffin escaped being convicted, but his business practices were so reprehensible that in 1886 his monthly meeting disowned him. Coffin and his wife moved to Chicago, where he lived until his death in 1916. In later years he reemerged into the society, writing reminiscent and historical pieces for Quaker periodicals. His personal religious views became modernist. But his influence among Friends, especially in Indiana Yearly Meeting, was nil after 1884. See Timothy Nicholson to Thomas Kimber, 7th Mo. 4, 1885, First National Bank folder, Charles F. and Rhoda M. Coffin Papers (Archives, Earlham College, Richmond, Ind.); Whitewater Monthly Meeting complaint with Coffin's response, 9th Mo. 23, 1885, ibid.; Marcus Mote to Henry Hartshorne, 1st Mo. 21, 1885, box 11, Hartshorne Family Papers (Quaker Collection, Haverford); *Richmond* (Ind.) *Palladium,* Feb. 1, March 4, 1886, Sept. 30, 1895; Mary Coffin Johnson and Percival Brooks Coffin, *Charles F. Coffin: A Quaker Pioneer* (Richmond, Ind.: Nicholson, 1923), 183–201; Whitewater Monthly Meeting Men's Minutes, 2nd Mo. 25, 1886 (Archives, Earlham).

5. Evans et al., comps., "Dictionary"; Rees, *Seth Cook Rees,* 54–55; Richard C. Sartwell, "The Influence of Leading Friends in Ohio Yearly Meeting of Friends, Evangelical, 1854–1919" (M. A. thesis, Earlham School of Religion, 1974), 107. Water baptism last became an issue when Dougan Clark, Jr., underwent the rite in 1894. Whitewater Monthly Meeting, where Clark held his membership, moved to depose him from the ministry amid considerable controversy and bitterness. The case dragged on for a year, finally lapsing when it became apparent that Clark was fatally ill. See "The Baptism of Dr. Dougan Clark," *American Friend,* 9th Mo. 27, 1894, pp. 246–48; Allen Jay to Rufus M. Jones, 9th Mo. 5, 1895, box 1, Rufus M. Jones Papers (Quaker Collection, Haverford); E. Gurney Hill et al. to Jones, 10th Mo. 8, 1894, with attachments, ibid.; Timothy Nicholson to Jones, 1st Mo. 12, 14, 4th Mo. 6, 6th Mo. 24, 7th Mo. 3, 19, 27, 8th Mo. 1, 1895, with attachments, ibid.

6. David C. LeShana, *Quakers in California: The Impact of 19th-Century Revivalism on Western Quakerism* (Newberg, Ore.: Barclay, 1969), 103–5; Teresa P. Wood to Chas. E. Cox, 9th Mo. 12, 1898, box 2, Jones Papers; A. Rosenberger to

Jones, Jan. 18, 1899, ibid.; A. T. Murray to Jones, 1st Mo. 11, 1899, ibid.; S. A. Wood to Jones, 2nd Mo. 18, 1899, ibid.; Timothy Nicholson to Joel Bean, 9th Mo. 26, 10th Mo. 6, 1898, box 4, Joel Bean Papers (Friends Historical Library, Swarthmore College, Swarthmore, Pa.).

7. Elbert Russell, *The History of Quakerism* (New York: Macmillan, 1942), 491–94.

8. William R. Hutchison, *The Modernist Impulse in American Protestantism* (Cambridge: Harvard University Press, 1976), 113; Hugh Barbour, "William Penn: Model of Protestant Liberalism," *Church History*, 48 (June 1979), 156–75. For a typical Hicksite reaction to the revival, see "In the West," *Journal*, 11th Mo. 8, 1882, p. 340. For Hicksite acceptance of modernism and identification with liberal religion, see, for example, William M. Jackson, *The Higher Criticism and the Relation of Its Result to Quakerism* (Philadelphia: Young Friends Association, 1895); and Thomas Elwood Longshore, *The Higher Criticism in Theology and Religion, Contrasted with Ancient Myths and Miracles as Factors in Human Evolution, and Other Essays on Reform* (New York: C. P. Somerby, 1892).

9. Hutchison, *Modernist Impulse*, 2.

10. Nereus Mendenhall letter, *Friends' Review*, 10th Mo. 20, 1892, pp. 204–5; Nereus Mendenhall to "Dear Friend," 7th Mo. 5, 1893, box 2, Hobbs-Mendenhall Papers (Southern Historical Collection, University of North Carolina, Chapel Hill); Mary M. Hobbs, "Nereus Mendenhall," in *Quaker Biographies*, ser. 2 (5 vols., Philadelphia, 1921–1926), V, 294–301; Margaret Davis Winslow, *A Gift from Grandmother* (n.p., 1957), 1; Nereus Mendenhall, *The Clue of Faith, in Science and Life. An Address before the Alumni Association of Haverford College, 24th of 6th Month 1879* (n.p., n.d.).

11. Jones lacks a major scholarly biography. The best available work is Elizabeth Gray Vining, *Friend of Life: A Biography of Rufus M. Jones* (Philadelphia: J. B. Lippincott, 1958). Jones told his own story in three autobiographical volumes: *Finding the Trail of Life* (New York: Macmillan, 1926); *The Trail of Life in College* (New York: Macmillan, 1929); and *The Trail of Life in the Middle Years* (New York: Macmillan, 1934).

12. Jones, *Trail of Life in the Middle Years*, 50–52; Byron Lindley Osborne, *The Malone Story: The Dream of Two Quaker Young People* (Canton, Ohio, 1970), 23–24; "Memorandum of the Conclusions of a Conference Held in New York, 5th Mo. 26, 1894, between J. Walter Malone, P. W. Raidabaugh, Isaac Sharpless, Allen Thomas, Rufus M. Jones, and James Wood," box 1, Jones Papers; Jones to Allen Jay, Feb. 1894, box 38A, ibid. It is important to keep in mind that the *American Friend* was privately owned rather than controlled by any Quaker group, even though it was endorsed by most of the yearly meetings as the denominational journal.

13. Eli Reece to Rufus M. Jones, 10th Mo. 3, 1894, box 1, Jones Papers; J. Henry Bartlett to Jones, 9th Mo. 20, 1894, ibid.; David Hadley to Jones, 1st Mo. 26, 1895, ibid.; J. Walter Malone to Jones, 1st Mo. 21, 1895, ibid.; Timothy Nicholson to Jones, 1st Mo. 6, 1896, ibid.; Philip S. Benjamin, *The Philadelphia Quakers in the Industrial Age, 1865–1920* (Philadelphia: Temple University Press, 1976), 178–80.

14. Vining, *Friend of Life*, 69–73; Elisabeth Isichei, *Victorian Quakers* (Oxford: Clarendon, 1970), 32–40. See also [Francis Frith, William Pollard, and William Edward Turner], *A Reasonable Faith: Short Essays for the Times* (London: Macmillan, 1884); and John Wilhelm Rowntree, *Essays and Addresses*, ed. Joshua Rowntree (London: Headley Brothers, 1905).

15. Vining, *Friend of Life*, 85–90. For the men under whom Jones studied at Harvard, see Bruce Kuklick, *The Rise of American Philosophy: Cambridge, Massachusetts, 1860–1930* (New Haven: Yale University Press, 1977), 229–401. For Francis

G. Peabody, see Sydney E. Ahlstrom, *A Religious History of the American People* (New Haven: Yale University Press, 1972), 795.

16. Rufus M. Jones, "Our Only Hope," *Christian Worker*, 6th Mo. 14, 1888, p. 278; "The Need of Thinking," *American Friend*, 7th Mo. 25, 1907, p. 466; "Some Tendencies of Recent Times," ibid., 3rd Mo. 29, 1900, p. 291; "Christ and Modern Thought," ibid., 10th Mo. 7, 1897, p. 933; Rufus M. Jones, *The Double Search: Studies in Atonement and Prayer* (Philadelphia: John C. Winston, 1906), 21–22.

17. "The Real Test of Inspiration," *American Friend*, 2nd Mo. 7, 1901, p. 148; "The Scriptures," ibid., 2nd Mo. 28, 1907, p. 131; "Either—Or," ibid., 12th Mo. 13, 1906, p. 803.

18. "Creeds," *Friends' Review*, 11th Mo. 9, 1893, p. 243; "Editorial Letter," *American Friend*, 7th Mo. 18, 1901, p. 676; "Beware of Discord Makers," ibid., 5th Mo. 12, 1898, pp. 437–38; Rufus M. Jones, *Practical Christianity: Essays on the Practice of Religion* (Philadelphia: John C. Winston, 1899), 185–87; Rufus M. Jones to Joel Bean, 10th Mo. 18, 1898, box 4, Bean Papers.

19. Jones, *Double Search*, 10–15; Rufus M. Jones, *A Dynamic Faith* (London: Headley Brothers, 1901), 29, 76–78.

20. "The Blood of Christ Cleanses from Sin," *American Friend*, 11th Mo. 12, 1903, pp. 771–72; Luke Woodard to Rufus M. Jones, 8th Mo. 2, 1901, box 3, Jones Papers; Jones, *Double Search*, 39–41, 43–44, 70–84.

21. Rufus M. Jones to Mary M. Hobbs, 12th Mo. 19, 1907, box 1, Hobbs-Mendenhall Papers (Southern Historical Collection); "When Is a Person Saved?" *American Friend*, 1st Mo. 16, 1908, p. 35; Jones, *Dynamic Faith*, 32–41; Rufus M. Jones, *Social Law in the Spiritual World: Studies in Human and Divine Inter-Relationship* (1904; reprint, London: Swarthmore, 1923), 123–40. For an analysis of Jones's mysticism, see Augustine J. Caffrey, "The Affirmation Mysticism of Rufus Matthew Jones" (D.S.T. diss., Catholic University of America, 1967), 174–239.

22. Jones, *Dynamic Faith*, 30–31; Jones, *Practical Christianity*, 43–44, 89–90, 95–98, 179–83.

23. My understanding of modernism has been guided by Hutchison, *Modernist Impulse*; and Ferenc Morton Szasz, *The Divided Mind of American Protestantism, 1880–1930* (University: University of Alabama Press, 1982).

24. Elbert Russell, *Quaker: An Autobiography* (Jackson, Tenn.: Friendly Press, 1956), 1–90.

25. Ibid., 80–114.

26. Elbert Russell, *Jesus of Nazareth in the Light of Today* (Philadelphia: John C. Winston, 1909), 9–10. For an example of reaction, see "Timely Topics," *Evangelical Friend*, April 21, 1910, pp. 3–4.

27. Elbert Russell, "The Principle of Progressive Revelation in Scripture," *American Friend*, 1st Mo. 25, 1900, pp. 77–79; Elbert Russell to Levi T. Pennington, Feb. 24, 1907, P folder, Elbert Russell Papers (Archives, Earlham); *Minutes and Proceedings of the Five Years Meeting of the American Yearly Meetings of Friends Held in Richmond, Indiana, Tenth Mo. 15 to Tenth Mo. 21, 1907* (Philadelphia: John C. Winston, 1908), 421–22, 424.

28. *Elbert Russell*, 97.

29. Frances Renfrow Doak, *Mary Mendenhall Hobbs* (Greensboro, N.C.: n.p., 1955); Paula Staahls Martin and Kathy Warden Manning, *Women of Guilford: A Study of Women's Contributions, 1740–1979* (Greensboro, N.C.: Women of Guilford, 1979), 73–77. For the context of Mary M. Hobbs's life and activities, see Anne Firor Scott, *The Southern Lady: From Pedestal to Politics, 1830–1930* (Chicago: University of Chicago Press, 1970).

30. Mary M. Hobbs to "Dear Roxie," 1st Mo. 8, 1901, box 2, Hobbs-Mendenhall

Papers (Friends Historical Collection, Guilford College, Greensboro, N.C.); Howard H. Brinton, "Friends for Seventy-Five Years," *Bulletin of Friends Historical Association*, 49 (Spring 1960), 13–15; "A Symposium: 'The Greatest Need of North Carolina Yearly Meeting' and How to Meet It," *Friends Messenger*, 1 (3rd Mo. 1904), 1.

31. Hobbs to "Dear Roxie,"; Mary M. Hobbs, "An Absentee God," box 3, Hobbs-Mendenhall Papers (Southern Historical Collection); Mary M. Hobbs, "Membership," box 2, Mary Mendenhall Hobbs Papers (Friends Historical Collection, Guilford); Mary M. Hobbs to Rufus M. Jones, 2nd Mo. 13, 1899, box 2, Jones Papers; Mary M. Hobbs, "Thus Saith the Lord," *American Friend*, 3rd Mo. 17, 1904, p. 176.

32. I have identified the modernists from three major sources: the correspondence in the Jones and Russell Papers; articles in the *American Friend* from 1894 to 1920; and the printed minutes of the Five Years Meeting for 1902 and 1907. Biographical information for all may be found in Evans et al., comps., "Dictionary."

33. Jones, *Trail of Life in the Middle Years*, 26–30; [Thomas], *Richard H. Thomas*, 310–11; *Elbert Russell*, 101, 120; Allen Jay to James Wood, 1st Mo. 4, 1907, box 5, Jones Papers; Charles E. Tebbetts to Jones, 7th Mo. 3, 1906, ibid.; Elbert Russell to Charles F. Coffin, March 24, 1915, Letters to and from Charles F. and Rhoda M. Coffin folder, Coffin Papers; *Autobiography of Allen Jay, Born 1831, Died 1910* (Philadelphia: John C. Winston, 1910), 363, 367, 403.

34. Rufus M. Jones to Elbert Russell, 8th Mo. 15, 1898, J folder, Russell Papers; Albert J. Brown to Jones, Aug. 23, 1903, box 4, Jones Papers; Charles E. Tebbetts to Jones, 1st Mo. 7, 1905, ibid.; Rufus M. Jones to Elizabeth B. Jones, Aug. 10, 1902, box 38D, ibid.

35. "Is It Safe to Neglect History?" *American Friend*, 12th Mo. 5, 1901, p. 1156; "A Call to Young Friends," ibid., 8th Mo. 18, 1904, p. 539; "New York Yearly Meeting," ibid., 6th Mo. 7, 1906, p. 373; Mary Mendenhall Hobbs, "A Need and a Suggestion," ibid., 5th Mo. 27, 1902, pp. 477–79; Rufus M. Jones to John Wilhelm Rowntree, 2nd Mo. 9, 1904, box 38A, Jones Papers.

36. Mary M. Hobbs to Allen D. Hole, [1907], box 1, Hobbs Papers; R. M. J., "The New Quakerism," *American Friend*, 11th Mo. 3, 1910, pp. 695–96; George A. Barton, "The Divine Immanence," ibid., 6th Mo. 6, 1895, pp. 549–50; Allen D. Hole, *The Place of the Quaker Message in Modern Life* (Richmond, Ind.: Central Book and Tract Committee, 1909), 12–13; *New York Yearly Meeting Minutes, 1907*, pp. 7–8; Jones, *Social Law*, 141–57.

37. *Proceedings of a Conference of Friends Held in Indianapolis, Indiana, 1897* (Philadelphia: *American Friend*, 1898), 487; James Wood, *The Distinguishing Doctrines of the Society of Friends* (New York: Friends Book and Tract Committee, 1898), 12–15; Lindley M. Stevens, "What Time Is It?" *American Friend*, 7th Mo. 21, 1904, p. 476.

38. Jones, *Trail of Life in the Middle Years*, 42–43; *Elbert Russell*, 102.

39. "Is True Religion Emotional?" *American Friend*, 9th Mo. 15, 1898, pp. 863–64; R. M. J., "A Serious Call," ibid., 1st Mo. 24, 1907, p. 51; *Proceedings . . . 1907*, pp. 235, 245–46; Elbert Russell to William P. Pinkham, Dec. 24, 1905, P folder, Russell Papers; Mary M. Hobbs to Rufus M. Jones, 2nd Mo. 13, 1899, box 2, Jones Papers.

40. "A Visit in the Central West," *American Friend*, 8th Mo. 28, 1902, p. 688; "News from the Field," ibid., 1st Mo. 5, 1899, p. 19; "Things of Interest among Ourselves," ibid., 2nd Mo. 27, 1908, p. 141; C. E. Newlin letter, ibid., 2nd Mo. 21, 1901, p. 178; "Correspondence between Yearly Meetings," ibid., 5th Mo. 12, 1898, pp. 435–36; "Yearly Meeting Epistles," ibid., 5th Mo. 26, 1904, p. 343; Edwin B. Bronner, "A Time of Change: Philadelphia Yearly Meeting, 1861–1914," in *Friends*

in the Delaware Valley: Philadelphia Yearly Meeting, 1681–1981, ed. John M. Moore (Haverford, Pa.: Friends Historical Association, 1981), 132–34; "Report of a Yearly Meeting Held in New York," *Evangelical Friend*, July 27, 1905, p. 128; Rufus M. Jones to "Dear Friend," 10th Mo. 20, 1900, box 38A, Jones Papers; Rufus M. Jones to Thomas Hodgkin, 1st Mo. 4, 1899, ibid.

41. *Minutes and Proceedings of the Five Years Meeting of the American Yearly Meetings Held in Indianapolis, Indiana, 1902* (Philadelphia: John C. Winston, 1903), 37–38; Russell, *History of Quakerism*, 475–76, 538; *Iowa Yearly Meeting Minutes, 1900*, p. 45.

42. "Kingdom of the Spirit," *American Friend*, 11th Mo. 28, 1895, p. 1142; *Proceedings . . . 1897*, p. 151.

43. *Elbert Russell*, 120–21, 125; *Proceedings . . . 1897*, p. 25; Thomas Newlin, "The Ideal Church," *American Friend*, 7th Mo. 3, 1902, p. 558.

44. "Christian Endeavour Department," *American Friend*, 6th Mo. 22, 1899, p. 586; "Reflections of a Voter," ibid., 11th Mo. 13, 1902, p. 881; "The Uprising of a City," ibid., 3rd Mo. 9, 1905, p. 155; *Elbert Russell*, 135–43; Mary M. Hobbs essay on Woodrow Wilson, n.d., box 3, Hobbs-Mendenhall Papers (Southern Historical Collection).

45. Elizabeth L. Comstock to Joshua L. Baily, [1889], box 2, Joshua L. Baily Papers (Quaker Collection, Haverford); B. L. Wick, *Sketch of the Life of Archibald Crosbie* (Cedar Rapids, Iowa: n.p., n.d.); editorial, *Friends' Review*, 10th Mo. 3, 1885, p. 137; ibid., 2nd Mo. 2, 1888, p. 424; ibid., 7th Mo. 21, 1892, p. 825; "Social Reform Not Socialism," ibid., 6th Mo. 4, 1891, p. 712; Kathaleen J. Carter to Thomas D. Hamm, Sept. 27, 1984 (in author's possession); Richard Eugene Wood, "Evangelical Quakers in the Mississippi Valley, 1854–1894" (Ph.D. diss., University of Minnesota, 1985), 267–69; Arthur Dewey Rush, "The Community of Haviland, Kansas: Its Early History and Development" (M.S. thesis, Fort Scott State College, 1942), 43–44. For the mugwumps, see John G. Sproat, *"The Best Men": Liberal Reformers in the Gilded Age* (New York: Oxford University Press, 1968). For the close parallel of Quaker attitudes toward economic reform with those of other Protestants in this era, see Henry F. May, *The Protestant Churches and Industrial America* (New York: Harper Brothers, 1949), 91–111.

46. "Love of Country," *American Friend*, 7th Mo. 19, 1894, p. 6; "The Supremacy of Love," ibid., 5–6; J. E. R., "A Dangerous Tyranny," ibid., 8th Mo. 2, 1894, p. 54. For similar reactions to the Pullman strike from other religious editors, see May, *Protestant Churches*, 108–10.

47. Benjamin, *Philadelphia Quakers*, 89–90; Isaac Sharpless to Mary Mendenhall Hobbs, 7th Mo. 17, 1912, box 1, Hobbs Papers; Mary Mendenhall Hobbs essay on the social gospel, n.d., box 3, Hobbs-Mendenhall Papers (Friends Historical Collection, Guilford); Eula Dixon, "How the Other Half Lives," *Guilford Collegian*, 9 (May 1897), 266–70; Alice B. Paige, "The Sweating System," *American Friend*, 8th Mo. 29, 1895, pp. 830–31; Elbert Russell, "The New Struggle for Liberty," ibid., 7th Mo. 25, 1912, pp. 470–72; Elbert Russell, "The Shadow of Anarchism," ibid., 8th Mo. 8, 1912, pp. 502–4; Elbert Russell, "The Massacre of the Innocents," ibid., 8th Mo. 22, 1912, pp. 538–39; *Proceedings . . . 1897*, p. 148; *Proceedings . . . 1907*, pp. 278–86, 353–73; *New York Yearly Meeting Minutes, 1907*, pp. 6–7.

48. *Proceedings . . . 1897*, pp. 148–49, 152–54; Ellison R. Purdy, "The Complement of Quakerism," *American Friend*, 1st Mo. 8, 1903, p. 520; Benjamin, *Philadelphia Quakers*, 208–9. To place modernist Friends in the larger context of Progressive attitudes toward the economic order, see Robert H. Wiebe, *The Search for Order, 1877–1920* (New York: Hill and Wang, 1967), 207–8; James Weinstein, *The Corporate Ideal in the Liberal State, 1900–1918* (Boston: Beacon, 1968); and Gabriel Kolko,

The Triumph of Conservatism: A Reinterpretation of American History, 1900–1916 (New York: Free Press, 1963).

49. Vining, *Friend of Life*, 88; Washington Gladden, "The Kingdom," *American Friend*, 11th Mo. 15, 1894, p. 429; "The Church in Modern Society," ibid., 9th Mo. 10, 1908, p. 584; *Elbert Russell*, 135–36. For the social gospel movement generally, see Richard C. White, Jr., and C. Howard Hopkins, *The Social Gospel: Religion and Reform in Changing America* (Philadelphia: Temple University Press, 1976).

50. Allen Jay to Rufus M. Jones, 1st Mo. 17, 24, 1907, box 5, Jones Papers. For a good example of such condescension, see "A Ministry of Simple Faith," *American Friend*, 2nd Mo. 5, 1903, p. 88.

51. See *Evangelical Friend* for 1905–1910; and Rees, *Seth Cook Rees*, 54–55.

52. Osborne, *Malone Story*, 8–16. Dr. Osborne, Malone's son-in-law, spoke with me at length about Walter Malone on Sept. 9, 1983.

53. Osborne, *Malone Story*, 18–21, 53–62.

54. Ibid., 71, 73–74, 79; W. P. P., "Personal Letter," *Evangelical Friend*, Aug. 26, 1909, p. 1.

55. Arthur O. Roberts, *The Association of Evangelical Friends: A Story of Quaker Renewal in the Twentieth Century* (Newberg, Ore.: Barclay, 1975), 5; Simeon O. Smith, *Biography of William M. Smith and History of Union Bible Seminary* (Westfield, Ind.: Union Bible Seminary, 1982), 58, 72; Charles H. Brackett, "The History of Azusa College and the Friends, 1900–1965" (M.A. thesis, University of Southern California, 1967).

56. See, for example, the address by Walter Malone in *Proceedings . . . 1897*, pp. 332–35.

57. William P. Pinkham, *The Lamb of God; or, the Scriptural Philosophy of the Atonement* (Cleveland: Cleveland Bible Training School, 1895), 8–9; William P. Pinkham, "The Divine Immanence," *Soul Winner*, March 27, 1902, pp. 147–48; J. Walter Malone, "George Adam Smith and Dr. Cadman at Northfield," *American Friend*, 10th Mo. 5, 1899, p. 946; Luke Woodard, "Some Thoughts for the Thoughtful," ibid., 10th Mo. 7, 1897, p. 949; William P. Pinkham letter, ibid., 4th Mo. 6, 1905, p. 235; "If a Son Asks Bread—," *Evangelical Friend*, Feb. 4, 1909, p. 1; Edward Mott to Elbert Russell, 2nd Mo. 12, 1908, M folder, Russell Papers.

58. W. P. P., "Personal Letter," 1; John Henry Douglas letter, *Evangelical Friend*, Nov. 1, 1906, p. 698; David Hadley, "Essential Points of Quaker Doctrine," ibid., Jan. 10, 1907, pp. 19–21; Esther Tuttle Pritchard, "The Essentials," *American Friend*, 3rd Mo. 29, 1900, p. 294. See also the extensive files of letters from Pinkham in the Jones and Russell papers.

59. "Alarming Heterodoxy," *Witness and Training School* News, 3 (June-July 1903), 8; Jacob Baker, *Incidents of My Life and Work of 84 Years* (Richmond, Ind.: Nicholson, 1911), 165–66; Jones, *Trail of Life in the Middle Years*, 227–28; Isaac T. Gibson letter, *Evangelical Friend*, July 29, 1909, p. 13; Byron J. Rees, *Hulda: The Pentecostal Prophetess; or, A Sketch of the Life and Triumph of Mrs. Hulda A. Rees, together with Seventeen of Her Sermons* (Philadelphia: Christian Standard Company, 1898), 73–74; "Iowa Yearly Meeting," *American Friend*, 9th Mo. 20, 1894, p. 231.

60. Lydia C. Williams-Cammack and Truman C. Kenworthy, *Life and Works of Amos M. Kenworthy* (Richmond, Ind.: Nicholson, 1918), 217–18; "The Whitewater Centennial at Richmond, Ind.," *Evangelical Friend*, March 3, 1909, pp. 1–4; Luke Woodard, "Some Observations," ibid., July 1, 1909, pp. 2–3; "Friends Peace Conference," *Soul Winner*, Jan. 9, 1902, p. 15; Baker, *Incidents*, 111–12, 175; Luke Woodard, *A Historical Sketch of the Schism in the Friends' Church in 1827–1828 Known as the "Hicksite Separation"* (Plainfield, Ind.: Publishing Association of Friends, 1912).

61. Edgar P. Ellyson, "Why I Am Opposed to Church Amusements," *American Friend*, 1st Mo. 10, 1895, p. 41; J. Walter Malone, "Russia and Her Retribution," *Soul Winner*, May 18, 1905, p. 277; F. E. Marsh, "Is the Lord's Coming Near?" *Evangelical Friend*, Feb. 8, 1906, pp. 88–89; *Ohio Yearly Meeting Minutes, 1905*, p. 75.

62. *Proceedings . . . 1897*, pp. 175–79; George M. Marsden, *Fundamentalism and American Culture: The Shaping of Twentieth-Century Evangelicalism, 1870–1925* (New York: Oxford University Press, 1980), 124–38; Seth C. Rees, *Fire from Heaven* (Cincinnati: God's Revivalist, 1899), 33, 67, 157–58; editorial, *Evangelical Friend*, Dec. 6, 1906, pp. 769–70.

63. Baker, *Incidents*, 145–47; "Life Line," *Soul Winner*, March 23, 1905, p. 152; "Christianity and Moral Reforms," *Evangelical Friend*, Feb. 22, 1906, pp. 114–15.

64. *Proceedings . . . 1897*, pp. 332–33; "True Revivals," *Evangelical Friend*, March 10, 1910, p. 2; William J. Doherty, "Demon Possession in the Twentieth Century," ibid., July 13, 1905, p. 105; A. M. Hills, "Satan's Devices, or the Extremist and the Fanatic," ibid., May 3, 1906, pp. 277–78; "True Conservatism," ibid., March 5, 1908, p. 147; "Camp Meeting Life," *Soul Winner*, June 5, 1902, p. 266; David Hadley to Rufus M. Jones, March 19, 1899, box 2, Jones Papers; *Iowa Yearly Meeting Minutes, 1908*, p. 17; *California Yearly Meeting Minutes, 1905*, pp. 21–22; ibid., 1906, pp. 104–5.

65. Luke Woodard, *Autumn Gleanings* (Richmond, Ind.: Nicholson, 1914), 105–10; J. T. Hoover, "A Football Team or Pugilism, Which?" *Evangelical Friend*, Jan. 25, 1906, p. 53; editorial, *Soul Winner*, May 8, 1902, p. 222; Edgar P. Ellyson, "Holding Out,' " *American Friend*, 2nd Mo. 21, 1895, pp. 179–80; Walter C. Rush to Rufus M. Jones, Dec. 21, 1897, box 2, Jones Papers; Anna J. Winslow, *Jewels from My Casket* (n.p., 1910), 176–77.

66. Charles Edwin Jones, *Perfectionist Persuasion: The Holiness Movement and Methodism, 1867–1936* (Metuchen, N.J.: Scarecrow, 1974), 79–88; Woodard, *Autumn Gleanings*, 210–11; Edward Mott, *Sixty Years of Gospel Ministry* (Portland, Ore.: n.p., 1947), 55–57, 60; "D. L. Moody's World-Wide Influence in Christian Work," *Evangelical Friend*, Feb. 8, 1906, p. 86; "The Drift," ibid., March 5, 1908, p. 148; "A Good Example," ibid., April 1, 1909, p. 1; "The Holiness Movement," ibid., Nov. 11, 1908, pp. 1–2; Robert Mapes Anderson, *Vision of the Disinherited: The Making of American Pentecostalism* (New York: Oxford University Press, 1980), 35–36, 48, 63; Marsden, *Fundamentalism and American Culture*, 43–138.

67. Jones, *Trail of Life in the Middle Years*, 159–60; "Sound the Alarm," *Evangelical Friend*, Aug. 1, 1907, p. 481.

68. Jones, *Trail of Life in the Middle Years*, 72–76; Ira C. Johnson to Rufus M. Jones, Jan. 8, 1907, box 5, Jones Papers; Johnson to Elbert Russell, Dec. 5, 1906, J folder, Russell Papers. For an account of Jones's visit to the home of an impoverished family in Mooresville, Indiana, where on an August night he shared a feather bed with a very fat farmer in flannel longjohns, see Rufus M. Jones to Elizabeth B. Jones, 8th Mo. 15, 1902, box 38D, Jones Papers.

69. Dougan Clark and Joseph H. Smith, *David B. Updegraff and His Work* (Cincinnati: M. W. Knapp, 1895), 191–94; *Proceedings . . . 1907*, pp. 375–89; *Elbert Russell*, 120.

70. John H. Douglas to Rufus M. Jones, 5th Mo. 5, 1895, box 1, Jones Papers; Douglas to Jones, 12th Mo. 8, 1897, Jan. 16, 1900, box 2, ibid.; Arthur Peacock to Jones, 12th Mo. 16, 1898, ibid.; Jacob Baker to Jones, 5th Mo. 27, 1901, box 3, ibid.; David Hadley to Jones, Aug. 20, 1901, ibid.

71. Thomas Newlin to Jones, 7th Mo. 5, 1896, box 1, Jones Papers; Newlin to

Jones, 8th Mo. 16, 1897, box 2, ibid.; Irving King to Jones, 1st Mo. 13, 1900, ibid.; *Elbert Russell*, 101–4, 106.

72. Allen Jay to Eli Jay, 6th Mo. 23, 1900, with attached program, box 1, Eli and Mahalah Jay Family Papers (Archives, Earlham); Joel Bean, "The Summer School at Haverford, 1900," box 8, Bean Papers; [Thomas], *Richard H. Thomas*, 361–63; Jones, *Trail of Life in the Middle Years*, 115–17; Esther Tuttle Pritchard, "The Summer School and Its Extension Work: A Rejoinder," *American Friend*, 4th Mo. 25, 1901, p. 390; "Letter from Esther Tuttle Pritchard," ibid., 3rd Mo. 21, 1901, p. 270; William P. Pinkham, "A Reasonable Inquiry," ibid., 1st Mo. 8, 1901, p. 7.

73. Rufus M. Jones to Elizabeth B. Jones, 1st Mo. 2, 1902, Box 38D, Jones Papers; Allen Jay to Rufus M. Jones, 7th Mo. 19, 1901, box 3, ibid.; Joseph Moore to Rufus M. Jones, 1st Mo. 21, 1901, ibid.; George A. Barton to Rufus M. Jones, 5th Mo. 23, 1901, ibid.; R. L. Kelly to Jones, 1st Mo. 18, 1901, ibid.; "Editorial Letter," *American Friend*, 7th Mo. 18, 1901, p. 676; *Elbert Russell*, 105–6.

74. For Newlin, see R. W. Kelsey to Russell, 1st Mo. 19, 1903, K folder, Russell Papers.

75. J. H. Douglas letter, *Western Work*, 3 (June 1899), 7; "Some Necessary Corrections," *Evangelical Friend*, Dec. 3, 1908, p. 2. For the training schools, see Roberts, *Association of Evangelical Friends;* Smith, *Biography of William M. Smith and History of Union Bible Seminary;* and Brackett, "History of Azusa College and the Friends."

76. "Editorial," *Evangelical Friend*, June 1, 1905, pp. 1–2. The *Soul Winner*, which began publishing in 1902, was the successor to another Malone publication, the *Bible Student*, founded in 1897. Wood, "Evangelical Quakers," 264–65. The *Witness and Training School News* was first published in 1900. In 1908 it became the *Pacific Friend*.

77. Edith Marie Stubbs to Rufus M. Jones, May 8, 1905, box 5, Jones Papers; Allen Jay to James Wood, 1st Mo. 4, 1907, ibid.; Jay to Jones, 1st Mo. 16, 1907, ibid.

78. My characterization of these yearly meetings is based on their minutes for 1900 to 1910 and on the periodicals for the same years.

79. Rufus M. Jones to John Wilhelm Rowntree, Jan. 30, May 20, 1902, box 38D, Jones Papers; Rufus M. Jones to Elizabeth B. Jones, Jan. 30, Aug. 10, 1902, ibid.; Levi D. Barr to Rufus M. Jones, June 4, 1904, box 4, ibid.; W. P. Pinkham to Rufus M. Jones, 4th Mo. 13, 1903, ibid.; *Elbert Russell*, 115–17; "Notes of Earlham Institute," *Evangelical Friend*, Aug. 24, 1905, pp. 193–94.

80. Cf. *American Friend* and *Evangelical Friend* for 1906. See also P. W. Raidabaugh to Rufus M. Jones, 2nd Mo. 27, 1907, box 5, Jones Papers; Rayner W. Kelsey to Jones, 2nd Mo. 1, 1907, ibid.; Charles E. Tebbetts to Jones, 7th Mo. 3, 1906, ibid.; Allen Jay to James Wood, 1st Mo. 4, 1907, ibid.; Jay to Jones, 1st Mo. 16, 1st Mo. 24, 1907, ibid.; "Thoughts for the New Year," *Evangelical Friend*, Jan. 3, 1907, pp. 1–2; and *California Yearly Meeting Minutes, 1906*, pp. 91–92.

81. William Wade Hinshaw, ed., *Encyclopedia of American Quaker Genealogy* (6 vols., Ann Arbor: Edwards Brothers, 1936–1950), IV, 976–77; "My Conversion and Call," *New Acts*, Oct. 1904, pp. 3–6; "Our Missionary Party," ibid., p. 2; *Ohio Yearly Meeting Minutes, 1891*, p. 35; ibid., 1902, p. 21; Alliance Monthly Meeting Minutes, June 7, 1901 (Archives, Malone College, Canton, Ohio).

82. L. R. Lupton, "Origin, Review, and Prospects of the World Evangelization Company," *New Acts*, Feb. 15, 1906, pp. 1–4; "Modern Apostolic Acts," ibid., Oct. 1904, pp. 1–2. The only known surviving file of the *New Acts* is in the Friends Historical Collection at Guilford College. Initially a monthly, it became a weekly soon after it was founded. For the journey to Africa, see William M. Smith, *Chapters*

from the New Acts: An Account of the First Missionary Journey of the World Evangelization Company to Africa (Alliance, Ohio: n.p., n.d.).

83. "Brought to Completion," *New Acts*, Feb. 1, 1906, pp. 1–4; "Present Problem of Faith," ibid., May 31, 1906, pp. 3–4; "Practicing Faith," ibid., June 31, 1906, pp. 1–3; "A Cyclone's Breath," ibid., June 14, 1906, pp. 1–2; "To Stop for Prayer," ibid., Sept. 27, 1906, p. 3; Levi R. Lupton, "Testimony: My Personal Experience," ibid., Feb. 1907, p. 3; "Prophetic Announcements," ibid., June 1907, pp. 6–7; "Holiness Bible School Leader Receives Pentecost," *Apostolic Faith*, Feb.–March 1907, p. 5; Damascus Quarterly Meeting of Ministry and Oversight Minutes, 5th Mo. 11, 8th 10, 1906 (Archives, Malone). The *New Acts* became a monthly again after Lupton's conversion to pentecostalism.

84. Lupton, "Testimony," 3; "Prophetic Announcements," 6–7; Smith, *Biography of William M. Smith*, 51–58.

85. "Newspaper Accounts of the Recent Outbreak of Tongues," *American Friend*, 1st Mo. 24, 1907, p. 56.

86. "The Gift of Tongues," *Evangelical Friend*, Jan. 10, 1907, p. 17; "The Facts in the Case," ibid., Feb. 7, 1907, pp. 83, 86–87; "The Lupton Case," ibid., Feb. 14, 1907, p. 99; "Statement of Friends Bible Institute," ibid.; J. W. Malone, "Speaking in Tongues or What Saith the Scripture," ibid., June 11, 1908, p. 373; Damascus Quarterly Meeting of Ministry and Oversight Minutes, 2nd Mo. 8, 1907; Smith, *Biography of William M. Smith*, 58.

87. "The 'Tongue' Movement," *Pacific Friend*, 2nd Mo. 15, 1908, pp. 3–4; "Speaking with Tongues," ibid., 4th Mo. 2, 1908, p. 9; "Tongues in the Light of the Gospel," *Evangelical Friend*, Oct. 1, 1908, p. 619; Aaron M. Bray to Rufus M. Jones, 1st Mo. 31, 1907, box 5, Jones Papers; Williams-Cammack and Kenworthy, *Life and Work of Amos M. Kenworthy*, 189–91; Homer A. Tomlinson, ed., *Diary of A. J. Tomlinson* (3 vols., New York: Church of God, World Headquarters, 1949), I, 14–20. The connections between holiness Friends and the early pentecostal movement remain largely unexplored, but some links are apparent. Charles F. Parham, considered by many the founder of modern pentecostalism, was deeply influenced by the holiness Quaker family into which he married in Kansas. He was familiar with Walter Malone and included some Friends among his early followers. Mary Woodworth Etter, another early pentecostal leader, was also a former Quaker. Anderson, *Vision of the Disinherited*, 36, 47–51. Tomlinson's relationship with Friends after 1900 is difficult to ascertain. He lived in areas of North Carolina and Tennessee in which there were no Friends meetings and so identified with various holiness groups there. In his travels, however, he continued to preach in Friends meetings and churches, even after he had become known as a pentecostal, and kept up connections with such holiness Quaker stalwarts as Seth Rees and Charles Stalker. Tomlinson, ed., *Diary of A. J. Tomlinson*, I, 23–24, 90, 207; Anderson, *Vision of the Disinherited*, 253.

88. R. M. J., "Speaking with Tongues," *American Friend*, 1st Mo. 17, 1907, p. 31; R. M. J., "A Serious Call," ibid., 1st Mo. 24, 1907, pp. 52–53.

89. "A Serious Call," *Evangelical Friend*, Feb. 7, 1907, pp. 81–83; R. M. J., "One More Serious Call," *American Friend*, 2nd Mo. 21, 1907, pp. 115–16; R. M. J., "Editorial Letter," ibid., 116; Vining, *Friend of Life*, 121–22; Thomas Newlin to Rufus M. Jones, March 20, 1907, box 5, Jones Papers; Rufus M. Jones to Elizabeth B. Jones, 1st Mo. 27, 1st Mo. 29, 2nd Mo. 2, 1907, box 39, ibid.

90. C. E. Newlin to Rufus M. Jones, 9th Mo. 18, 1907, box 5, Jones Papers; Rufus M. Jones to Elizabeth B. Jones, 10th Mo. 17, 1907, box 39, ibid.; *Elbert Russell*, 119–20; *Proceedings . . . 1907*, pp. 212–21; "The Five Years Meeting—A Review," *American Friend*, 10th Mo. 31, 1907, p. 695; Rufus M. Jones to Russell, 11th Mo. 15,

1907, J folder, Russell Papers. For holiness impressions of the 1907 Five Years Meeting, see Mott, *Friends Church*, 41–46.

91. Although now two decades old, an excellent introduction to the varieties of American Quakerism today is Edwin B. Bronner, ed., *American Quakers Today* (Philadelphia: Friends World Committee, 1966). Also helpful are the essays in Francis B. Hall, ed., *Quaker Worship in North America* (Richmond, Ind.: Friends United Press, n.d.).

92. Bronner, ed., *American Quakers Today*, 11–30, 32–42, 58–84. Symptomatic of the continuing diversity within Friends United Meeting is the devotion of the September 1984 issue of its periodical, *Quaker Life,* to the Quaker "search for identity."

93. For my understanding of Westfield after 1900, I have been guided by conversations with Willard C. Heiss of Indianapolis; with Joseph G. and Leanna (Barker) Roberts of Westfield; and with Olive Osborne of North Canton, Ohio; and, of course, by [James Baldwin], *In My Youth: From the Posthumous Papers of Robert Dudley* (Indianapolis: Bobbs-Merrill, 1914). For William M. Smith, see Smith, *Biography of William M. Smith.* For the separation, see Harold N. Tollefson, "The Separation at Westfield, Indiana," typescript, 1975 (in author's possession).

Bibliography

MANUSCRIPT COLLECTIONS

Ethel Bevan, Haviland, Kans.
Stacy E. Bevan Papers

Manuscripts Department, Duke University Library, Durham, N.C.
Simeon Barker Papers
Thomas Hinshaw Papers
W. Rufus Kersey, comp. "Documents Dealing with the Life and Work of John Henry
Douglas, Quaker Evangelist, 1832–1919." Typescript. N.d.
Robert and Newton D. Woody Papers

Archives, Earlham College, Richmond, Ind.
Charles F. and Rhoda M. Coffin Papers
Duck Creek Monthly Meeting Membership Book
Duck Creek Monthly Meeting Men's and Women's Minutes
Earlham Students Collection
David Huddleston Papers
Indiana Yearly Meeting of Ministers and Elders Minutes
Indiana Yearly Meeting for Sufferings Minutes
Individual Friends Collection
Allen Jay Papers
Eli and Mahalah Jay Family Papers
Joseph Moore Papers
New Garden Monthly Meeting Men's and Women's Minutes
Timothy Nicholson Papers
Elbert Russell Papers
Springfield Monthly Meeting Men's and Women's Minutes
Walnut Ridge Monthly Meeting Men's Minutes
White River Monthly Meeting Men's and Women's Minutes
Whitewater Monthly Meeting Men's and Women's Minutes

Friends Historical Collection, Guilford College, Greensboro, N.C.
John Beals Collection
Cane Creek Monthly Meeting Men's and Women's Minutes
Addison Coffin Papers
Deep Creek Monthly Meeting Men's and Women's Minutes
Deep River Monthly Meeting Men's and Women's Minutes
Haworth Family Papers
Lewis Lyndon Hobbs Papers
Mary Mendenhall Hobbs Papers
Hobbs-Mendenhall Papers
Allen Jay Papers
Lost Creek Monthly Meeting Men's and Women's Minutes
Meeting for Sufferings Minutes and Papers

New Garden Monthly Meeting Men's Minutes'
David E. Sampson Memorial
Springfield Monthly Meeting Men's and Women's Minutes
Elmina Foster Coffin Wilson. "Reminiscence of New Garden Boarding School."
     Typescript. N.d.
John W. and Mary C. Woody Family Papers.

Quaker Collection, Haverford College, Haverford, Pa.
Joshua L. Baily Papers
Charles Evans Papers
William Bacon Evans et al., comps. "Dictionary of Quaker Biography." Typescript.
     N.d.
Hartshorne Family Papers
Rufus M. Jones Papers
Miscellaneous Letters Collection
Rhoads Family Papers
Tallcot Family Papers
Taylor Family Papers
Updegraff Family Papers

Haviland Records Room, New York, N.Y.
New York Yearly Meeting Representative Meeting (Orthodox) Minutes and Papers

Willard C. Heiss, Indianapolis
Oliver Albertson Diaries
Darius B. Cook. "History of the Cook and Bowles Families." Typescript. Ca. 1930.
Benjamin Cox Diary
John Jones Diary
Margaret Jones Diary
Randolph County Temperance Society Records
Nixon Rush Memoirs
Lydia Bond Wasson Diary

Henry County Historical Society, New Castle, Ind.
Elijah Coffin Scrapbook
Genealogy Files
Daniel Newby. "Memoranda of Old Rich Square." 1921
Henry W. Painter. "History of Spiceland Quarterly Meeting." Typescript. 1921.
Spiceland Auxiliary to the Bible Association of Friends in America Records

Indiana Historical Society Library, Indianapolis
Eleazer Bales Collection
Nathan H. Clark Papers
Reuben Green Papers
Willard C. Heiss, comp. "Pickett-Allen Family Letters"
Rebecca Russell Diary
Martha White Talbert Diary

Indiana Division, Indiana State Library, Indianapolis
Isaac W. and Benjamin B. Beeson Papers

George Chittenden Papers
George Evans. "Letters from George Evans to His Family and Particular Friends at Spiceland, Indiana." Typescript. 1839–1840.
Joseph John Gurney Letter to Spiceland Monthly Meeting. 1837.
Merritt Harrison Papers
Mill Creek Social Circle and Bible School Minutes
Susan B. Unthank Papers

Manuscripts Department, Kansas State Historical Society, Topeka
Herman Newman Collection

Archives, Malone College, Canton, Ohio
Adrian Literary and Missionary Society Minutes
Adrian Monthly Meeting Minutes
Alliance Monthly Meeting Minutes
Damascus Quarterly Meeting for Ministry and Oversight Minutes
Goshen Monthly Meeting Men's and Women's Minutes
Ohio Yearly Meeting for Sufferings and Representative Meeting Minutes

Byron L. Osborne, North Canton, Ohio
J. Walter Malone. "Autobiography." N.d.

George F. Parker, Bakersfield, Calif.
Macy-Parker Family Letters

Joseph G. and Leanna Roberts, Westfield, Ind.
Conservative Friends Sermon Transcripts

Southern Historical Collection, University of North Carolina, Chapel Hill
Hobbs-Mendenhall Papers
Watson-Nicholson Papers

Friends Historical Library, Swarthmore College, Swarthmore, Pa.
Joel Bean Papers
Bettle Family Papers
Coffin Family Papers
Furnas Family Papers
Griffith Family Papers
William Wade Hinshaw Collection
William Hobson Papers
Susanna and Lydia Hockett Commonplace Book
Kite-Bassett Papers
Stratton Papers
John Greenleaf Whittier Collection
Wood Family Papers

Wilmington College Library, Wilmington, Ohio
Caesars Creek Monthly Meeting Women's Minutes
Center Monthly Meeting Men's and Women's Minutes

Yadkin County Public Library, Yadkinville, N.C.
Kathryn Dobbins Huggins Genealogical Collection

Documents in Author's Possession
Augustus W. Benedict Letters. 1986.
John D. Carter. "Autobiography." Typescript. N.d.
Mildred Henley Calvert Letter. 1984.
Kathaleen Johnson Carter Letters. 1984–1986.
Gurney B. Reece Letters. 1981–1984.
Harold N. Tollefson. "The Separation at Westfield, Indiana." Typescript. 1975.
Richard E. Wood. "The Emergence of Revivalistic, Pastoral Quakerism in Mid-
    western America, 1850–1890: Creative Response or Tragic Accommodation?"
    Typescript. 1976.

INTERVIEWS

Heiss, Willard C. Indianapolis. Various dates, 1981–1987.
Osborne, Dr. and Mrs. Byron L. North Canton, Ohio. Sept. 9, 1983.
Peirce, Robert A. and Elsie (Davis). Dalton, Ind. Various dates, 1981–1985.
Roberts, Joseph G. and Leanna (Barker). Westfield, Ind. July 16, 1983. April 12,
    1986.

PERIODICALS

Quaker and Other Denominational Periodicals
American Friend. Richmond, Ind. 1867–1868.
———. Philadelphia and Richmond, Ind. 1894–1925.
Apostolic Faith. Houston. 1906–1908.
British Friend. London and Glasgow. 1870–1900.
Christian Worker. New Vienna, Ohio, and Chicago. 1871–1894.
Evangelical Friend, Cleveland, 1905–1912.
Freedmen's Record. Richmond, Ind. 1865–1866.
Friend. Philadelphia. 1827–1910.
Friends' Expositor. Mount Pleasant, Ohio. 1887–1892.
Friends' Intelligencer. Philadelphia. 1870–1880.
Friends' Messenger. High Point, N.C. 1904–1908.
Friends' Review. Philadelphia. 1847–1894.
Gospel Expositor. Columbus, Ohio. 1883–1884.
Guilford Collegian. Greensboro, N.C. 1897.
Journal. Philadelphia. 1882.
Miscellaneous Repository. Mount Pleasant, Ohio. 1828–1833.
Nebraska Friend. Central City, Nebr. 1906–1907.
New Acts. Alliance, Ohio. 1904–1908.
Pacific Friend. Whittier, Calif. 1908–1910.
Present-Day Papers. York, Eng. 1899–1902.
Primitive Friend. Emporia, Kans. 1883–1884.
Quaker. Indianapolis. 1921–1922.
Soul Winner. Cleveland. 1902–1905.
Southern Friend. Richmond, Va. 1864–1865.
Star and Crown. Indianapolis. 1885–1886.
Western Friend. Cincinnati. 1848–1849.
———. Quakervale, Kans. 1879–1890.

Western Work. Oskaloosa, Iowa. 1897–1912.
Witness and Training School News. Huntington Park, Calif. 1900–1907.

Newspapers
New Castle (Ind.) *Courier*. 1840–1904.
Richmond (Ind.) *Item*. 1884–1886.
Richmond (Ind.) *Palladium*. 1837–1850.
Wayne County Record. Centerville, Ind. 1840–1842.
Winchester (Ind.) *Journal*. 1868–1880.

PUBLISHED RECORDS AND MINUTES OF QUAKER GROUPS AND ORGANIZATIONS

Monthly Meeting Records
Heiss, Willard C., ed. *Abstracts of the Records of the Society of Friends in Indiana*. 7 vols. Indianapolis: Indiana Historical Society, 1962–1977.
Hinshaw, William Wade, ed. *Encyclopedia of American Quaker Genealogy*. 6 vols. Ann Arbor: Edwards Brothers, 1936–1950.

Yearly Meeting Minutes (Orthodox, or Gurneyite)
Baltimore. 1870–1895.
California. 1893–1910.
Indiana. 1821–1910.
Iowa. 1863–1910.
Kansas. 1872–1910.
New England. 1871–1900.
New York. 1855–1910.
Ohio. 1860–1910.
Oregon. 1892–1910.
Philadelphia. 1845–1860. 1870–1885.
Western. 1858–1910.
Wilmington. 1892–1910.

Minutes and Proceedings of the Five Years Meeting and Forerunners
Proceedings, Including the Declaration of Christian Doctrine, of the General Conference of Friends Held in Richmond, Ind., U.S.A., 1887. Richmond, Ind.: Nicholson, 1887.
Proceedings of the Conference of Friends of America, Held in Indianapolis, Indiana, 1892. Richmond, Ind.: Nicholson, 1892.
Proceedings of the Conference of Friends of America Held in Indianapolis, Indiana, 1897. Philadelphia: American Friend, 1898.
Minutes and Proceedings of the Five Years Meeting of the American Yearly Meetings Held in Indianapolis, Indiana, 1902. Philadelphia: John C. Winston, 1903.
Minutes and Proceedings of the Five Years Meeting of the American Yearly Meetings of Friends Held in Richmond, Indiana, Tenth Mo. 15 to Tenth Mo. 21, 1907. Philadelphia: John C. Winston, 1908.

Miscellaneous Records of Quaker Groups
Bible Association of Friends in America. *Annual Report*. Philadelphia, 1832–1845.

Minutes of the Ministerial Conference of Western Yearly Meeting of Friends Held at Bloomingdale, Ind., Eleventh Mo. 1880. Indianapolis: Baker and Randolph, 1881.

Minutes of the Ministerial Conference of Western Yearly Meeting of Friends, Held at Westfield, Hamilton County, Ind., Eleventh Month, 1881. Indianapolis: Baker and Randolph, 1881.

Report of the Committee on Education to the Yearly Meeting. Philadelphia: n.p., 1844.

Disciplines

Baltimore Yearly Meeting. *Discipline of the Yearly Meeting of Friends Held in Baltimore for the Western Shore of Maryland, Virginia, and the Adjacent Parts of Pennsylvania, as Revised and Adopted in 1865.* Baltimore: J. B. Rose, 1865.

———. *Discipline of the Yearly Meeting of Friends Held in Baltimore, for the Western Shore of Maryland, Virginia, and the Adjacent Parts of Pennsylvania, as Revised and Adopted in 1876.* Baltimore: Wm. K. Boyle, 1877.

Indiana Yearly Meeting. *The Discipline of the Society of Friends of Indiana Yearly Meeting.* Cincinnati: Achilles Pugh, 1839.

———. *The Discipline of the Society of Friends of Indiana Yearly Meeting.* Cincinnati: Achilles Pugh, 1854.

———. *The Discipline of the Society of Friends of Indiana Yearly Meeting.* Richmond, Ind.: E. Morgan and Sons, 1864.

———. *The Discipline of the Society of Friends of Indiana Yearly Meeting.* New Vienna, Ohio: Friends Publishing House, 1878.

———. *Discipline of the Society of Friends of Indiana Yearly Meeting.* Richmond, Ind.: Nicholson, 1892.

Iowa Yearly Meeting. *The Discipline of the Society of Friends of Iowa Yearly Meeting.* Chicago: n.p., 1865.

———. *The Discipline of Iowa Yearly Meeting of the Society of Friends.* New Vienna, Ohio: Friends Publishing House, 1876.

New England Yearly Meeting. *Doctrines, Christian Advices, Rules of Discipline of New England Yearly Meeting of Friends.* New Bedford, Mass.: E. Anthony, 1872.

New York Yearly Meeting. *Discipline of the Yearly Meeting of Friends Held in New-York for the State of New-York and Parts Adjacent as Revised and Adopted, in the Sixth Month, 1810.* New York: Mahlon Day, 1836.

———. *Discipline of the Society of Friends of New-York Yearly Meeting.* New York: Samuel S. and William Wood, 1859.

———. *Discipline of the Society of Friends of New York Yearly Meeting.* New York: John F. Trout, 1876.

North Carolina Yearly Meeting. *The Discipline of the Society of Friends of North-Carolina Yearly Meeting, Revised 1869.* Greensboro, N.C.: Patriot Office, 1870.

———. *The Discipline of the Society of Friends of North Carolina Yearly Meeting, Revised 1876.* Columbus: Friends Publishing House, 1880.

Ohio Yearly Meeting. *Discipline of the Society of Friends of Ohio Yearly Meeting.* Mount Pleasant, Ohio: Elisha Bates, 1819.

———. *The Discipline of the Religious Society of Friends of Ohio Yearly Meeting, Revised by the Meeting Held at Mount Pleasant, in the Year 1859.* Cincinnati: Achilles Pugh, 1860.

————. *The Discipline of Ohio Yearly Meeting of the Society of Friends. Revised by a Committee of the Yearly Meeting in 1876*. New Vienna, Ohio: Friends Publishing House, n.d.

Philadelphia Yearly Meeting. *Rules of Discipline of the Yearly Meeting of Friends Held in Philadelphia*. Philadelphia: J. Mortimer, 1828.

Western Yearly Meeting. *The Discipline of the Society of Friends of Western Yearly Meeting*. Indianapolis: Douglass and Conner, 1866.

————. *The Discipline of the Society of Friends of Western Yearly Meeting*. Columbus: Friends Publishing House, 1879.

DOCTRINAL WORKS AND STATEMENTS

Action of the Several Yearly Meetings of Friends, relative to the Secession from New England Yearly Meeting. Philadelphia: n.p., 1846.

Address to Friends, Prepared by the Committees of New York, New England, Baltimore, North Carolina, and Indiana, at Baltimore in Fifth Month 1851. New York: James Egbert, 1852.

Address to the Society of Friends. N.p., 1855.

Arnett, Thomas. *Address to the Christian Traveler in Every Evangelical Denomination, and to Others; Containing Devout Meditations and Remarks on Various Subjects; with Occasional Religious Exercises*. Cincinnati: Achilles Pugh, 1872.

Barbour, Hugh, and Arthur O. Roberts, eds. *Early Quaker Writings, 1650–1700*. Grand Rapids: Eerdmans, 1973.

Bates, Elisha. *The Doctrines of Friends; or, Principles of the Christian Religion, as Held by the Society of Friends—Commonly Called Quakers*. Mount Pleasant, Ohio, 1868.

————. *An Examination of Certain Proceedings and Principles of the Society of Friends, Called Quakers*. St. Clairsville, Ohio, 1837.

Brown, E. Howard, and Ruth E. Brown. *Young People's History of the Friends Church*. Chicago: Publishing Association of Friends, 1899.

Clark, Dougan, Jr. *Address by Dr. Dougan Clark*. N.p., 1858.

————. *The Holy Ghost Dispensation*. Chicago: Publishing Association of Friends, 1892.

————. *Instructions to Christian Converts*. Chicago: Publishing Association of Friends, 1889.

————. *The Offices of the Holy Spirit*. Philadelphia: National Publishing Association for the Promotion of Holiness, n.d.

————. *The Theology of Holiness*. Boston: McDonald and Gill, 1893.

Clarkson, Thomas. *A Portraiture of Quakerism, Taken from a View of Moral Education, Discipline, Peculiar Customs, Religious Principles, Political and Civil Economy, and Character of the Society of Friends*. 3 vols. New York: Samuel Stansbury, 1806.

Coffin, Elijah. *The Mother's Catechism of Christian Doctrine and Practice: Designed for the Use of Families and Schools*. Richmond, Ind.: Central Book and Tract Committee, 1859.

————, comp. *Scripture Exercises Consisting of Questions on the Gospel according to Luke and John in Harmony*. Cincinnati: E. Morgan and Sons, 1859.

Comly, John, and Isaac Comly, eds. *Friends' Miscellany: Being a Collection of Essays and Fragments, Biographical, Epistolary, Narrative, and Historical*. 12 vols. Philadelphia, 1834–1839.

Concise Statement of the Christian Doctrines of the Society of Friends. Richmond, Ind.: Central Book and Tract Committee, 1855.

Cox, Samuel Hanson. *Quakerism Not Christianity; or, Reasons for Renouncing the Doctrine of Friends*. New York: D. Fanshaw, 1833.

Document Issued by the Conference of Friends, Held in Baltimore, 7th Mo. 1849. With Some Remarks Thereon. Philadelphia: John Penington, 1850.

Edgerton, Jesse. *The New Quakerism*. N.p., 1900.

————. *Why Am I a Friend?* N.p., 1893.

Edgerton, Joseph. *Address to the Members of the Society of Friends*. Richmond, Ind.: n.p., 1841.

Edgerton, Walter. *A History of the Separation in Indiana Yearly Meeting of Friends in the Winter of 1842 and 1843 on the Anti-Slavery Question*. Cincinnati: Achilles Pugh, 1856.

————. *Modern Quakerism Examined and Contrasted with That of the Ancient Type*. Indianapolis: Printing and Publishing House, 1876.

————. *Walter Edgerton's Disownment by Spiceland Monthly Meeting*. N.p., 1877.

Ellyson, Edgar P. *Holding Out: Written Especially for Young Converts; also for New Arrivals in the Land of Canaan*. Cincinnati: Revivalist, 1896.

Epistles and Testimonies Issued by the Yearly Meetings of Friends in North America Setting Forth Their Belief in the Holy Scriptures and in the Divinity and Offices of Our Lord and Saviour Jesus Christ. Philadelphia: n.p., 1828.

[Evans, Charles]. *Considerations Addressed to the Members of the Yearly Meeting of Friends of Philadelphia*. Philadelphia: John Penington, 1846.

Evans, Thomas. *An Exposition of the Faith of the Religious Society of Friends, Commonly Called Quakers in the Fundamental Doctrines of the Christian Religion, Principally Selected from Their Early Writings*. Philadelphia: Kimber and Sharpless, 1828.

Evans, William, and Thomas Evans, comps. *The Friends Library: Comprising Journals, Doctrinal Treatises, and Other Writings of Members of the Religious Society of Friends*. 14 vols. Philadelphia, 1837–1850.

Experience of J. H. Merle D'Aubigne in the Work of Conversion. Richmond, Ind.: Central Book and Tract Committee, 1861.

Finney, Charles G. *Lectures on Revivals of Religion*. New York: Goodrich, 1868.

Fox, George. *Works*. 8 vols. Philadelphia: Marcus T. C. Gould, 1831.

[Frith, Francis, William Pollard, and William Edward Turner]. *A Reasonable Faith: Short Essays for the Times*. London: Macmillan, 1884.

Gurney, Joseph John. *Essays on the Doctrines, Evidences, and Practical Operation of Christianity*. Philadelphia: Longstreth, 1884.

————. *Letter to Friends of the Monthly Meeting of Adrian, Michigan*. New York: Mahlon Day and Co., 1839.

————. *Observations on the Distinguishing Views and Practices of the Society of Friends*. New York: Mahlon Day and Co., 1840.

Harvey, Cyrus W. *The Baptism of the Holy Spirit for Salvation: A Treatment of the Doctrine of Baptisms from Greek Usage, History, and Scripture*. Wichita, 1906.

————. *An Historic Parallel, or George Fox and Martin Luther as Reformers*. Baxter Springs, Kans., 1878.

————. *The Message of Quakerism and Its Relation to Modern Times*. N.p., n.d.

————. *An Open Letter to David B. Updegraff on Toleration and John's Baptism*. Quakervale, Kans.: *Western Friend*, 1887.

————. *The Resurrection as Taught by Early Friends*. Quakervale, Kans., 1882.

————. *Revised Criticism on the Ohio Minutes*. Quakervale, Kans.: n.p., 1880.

Hobbs, Barnabas C. *Baptism: What Was It in the Old Testament? What Was It in the New Testament?* Glasgow: Robert Smeal, 1879.

————. *Earlham Lectures*. Richmond, Ind.: Nicholson, 1885.

————. *School Friend, Fourth Book. Reading Exercises for the Use of Schools*. Cincinnati: n.p., 1854.

Hodgson, William. *An Examination of the Memoirs and Writings of Joseph John Gurney*. Philadelphia, 1856.

————. *The Society of Friends in the Nineteenth Century: A Historical View of the Successive Convulsions and Schisms Therein during That Period*. 2 vols. Philadelphia, 1875–1876.

Hole, Allen D. *The Place of the Quaker Message in Modern Life*. Richmond, Ind.: Central Book and Tract Committee, 1909.

Hole, Israel P. *A Discourse Delivered in Ohio Yearly Meeting of Friends, 9th Mo. 1st, 1885, in Answer to Arguments by D. B. Updegraff, in Favor of the Ordinances*. Columbus: William G. Hubbard, 1885.

Hubbard, Jeremiah. *An Exhortation to the Families, and More Particularly to the Heads of Families That Constitute North Carolina Yearly Meeting of Friends*. Greensboro, N.C.: William Swaim, 1833.

Hunt, David. *Essays on Religious Subjects: Including the Ordinances, Deity of Our Lord and Savior Jesus, Resurrection of the Dead, Etc*. New Vienna, Ohio, 1874.

In the Court of Appeal. Appeal from the Chancery Division of the High Court of Justice. Between John T. Dorland and Others Plaintiffs (Appellants) and Gilbert Jones and Others, Defendants (Respondents). Appeal Book. Belleville, Ont.: Ontario Steam Printing, 1884.

Indiana Yearly Meeting. *An Appeal for the Rights of Conscience*. Richmond, Ind.: n.p., 1863.

————. *Testimony and Epistle of Advice*. N.p., 1827.

Is It Calumny? or, Is It Truth? An Examination of a Pamphlet Entitled Calumny Refuted, or a Glance at John Wilbur's Book. Philadelphia: John Penington, 1846.

Jackson, William M. *The Higher Criticism and the Relation of Its Result to Quakerism*. Philadelphia: Young Friends Association, 1895.

Janney, Samuel M. *An Examination of the Causes Which Led to the Separation of the Religious Society of Friends in America in 1827–28*. Philadelphia: T. Ellwood Zell, 1868.

Jenkins, Stella Frances. *An Interpretation of the Gospel According to Friends: A Sketch*. Kansas City, Mo.: Charles E. Brown, n.d.

Jones, Augustine. *The Principles, Methods, and History of the Society of Friends*. Lynn, Mass.: George C. Herbert, 1874.

Jones, Rufus M. *The Double Search: Studies in Atonement and Prayer*. Philadelphia: John C. Winston, 1906.

————. *A Dynamic Faith*. London: Headley Brothers, 1901.

————. *Practical Christianity*. Philadelphia: John C. Winston, 1899.

————. *Social Law in the Spiritual World: Studies in Human and Divine Inter-Relationship*. 1904. London: Swarthmore, 1923.

Kenworthy, Jesse. *Copy of a Letter Addressed to a Friend in Philadelphia*. N.p., n.d.

Kimber, Thomas. *Historical Essays on the Worship of God and the Ministry of Our Lord and Savior; on the Early Christian Church, A.D. 50–150; on the Apostle Paul, and the Gentile Churches*. New York: Taber, 1889.

————. *The True Christian Theology of the Early Friends: An Essay Read before the*

Professors and Students of Earlham College, Richmond, Ind., Fifth Month 15th, 1880. New York: Central Tract Committee of New York Yearly Meeting, 1880.

Kite, John L. *Separation from the Religious Society of Friends.* Philadelphia: n.p., 1859.

Lamborn, Thomas. *Mystery Babylon Somewhat Exposed: The Standing of the Church Referred To and the True Seed Encouraged.* New Garden, Pa.: n.p., 1858.

Lewis, Enoch. *Ohio Yearly Meeting 1854.* n.p., n.d.

Longshore, Thomas Elwood. *The Higher Criticism in Theology and Religion, Contrasted with Ancient Myths and Miracles as Factors in Human Evolution, and Other Essays on Reform.* New York: C. P. Somerby, 1892.

Marshall, David. *Justification and Sanctification Inseparable in the Work of Redemption.* Carthage, Ind.: n.p., 1881.

Maule, Joseph E. *An Earnest Appeal to All Those Who Desire the Maintenance of the Ancient Doctrines and Testimonies of the Gospel as Held by the Primitive Friends.* Philadelphia: n.p., 1872.

————. *A Serious Review, Affectionately Recommended to the Careful Examination of Friends.* Philadelphia: William S. Young, 1860.

————. *Some Extracts and Remarks on Acknowledging Meetings of Separatists as Though They Were Meetings of Friends.* Philadelphia: William S. Young, 1859.

Maule, Joshua. *A Plea for the Unchangeable Truth Addressed to Friends.* Colerain, Ohio: n.p., 1860.

Mendenhall, Nereus. *The Clue of Faith, in Science and Life. An Address before the Alumni Association of Haverford College, 24th of 6th Month 1879.* N.p., n.d.

Mott, Edward. *The Friends Church in the Light of Its Recent History.* Portland, Ore.: Loomis Printing, n.d.

Narrative of the Facts and Circumstances That Have Tended to Produce a Secession from the Society of Friends in New England Yearly Meeting. Providence: Knowles and Vose, 1845.

New England Yearly Meeting. *A Declaration of New-England Yearly Meeting of Friends upon Various Christian Subjects.* Providence: Knowles and Vose, 1845.

————. *Narrative of Facts and Circumstances That Have Tended to Produce a Secession from the Society of Friends, in New England Yearly Meeting.* Providence: Knowles and Vose, 1845.

————. *A Vindication of the Disciplinary Proceedings of New England Yearly Meeting of Friends.* Boston: Damrell and Moore, 1852.

New York Monthly Meeting. *Address of the New York Monthly Meeting of Friends to Its Members.* New York: William Wood, 1863.

Nicholson, William. *Christian Conversion: Its Nature and Results and Some of Its Relations to Certain Other Topics.* Richmond, Ind.: Nicholson, 1884.

On the Nature and Efficacy of the Cross of Christ. Philadelphia: Tract Association of Friends, 1832.

On the Practical Importance of Faith in the Divinity of Christ. Philadelphia: William Salter, 1832.

Penn, William. *No Cross, No Crown: A Discourse Showing the Nature and Discipline of the Holy Cross of Christ, and That Denial of Self, and Daily Bearing of Christ's Cross, Is the Way Alone to the Rest and Kingdom of God.* London: Benjamin Clark, 1682.

Philadelphia Yearly Meeting. *An Address to Its Own Members and to the Members of Our Society Elsewhere, Issued by the Yearly Meeting of Friends, Fourth Month 18th, 1883.* Philadelphia: Friends Book Store, 1883.

————. *The Ancient Testimony of the Religious Society of Friends, Commonly Called Quakers, Respecting Some of Their Christian Doctrines and Practices*. Philadelphia: Joseph Rakestraw, 1843.

————. *An Appeal for the Ancient Doctrines of the Society of Friends*. Philadelphia: Joseph Kite, 1847.

————. *Report in Relation to the Facts and Causes of the Division which Occurred in New England Yearly Meeting in the Year 1845*. Philadelphia, 1847.

Pinkham, William P. *The Lamb of God; or, The Scriptural Philosophy of the Atonement*. Cleveland: Cleveland Bible Training School, 1895.

Rees, Seth C. *Fire from Heaven*. Cincinnati: God's Revivalist, 1899.

————. *The Holy War*. Cincinnati: God's Bible School and Revivalist, 1904.

————. *The Ideal Pentecostal Church*. Cincinnati: M. W. Knapp, 1897.

Rowntree, John Wilhelm. *Essays and Addresses*. Ed. Joshua Rowntree. London: Headley Brothers, 1905.

Russell, Elbert. *Jesus of Nazareth in the Light of Today*. Philadelphia: John C. Winston, 1909.

Smiley, Sarah F. *The Fulness of Blessing; or, The Gospel of Christ, as Illustrated from the Book of Joshua*. New York: Anson D. F. Randolph, 1876.

Smith, Hannah Whitall. *The Christian's Secret of a Happy Life*. Boston: Willard Tract Repository, 1875.

Smith, William M. *The Bible History of World Government and a Forecast of Its Future from Bible Prophecy*. Cincinnati: Winfred R. Cox, 1919.

————. *Chapters from the New Acts: An Account of the First Missionary Journey of the World Evangelization Company of Africa—1904–5*. Alliance, Ohio: n.p., n.d.

————. *Nicolaitanism: The Thing That Jesus Hates; and Laodiceanism, The Thing That Makes Jesus Sick*. N.p., n.d.

Stalker, Charles H. *Twice around the World with the Holy Ghost; or, The Impressions and Convictions of the Mission Field*. Columbus, Ohio, 1906.

Tallcot, Joseph. *The Friendly Visitant for Parents and Children*. 2 vols. Philadelphia: Henry Longstreth, n.d.

Testimony of the Society of Friends on the Continent of North America. Philadelphia: Friends' Book Store, 1830.

Thomas, Francis W. *An Address to the Religious Society of Friends*. Richmond, Ind.: Central Book and Tract Committee, 1863.

Thomas, Richard H. *Penelve; or, Among the Quakers*. London: Headley Brothers, 1898.

Thoughts on Growth in Grace. Richmond, Ind.: n.p., n.d.

Updegraff, David B. *An Address to Ohio Yearly Meeting on the Ordinances, and the Position of Friends Generally in Relation to Them*. Columbus: William G. Hubbard, 1885.

————. *David B. Updegraff on the Ordinances: An Interview*. Richmond, Ind.: n.p., 1886.

————. *Old Corn; or, Sermons on the Spiritual Life*. Boston: McDonald and Gill, 1892.

————. *Open Letters for Interested Readers*. Philadelphia: n.p., 1880.

Waring, William. *A Call to the Fountain: To Turn from Shadow and Imitation, and to Press after Substance; The Power That Quickens—The Life That Is Eternal*. Philadelphia: Smith, English, 1873.

Western Yearly Meeting [Conservative]. *A Salutation of Love, to All True Friends*. N.p., 1878.

Wilbur, John. *Letters to a Friend on Some of the Primitive Doctrines of Christianity*. London: Harvey and Darton, 1832.

————. *A Narrative and Exposition of the Late Proceedings of New England Yearly Meeting, with Some of Its Subordinate Meetings and Their Committee, in Relation to the Doctrinal Controversy Now Existing in the Society of Friends*. New York: Piercy and Reed, 1845.

Wood, James. *The Distinguishing Doctrines of the Society of Friends*. New York: Friends Book and Tract Committee, 1898.

Woodard, Luke. *Autumn Gleanings*. Richmond, Ind.: Nicholson, 1914.

————. *Gathered Fragments*. Columbus: Joseph H. Miller, 1883.

————. *A Historical Sketch of the Schism in the Friends' Church in the Years 1827–1828 Known as the "Hicksite Separation"*. Plainfield, Ind.: Publishing Association of Friends, 1912.

————. *The Morning Star! A Treatise on the Nature, Offices, and Works of the Lord Jesus Christ*. New Vienna, Ohio: Friends Publishing House, 1875.

————. *What Is Truth?*. Auburn, N.Y.: Knapp et al., 1901.

JOURNALS, MEMOIRS, AUTOBIOGRAPHIES, AND REMINISCENCES

American Annual Monitor; or, Obituary of the Members of the Society of Friends in America. 6 vols. New York: Samuel S. and William Wood, 1858–1863.

Arnett, Thomas. *Journal of the Life, Travels, and Gospel Labors of Thomas Arnett*. Chicago: Publishing Association of Friends, 1884.

Bailey, Hannah J. *Reminiscences of a Christian Life*. Portland, Me.: Hoyt, Fogg, and Donham, 1885.

Baker, Jacob. *Incidents of My Life and Work of 84 Years*. Richmond, Ind.: Nicholson, 1911.

[Baldwin, James]. *In My Youth: From the Posthumous Papers of Robert Dudley*. Indianapolis: Bobbs-Merrill, 1914.

Beals, Charles E. *Benjamin F. Trueblood: Prophet of Peace*. New York: Mosher, 1916.

[Bettle, Samuel, Jr.]. *Extracts from Memoranda of Jane Bettle, with a Short Memoir concerning Her*. Philadelphia: Joseph and William Kite, 1843.

Binford, Gurney. *As I Remember It: 43 Years in Japan*. N.p., 1950.

Braithwaite, Joseph Bevan, ed. *Memoirs of Joseph John Gurney; With Selections from His Journal and Correspondence*. 2 vols. Philadelphia: Lippincott, and Grambo, 1855.

Branson, Ann. *Journal of Ann Branson, a Minister of the Gospel in the Society of Friends*. Philadelphia: Wm. H. Pile's Sons, 1892.

Brinton, Howard H. "Friends for Seventy-Five Years." *Bulletin of Friends Historical Association*. 49 (Spring 1960), 1–20.

————, ed. "The Revival Movement in Iowa: A Letter from Joel Bean to Rufus M. Jones." *Bulletin of Friends Historical Association*. 50 (Fall 1961), 102–10.

[Butler, Josiah et al.]. *John Butler: A Sketch of His Life*. Columbus: William G. Hubbard, 1890.

Clark, Dougan, and Joseph H. Smith. *David B. Updegraff and His Work*. Cincinnati: M. W. Knapp, 1895.

Coffin, Addison. *Life and Travels of Addison Coffin*. Cleveland: William G. Hubbard, 1897.

Coffin, Levi. *Reminiscences of Levi Coffin, the Reputed President of the Underground Railroad*. Cincinnati: Robert Clark, 1880.

Conger, O. T., ed. *Autobiography of a Pioneer: The Nativity, Experiences, Travels, and Ministerial Labors of Rev. Samuel Pickard, the "Converted Quaker," containing Stirring Incidents and Practical Thoughts, with Sermons by the Author.* Chicago: Church and Goodman, 1866.

Cope, Gilbert S. *Genealogy of the Sharpless Family, Descended from John and Jane Sharpless, Settlers Near Chester, Pa., 1682.* Philadelphia, 1887.

Cox, Eliza Armstrong. *Looking Back Over the Trail.* N.p.: Woman's Missionary Association of Friends in America, 1927.

Cross, Barbara M., ed. *The Autobiography of Lyman Beecher.* 2 vols. Cambridge: Harvard University Press, 1961.

Deem, T. B. *Olden Spiceland.* N.p., 1934.

Doak, Frances Renfrow. *Mary Mendenhall Hobbs.* Greensboro, N.C.: Guilford College, 1955.

Dobkin, Marjorie Horsepian, ed. *The Making of a Feminist: Early Journals and Letters of M. Carey Thomas.* Kent, Ohio: Kent State University Press, 1979.

Dunn, Richard H., ed. *The Papers of William Penn.* 5 vols. to date. Philadelphia: University of Pennsylvania Press, 1982– .

Elliott, Errol T. *Life Unfolding: The Spiritual Pilgrimage of a Quaker Plainsman.* Richmond, Ind.: Friends United Press, 1975.

Evans, Joshua. *A Journal of the Life, Travels, Religious Exercises, and Labours in the Work of the Ministry of Joshua Evans, Late of Newton Township, Gloucester County, New Jersey.* Byberry, Pa.: John Comly, 1837.

Evans, William. *Journal of the Life and Religious Services of William Evans, a Minister of the Gospel in the Society of Friends.* Philadelphia: Friends Book Store, 1870.

Finney, Charles G. *Memoirs of Rev. Charles G. Finney.* New York: A. S. Barnes, 1876.

Frame, Nathan T., and Esther G. Frame. *Reminiscences of Nathan T. and Esther G. Frame.* Cleveland: Britton, 1907.

Hare, Caroline, comp. *Life and Letters of Elizabeth L. Comstock.* London: Headley Brothers, 1895.

Harlan, Alpheus H. *History and Genealogy of the Harlan Family and Particularly of the Descendants of George and Michael Harlan, Who Settled in Chester County, Pennsylvania, in 1687.* Baltimore, 1914.

Harrison, Eliza Cope. *Philadelphia Merchant: The Diary of Thomas P. Cope, 1800–1851.* South Bend, Ind.: Gateway, 1978.

Harvey, Julianna, comp. *Memorial of Cyrus W. Harvey.* Philadelphia: Friends Book Store, 1920.

Haviland, Laura S. *A Woman's Life-Work: Labors and Experiences.* Chicago: C. V. Waite, 1887.

Healy, Christopher. *Memoir of Christopher Healy, Taken Principally from His Own Memoranda.* Philadelphia: Friends Book Store, 1886.

Hicks, Elias. *Letters of Elias Hicks.* Philadelphia: T. Ellwood Zell, 1861.

Hoag, Joseph. *Journal of the Life of Joseph Hoag, an Eminent Minister of the Gospel in the Society of Friends.* Auburn, N.Y.: Knapp and Peck, 1861.

Hobbs, B. C., ed. *Autobiography of William Hobbs.* Indianapolis: John Woolman Press, 1962.

Hodgson, William. *Selections from the Letters of Thomas B. Gould, a Minister of the Gospel in the Society of Friends; with Memoirs of His Life.* Philadelphia: C. Sherman and Son, 1860.

Hoover, Henry. *Sketches and Incidents, Embracing a Period of Fifty Years*. Indianapolis: John Woolman Press, 1962.

Hubbard, Jeremiah. *Forty Years among the Indians*. Miami, Okla.: Phelps, 1913.

Hull, Henry. *Memoirs of the Life and Religious Labors of Henry Hull, a Minister of the Gospel in the Society of Friends, Late of Stanford in the State of New York*. Philadelphia: Friends' Book Store, 1864.

Hunt, Nathan. *A Brief Memoir of Nathan Hunt: Chiefly Extracted from His Journal and Letters*. Philadelphia: Uriah Hunt and Son, 1858.

Jay, Allen. *Autobiography of Allen Jay, Born 1831, Died 1910*. Philadelphia: John C. Winston, 1910.

Johnson, Mary Coffin, ed. *Life of Elijah Coffin*. Cincinnati: E. Morgan and Sons, 1863.

————, ed. *Rhoda M. Coffin: Her Reminiscences, Addresses, Papers, and Ancestry*. New York: Grafton, 1910.

———— and Percival Brooks Coffin. *Charles F. Coffin: A Quaker Pioneer*. Richmond, Ind.: Nicholson, 1923.

Jones, Rufus M. *Eli and Sybil Jones and Their Work*. Philadelphia: John C. Winston, 1889.

————. *Finding the Trail of Life*. New York: Macmillan, 1926.

————. *The Trail of Life in College*. New York: Macmillan, 1929.

————. *The Trail of Life in the Middle Years*. New York: Macmillan, 1934.

[King, Francis T.]. *Memoir of Elizabeth T. King. With Extracts from Her Letters and Journal*. Baltimore: Armstrong and Berry, 1859.

Kite, Thomas. *Memoirs and Letters of Thomas Kite, a Minister of the Gospel in the Society of Friends*. Philadelphia: Friends' Book Store, 1883.

Lewis, David J. *Word and Work of David J. Lewis*. Cincinnati: M. W. Knapp, 1900.

Maule, Joshua. *Transactions and Changes in the Society of Friends, and Incidents in the Life and Experience of Joshua Maule*. Philadelphia: J. B. Lippincott, 1886.

Memorials concerning Deceased Friends: Members of Philadelphia Yearly Meeting. Philadelphia: Friends' Book Store, 1875.

Memorials of Deceased Friends, Who Were Members of Indiana Yearly Meeting. Cincinnati: Achilles Pugh, 1857.

Mott, Edward. *Sixty Years of Gospel Ministry*. Portland, Ore.: n.p., 1947.

Mott, Frank Luther. "Quaker Boy." *Palimpsest*. 43 (Aug. 1962), 305–26.

Mott, Richard F., ed. *Memoir and Correspondence of Eliza P. Gurney*. Philadelphia: J. B. Lippincott, 1886.

[Murray, Ruth S.]. *Under His Wings: A Sketch of the Life of Robert Lindley Murray*. New York: Anson D. F. Randolph, 1876.

New Garden Monthly Meeting, Ohio (Conservative). *A Brief Account of Esther Fowler: A Valued Minister in the Society of Friends*. [Barnesville, Ohio: n.p., 1923].

Newlin, Joel, comp. *Some Account of the Life and Religious Labors of Eli Newlin, a Minister of the Gospel in the Society of Friends*. Indianapolis: William B. Burford, 1890.

Noyes, Katharine Macy, ed. *Jesse Macy: An Autobiography*. Springfield, Ill.: Charles C. Thomas, 1933.

O'Neall, John Belton. *The Annals of Newberry, Historical, Biographical, and Anecdotal*. Charleston, S.C.: S. G. Courtenay, 1859.

Osborn, Charles. *Journal of That Faithful Servant of Christ, Charles Osborn, Containing an Account of Many of His Travels and Labors in the Ministry, and His Trials and Exercises in the Service of the Lord, and in Defense of the Truth, as It Is in Jesus*. Cincinnati: Achilles Pugh, 1854.

Parham, Sarah T. *The Life of Charles F. Parham*. Joplin, Mo.: Tri-State Printing Company, 1930.

Pennington, Levi T. *Rambling Recollections of Ninety Happy Years*. Portland, Ore.: Metropolitan Press, 1967.

Phillips, Clifton J., ed. "Charles A. Beard's Recollections of Henry County, Indiana." *Indiana Magazine of History*. 55 (March 1959), 17–24.

Pickard, John B., ed. *The Letters of John Greenleaf Whittier*. 3 vols. Cambridge, Mass.: Belknap, 1975.

Plainfield Monthly Meeting, Ind. [Conservative]. *Memorial of Plainfield Monthly Meeting of Friends, concerning Our Dear Friend, Eleazer Bales, Deceased*. N.p., 1887.

Quaker Biographies. Ser. 2. 5 vols. Philadelphia: Friends' Book Store, 1921–1926.

Rees, Byron J. *Hulda: The Pentecostal Prophetess; or, A Sketch of the Life and Triumph of Mrs. Hulda A. Rees, together with Seventeen of Her Sermons*. Philadelphia: Christian Standard Company, 1898.

Rees, Paul S. *Seth Cook Rees: The Warrior Saint*. Indianapolis: Pilgrim Book Room, 1934.

Russell, Elbert. *Elbert Russell, Quaker: An Autobiography*. Jacksonville, Tenn.: Friendly Press, 1956.

Schooley, George A., ed. *The Journal of Dr. William Schooley: Pioneer Physician, Quaker Minister, Abolitionist, Philosopher, and Scholar, 1794–1860, Somerton, Belmont County, Ohio*. Zanesville, Ohio, 1977.

Seebohm, Benjamin, ed. *Memoirs of the Life and Gospel Labours of Stephen Grellet*. 2 vols. Philadelphia: Henry Longstreth, 1860.

Smith, Hannah Whitall. *John M. Whitall: The Story of His Life*. Philadelphia: n.p., 1879.

———. *My Spiritual Autobiography; or, How I Discovered the Unselfishness of God*. New York: Revell, 1903.

Smith, Logan Pearsall, ed. *Philadelphia Quaker: The Letters of Hannah Whitall Smith*. New York: Harcourt-Brace, 1950.

Smith, Simeon O., comp. *Biography of William M. Smith and History of Union Bible Seminary*. Westfield, Ind.: Union Bible Seminary, 1982.

Stanton, William Henry. *A Book Called Our Ancestors the Stantons*. Philadelphia: n.p., 1922.

Tallcot, Joseph. *Memoirs of Joseph Tallcot*. Auburn, N.Y.: Miller, Orton, and Mulligan, 1855.

[Thomas, Anna B.]. *Richard H. Thomas, M.D.: Life and Letters*. London: Headley Brothers, 1905.

Thomas, Martha C. *Memoir of Martha C. Thomas, Late of Baltimore, Maryland*. Richmond, Ind.: Central Book and Tract Committee, n.d.

Thomasson, Eunice, comp. *Some Account of the Life and Religious Services of Joseph Edgerton, a Minister of the Gospel in the Society of Friends, with Extracts from His Correspondence*. Philadelphia: William H. Pile, 1885.

Tomlinson, Homer A., ed. *Diary of A. J. Tomlinson*. 3 vols. New York: Church of God, World Headquarters, 1949.

Wallis, Charles L., ed. *Autobiography of Peter Cartwright*. Nashville: Abingdon, 1956.

Warner, Stafford Allen. *Yardley Warner: The Freedman's Friend. His Life and Times*. Didcot, Eng.: Wessex, n.d.

Whitman, Walt. "Notes (Such as They Are) Founded on Elias Hicks." In *The Complete Prose Works of Walt Whitman*, VI, 241–80. Ed. Richard Maurice Burke et al. 10 vols. New York: G. H. Putnam, 1902.

Wick, B. L. *Sketch of the Life of Archibald Crosbie*. Cedar Rapids, Iowa: n.p., n.d.

Wilbur, John. *Journal of the Life of John Wilbur, a Minister of the Gospel in the Society of Friends; with His Correspondence*. Providence: George H. Whitney, 1859.

Williams, Jesse, and Hannah Williams. *Memoirs of Jesse and Hannah Williams, Late of Plymouth, Montgomery County, Pennsylvania*. Philadelphia: William H. Pile, 1875.

Williams, William. *Journal of the Life, Travels, and Gospel Labours of William Williams, Dec., a Minister of the Society of Friends, Late of White-Water, Indiana*. Cincinnati: Lodge, L'Hommedieu, and Hammond, 1828.

Williams-Cammack, Lydia M., and Truman C. Kenworthy. *Life and Works of Amos M. Kenworthy*. Richmond, Ind.: Nicholson, 1918.

Wilson, Joseph C. et al. *A Brief Sketch of the Lives of Jonathan and Drusilla Wilson*. Plainfield, Ind.: Publishing Association of Friends, 1909.

Winslow, Anna J. *Jewels from My Casket*. N.p., 1910.

Winslow, Margaret Davis. *A Gift from Grandmother*. N.p., 1957.

Woodard, Luke. *Sketches of a Life of 75 in Three Parts: Biographical, Historical, and Descriptive*. Richmond, Ind.: Nicholson, 1907.

Woodard, Solomon B. *Story of a Life of Ninety Years: Biographical and Descriptive*. Richmond, Ind.: Nicholson, 1928.

Woodward, Walter C. *Timothy Nicholson: Master Quaker*. Richmond, Ind.: Nicholson, 1928.

TRAVEL ACCOUNTS

Backhouse, Hannah Chapman. *Extracts from the Journals and Letters of Hannah Chapman Backhouse*. London: Richard Barrett, 1858.

Borome, Joseph A. "John Candler's Visit to America." *Bulletin of Friends Historical Association*. 48 (Spring 1959), 21–62.

Bronner, Edwin B., ed. *An English View of American Quakerism: The Journal of Walter Robson*. Philadelphia: American Philosophical Society, 1970.

Budge, Frances Anne. *Isaac Sharp: An Apostle of the Nineteenth Century*. London: Headley Brothers, 1898.

Galleway, Elizabeth L., ed. *Travels of Robert and Sarah Lindsey*. London: Samuel Harris, 1886.

Jackson, Sheldon G. "English Quakers Tour Kansas in 1858." *Kansas Historical Quarterly*, 13 (Feb. 1944), 36–52.

Littleboy, Richard. "Notes of a Visit to the Yearly Meetings of Friends in Western America." *Friends' Quarterly Examiner*. 13 (4th Mo. 1879), 276–92.

Newman, Henry Stanley. *Memories of Stanley Pumphrey*. New York: Friends Book and Tract Committee, 1883.

Seebohm, Benjamin, ed. *Memoirs of William Forster*. 2 vols. London: Alfred W. Bennett, 1865.

[Seebohm, Frederic W., et al., comps.]. *Private Memoirs of B. and E. Seebohm*. London: Provost, 1873.

Tallack, William. *Friendly Sketeches in America*. London: A. W. Bennett, 1861.

[Thomas, Anna B.]. *J. Bevan Braithwaite: A Friend of the Nineteenth Century*. London: Hodder and Stoughton, 1909.

Thornbrough, Gayle, ed. *A Friendly Mission: John Candler's Letters from America, 1853–1854*. Indianapolis: Indiana Historical Society, 1951.

THESES AND DISSERTATIONS

Anscombe, Francis Charles. "The Contribution of the Quakers to the Reconstruction of the Southern States." Ph.D. diss., University of North Carolina, 1926.

Beeth, Howard N. "Outside Agitators in Southern History: The Society of Friends, 1656–1800." Ph.D. diss., University of Houston, 1984.

Bickley, William Phillips. "Education as Reformation: An Examination of Orthodox Quakers' Formation of the Haverford School Association and Founding of Haverford School, 1815–1840." Ed.D. diss., Harvard University, 1983.

Brackett, Charles H. "The History of Azusa College and the Friends, 1900–1965." M.A. thesis, University of Southern California, 1967.

Buys, John William. "Quakers in Indiana in the Nineteenth Century." Ph.D. diss., University of Florida, 1973.

Caffrey, Augustine J. "The Affirmation Mysticism of Rufus M. Jones." D.S.T. thesis, Catholic University of America, 1967.

Fisher, B. Eugene. "A Study of Toleration among Midwest Quakers, 1850–1900." M.A. thesis, Earlham School of Religion, 1972.

Goldsmith, Myron Dee. "William Hobson and the Founding of Quakerism in the Pacific Northwest." Ph.D. diss., Boston University, 1962.

Good, Donald G. "Elisha Bates: American Quaker Evangelical in the Early Nineteenth Century." Ph.D. diss., University of Iowa, 1967.

Gray, Harold Lee. "An Investigation of the Causes of Separation in Indiana Yearly Meeting of Friends in 1843." M.A. thesis, Indiana Central College, 1970.

Hay, Alexander H. "The Rise of the Pastoral System in the Society of Friends, 1850–1900." M.A. thesis, Haverford College, 1938.

Hilty, Hiram H. "North Carolina Quakers and Slavery." Ph.D. diss., Duke University, 1969.

Holtzclaw, Louis Ray. "Newport, Indiana: A Study of Quaker Antebellum Reform." Ed.D. diss., Ball State University, 1975.

Minear, Mark E. "The Richmond Conference of 1887." M.A. thesis, Earlham School of Religion, 1984.

Norton, James H. "Quakers West of the Alleghenies and in Ohio to 1861." Ph.D. diss., Case Western Reserve University, 1965.

Roberts, Arthur Owen. "The Concepts of Perfection in the History of the Quaker Movement." B.D. thesis, Nazarene Theological Seminary, 1951.

Rush, Arthur Dewey. "The Community of Haviland, Kansas: Its Early History and Development." M.S. thesis, Fort Scott State College, 1942.

Sartwell, Richard C. "The Influence of Leading Friends in Ohio Yearly Meeting of Friends, Evangelical, 1854–1919." M.A. thesis, Earlham School of Religion, 1974.

Selleck, Ronald Eugene. "I Shall Not Pass This Way Again: A Study of Stephen Grellet's Life and Thought." Ph.D. diss., University of Chicago, 1985.

Stanley, S. Lindley. "A History of the Quaker Settlement at Hesper, Kansas." M.S. thesis, Kansas State Teachers College, 1937.

Wood, Richard Eugene. "Evangelical Quakers in the Mississippi Valley, 1854–1894." Ph.D. diss., University of Minnesota, 1985.

Worrall, Arthur John. "New England Quakerism, 1656–1830." Ph.D. diss., Indiana University, 1969.

BOOKS AND ARTICLES

Abzug, Robert H. *Passionate Liberator: Theodore Dwight Weld and the Dilemma of Reform*. New York: Oxford University Press, 1980.

Ahlstrom, Sydney E. *A Religious History of the American People*. New Haven: Yale University Press, 1972.

Anderson, Robert Mapes. *Vision of the Disinherited: The Making of American Pentecostalism*. New York: Oxford University Press, 1979.

Atherton, Lewis. *Main Street on the Middle Border*. Bloomington: Indiana University Press, 1954.

Bacon, Margaret Hope. *Valiant Friend: The Life of Lucretia Mott*. New York: Walker, 1980.

Barbour, Hugh. *The Quakers in Puritan England*. New Haven: Yale University Press, 1964.

―――. "William Penn: Model of Protestant Liberalism." *Church History*. 48 (June 1979), 156–75.

Bauman, Richard. *For the Reputation of Truth: Politics, Religion, and Conflict among the Pennsylvania Quakers, 1750–1800*. Baltimore: Johns Hopkins University Press, 1972.

Beauregard, Erving E. *Old Franklin: The Eternal Touch: A History of Franklin College, New Athens, Harrison County, Ohio*. Lanham, Md.: University Press of America, 1983.

Bedell, L. Frank. *Quaker Heritage: Friends Coming into the Heart of America: A Story of Iowa Conservative Yearly Meeting*. Cedar Rapids, Iowa, 1966.

Beebe, Ralph K. *A Garden of the Lord: A History of Oregon Yearly Meeting of Friends Church*. Portland, Ore.: n.p., 1968.

Benjamin, Philip S. *The Philadelphia Quakers in the Industrial Age, 1865–1920*. Philadelphia: Temple University Press, 1976.

Berg, Barbara. *The Remembered Gate: Origins of American Feminism: The Woman and the City, 1800–1860*. New York: Oxford University Press, 1978.

Bill, J. Brent. *David B. Updegraff: Quaker Holiness Preacher*. Richmond, Ind.: Friends United Press, 1983.

Boller, Paul F., Jr. *American Thought in Transition: The Impact of Evolutionary Naturalism, 1865–1900*. Washington, D.C.: University Press of America, 1983.

Bradley, A. Day. "New York Yearly Meeting at Poplar Ridge and the Primitive Friends." *Quaker History*. 68 (Autumn 1979), 75–82.

Brinton, Howard H. *Friends for 300 Years: The History and Beliefs of the Society of Friends since George Fox Started the Quaker Movement*. New York: Harper, 1952.

―――, ed. *Children of Light: In Honor of Rufus M. Jones*. New York: Macmillan, 1938.

Brock, Peter. *Pacifism in the United States from the Colonial Era to the First World War*. Princeton: Princeton University Press, 1968.

―――. *Pioneers of the Peaceable Kingdom*. Princeton: Princeton University Press, 1970.

Bronner, Edwin B. "Distributing the Printed Word: The Tract Association of Friends, 1816–1966." *Pennsylvania Magazine of History and Biography*. 91 (July 1967), 342–54.

―――. *William Penn's "Holy Experiment": The Founding of Pennsylvania, 1681–1701*. Philadelphia: Temple University Press, 1962.

―――, ed. *American Quakers Today*. Philadelphia: Friends World Committee, 1966.

Brown, Richard D. *Modernization: The Transformation of American Life, 1607–1865*. New York: Hill and Wang, 1976.

Cadbury, Henry J. "Negro Membership in the Society of Friends." *Journal of Negro History*. 21 (April 1936), 151–213.

Carroll, Kenneth L. "Singing in the Spirit in Early Quakerism." *Quaker History*. 73 (Spring 1984), 1–13.

Carter, Paul A. *The Spiritual Crisis of the Gilded Age*. DeKalb: Northern Illinois University Press, 1971.

Cartland, Fernando G. *Southern Heroes; or, The Friends in Wartime*. Cambridge, Mass.: Riverside, 1895.

Clark, Minnie B. "Barnabas Coffin Hobbs." *Indiana Magazine of History*. 19 (Sept. 1923), 282–90.

Clarke, Grace Julian. *George W. Julian*. Indianapolis: Indiana Historical Commission, 1923.

Conforti, Joseph. "Jonathan Edwards' 'Most Popular Work': The Life of David Brainerd' and Nineteenth-Century Evangelical Culture." *Church History*. 54 (June 1985), 188–203.

Cook, Darius B. *History of Quaker Divide*. Dexter, Iowa: *Dexter Sentinel*, 1914.

Cooper, William. "Joseph Moore: Quaker Evolutionist." *Indiana Magazine of History*. 72 (June 1976), 123–37.

Cox, John, Jr. *Quakerism in the City of New York*. New York: n.p., 1930.

Cremin, Lawrence A. *American Education: The National Experience, 1783–1876*. New York: Harper and Row, 1980.

Cross, Whitney R. *The Burned-Over District: The Social and Intellectual History of Enthusiastic Religion in Western New York, 1800–1850*. Ithaca: Cornell University Press, 1950.

Curtis, Peter H. "A Quaker and the Civil War: The Life of James Parnell Jones." *Quaker History*. 67 (Spring 1978), 35–41.

Davis, David Brion. *The Problem of Slavery in the Age of Revolution, 1770–1823*. Ithaca: Cornell University Press, 1975.

Dawley, Alan. *Class and Community: The Industrial Revolution in Lynn*. Cambridge: Harvard University Press, 1976.

Densmore, Christopher. "Quaker Publishing in New York State, 1784–1860." *Quaker History*. 74 (Fall 1985), 37–55.

Dieter, Melvin Easterday. *The Holiness Revival of the Nineteenth Century*. Metuchen, N.J.: Scarecrow, 1980.

Doherty, Robert W. *The Hicksite Separation: A Sociological Analysis of Religious Schism in Early Nineteenth-Century America*. New Brunswick: Rutgers University Press, 1967.

Dolan, Jay P. *Catholic Revivalism: The American Experience, 1830–1900*. Notre Dame: University of Notre Dame Press, 1978.

Drake, Thomas E. *Quakers and Slavery in America*. New Haven: Yale University Press, 1950.

Dunn, Mary Maples. "Saints and Sisters: Congregational and Quaker Women in the Early Colonial Period." *American Quarterly*. 30 (Winter 1978), 582–601.

———. *William Penn: Politics and Conscience*. Princeton: Princeton University Press, 1967.

Elliott, Errol T. *Quaker Profiles from the American West*. Richmond, Ind.: Friends United Press, 1972.

———. *Quakers on the American Frontier*. Richmond, Ind.: Friends United Press, 1969.

Emerson, Elizabeth H. "Barnabas C. Hobbs: Midwestern Quaker Minister and Educator." *Quaker History.* 49 (Spring 1960), 21–35.

Epstein, Barbara Leslie. *The Politics of Domesticity: Women, Evangelism, and Temperance in Nineteenth-Century America.* Middletown, Conn.: Wesleyan University Press, 1981.

Evans, William Bacon. *Jonathan Evans and His Time, 1759–1839: A Bi-Centennial Biography.* Boston: Christopher, 1959.

Foner, Eric. *Free Soil, Free Labor, Free Men: The Ideology of the Republican Party before the Civil War.* New York: Oxford University Press, 1970.

Forbush, Bliss. *Elias Hicks: Quaker Liberal.* New York: Columbia University Press, 1956.

———. *A History of Baltimore Yearly Meeting of Friends: Three Hundred Years of Quakerism in Maryland, Virginia, the District of Columbia, and Central Pennsylvania.* Baltimore: Baltimore Yearly Meeting, 1972.

Foreign Mission Work of American Friends: A Brief History of Their Work from the Beginning to the Year 1912. N.p.: American Friends Board of Foreign Missions, 1912.

Formisano, Ronald P. *The Birth of Mass Political Parties: Michigan, 1827–1861.* Princeton: Princeton University Press, 1971.

Frost, J. William. *The Quaker Family in Colonial America: A Portrait of the Society of Friends.* New York: St. Martin's, 1973.

———. *The Quaker Origins of Antislavery in America.* New York: Arno, 1979.

Gilbert, Dorothy Lloyd. *Guilford: A Quaker College.* Greensboro, N.C.: n.p., 1937.

Gragg, Larry Dale. *Migration in Early America: The Virginia Quaker Experience.* Ann Arbor: UMI Research, 1980.

Greven, Philip. *The Protestant Temperament: Patterns of Child-Rearing, Religious Experience, and the Self in Early America.* New York: Knopf, 1977.

Grubb, Edward. *Separations, Their Causes and Effects: Studies in Nineteenth-Century Quakerism.* London: Headley Brothers, 1914.

Hall, Francis B., ed. *Quaker Worship in North America.* Richmond, Ind.: Friends United Press, n.d.

Halttunen, Karen S. *Confidence Men and Painted Women: A Study of Middle-Class Culture in America, 1830–1870.* New Haven: Yale University Press, 1982.

Hamm, Thomas D. *The Antislavery Movement in Henry County, Indiana.* New Castle, Ind.: Henry County Historical Society, 1975.

Hammarburg, Melvyn. "Indiana Farmers and the Group Basis of Late Nineteenth-Century Political Parties." *Journal of American History.* 61 (June 1974), 91–115.

Handy, Robert T. *A Christian America: Protestant Hopes and Historical Realities.* New York: Oxford University Press, 1971.

———. *A History of the Churches in the United States and Canada.* New York: Oxford University Press, 1976.

Haskell, Thomas L. *The Emergence of Professional Social Science: The American Social Science Association and the Nineteenth-Century Crisis of Authority.* Urbana: University of Illinois Press, 1977.

Hatch, Nathan O., and Mark A. Noll, eds. *The Bible in America: Essays in Cultural History.* New York: Oxford University Press, 1982.

Hatcher, Sadie Bacon. *A History of Spiceland Academy, 1826 to 1921.* Indianapolis: Indiana Historical Society, 1934.

Hays, Samuel P. *The Response to Industrialism, 1885–1914.* Chicago: University of Chicago Press, 1957.

Heiss, Willard. *A Brief History of Western Yearly Meeting of Conservative Friends and the Separation of 1877.* Indianapolis: John Woolman Press, 1963.

Hendricks, Charles C. "The Influence of Joseph Moore and the Baltimore Association on North Carolina Quakers." *Southern Friend*. 2 (Autumn 1980), 71–83.

Henretta, James A. "Families and Farms: *Mentalité* in Pre-Industrial America." *William and Mary Quarterly*. Ser. 3. 35 (Jan. 1978), 3–32.

Henry, Stuart C. *Unvanquished Puritan: A Portrait of Lyman Beecher*. Grand Rapids: Eerdmans, 1973.

Hickey, Damon D. "Progressives and Conservatives Search for Order: The Division of North Carolina Quakers." *Southern Friend*. 6 (Spring 1984), 17–35.

Hilty, Hiram H. "Zenas L. Martin: Quaker Pioneer in Cuba." *Quaker History*. 59 (Fall 1970), 81–97.

Hinshaw, Seth B. *The Carolina Quaker Experience, 1665–1985: An Interpretation*. Greensboro, N.C.: North Carolina Friends Historical Society, 1985.

History of Wayne County, Indiana. 2 vols. Chicago: Interstate, 1884.

Howe, Daniel Walker. *The Political Culture of the American Whigs*. Chicago: University of Chicago Press, 1979.

Hutchison, William R. *The Modernist Impulse in American Protestantism*. Cambridge: Harvard University Press, 1976.

Illick, Joseph E. " 'Some of Our Best Indians Are Friends': Quaker Attitudes and Actions regarding Western Indians during the Grant Administration." *Western Historical Quarterly*. 2 (July 1971), 283–94.

Ingle, H. Larry. *Quakers in Conflict: The Hicksite Reformation*. Knoxville: University of Tennessee Press, 1986.

Isaac, Rhys. *The Transformation of Virginia, 1740–1790*. Chapel Hill: University of North Carolina Press, 1982.

Isichei, Elisabeth. *Victorian Quakers*. Oxford: Clarendon, 1970.

Jackson, Sheldon Glenn. *A Short History of Kansas Yearly Meeting of Friends*. Wichita: Day's Print Shop, 1946.

———. *Quaker Pioneers in the Cherokee Strip: The Life and Times of Alvin and Laura Coppock*. Azusa, Calif: Azusa Pacific University Press, 1982.

James, Sydney V. *A People among Peoples: Quaker Benevolence in Eighteenth-Century America*. Cambridge: Harvard University Press, 1963.

Johnson, Paul E. *A Shopkeeper's Millennium: Society and Revivals in Rochester, New York, 1815–1837*. New York: Hill and Wang, 1978.

Jones, Charles Edwin. *Perfectionist Persuasion: The Holiness Movement and Methodism, 1867–1936*. Metuchen, N.J.: Scarecrow, 1974.

Jones, Charles Edwin, comp. *A Guide to the Study of the Holiness Movement*. Metuchen, N.J.: Scarecrow, 1974.

Jones, Louis Thomas. *The Quakers of Iowa*. Iowa City: Clio, 1914.

Jones, Rufus M. *Haverford College: A History and an Interpretation*. New York: Macmillan, 1933.

———. *The Later Periods of Quakerism*. 2 vols. London: Macmillan, 1921.

Keller, Robert H. *American Protestantism and United States Indian Policy, 1869–1882*. Lincoln: University of Nebraska Press, 1983.

Kelley, Robert H. *The Cultural Pattern in American Politics: The First Century*. New York: Knopf, 1979.

Kennedy, Thomas C. "Southland College: The Society of Friends and Black Education in Arkansas." *Arkansas Historical Quarterly*. 42 (Autumn 1983), 207–38.

Ketring, Ruth Anna. *Charles Osborn in the Anti-Slavery Movement*. Columbus: Ohio State Archaeological and Historical Society, 1937.

Kleppner, Paul. *The Cross of Culture: A Social Analysis of Midwestern Politics, 1850–1900*. New York: Free Press, 1970.

Knollenberg, Bernhard. *Pioneer Sketches of the Upper Whitewater Valley: Quaker Stronghold of the West*. Indianapolis: Indiana Historical Society, 1945.

Kolko, Gabriel. *The Triumph of Conservatism: A Reinterpretation of American History, 1900–1916*. New York: Free Press, 1963.

Kuklick, Bruce. *The Rise of American Philosophy: Cambridge, Massachusetts, 1860–1930*. New Haven: Yale University Press, 1977.

Kutolowski, Kathleen Smith. "Antimasonry Reexamined: Social Bases of the Grass-Roots Party." *Journal of American History*. 71 (Sept. 1984), 269–93.

LeShana, David C. *Quakers in California: The Effects of 19th-Century Revivalism on Western Quakerism*. Newberg, Ore.: Barclay, 1969.

McDaniel, Ethel Hittle. *The Contribution of the Society of Friends to Education in Indiana*. Indianapolis: Indiana Historical Society, 1939.

McLoughlin, William G. *Modern Revivalism: Charles Grandison Finney to Billy Graham*. New York: Ronald, 1959.

McPherson, James M. *Ordeal by Fire*. New York: Knopf, 1982.

Marietta, Jack D. *The Reformation of American Quakerism, 1748–1783*. Philadelphia: University of Pennsylvania Press, 1984.

Marsden, George M. *Fundamentalism and American Culture: The Shaping of Twentieth-Century Evangelicalism, 1870–1925*. New York: Oxford University Press, 1980.

Martin, Paula Staahls, and Kathy Warden Manning. *Women of Guilford: A Study of Women's Contributions, 1740–1979*. Greensboro, N.C.: Women of Guilford, 1979.

Mathews, Donald G. *Religion in the Old South*. Chicago: University of Chicago Press, 1977.

May, Henry F. *The Protestant Churches and Industrial America*. New York: Harper Brothers, 1949.

Mekeel, Arthur J. *Quakerism and a Creed*. Philadelphia: Friends' Book Store, 1936.

Miller, Perry. *The Life of the Mind in America from the Revolution to the Civil War*. New York: Harcourt Brace Jovanovich, 1965.

Milner, Clyde A. II. *With Good Intentions: Quaker Work among the Pawnees, Otos, and Omahas in the 1870s*. Lincoln: University of Nebraska Press, 1982.

Moore, John M., ed. *Friends in the Delaware Valley: Philadelphia Yearly Meeting, 1681–1981*. Haverford, Pa.: Friends Historical Association, 1981.

Moore, R. Laurence. *Religious Outsiders and the Making of Americans*. New York: Oxford University Press, 1986.

Moorhead, James H. "Between Progress and Apocalypse: A Reassessment of Millennialism in American Religious Thought, 1800–1880." *Journal of American History*. 71 (Dec. 1984), 425–42.

Morlan, Charles P., comp. *A Brief History of Ohio Yearly Meeting of the Religious Society of Friends (Conservative)*. N.p., 1959.

Nelson, Jacquelyn S. "The Military Response of the Society of Friends in Indiana to the Civil War." *Indiana Magazine of History*. 81 (June 1985), 101–30.

Osborne, Byron Lindley. *The Malone Story: The Dream of Two Quaker Young People*. Canton, Ohio, 1970.

Perry, Lewis. *Intellectual Life in America: A History*. New York: Franklin Watts, 1984.

Rank, Albert. *History of the Brethren Church*. Ashland, Ohio: Brethren Publishing Company, 1968.

Ratcliff, Richard P. *The Quakers of Spiceland, Henry County, Indiana: A History of Spiceland Friends Meeting, 1828–1968*. New Castle, Ind.: Community Printing, 1968.

Rawley, James A. "Joseph John Gurney's Mission to America, 1837–1840." *Mississippi Valley Historical Review*. 49 (March 1963), 653–74.

Riker, Dorothy, and Gayle Thornbrough, comps. *Indiana Election Returns, 1816–1851*. Indianapolis: Indiana Historical Bureau, 1960.

Robert, Arthur O. *The Association of Evangelical Friends: A Story of Quaker Renewal in the Twentieth Century*. Newberg, Ore.: Barclay, 1975.

Russell, Elbert. *The History of Quakerism*. New York: Macmillan, 1942.

———. *The Separation after a Century*. Philadelphia: Friends' Intelligencer, 1928.

Ryan, Roderick N. "Moral Reform and Democratic Politics: The Dilemma of Roberts Vaux." *Quaker History*, 59 (Spring 1970), 3–14.

Sandeen, Ernest R. *The Roots of Fundamentalism: British and American Millenarianism, 1800–1930*. Chicago: University of Chicago Press, 1970.

Schlabach, Theron F. "The Humble Become 'Aggressive Workers': Mennonites Organize for Mission, 1880–1910." *Mennonite Quarterly Review*. 52 (April 1978), 91–112.

———. "Mennonites, Revivalism, Modernity—1683–1850." *Church History*. 48 (Dec. 1979), 398–415.

Scott, Anne Firor. *The Southern Lady: From Pedestal to Politics, 1830–1930*. Chicago: University of Chicago Press, 1970.

Semi-Centennial of Western Yearly Meeting of Friends Church, Plainfield, Indiana, Ninth Month 23, 1908. Plainfield, Ind.: Publishing Association of Friends, 1908.

Smith, Thomas H. "Ohio Quakers and the Mississippi Freedmen: 'A Field to Labor.' " *Ohio History*. 78 (Summer 1969), 159–71.

Smith, Timothy L. *Called unto Holiness: The Story of the Nazarenes*. Kansas City, Mo.: Nazarene Publishing House, 1962.

———. *Revivalism and Social Reform: American Protestantism on the Eve of the Civil War*. New York: Harper and Row, 1965.

———. "Righteousness and Hope: Christian Holiness and the Millennial Vision in America, 1800–1900." *American Quarterly*. 31 (Spring 1979), 21–45.

Snyder, Edward D. "Whittier and the Unitarians." *Quaker History*. 49 (Fall 1970), 111–16.

Soderlund, Jean R. *Quakers and Slavery: A Divided Spirit*. Princeton: Princeton University Press, 1985.

Sproat, John G. *"The Best Men": Liberal Reformers in the Gilded Age*. New York: Oxford University Press, 1968.

Strachey, Barbara. *Remarkable Relations: The Story of the Pearsall Smith Women*. London: Gollancz, 1980.

Swift, David E. *Joseph John Gurney: Banker, Reformer, and Quaker*. Middletown, Conn.: Wesleyan University Press, 1962.

Szasz, Ferenc Morton. *The Divided Mind of Protestant America, 1880–1930*. University: University of Alabama Press, 1982.

Taber, William P. *Be Gentle, Be Plain: A History of Olney*. [Barnesville, Ohio]: Olney School, 1976.

———. "The Expanding World of the Ohio Wilburite Quakers in the Latter Part of the Nineteenth Century." *Quaker History*. 56 (Spring 1967), 18–33.

———. *The Eye of Faith: A History of Ohio Yearly Meeting, Conservative*. Barnesville, Ohio: Ohio Yearly Meeting, 1985.

Thomas, Allen C., and Richard H. Thomas. *A History of the Friends in America*. Philadelphia: John C. Winston, 1894.

Thompson, Donald C., comp. *Indiana Authors and Their Books*. 3 vols. Crawfordsville, Ind.: Wabash College, 1966–1981.

Thornburg, Opal. *Earlham: The Story of the College, 1847–1962*. Richmond, Ind.: Earlham College Press, 1963.

Tolles, Frederick B. *Meeting House and Counting House: The Quaker Merchants of Colonial Philadelphia, 1682–1763*. Chapel Hill: University of North Carolina Press, 1948.

———. "The New Light Quakers of Lynn and New Bedford." *New England Quarterly*. 32 (Sept. 1959), 291–319.

———. *The Quakers and the Atlantic Culture*. New York: Harper and Row, 1960.

Tucker, Ebenezer C. *History of Randolph County, Indiana: With Illustrations and Biographical Sketches of Some of the Prominent Men and Pioneers*. Chicago: A. E. Kingman, 1882.

Tuveson, Ernest Lee. *Redeemer Nation: The Idea of America's Millennial Role*. Chicago: University of Chicago Press, 1968.

Tyrrell, Ian R. *Sobering Up: From Temperance to Prohibition in Antebellum America, 1800–1860*. Westport, Conn.: Greenwood, 1979.

Vining, Elizabeth Gray. *Friend of Life: A Biography of Rufus M. Jones*. Philadelphia: J. B. Lippincott, 1958.

Wacker, Grant. "The Holy Spirit and the Spirit of the Age in American Protestantism, 1880–1910." *Journal of American History*. 72 (June 1985), 45–62.

Walters, Ronald G. *American Reformers, 1815–1860*. New York: Hill and Wang, 1978.

Watson, S. Arthur. *Penn College: A Product and a Producer*. Oskaloosa, Iowa: William Penn College, 1971.

Weber, Timothy P. *Living in the Shadow of the Second Coming: American Premillennialism, 1875–1925*. New York: Oxford University Press, 1979.

Weeks, Stephen B. *Southern Quakers and Slavery: A Study in Institutional History*. Baltimore: Johns Hopkins University Press, 1896.

Weinstein, James. *The Corporate Ideal in the Liberal State, 1900–1918*. Boston: Beacon, 1918.

Westerhoff, John H. III. *McGuffey and His Readers: Piety, Morality, and Education in Nineteenth-Century America*. Nashville: Abingdon, 1977.

White, Ronald C., Jr., and C. Howard Hopkins. *The Social Gospel: Religion and Reform in Changing America*. Philadelphia: Temple University Press, 1976.

Wiebe, Robert H. *The Search for Order, 1877–1920*. New York: Hill and Wang, 1967.

Williams, Walter R. *The Rich Heritage of Quakerism*. Grand Rapids: Eerdmans, 1962.

Worrall, Arthur J. *Quakers in the Colonial Northeast*. Hanover, N.H.: University Press of New England, 1980.

Zuber, Richard L. "Conscientious Objectors in the Confederacy: The Quakers of North Carolina." *Quaker History*. 67 (Spring 1978), 1–19.

Index

Abolition: Quaker disassociation from, 27; Quaker schism over, 32; Quaker support of, 61

American Friend: as source of factionalism, 166, 167; at war with *Evangelical Friend,* 169

Anti-intellectualism, 8

Antislavery. *See also* Abolition; of Charles Osborn, 32; and evangelical Quakers, 24, 61; of Gurneyites, 50, 61; and Quaker thought, 10; vote for George W. Julian, 61; and Walter Edgerton, 32; Wilburite-Gurneyite conflicts over, 33

An Appeal for the Rights of Conscience, 67

Atonement: evangelical views on, 86; and opposition to Hicksites, 19; in Quaker belief, 17; renewal Quaker emphasis on, 49

Baldwin, James: father of, 41; and literary re-creation of Quakers, xiii; on Quaker plain life, 9

Balkwill, Helen, 130

Baptism: Helen Balkwill's position on, 130; of the Holy Spirit, 4, 5, 88, 130; opposition to water baptism, 130, 131; Quaker view of, 4; and tribulation, 4

Barclay, William, 122

Bean, Joel, 117; controversy surrounding, 139–43, 145–46; deposition of, 142

Benevolence, and plain life, 10

Bible: authority of, 18; the Bible Association of Friends in America, 25; Elias Hicks's view of, 16; evangelical view of, 86; "First Day Schools for Scriptural Instruction," 26; Gurneyite claims for, 29; Gur-

neyite emphasis on, 49; Hicksite "heresy" on, 19; "higher criticism" of, 109; and holiness crusade against modernism, 161; Joseph Gurney's view of, 21; Joseph Tallcot on, 25; literalism on ordinances, 133; moderate view of, 114; modernist views of Elbert Russell, 152; modernist views of Mary Mendenhall Hobbs, 153; Nereus Mendenhall's view of, 147; Quaker emphasis on, 25; Quaker literalism on, 147; Quaker view of, 16, 17; renewal emphasis on, 49; Rufus M. Jones's critical view of, 149; Wilburite attitudes toward, 30

Christ: Conservative Friends on, 100; Hicksite "heresy" on, 19; Quaker emphasis on, 18; Quaker view of, 16, 17

Christian Worker, 103

Clark, Dougan, Jr.: as editor, 106; radical teachings of, 87; as revival theologian, 82; and water baptism controversy, 220n

Coffin, Charles F.: Bureau of Indian Affairs offered, 58; business practices of, 220n; early life of, 46; emphasis on Bible of, 49; as friend of John Douglas, 82; renewal reform of, 60

Coffin, Rhoda M.: career of, 47; early life of, 46; as friend of John Douglas, 82; renewal reform of, 60

Communion, Quaker opposition to, 130

Conservative Friends, 99–102. *See also* Wilburites; against politics, 101; attacked by revivalists, 109; authority of Bible among, 100; Cyrus Harvey in, 100, 101; divinity of Christ for, 100; eschew voting, 101; holi-